Lecture Notes in Artificial Intelligence   9744

Subseries of Lecture Notes in Computer Science

More information about this series at http://www.springer.com/series/1244

Dylan D. Schmorrow · Cali M. Fidopiastis (Eds.)

Foundations of Augmented Cognition: Neuroergonomics and Operational Neuroscience

10th International Conference, AC 2016
Held as Part of HCI International 2016
Toronto, ON, Canada, July 17–22, 2016
Proceedings, Part II

 Springer

Editors
Dylan D. Schmorrow
Soar Technology Inc.
Vienna, VA
USA

Cali M. Fidopiastis
Design Interactive, Inc.
Orlando, FL
USA

ISSN 0302-9743 ISSN 1611-3349 (electronic)
Lecture Notes in Artificial Intelligence
ISBN 978-3-319-39951-5 ISBN 978-3-319-39952-2 (eBook)
DOI 10.1007/978-3-319-39952-2

Library of Congress Control Number: 2016940364

LNCS Sublibrary: SL7 – Artificial Intelligence

Printed on acid-free paper

This Springer imprint is published by Springer Nature
The registered company is Springer International Publishing AG Switzerland

Foreword

The 18th International Conference on Human-Computer Interaction, HCI International 2016, was held in Toronto, Canada, during July 17–22, 2016. The event incorporated the 15 conferences/thematic areas listed on the following page.

A total of 4,354 individuals from academia, research institutes, industry, and governmental agencies from 74 countries submitted contributions, and 1,287 papers and 186 posters have been included in the proceedings. These papers address the latest research and development efforts and highlight the human aspects of the design and use of computing systems. The papers thoroughly cover the entire field of human-computer interaction, addressing major advances in knowledge and effective use of computers in a variety of application areas. The volumes constituting the full 27-volume set of the conference proceedings are listed on pages IX and X.

I would like to thank the program board chairs and the members of the program boards of all thematic areas and affiliated conferences for their contribution to the highest scientific quality and the overall success of the HCI International 2016 conference.

This conference would not have been possible without the continuous and unwavering support and advice of the founder, Conference General Chair Emeritus and Conference Scientific Advisor Prof. Gavriel Salvendy. For his outstanding efforts, I would like to express my appreciation to the communications chair and editor of *HCI International News*, Dr. Abbas Moallem.

April 2016   Constantine Stephanidis

HCI International 2016 Thematic Areas and Affiliated Conferences

Thematic areas:

- Human-Computer Interaction (HCI 2016)
- Human Interface and the Management of Information (HIMI 2016)

Affiliated conferences:

- 13th International Conference on Engineering Psychology and Cognitive Ergonomics (EPCE 2016)
- 10th International Conference on Universal Access in Human-Computer Interaction (UAHCI 2016)
- 8th International Conference on Virtual, Augmented and Mixed Reality (VAMR 2016)
- 8th International Conference on Cross-Cultural Design (CCD 2016)
- 8th International Conference on Social Computing and Social Media (SCSM 2016)
- 10th International Conference on Augmented Cognition (AC 2016)
- 7th International Conference on Digital Human Modeling and Applications in Health, Safety, Ergonomics and Risk Management (DHM 2016)
- 5th International Conference on Design, User Experience and Usability (DUXU 2016)
- 4th International Conference on Distributed, Ambient and Pervasive Interactions (DAPI 2016)
- 4th International Conference on Human Aspects of Information Security, Privacy and Trust (HAS 2016)
- Third International Conference on HCI in Business, Government, and Organizations (HCIBGO 2016)
- Third International Conference on Learning and Collaboration Technologies (LCT 2016)
- Second International Conference on Human Aspects of IT for the Aged Population (ITAP 2016)

Conference Proceedings Volumes Full List

1. LNCS 9731, Human-Computer Interaction: Theory, Design, Development and Practice (Part I), edited by Masaaki Kurosu
2. LNCS 9732, Human-Computer Interaction: Interaction Platforms and Techniques (Part II), edited by Masaaki Kurosu
3. LNCS 9733, Human-Computer Interaction: Novel User Experiences (Part III), edited by Masaaki Kurosu
4. LNCS 9734, Human Interface and the Management of Information: Information, Design and Interaction (Part I), edited by Sakae Yamamoto
5. LNCS 9735, Human Interface and the Management of Information: Applications and Services (Part II), edited by Sakae Yamamoto
6. LNAI 9736, Engineering Psychology and Cognitive Ergonomics, edited by Don Harris
7. LNCS 9737, Universal Access in Human-Computer Interaction: Methods, Techniques, and Best Practices (Part I), edited by Margherita Antona and Constantine Stephanidis
8. LNCS 9738, Universal Access in Human-Computer Interaction: Interaction Techniques and Environments (Part II), edited by Margherita Antona and Constantine Stephanidis
9. LNCS 9739, Universal Access in Human-Computer Interaction: Users and Context Diversity (Part III), edited by Margherita Antona and Constantine Stephanidis
10. LNCS 9740, Virtual, Augmented and Mixed Reality, edited by Stephanie Lackey and Randall Shumaker
11. LNCS 9741, Cross-Cultural Design, edited by Pei-Luen Patrick Rau
12. LNCS 9742, Social Computing and Social Media, edited by Gabriele Meiselwitz
13. LNAI 9743, Foundations of Augmented Cognition: Neuroergonomics and Operational Neuroscience (Part I), edited by Dylan D. Schmorrow and Cali M. Fidopiastis
14. LNAI 9744, Foundations of Augmented Cognition: Neuroergonomics and Operational Neuroscience (Part II), edited by Dylan D. Schmorrow and Cali M. Fidopiastis
15. LNCS 9745, Digital Human Modeling and Applications in Health, Safety, Ergonomics and Risk Management, edited by Vincent G. Duffy
16. LNCS 9746, Design, User Experience, and Usability: Design Thinking and Methods (Part I), edited by Aaron Marcus
17. LNCS 9747, Design, User Experience, and Usability: Novel User Experiences (Part II), edited by Aaron Marcus
18. LNCS 9748, Design, User Experience, and Usability: Technological Contexts (Part III), edited by Aaron Marcus
19. LNCS 9749, Distributed, Ambient and Pervasive Interactions, edited by Norbert Streitz and Panos Markopoulos
20. LNCS 9750, Human Aspects of Information Security, Privacy and Trust, edited by Theo Tryfonas

Augmented Cognition

Program Board Chairs: **Dylan D. Schmorrow, USA, Cali M. Fidopiastis, USA**

- Robert Abbott, USA
- Rosario Bruno Cannavò, Italy
- David Combs, USA
- Andrew J. Cowell, USA
- Martha Crosby, USA
- Priya Ganapathy, USA
- Rodolphe Gentili, USA
- Michael W. Hail, USA
- Monte Hancock, USA
- Ion Juvina, USA
- Philip Mangos, USA
- David Martinez, USA
- Santosh Mathan, USA
- Chang Soo Nam, USA
- Banu Onaral, USA
- Robinson Pino, USA
- Lauren Reinerman-Jones, USA
- Victoria Romero, USA
- Jose Rouillard, USA
- Amela Sadagic, USA
- Patricia Shewokis, USA
- Paula Alexandra Silva, USA
- Anna Skinner, USA
- Robert Sottilare, USA
- Ann Speed, USA
- Roy Stripling, USA
- Eric Vorm, USA
- Peter Walker, USA

The full list with the program board chairs and the members of the program boards of all thematic areas and affiliated conferences is available online at:

http://www.hci.international/2016/

HCI International 2017

The 19th International Conference on Human-Computer Interaction, HCI International 2017, will be held jointly with the affiliated conferences in Vancouver, Canada, at the Vancouver Convention Centre, July 9–14, 2017. It will cover a broad spectrum of themes related to human-computer interaction, including theoretical issues, methods, tools, processes, and case studies in HCI design, as well as novel interaction techniques, interfaces, and applications. The proceedings will be published by Springer. More information will be available on the conference website: http://2017. hci.international/.

General Chair
Prof. Constantine Stephanidis
University of Crete and ICS-FORTH
Heraklion, Crete, Greece
E-mail: general_chair@hcii2017.org

http://2017.hci.international/

Contents – Part II

Human Cognition and Behavior in Complex Tasks and Environments

Interaction in Augmented Cognition

Social Cognition

Contents – Part I

Augmented Cognition in Training and Education

Agent-Based Practices for an Intelligent Tutoring System Architecture

Keith Brawner$^{(\boxtimes)}$, Greg Goodwin, and Robert Sottilare

Army Research Laboratory, Adelphi, USA
{keith.w.brawner.civ,gregory.a.goodwin6.civ,
robert.a.sottilare.civ}@mail.mil

Abstract. The Generalized Intelligent Framework for Tutoring (GIFT) project is partially an effort to standardize the systems and processes of intelligent tutoring systems. In addition to these efforts, there is emerging research in agent-driven systems. Agent-based systems obey software and messaging communication protocols and accomplish objectives to the original system, but have different architectural structure. This paper describes the upcoming research changes for GIFT, from a module-driven system to an agent-driven system, the reasons for wanting to do so, the advantages of the change, some initial technical approaches which encapsulate current functionality, and the types of research that this change will enable in the future.

Keywords: Intelligent tutorins systems · Agent based systems · eLearning · mLearning · Software-as-a-service

1 Introduction

The Generalized Intelligent Framework for Tutoring (GIFT) is a science and technology project whose goal is to reduce the technical cost time and skills required to author intelligent tutoring systems (ITS) and to increase the effectiveness of automated instruction in new domains [1]. This is accomplished through the implementation of four primary principles: domain independence, componentization, generalized ITS authoring tools, and automation. A core design philosophy of GIFT is to separate domain-dependent from domain-independent components. This allows the same tutoring infrastructure to be used to train car repair, or medical triage, or team situational awareness, and reduces the number of unique ITS components. Under the principle of componentization, the modules in GIFT, their functions and the messages exchanged between them are standardized to simplify tutor creation and modification. Using this design, an ITS author does not need to have computer programming or instructional system design skills to create a functional ITS.

Componentization simplifies design and processes through constrained input/output sets. The constraint of these input/output sets, in turn, renders them easier to automate or self-construct. Recent projects involving GIFT attempt to build a "policy" which maps inputs to outputs in a few fashions. As a few examples, an instructional policy may recommend immediate or delayed feedback based on a profile of a learner, a learner profile may choose the frequency with which to communicate information to an

© Springer International Publishing Switzerland 2016
D.D. Schmorrow and C.M. Fidopiastis (Eds.): AC 2016, Part II, LNAI 9744, pp. 3–12, 2016.
DOI: 10.1007/978-3-319-39952-2_1

instructional module, or a model of the domain may choose specific implementations of feedback (in game, avatar-driven, flashing, etc.). These policies can be constructed, based on historical data, via software process or modified based on the observations of student state and instructional effects.

Just as componentization simplifies the engineering design space of its components, the creation of policy-driven input/output functions is easier to automate. Techniques for automatically creating agent-driven input/output policies are well studied in the reinforcement learning literature, including techniques such as neural networks, entropy-reducing decision trees, Markov processes, and others. However, in a system like GIFT with disparate processes, input/output options, and data sources, these techniques result in policies that are customized towards each module. A general-purpose solution for optimizing the finite-action set is preferred. Over time, ITSs have developed from custom-crafted systems into systems of interchangeable parts and into systems of software-customized policies. In this paper we will outline the next step of ITS evolution into true agent-based systems, which construct their own policies.

This paper briefly reviews the history of the creation of agent-based ITS, agent-based frameworks for educational purposes, how an agent-based and policy-driven system can be constructed over top of an existing modular system (i.e. GIFT), the advantages and disadvantages of doing so, and initial planning steps of implementation. The paper presents draft designs for interoperability and communication as well as sample technologies for general-purpose adaptation in the presence of data for the purpose of gaining knowledge or optimizing instruction.

2   Existing Work with Agent Frameworks and Intelligent Tutoring Systems (ITS)

In order to frame the discussion of the emergence and development of an agent-based system, there should be a discussion of what defines an agent, and how the term is used. Franklin and Graesser present the essence of agency as having components of sensing the environment, acting upon it, having a sense of time, and pursuing goals [2]. They also state that such agents can be composed of multiple sub-agents, each meeting the above criteria. Based on this definition, the modules of GIFT do not currently have all the traits of agents, but do meet some of the criteria. GIFT modules have information from the environment (the system) and produce outputs, however they individually do not always have a means of assessing the impact of that output on the environment (knowing if they have achieved a goal). A plug-in, or within-module process, which is able to track within-module data, determine the module output, serve the goal of the module (usually modeling), and adjust itself over time would enable GIFT modules to meet the criteria of agents set for by Franklin and Graesser.

The idea of using a framework of cooperative agents as part of an intelligent tutoring system is not new. The problems faced by the field in 1995 were similar to the problems faced with modern-day systems (e.g., lack of reuse, lack of standards, and lack of flexibility). Overcoming these problems by creating a modular framework of agents to provide tutoring capabilities, was the objective of the Generic Instructional Architecture (GIA) project [3]. The GIA and GIFT projects share similar goals, but where GIFT attempts to modularize and then automate, GIA attempts automation directly. In a system such as GIA, the Agent Communication Language (ACL) forms the backbone of communication, with agents advertising their functionalities, availability, and ontology for communication. However, the lack of call for specific agents, or specific groups and types of agents, adds, rather than cuts, from developmental time of a system. Not specifying the required agents, policies, and functions, results in a lack of development for specific system instantiation. This weakness is present in the lack of adoption of the system for in-the-wild tutoring.

Gascueña presents another agent-based system composed of a Student, Domain, Pedagogical, and Educational Module, similar to structure adopted by the GIFT project [4]. Each module in Gascueña's system could have multiple agents and each agent its own software program which can provide recommendation on the output or action of the total module. Examples of these agents include Pedagogical agents for Preferences, Accounting, Exercises, and Tests. Other researchers have proposed similar designs that include Assistant, Evaluation, and Pedagogical agents [5], or may divide these agent capabilities into services such as a Domain, User, Adaptation, and Application Service [6]. GIFT handles functions such as Adaptation and Application through optional and additional plug-in services, which are updated based on outcomes from processing system outputs. However, currently neither GIFT nor Gascueña provide a suggestion of conflict management between recommend agent actions. Overly specifying functions, agents, and policies results in a tightly bound system where few functions can be added.

Inside of the framework of an educational system, additional agents beyond the above are needed that function to enable content/training delivery to a student. The previously mentioned agents only function as part of online instructional management while greater functionality is needed for full individualization. Examples of the types of needed agents are provided by Lin et al. [7] who describe a series of external agents running outside the core instructional loop. These include an adviser agent, which advises the next content to view, a collaboration agent, for collaborating with peers, a course planning agent, which plans a student path through a course, a course delivery agent, which accommodates different delivery styles, and several others. These agents are managed by an agent management and deployment service. Other work, such as Regan's Training and Learning Architecture (TLA) [8], or the Personalized Assistance for Learning (PAL) [9] effort describe the system-of-systems approach to agent construction. Further work examples can be seen in the Dynamic Tailoring System (DTS), which provides an agent derived from the Soar cognitive architecture programmed for the purpose of pedagogy and scaffolding [10]. These systems show the flexibility required for addition, but, like GIA, cannot function as a pure delivery system.

Each of these systems discussed so far has either (a) not specified the functions which are required for agents (e.g. recommendation agent), or (b) overly specified the information for agents (e.g. domain hinting agent). The problem with not specifying the requirements for agency adequately is that it makes it impossible for the system to be adopted as an agent-based system. On the other hand, when the functions are too constrained, they become less flexible and this limits the manner of system expansion. As we look to ways of transforming GIFT to an agent-based system, it is important to provide specifications for the addition of new agents without being overly restrictive on how those agents will function within the GIFT environment. One of the primary advantages of GIFT is that very little new ITS functionality is dictated, existing functions are standardized, and the ability to expand is clearly defined.

3 Online Agents and Online Learning

Terms such as "microadaptive instruction" or "inner instructional loop" may refer to one or more tutoring actions taken with the student. These actions may include hinting, prompting, metacognitive reflection, and others. All these actions are provided to help the learner overcome an impasse in problem solving. For the systems able to assign multiples of these actions (i.e. a service which recommends hinting conflicting with a service recommending prompting), there is a mitigation function to help make sure that all available instructional actions are not taken simultaneously. As an example, AutoTutor Lite uses a cycle of pump → hint → prompt → assert as the student progressively needs more content or assistance [11]. Generally speaking, these online actions are taken in order to nudge, rather than didactically instruct, the student towards the preferred manner of thinking on problem solving. The online and real-time components of these decisions deal with data and decisions which are of small grain size, or of small individual impact.

3.1 Learning Agents

The typical approach for the creation of an intelligent tutoring system follows a relatively simple process. First, a system is developed and deployed into a production setting while using a baseline (usually manually created) process. Second, the learner data for this system is analyzed using an approach such as a Bayesian network, reinforcement learning algorithm, or equivalent. Third, the findings are used to improve the initial models, which serve as the baseline for the next version of the system. This collect-model-update cycle varies for different ITS. Many systems have followed this approach for affective learner modeling [12], domain modeling [13], or instructional modeling [14].

An alternative approach for creating an ITS is to develop agents which can learn in the presence of new data. While this approach reduces human control of the final model, and perhaps reduces scientific validity, it generally produces improved model quality [14]. This is because an agent-based ITS can continuously improve its underlying models based on ground truth observations, customized to the actual content delivered. An example of such a system is one which begins to build an initial model from available data/decisions, modifies or customizes the model for a new student, and puts the new model into practice immediately. It makes most use of policy information compatible with multiple instructional domains, allows configuration from observed evidence, and can potentially share this knowledge with other similar agents and processes.

3.2   Potential Implementations

GIFT is based on the learning effect chain, whereby learner data informs learner states which inform instructional strategy selection which influence learning gains [1]. This chain is instantiated in the GIFT software as a Domain Module which informs a Learner Module which informs a Pedagogical Module which selects instructional strategies which are implemented as instructional tactics in the Domain Module. Each portion of data is passed in real-time in order to deliver content to the student. The most basic implementation of agent policies is to add a policy-handling component to the existing structure. The left side of Fig. 1 shows how these items exist in current GIFT architecture, while right side of Fig. 1 shows the addition of policy information. Figure 2 shows an in-depth implementation of the concept of policy overlay to existing functionality.

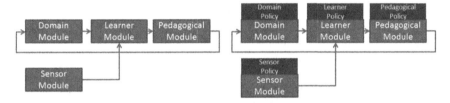

Fig. 1. The addition of a policy component to the existing GIFT structure in order to accommodate real-time agent functionality.

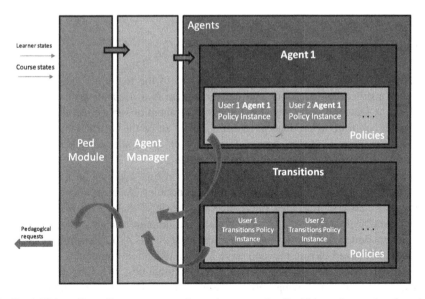

Fig. 2. Addition of a policy component shown in greater detail within an instructional module (pedagogical policy)

However, as agents and agent-based practices are added to GIFT, a manner of representation is needed, this is especially prevalent for a changing structure over time, such as when a policy is learned for a specific class of users over a large series of interactions. A manner of autonomously changing system behavior can be added through the addition of a policy component as an overlay to the module. In this manner, the initial module configuration (via various configuration files) can be referenced in mutable policy, changed in the presence of new data, and de-conflicted in the event of conflict. The addition of this type of policy information enables additional features and functions to be supported. Examples of these behaviors for specific model instantiations are presented in Table 1.

Table 1. Listing of modules, example module policies, and data sources for model updates

Module	Policy example	Cause for alteration
Domain module	Selection of instructional tactic, selecting a shorter segment instead of a longer one	Time available for student
Domain module	Generation of an after action review (AAR) as part of a sequence of content	Student actions
Learner module	Prediction of student state, based on difficulty of concepts (mined from previous example)	Updated assessment of individual student, classroom, or introduction of new data source
Pedagogical module	Selection among conflicting instructional policies ("hint" or "prompt")	Varying observed effects dependent on authored quality

4 Offline Agents and Services

In contrast to online agents which perform as part of the real-time decision loop for managing instructional decisions and delivery, there is a need for offline agents and services. The factors driving the need for an offline agent or service include output that takes too much time to produce in real-time, the size of the instructional decision is larger than a single time-step, a need to reach back to an alternative data source, or output that is appropriate for multiple online modules.

The expansion of the GIFT architecture shown in Fig. 1 allows for a single policy which links to other policy components in other modules. As an example, a policy of "progressive mastery" (teaching one concept to mastery, then moving to the second concept) can be linked across the pedagogical and domain modules in order to coordinate instruction. Such a policy would require components to be present in both of the key areas, initialized at runtime, and have a communication component for synchronization. This policy add-on enables two core functionalities: switching policies based on observed results, and having policies based on multiple module functionality. This addition of a policy component, although simple, provides significant capability.

4.1   Functions and Features

The Advanced Distributed Learning (ADL) group has put together a number of technologies for providing underlying standards for the next generation of intelligent tutoring systems. Some examples of the offline services offered by agents include items such as the Learning Registry, which is an indexing service which extends to a number of publishers for the point of being able to integrate content, as a reusable learning object, into various learning systems. On top of this layer, it is anticipated that offline agents can be constructed to provide additional information on the content (e.g. metadata, paradata, learning object descriptors) or to provide content-matching services between the users and the content. The accumulated products of these offline agents would have be available to the online services and agents such that online services could make use of them. As new offline agents are developed to provide new products, online ITS agents would simply require new policies to enable them to make appropriate use of those new products.

Finally, it is possible that some policies may be developed offline but utilized online. For example, some instructional decisions may require information gathered across several modules, or may be based on products compiled from other offline agents but that inform decisions made in an online environment. Such information may require the use of a policy component which is constructed offline, but shared in an online environment. This type of function would learn from many different instructional decisions from many learners in many domains, with varying amount of learner history.

4.2   Potential Implementations

Unlike online agent, policies, and services, GIFT has no prescribed structure for the implementation and communication of offline components. Provided that formats and configurations are suitable for online instantiations, there is no requirement for offline standardization at this time. This leaves the offline implementations free to use all data

Table 2. Module-specific services and policies for GIFT

Module using agent/service	Service/policy example	Data source
Domain module	Creation of customized scenarios around instructional needs	Bank of specific, instructionally valid, examples
Domain module	Pre-generation of hints, loaded in for selection at runtime	Domain-specific text corpus, learning objectives
Domain module	Recommendation service	Based on learner learning goals
Learner module	Modeling of competencies and mapping to taught concepts	Learner record store, trace data of transferability of skills from previous sessions
Pedagogical module	Update to instructional model for a specific domain	History of many learners across many courses

available and all standard formats. The limitations on offline services are more relaxed, and examples of various potential services are provided in Table 2.

5   Efforts Towards Unification and an Interoperable Learning Ecosystem

One of the core concepts behind the GIFT architecture has been to unify the various commonly used portions of intelligent tutoring systems. This effort now allows for the incorporation of agents and policy components which can be expanded across each of its core modules, and across offline and online processes. However, GIFT is not unique in its role to attempt standardization among various services. Techniques such as those implemented in the Open Agent Architecture (OAA) serve as brokering functions between application agents, meta-agents (facilitate coordination with other agents), and user agents. The typical functions from this and similar systems from various frameworks include the user side (front end), processing side (back end), and functionality side (module purposes).

Not only do we seek to unify commonly used portions of intelligent tutoring systems, but also to enable GIFT to be interoperable with the larger learning ecosystem. As described above, the ADL group has been developing standards and agents (e.g., PAL, TLA) for such a purpose. As more of these services are developed by various groups, the risk is that interoperability challenges will multiply. In such an increasingly diverse and complex ecosystem, the need for intelligent agents will only grow. Agents will be needed to broker the needs of systems like GIFT and the potential catalogue of services available in the larger learning ecosystem. As an example, the Virtual Human Toolkit (VHTk) provides the functionality to model the various aspects of virtual humans. This functionality includes aspects and services such as speech processing, emotional modeling of the learner, emotional modeling of the virtual human, the gestures of the virtual human, rendering, and other services. It has been used in many tutoring or learning programs [15]. This particular product/package provides for the integration of many functional back-end features required for human modeling. Virtual humans serve as a good example of agents or agent based systems that would routinely interact with an ITS like GIFT. Currently GIFT has limited ability to operate with the VHTk through basic service calls to supporting functionality. However, in a more agent based GIFT, this would be accomplished much more easily by creating the necessary policies via the VHTk, having them represented within modules, and delivering them to the students.

A final example of services being developed in the larger learning ecosystem is the Generalized Learning Utilities (SuperGLU). This is a collection of back-end services and features developed through Office of Naval Research initiative funding to provide functionality for offline processes and policies [16]. These services include the communication of learner performance data, through the xAPI standard [8], the ability to add agents without knowledge of the other agent components, and the overall integration of various tutoring services and data structures. SuperGLU is additionally intend to work with LearnSphere, as an effort to unite the storage and processing of data generated by tutoring systems.

6 Conclusion and Future Research

Transforming GIFT into an agent-based system has both advantages and some disadvantages. The anticipated benefits include the simplification of development through automating the creation and refinement of underlying models and to simplify interoperability with a larger learning ecosystem. A potential disadvantage is that as agents take over the task of refining models and managing interactions among different systems, humans become monitors and managers of system development rather than architects. There is some risk that this would result in humans being less effective or efficient in troubleshooting or in making system-wide changes that might improve performance, considering the additional complications of having a system which changes over time.

The benefits of making GIFT into a learning agent-based system are enticing. Developing learner and pedagogy models through research is time and resource intensive. Developing intelligent learning agents that can in effect figure out what works and automatically improve those models could potentially save huge amounts of time and resources. Furthermore the larger learning ecosystem is an ever changing entity. Using intelligent, learning agents to constantly search that ecosystem and establish interfaces between GIFT and new and changing services and agents in that ecosystem would also save substantial resources.

On the other hand, the risks of converting GIFT (or any system) into an agent-based system should not be overlooked. As humans manage system evolution by changing system rewards through new or revised policies, there is always the risk that those changes may not have the intended effect on learning performance. For example, suppose a policy was created to reduce time to train one module in a course without decreasing performance in that module. Suppose the policy change was successful, but a second order consequence was that there was a decrement in student performance on another module in the same course. Single-minded focus on limited metrics can result in unintended effects on other, unmeasured, items. To troubleshoot such issues, it will be necessary for system managers to be able to understand why those policy changes had those effects. This would not be a simple problem to solve and it would be more difficult if managers could not see or understand what the agent had done to reduce training time for the targeted module. Add to this the possibility that multiple agents could be making changes to different models at the same time, and one can see that untangling the causes and effects on overall system performance could be quite difficult. Thus it will be important to develop ways for agents to provide system managers with human-readable reports on changes made to the system as well as other agent activities. These and perhaps other challenges lie ahead as we implement an agent-based design for GIFT.

References

1. Sottilare, R.A., Brawner, K.W., Goldberg, B.S., Holden, H.A.: The Generalized Intelligent Framework for Tutoring (GIFT). US Army Research Laboratory (2012)
2. Franklin, S., Graesser, A.: Is it an agent, or just a program?: a taxonomy for autonomous agents. In: Jennings, N.R., Wooldridge, M.J., Müller, J.P. (eds.) ECAI-WS 1996 and ATAL 1996. LNCS, vol. 1193, pp. 21–35. Springer, Heidelberg (1997)
3. Cheikes, B.A.: Gia: an agent-based architecture for intelligent tutoring systems. In: Proceedings of the CIKM 1995 Workshop on Intelligent Information Agents. Citeseer (1995)
4. Gascueña, J.M., Fernández-Caballero, A.: An agent-based intelligent tutoring system for enhancing e-learning/e-teaching. Int. J. Instr. Technol. Distance Learn. **2**, 11–24 (2005)
5. Lopes, C.R.: A multiagent architecture for distance education systems. In: Null, p. 368. IEEE (2003)
6. Chepegin, V., Aroyo, L., De Bra, P., Houben, G.: CHIME: service-oriented framework for adaptive web-based systems. In: Conferentie Informatiewetenschap, pp. 29–36. Citeseer (2003)
7. Lin, F., Holt, P., Leung, S., Hogeboom, M., Cao, Y.: A multi-agent and service-oriented architecture for developing integrated and intelligent web-based education systems. In: International Workshop on Applications of Semantic Web Technologies for E-Learning at the International Conference on Intelligent Tutoring Systems (2004)
8. Regan, D.A.: The training and learning architecture: infrastructure for the future of learning. In: Invited Keynote International Symposium on Information Technology and Communication in Education (SINTICE), Madrid, Spain (2013)
9. Regan, D., Raybourn, E.M., Durlach, P.: Learning modeling consideration for a personalized assistant for learning (PAL). In: Design Recommendations for Adaptive Intelligent Tutoring Systems: Learner Modeling, vol. 1 (2013)
10. Wray, R.E., Woods, A.: A cognitive systems approach to tailoring learner practice. In: Proceedings of the Second Annual Conference on Advances in Cognitive Systems ACS, p. 38 (2013)
11. D'mello, S., Graesser, A.: Autotutor and affective autotutor: learning by talking with cognitively and emotionally intelligent computers that talk back. ACM Trans. Interact. Intell. Syst. (TiiS) **2**, 23 (2012)
12. Ramirez, G.A., Baltrušaitis, T., Morency, L.-P.: Modeling latent discriminative dynamic of multi-dimensional affective signals. In: D'Mello, S., Graesser, A., Schuller, B., Martin, J.-C. (eds.) ACII 2011, Part II. LNCS, vol. 6975, pp. 396–406. Springer, Heidelberg (2011)
13. Duong, H., Zhu, L., Wang, Y., Heffernan, N.: A prediction model that uses the sequence of attempts and hints to better predict knowledge: "better to attempt the problem first, rather than ask for a hint". In: Educational Data Mining 2013 (2013)
14. Liu, Y.-E., Mandel, T., Brunskill, E., Popovic, Z.: Trading off scientific knowledge and user learning with multi-armed bandits. In: Educational Data Mining, London, UK (2014)
15. Lane, H.C., Hays, M., Core, M., Gomboc, D., Forbell, E., Auerbach, D., Rosenberg, M.: Coaching intercultural communication in a serious game. In: Proceedings of the 16th International Conference on Computers in Education, pp. 35–42 (2008)
16. Benjamin, N., Xiangen, H., Graesser, A., Zhiqiang, C.: Autotutor in the cloud: a service-oriented paradigm for an interoperable natural-language its. J. Adv. Distrib. Learn. Technol. **2**, 49–63 (2014)

Intelligent Tutoring Gets Physical: Coaching the Physical Learner by Modeling the Physical World

Benjamin Goldberg[✉]

U.S. Army Research Laboratory-Human Research and Engineering Directorate,
Orlando, FL, USA
benjamin.s.goldberg.civ@mail.mil

Abstract. Extending the application of intelligent tutoring beyond the desktop and into the physical world is a sought after capability. If implemented correctly, Artificial Intelligence (AI) tools and methods can be applied to support personalized and adaptive on-the-job training experiences as well as assist in the development of knowledge, skills and abilities (KSAs) across athletics and psychomotor domain spaces. While intelligent tutoring in a physical world is not a traditional application of such technologies, it still operates in much the same fashion as all Intelligent Tutoring Systems (ITS) in existence. It takes raw system interaction data and applies modeling techniques to infer performance and competency while a learner executes tasks within a scenario or defined problem set. While a traditional ITS observes learner interaction and performance to infer cognitive understanding of a concept and procedure, a physical ITS will observe interaction and performance to infer additional components of behavioral understanding and technique. A question the authors address in this paper is how physical interactions can be captured in an ITS friendly format and what technologies currently exist to monitor learner physiological signals and free-form behaviors? Answering the question involves a breakdown of the current state-of-the-art across technologies spanning wearable sensors, computer vision, and motion tracking that can be applied to model physical world components. The breakdown will include the pros and cons of each technology, an example of a domain model the data provided can inform, and the implications the derived models have on pedagogical decisions for coaching and reflection.

Keywords: Intelligent tutoring systems · Physical modeling · Psychomotor · Wearable sensors

1 Introduction

The concept of Augmented Cognition (AugCog) is based on the application of technology to impart information on a user that is not inherently perceivable in the natural task environment. This information is intended to assist a user in executing a task by enhancing an individual's cognitive function in support of meeting a specified objective. From a training and education perspective, AugCog practices are associated with adaptive instructional techniques that augment the path an individual takes in learning a topic or skill and the type of coaching they receive along the way. These management

© Springer International Publishing Switzerland 2016
D.D. Schmorrow and C.M. Fidopiastis (Eds.): AC 2016, Part II, LNAI 9744, pp. 13–22, 2016.
DOI: 10.1007/978-3-319-39952-2_2

decisions are based on models configured to inform interactions across domain, learner, and pedagogical representations of a training space. These applications are traditionally referred to in the literature as Intelligent Tutoring Systems (ITS).

To date, majority of ITSs are built around strictly cognitive problem domains, with notable successes seen across an array of academic and military applications [1]. What is a sought after capability, and more achievable now than ever with advances in wearable technologies, is extending these practices to the physical world in pursuit of training psychomotor skills. This involves tasks that associate cognition with physical interaction to meet an established goal, and incorporates a combination of hand-eye coordination, muscle memory, and behavioral techniques that dictate performance and assessed acquisition of skill.

While this can be considered a novel extension of traditional ITS methods, its implementation doesn't vary significantly from systems of the past. It utilizes models built on domain and learner information to inform a pedagogical decision. In this instance, the domain isn't informed solely by performance and procedural information communicated by a training application; it now requires methods to collect task relevant behavioral measures that can be used to capture a physical technique and assess performance against a set of specified standards. The important component here is that the information collected must be done in a task's natural environment, where the physical actions can be performed with zero hindrances.

An area of interest to the research community is identifying data types required to model psychomotor interactions at a hand-eye coordination level, and how best to utilize available sensor technologies to instrument the learner and the training environment with data streams that can accurately track behavior. In this paper we discuss the facets associated with the development of a psychomotor adaptive training capability. This includes reviewing theory surrounding psychomotor learning and skill acquisition, how to enable assessment and coaching from a physical problem space, and what commercial off-the-shelf sensors can provide valuable data to infer skill.

2   Learning a New Skill and the Role of Coaching and Feedback

There are common tenets expressed in the literature associated with learning a new skill (see Fig. 1 for a mind map of variables associated with psychomotor skill development [2]). The first and foremost is that experience and practice trumps all. However, simply practicing a skill over and over does not necessarily lead to expert performance. How individuals progress in skill development is based on a number of factors. Anders Ericson's theory of deliberate practice highlights the following attributes of an effective practice event: (1) the event is designed to improve performance; (2) the individual has the ability to repeat the application over multiple trials; (3) the task requires high mental engagement; and (4) feedback is continuously made available that is designed to serve in a coaching capacity [3]. The fourth factor is critical when determining the implications of using ITSs to replace human counterparts to train psychomotor skills.

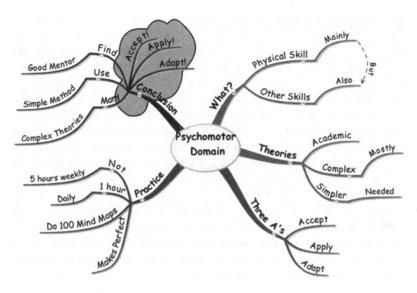

Fig. 1. The psychomotor domain as mind mapped by Faizel Mohidin [2]

Acquiring a new skill follows three primary phases of development, each building on top of the other: (1) beginner/novice phase where an individual tries to understand the cognitive and physical requirements of the activity to generate actions while avoiding errors; (2) the intermediate/journeyman phase where focused attention on task performance is no longer required and noticeable errors become increasingly rare; and (3) the expert phase where the execution of a skill becomes automated with minimal effort and exertion [4, 5]. How individuals progress through these three phases of skill acquisition and the rate at which they do so is dependent on the factors listed above.

From the coaching perspective, especially within the beginner/novice phase, how can an individual modify behavior if there is no way to effectively link actions to observed outcomes? During this phase of learning, behavioral tendencies are established and schemas are built in memory, making feedback to instill proper habits critical. In the traditional sense, a coach/instructor with knowledge in the domain will observe a learner, identify errors in their behavior as determined by a performance outcome, and provide feedback to correct errors and reinforce proper technique.

Utilizing technology to facilitate this inference procedure is challenging. It requires a machine to have the ability to consume perceptual information that associates with behaviors an expert human would assess, and models to determine how the captured data relates to a representation of desired behavior. This identified capability requires a representation of knowledge an expert works with to dictate coaching practices and warrants the utility of a deconstructed task analysis, breaking a domain down into its piece parts in a hierarchical structure of varying skills and applications.

2.1 Deconstructing a Psychomotor Domain

In terms of relating what's already been discussed to a real-world example, take the domain of basketball. When someone is attempting to learn basketball for the first time, the initial approach to instruction is focused on a set of fundamentals. These fundamentals set a foundation of required skills to successfully perform as an elite basketball player. In this instance you can decompose basketball into three physical fundamental skills: (1) dribbling, (2) passing, and (3) shooting. Each of these breakdown further into a set of sub-skills that ascend in complexity as you progress through practice opportunities (e.g., dribbling with your dominant hand, to dribbling with your non-dominant hand, to dribbling between hands, to dribbling between your legs, to dribbling behind your back, etc.). The desired end state is the development of muscle memory to automatically perform a task without dedicating cognitive function to make it happen. When you establish automated execution of fundamental behaviors, then an individual can progress to more complex scenarios requiring advanced application of a skill (e.g., dribbling while being defended). This is followed by practice opportunities to combine the application of skills to perform a higher level task.

This analogy can associate with almost all psychomotor domains of instruction, regardless if its association with job-related activities or athletics. Each domain can be deconstructed into a set of fundamental components that are performed when a situation warrants their execution. The goal of an automated ITS is to establish models of fundamental behaviors to make the assessment space manageable. While the assessment space of a domain is defined around a set of concepts and objectives, it is inherently dictated by the data one can collect.

3 Modeling the Physical World

Modeling a physical task requires an understanding of the physical environment that task is being performed within. The environment will determine the granularity level of data a model can be built from, and can range from a highly customized room built with sensing technologies to detect specific data feeds, to an open warehouse or gymnasium, to an open field in the wild. The ideal situation involves a task environment instrumented to inform both performance and behavior metrics that can assess causal relationships. But the ideal environment to support this methodology is rare. That is why establishing tools for collecting relevant information in a less controlled space is critical to the success of ITSs being used in the wild. In the following subsections, we will describe three modeling scenarios: (1) modeling a psychomotor task in a highly sensorized environment that is tightly-coupled, (2) modeling a psychomotor task in a confined space with no custom sensors that is loosely-coupled, and (3) modeling a psychomotor task in an unrestricted space out in the open.

In each scenario, sensor inputs will be identified. While the first scenario is based on an actual research project being conducted at the U.S. Army Research Laboratory, the latter two are presented as hypothetical applications. In this instance, we aim to identify notional applications of sensor technologies to monitor physical interaction and behaviors that can personalize training in physical spaces.

3.1 Modeling a Physical Task in a Highly Sensorized Environment

Highly sensorized training environments used to develop physical skills provide excellent opportunities to produce initial psychomotor ITS applications. In these scenarios, an environment is built with components to track predefined behaviors. These behaviors are tracked to allow instructors to better inform their decisions on what aspects of a skill to instruct, or in this instance use sensors to model task behaviors to automatically assess skill and trigger coaching feedback.

An example of this ideal scenario can be seen in work we're performing on the development of an adaptive marksmanship training capability [6]. For this project, we are working with the U.S. Army's Engagement Skills Trainer (EST; see Fig. 2). The EST is a simulated firing range that recreates the tasks executed on a live range in a safe/cost-effective setting. In our effort, we're focused on building an ITS to support the development of Basic Rifle Marksmanship (BRM) skills and fundamentals.

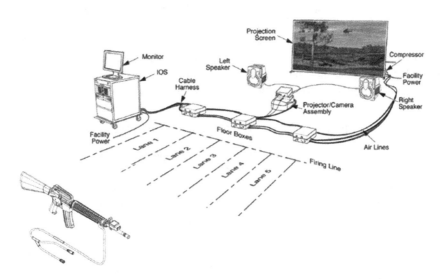

Fig. 2. The U.S. army engagement skills trainer

The EST offers an excellent testbed for this use case based on the features it provides. The system was developed to log data linked to both performance and behavioral metrics. In terms of BRM, the EST tracks performance across a set of grouping exercises that gauge metrics on group size and group accuracy. In addition to the performance metrics, the EST weapons are outfitted with sensor technologies that associate with behavioral properties. These include sensors to track: (1) the aim trace of the weapon barrel, (2) the distance the trigger travels in relation to time, (3) the cant angle of the rifle, and (4) the amount of pressure applied to the buttstock of the rifle.

With all of this contextual data, we were able to build models of expert behavior across a set of performers within the Army Marksmanship Unit's Service Rifle Team. The models were based on the four fundamentals of BRM outlined in the training field manual: (1) breathing, (2) trigger control, (3) body position, and (4) sight alignment.

The models are used as benchmarks to assess a trainee's behavior against to determine if they are properly performing the fundamentals of BRM procedures as deemed by a field of experts. To build out this prototype, we utilized the Generalized Intelligent Framework for Tutoring (GIFT).

Generalized Intelligent Framework for Tutoring (GIFT). GIFT is a domain-independent framework established to author, deliver, and evaluate ITS technologies [7]. It provides a set of standards to follow in creating models across a domain, learner, and pedagogical schema. In special instances, GIFT supports the consumption of sensor information to inform states not linked directly to system interaction data and can extend modeling techniques to monitor affective and physical attributes of a learner. For the adaptive marksmanship ITS, GIFT is configured to take in the EST data streams through the sensor module, where the data is filtered and processed in real-time to assess against the represented expert behaviors. This assessment is used to select a performance state for each of the BRM fundamentals, where those skills assessed as below expectation are used to guide the selection of coaching feedback to deliver. While we are making good progress on developing an ITS for teaching BRM, and the EST provides an ideal set of behavioral information, how to extend these methods into more advanced skills of marksmanship execution (i.e., hitting moving targets) need to be further conceptualized.

3.2   Modeling a Physical Task in a Confined Space with no Custom Sensors

In this scenario, psychomotor activity is believed to be performed in a controlled space designed to support task execution, but lacks the inclusion of customized sensors built to collect task relevant information. In this instance, we are interested in identifying technologies that can extend the assessment space of these environments to inform contextually relevant variables. This includes identifying what variables matter in consistently gauging performance and behavior across a wide range of tasks.

While each domain has unique assessment requirements, many can share similar data to infer completely different skill applications. This would depend on how the data is represented in a model and how that model is linked to a component and/or fundamental of a skill. The hope is to avoid building a set of custom sensors and to utilize commercial off-the-shelf sensing technologies. In a controlled space, the following technologies are believed to provide valuable information for modeling the physical world: (1) motion tracking and (2) wearable sensors.

In most instances, this scenario may be the most complex of the three. With the task being performed in a confined space, the characteristics of the task actions most likely associate with fine motor control over a set of environmental objects. For this reason, it is important to understand the current state of the art of what information can be made available for modeling purposes, and how that impacts the type of domains an ITS can currently support under these environmental conditions. An overarching assumption with all selected technologies is that they can communicate data in real-time to an architecture that can process and model its outputs, such as GIFT.

Motion Tracking. In many psychomotor tasks, monitoring the physical motions of an individual's movement and skeletal structure can go a long way into assessing their behavior. This is especially true in fitness training, athletics, and task-oriented domains that require precise movements to meet standard performance. Depending on the domain being trained, the body is constrained to certain movements and actions that can be executed in support of meeting a task objective. It is assumed under these conditions that behavioral characteristics can be modeled for determining proper execution. In this instance, logging data over a window of time as you observe a set of experts perform a task can be used to determine if there are trends in behavior that influence outcomes and proper techniques. If trends can be identified through statistical inference procedures, then models can be established to compare trainee data against in real-time to diagnose performance on a set of behaviors.

The challenge is using motion based information, which can be noisy in nature and not of appropriate validity in measuring precise movements, to build assessment models that operate in an ITS. Outfitting the environment with motion tracking technology can be used to quantifiably monitor user actions, which is a start. For the context of this paper, we associate motion tracking technology as a free standing system of cameras and sensors that can be placed throughout a confined space. The issue is that a technology of this nature limits the amount of space a task can be conducted within. That's why it's important to understand the characteristics of a domain to determine if this type of modeling technique is viable.

For implementation purposes, systems can be as complex as cameras placed throughout a training space that are designed to locate and track a set of reflective markers that can be placed on a number of items (e.g., placed on a bodysuit worn by a user or on interaction environment elements in an environment, like a baseball bat seen in the left image of Fig. 3). Motion tracking can also be supported by commercial products like the Microsoft Kinect 2, where no markers are required to capture and track an individual's skeletal structure, producing an image like the one seen on the right of Fig. 3. Regardless of the approach selected, motion tracking can be a nice option when the task environment is confined. There is still much work to.

Fig. 3. Motion tracking technologies: on left is motion tracking resulting from wearable bodysuit with mounted reflectors; on right is motion tracking resulting from Microsoft Kinect.

Wearable Sensors. Recent advancements in wearable technologies have made them a viable data source when considering inputs for informing models to train psychomotor skills. In the context of this paper, wearable sensors are any technology that can be unobtrusively attached to a user that logs physiological and behavioral measures. Common metrics collected by these devices include electrocardiogram/heartrate information, accelerometer data, gyroscope information, galvanic skin response, breathing patterns in some instances, and location data if GPS compliant.

The current application of these sensors within the commercial world is primarily for health tracking purposes. The combination of data channels can output metrics related to activity levels, stress, and sleep patterns. The market is very competitive, with a near endless selection of options ranging from the data they provide and the style of which they are worn.

From a training perspective, the research goal is to identify how best to use these technologies to collect information that can be used to guide skill acquisition of a physical task. Majority of the current products involve sensors that wear either around the wrist or ankle. These typically record a comprehensive set of physiological markers, behavioral movement data, and environmental factors such as temperature and UV exposure. While many of these provide valuable information to monitor activity and affective variables such as stress, they lack granular data sources linked to precision of movements from a motor-control angle.

However, that's not true for all wearable sensors. Products like the MOOV Now and Zepp Sports sensors provide real-time 3D motion tracking of a joint/limb on the human body (see Fig. 4). This information is logged and visualized for replay purposes. Current applications like Zepp allow you to replay your data feed side-by-side with data collected

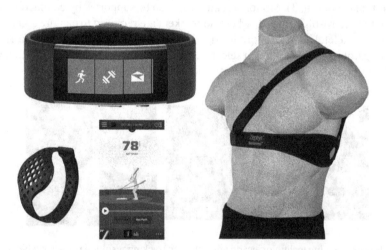

Fig. 4. Wearable sensing technologies: upper left is the Microsoft Band 2 [http://www.microsoft.com/microsoft-band]; lower left is the MOOV now activity bracelet that supports 3D motion tracking [http://welcome.moov.cc/] and the Zepp Baseball sensor output [http://www.zepp.com]; right is Zephyr Technologies' BioHarness 3 wearable sensor [http://www.zephyranywhere.com/].

from an expert for a comparative evaluation, but there is no coaching beyond that. Exploring modeling techniques that take these three dimensional tracking feeds and associate behavioral parameters in association with a task fundamental or objective is essential for ITSs supporting this interaction environment.

3.3   Modeling a Physical Task Out in the Open

In considering a physical domain performed in a boundless open environment, sensing technologies play a different role than seen in the confined space. In this instance, tasks are performed that require coordination of movements and activities over possible large distances, with factors of location, speed, acceleration, and terrain playing a role in how the task is performed. For an excellent review of this conceptual environment with a use case centered on land navigation, see Sottilare & LaViola, 2015 [8]. In their review, the authors present a set of 'smart glasses' and a feasibility analysis of their application in a live land navigation training scenario.

As the majority of smart glasses sync to a cellular device for processing purposes, the smart glasses themselves primarily serve as tools to present information to a user, with many options including simple text message overlays, objects placed to augment the visual environment, or videos containing instructional material. From a behavioral sensing standpoint, these smart glasses can utilize forward facing cameras to assess an individual's orientation within an environment, with the ability to make inferences on what someone should see based on a calculation of their visual field of view from a specified Global Positioning System (GPS) coordinate.

Beyond the smart glass inputs and outputs, the real sensing taking place in this training environment is provided through the phone, with this example providing GPS location data as tracked over a cellular network. With this information, assessment rules can be built in GIFT based on the data factors listed above. Zones of interest can also be established that can trigger situational awareness oriented tutorial interventions, forcing an individual to reflect on the situation and respond to a prompt that can be used to assess competency and trigger coaching interactions.

In these open environment training events, there can be a combination of open and confined task characteristics, where a sensing technology can be applied to track both location, as well as fine motor-movements. In this instance, computation on wearable sensors providing 3-D motion tracking, like the MOOV Now sensor described above, must be done on a mobile device. This requires GIFT modules to run locally, as the range on wearable sensors doesn't support long range distances. Computations must be performed on the cellular device, with behavioral state information communicated through the network in support of GIFT's learning effect chain. This approach to physical modeling is also critical for team-oriented training tasks. From this perspective, multiple entities can be tracked in a single environment. Formations can be monitored, and team oriented behaviors can be modeled to establish boundaries of acceptable performance.

4   Conclusion

In this paper, we present high-level hypothetical considerations that can be used to guide requirement discussions in the development of a psychomotor-based ITS. Modeling the physical world to support automated coaching of psychomotor skills is not by any means a simple task. As evident by the described modeling use cases, capturing data granular enough to inform accurate assessments is limited, even when customized environments are established. In addition, there are multiple architectural considerations that must be addressed to consume, process, and act upon behavioral information linked to a skill fundamental.

References

1. Kulik, J.A., Fletcher, J.: Effectiveness of intelligent tutoring systems: a meta-analytic review. Rev. Educ. Res. **86**(1), 42–78 (2016)
2. Mohidin, F.: Blooms Taxonomy – The Psychomotor Domain and Mind Mapping (No Date). http://www.mindmaptutor.com/blooms-taxonomy-the-psychomotor-domain-and-mind-mapping. Accessed 8 Jan 2016
3. Ericsson, K.A.: The influence of experience and deliberate practice on the development of superior expert performance. In: Cambridge Handbook of Expertise and Expert Performance, pp. 683–703 (2006)
4. Ericsson, K.A., Krampe, R.T., Tesch-Romer, C.: The role of deliberate practice in the acquisition of expert performance. Psychol. Rev. **100**(3), 363–406 (1993)
5. Fitts, P.M., Posner, M.I.: Human Performance. Brooks/Cole Publishing, Belmont (1967)
6. Goldberg, B., Amburn, C.: The application of GIFT in a psychomotor domain of instruction: a marksmanship use case. In: Proceedings of 3rd Annual GIFT Users Symposium, Orlando, FL (2015)
7. Goldberg, B., Sottilare, R., Brawner, K., Sinatra, A., Ososky, S.: Developing a generalized intelligent framework for tutoring (GIFT): informing design through a community of practice. In: Workshop at the 2015 International Conference on Artificial Intelligence in Education (AIED). Madrid, Spain (2015)
8. Sottlare, R., LaViola, J.: Extending intelligent tutoring beyond the desktop to the psychomotor domain. In: Proceedings of the Interservice/Industry Training Simulation and Education Conference (I/ITSEC), Orlando, FL (2015)

Measuring Stress in an Augmented Training Environment: Approaches and Applications

David Jones$^{(\boxtimes)}$ and Sara Dechmerowski

Design Interactive, Orlando, FL, USA
{david.jones,sara.dechmerowski}@desgninteractive.net

Abstract. Augmented reality (AR) and virtual reality (VR) training systems provide an opportunity to place learners in high stress conditions that are impossible in real life due to safety risks or the associated costs. Using physiological classifiers it is possible to continually measure the stress levels of learners within AR and VR training environments to adapt training based on their responses. This paper reviews stress measurement approaches, outlines an adaptive stress training model that can be applied to augment training and describes key characteristics and future research that is critical to realizing adaptive VR and AR training platforms that take into account learner stress levels.

Keywords: Adaptive training · Objective stress measurement · Training fidelity evaluation · High-stress training · Augmented Reality

1 Introduction

One goal of Augmented Reality (AR) training is to inject virtual objects and events into a live environment to allow trainees to acquire the targeted knowledge, skills, and abilities in a highly realistic environment. Two primary reasons to apply AR within a training program are to reduce the cost associated with live training entities and to create stressful conditions that could cause a significant level of risk if completed live. The goals and benefits of Virtual Reality (VR) training are a similar balance of creating highly realistic and potentially stressful conditions while controlling the risk and cost of training. The process of inducing stress within a controlled training environment is important when preparing learners to perform for high-stress conditions. Alternatively, there is utility in increasing levels of perceived stress and associated arousal within AR and VR environments in order to engage learners.

A variety of methods of inducing stress during training have been developed and evaluated [1–4] and resilience training and stress inoculation programs rely on those applications to elicit target states during training. For example, the U.S. Air Force's Stress Inoculation Training (SIT) program trains battlefield airmen to first understand the negative effects of stress, learn to detect and control stress responses, and finally practice skills taught under realistic high stress conditions [5]. Guidance followed during this program suggests that stressor intensity should be incrementally increased as task proficiency is demonstrated [6]. This approach ensures that trainees are not overwhelmed early which could interfere with skill acquisition while continuing to push learners operate under more and more realistic high-stress conditions [6].

© Springer International Publishing Switzerland 2016
D.D. Schmorrow and C.M. Fidopiastis (Eds.): AC 2016, Part II, LNAI 9744, pp. 23–33, 2016.
DOI: 10.1007/978-3-319-39952-2_3

The greatest challenge with creating training that balances learner stress levels lies in the ability to track learner stress levels over time.

This paper presents an approach to objectively measure stress levels during AR and VR training and reviews applications of the approach to optimize and evaluate training programs. The presented technology leverages a physiology-based stress classification algorithm that has the capability to objectively and unobtrusively capture real-time individualized stress data in a mobile environment with over 95 % accuracy. While originally designed to support Veteran mental health therapy, the algorithm, which uses a wrist-worn device to collect human physiology state provides a continuous realtime stress measure that can be used to optimize AR and VR training. The approach provides a more effective option to alternatives, including subjective stress ratings or cortisol analysis post-training.

Two key applications of the stress classifier are presented in this paper. The first application is the creation of adaptive AR and VR training systems that adjust stressors that are presented to learners based on their state and performance. The goal of this application is to balance stress with training progression during AR and VR training exercises. The second application included is the objective evaluation of AR and VR training event fidelity based on objective trainee responses, with the goal of optimizing future training events. In addition to reviewing frameworks to support the application of stress evaluation in AR and VR environments, a comparative evaluation of stress evaluation techniques is presented.

2 Measuring Stress

The most important and difficult step in creating a training platform that can adapt based on trainee stress is the effective evaluation of stress. Early measurements of psychological stress have relied upon written scales that leverage a battery of validated questions to elicit a rating of stress for each individual. These scales were initially developed to support clinical psychologists and fall within two general categories of measures: Measures of stressful life events that have occurred; and measures of the subjective evaluation of perceived stress and/or ability to cope with stress.

The use of life event scales date back to Holmes and Rahe's 1967 Schedule of Recent Experiences (SRE) which includes a checklist of 43 stressful life events such as the death of a spouse, divorce, or being fired from work [7]. Each of the life events that were experienced on that scale are counted and the total is used to provide a relative stress level for the person being evaluated. Since the inception of the SRE, longer batteries and a variety of specialized batteries have been developed for special groups such as children [8] or combatants within the Gulf War [9]. Because the scales that are used require a level of customization to the events that occur within the targeted population, this approach to measuring stress has the potential to lack consistency or sensitivity.

A second approach to measuring stress involves the use of perceived stress measures. The most commonly used perceived stress measure is the Perceived Stress Scale (PSS) [10]. The PSS includes questions that measure of how unpredictable, uncontrollable, and overloaded respondents lives are in combination with direct evaluations of experienced stress levels and is available in a four, ten, and fourteen item batteries.

Although perceived stress measures are more generalizable than life event scales and can be gathered more efficiently using the four item form, they still require some level of self-evaluation and cannot be continuously gathered without breaking the flow of training.

2.1 Physiological Stress Monitoring

To support the capabilities to unobtrusively modify training based on trainee stress and performance or objectively evaluate the effectiveness of a stressor to create targeted trainee states, it is critical to move away from written batteries and towards physiological measures of stress and negative arousal. Advances in wearable physiological sensors have made it possible to measure human states that are capable of quantifying stress [11, 12], including cardiovascular and respiratory measures and electrodermal activity. Because most tasks that AR and VR training are beneficial to train require physical activity, there is risk that those measures could contain noise during training. Particularly, because the same physiological states that are affected by increases in the sympathetic nervous system activity (which allows them the be effective stress measures [13]), also tend to fluctuate due to physical activity or environmental conditions, there is a need to cast a wider net when classifying stress, and take into account a variety of physiological and environmental sates simultaneously. Table 1 provides and overview of physiological states that are particularly useful for classifying stress, examples of conditions that could create noise in each data type, and references of previous efforts to apply each measure to classify stress.

Table 1. Physiological states, features, and sources of noise for stress classification

Measure	Features	Causes of noise	Reference
Skin conductance	Skin conductance level, phasic skin conductance response	Environmental and skin temperature, humidity	[12, 15–18]
ECG	Heart rate, heart rate variability	Physical movement and performance	[12, 14, 15]
Respiration	Breathing rate, breathing depth, respiratory sinus arrhythmia	Physical movement and performance	[14, 18]

Researchers recently developed a physiological classifier of stress that leverages a combination of skin conductance, cardiovascular features, skin temperature, and physical movement collected from an Empatica E3 band to serve as the core of a clinical stress therapy tool [19]. After collecting EDA and HRV data for participants under baseline conditions and under stressed conditions (created using the Trier Social Stress Test (TSST) protocol), a linear classifier (see Fig. 1) was trained to differentiate psychological stress vs. non-stressed conditions at over 95 % accuracy. In addition to leveraging multiple features listed in Table 1, the researchers leveraged gyroscopes to detect movement and skin temperature to detect temperature to discount components of the classifier when significant levels of noise were present.

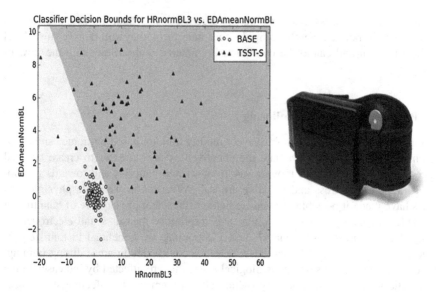

Fig. 1. Decision boundary for linear stochastic gradient descent- trained E3 classifier applied (left; reprinted from [19] with permission) and Empatica E3 band (right)

3 Leveraging Stress Measures to Improve Adaptive Training

Two of the key characteristics that are evaluated in AR and VR training applications are immersion and presence. Although throughout the history of VR and AR development there have been various interpretations of the terms, immersion generally refers to the level of fidelity of the sensory cues used within the environment while presence is a subjective response of the person experiencing the environment [20]. By this definition, it is apparent that fidelity can be objectively evaluated by comparing the visual, auditory, haptic, and olfactory cues present in a VR or AR environment to those in the live environment. Presence is a more difficult to objectively measure construct as it relies on the evaluation of the person experiencing the environment. To target this evaluation and move away from subjective ratings or presence, physiological data, including those that are described above to measure stress (e.g. change in heart rate and skin conductance) have been studies and demonstrated a correlation with presence measures over 15 years ago [21, 22].

In addition to measuring the sense of realism that VR and AR systems can instill, the use of physiological stress measures in combination with real-time performance can be used to drive adaptive training. Adaptive training has the potential to significantly optimize training efficiency [23] and based on the varied response of learners to stress exposure training, the process of adapting training based on individual responses to stressors holds even more potential. Originally designed as a clinical intervention for patients that required coping mechanisms for conditions like anger and phobic reactions, the goal of stress exposure training is to alleviate the negative effects of stress on performance by preparing personnel to perform tasks effectively under high-demand, high-stress conditions [24].

Figure 2 outlines a simplified stress appraisal process and includes two paths of stress response, one associated with the availability of effective coping mechanisms that results in normal performance and one that is associated with a stress appraisal that leads to a decrease in normal performance. VR and AR Stress Exposure Training seeks to build effective coping mechanisms through repeated presentation of stressors. In the therapy domain, this process is used to target a single phobia or condition with continuous support of a therapist throughout the process. When preparing for a wide array of stressors, such as preparing for battlefield stressors in an active combat environment, this task becomes more complicated because individuals react differently to environmental stressors based on past experiences and their appraisal of the situation [25].

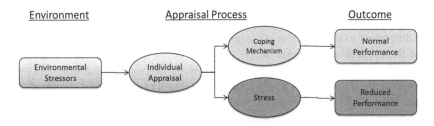

Fig. 2. Appraisal process and effects of stress

In order for the stress exposure therapy process to continually present new stressors within training to (1) determine the conditions that must be targeted in training and (2) repeat the exposure in a controlled environment that allows the development of effective coping mechanisms, it is critical that a performance and stress measurement feedback loop be created and used to drive future presentations of stressors. Stress training aims to teach the necessary skills for maintaining effective task performance under stress conditions and to enhance familiarity within the environment. Research on stress exposure training and the effects of stress provide the following guidance to the development of adaptive AR and VR training frameworks:

- Virtual training scenarios must continually be adapted to add various types of stress within the environment in order for trainees to develop coping mechanisms.
- In order ensure effective transfer of the coping strategies to the live environment, stress conditions must be similar to those found in the live environment.
- Because the goal of stress exposure training is to ensure effective task performance under stress, training must take into account the real-time performance of trainees to ensure that use of the system does not lead to negative training.

Figure 3 outlines an adaptive stressor process diagram that can be followed to control stressor presentation within VE and AR training platforms. The approach and architecture requires four key components in order to effectively drive stress training:

- Performance Evaluation- The ultimate goal of training is to improve learner performance. Although stress exposure training has the secondary goal of training performance under high stress conditions, optimizing performance must remain as the core goal of training. In order to ensure that negative training is avoided when inducing stress, it is critical to take into account trainee performance on targeted training objectives prior to evaluating learner stress states. The goal of the evaluation is for learner performance to remain high (or bounce back when performance drops) when new stressors are presented within the training scenario. For this to effectively work in a closed adaptive system, the performance evaluation metrics should be coded within the AR/VR training environment.

- Stress State Evaluation- Physiological stress monitoring provides a real-time and objective method to continuously track stress and the response to stressors within the AR/VR training environment. A wrist-worn stress monitoring approach similar to the one described above has the potential to evaluate stress when learners are in an environment that allows them to move around, such as an AR training space.

- Trainee State Classification- Once trainee performance and stress state is calculated, it's important to merge the data to support the determination of overall trainee state and the appropriate response of the training system to meet the targeted training goals. For example, the combination of good performance and a low stress state should be used to trigger a new stressor within the scenario while a combination of high stress and low performance should be used to reduce/remove the stressors present to allow trainee performance to normalize and avoid negative training.

- Stressor Activation/Deactivation Methods- In order for scenario adaptations to be applied based on performance and stress states, it is necessary to include hooks into the code to activate and deactivate stressors in real time. To meet this need, modular stressors that can be activated in real-time (e.g. reducing visual acuity of the scene, integrating additional enemies, etc.) must be designed and scripts developed to trigger them based on the evaluated trainee state.

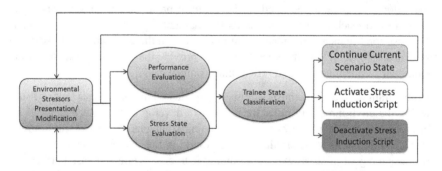

Fig. 3. Adaptive stress training process diagram

By applying a closed adaptive training cycle that can modify AR and VR training scenarios in real-time it is possible to create an ever-changing environment that pushes learners to create coping mechanisms for environmental stressors that they are expected to operate during the presentation of in a live transfer environment. The approach allows a variety of potential stressors to be presented in close succession and only continuing the focus on those that require additional coping strategies. If this approach is scaled to groups of learners, it is possible to garner knowledge regarding the effectiveness of each stressor to trigger targeted stress states on a more generalizable scale. This capability to evaluate stressor effectiveness is a second key benefit of objectively measuring stress within AR and VR training environments. By measuring the response to cues across trainees, it is possible to classify or order stressors based on their effectiveness of created targeted stress states. By evaluating additional characteristics of each trainee during this evaluation, it is possible to further classify the effectiveness of various stressor cues based on trainee characteristics such as expertise level or past experience with particular cues/conditions in a live environment. This subclassification of training stressor effectiveness has the potential to optimize the order and presentation of scenario stressors based on each trainee's specific experiences.

In order for the evaluation of stressor cues to be supported in real-time, an infrastructure must be developed to precisely track the presentation of cues in the training environment. Specifically, in addition to objective measures of stress, the following characteristics must be tracked in order to develop models of stressor effectiveness:

- Cue activation tracking- Within an AR environment stress induction cues can be triggered live or as an augmented component of the scenario. In order to evaluate the effects of cues and combination of cues accurately, a tracking system must be instantiated to track when live and augmented cues are triggered.
- Trainee characteristics- By tracking a database of trainee characteristics in addition to the stress response to various stressors as they are presented, it is possible to create a more precise prediction of the cues that will be responded to in similar ways during future training.

The approach of leveraging physiological data in combination with performance data to drive adaptive training augmentation has demonstrated significant value in previous research. For example, research has suggested that skin conductance response (SCR) as a measure of arousal can be used in combination with a contextual understanding of the training tasks that learners are completing to predict learning gains and modify adaptive tutoring systems [26]. Further research conducted at the Army Research Lab led to the development of an architecture, similar to that presented in Fig. 3, of personalized adaptive training that leverages a combination of trainee physiological state and performance to drive training adaptations [27].

4 Future Research

The research into adaptive training platforms that leverage physiological stress states to drive training augmentation shows potential to optimize training. In order to meet the potential of the approach, additional research is needed to improve stress classification and the application of stress evaluations in the adaptive training domain. Two particular areas that require additional research include the application of deep understanding of the effects of stress on learning and memories and the development of personalized measures of stress and ruggedized sensor arrays that further improve stress classification accuracy.

Learning and memory development occurs in stages, including initial memory encoding, consolidation, retrieval, and reconsolidation. Research shows that the presence of stress affects each stage of the memory/learning process in different ways [28–36]. Although factors aside from the timing of stress during the learning, recall, and reconsolidation process have effects on the process, the general understanding of the effects of stress on each stage of the process are outlined in Fig. 4. Future research on the integration of stress within VE an AR training environments should apply these basic constructs of learning and memory to create micro-adaptive training that not only adapts training to present the correct cues and conditions (as objectively evaluated), but also present them at the correct time. The goal of this application should be to prime learners to retain and consolidate new information or break the retrieval or reconsolidation of negatively trained actions and memories.

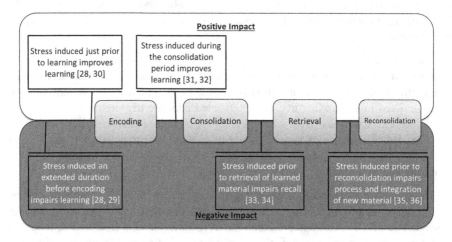

Fig. 4. Effects of stress on learning and recall process

A second avenue of research that is critical to improve the capabilities of VE and AR training systems to support adaptive stress training is the enhancement of classifiers of stress that are used to drive adaptations. Specifically, there is a need to develop approaches and systems to automate the development of personalized classifiers of stress and systems to evaluate the effects of stress training across studies and as learners move to a transfer environment. Finally, to meet this need, there is a need to develop new noninvasive hardware platforms that can measure the core features that can be used to classify stress while accounting for the noise that is associated with measuring stress in unpredictable environments. By continuing research in these domains, it will be possible to merge the power of adaptive training within AR and VR environments and objective stress measurement to better prepare people for high risk and high stress jobs and potentially reduce the impact of negative stress on people in those positions.

References

1. Bartone, P.: Resilience under military operational stress: can leaders influence hardiness? Mil. Psychol. **18**, 131–148 (2006)
2. Carroll, M., Hale, K., Stanney, K., Woodman, M., DeVore, L., Squire, P., Sciarini, L.: Framework for training adaptable and stress-resilient decision making. In: Interservice Training, Simulation, and Education Conference (I/ITSEC) (2012)
3. Jones, D., Hale, K., Dechmerowski, S., Fouad, H.: Creating adaptive emotional experience during VE training. In: Interservice Training, Simulation, and Education Conference (I/ITSEC) (2012)
4. Saunders, T., Driskell, J., Hall, J., Salas, E.: The effect of stress inoculation training on anxiety and performance. ARI Research Note, pp. 96–27 (1996)
5. Robson, S., Manacapilli, T.: Enhancing Performance Under Stress: Stress Inoculation Training for Battlefield Airmen. RAND Corporation, Santa Monica (2014)
6. Keinen, G., Friedland, N.: Training effective performance under stress: queries, dilemmas, and possible solutions. In: Driskell, J.E., Salas, E. (eds.) Stress and Human Performance, pp. 257–277. Erlbaum, Mahwah (1996)
7. Holmes, T.H., Rahe, R.H.: The social readjustment rating scale. J. Psychosom. Res. **11**(2), 213–218 (1967)
8. Grant, K.E., Compas, B.E., Thurm, A.E., McMahon, S.D., Gipson, P.Y.: Stressors and child and adolescent psychopathology: measurement issues and prospective effects. J. Clin. Child Adolesc. Psychol. **33**(2), 412–425 (2004)
9. Southwick, S.M., Morgan 3rd, C.A., Nicolaou, A.L., Charney, D.S.: Consistency of memory for combat-related traumatic events in veterans of Operation Desert Storm. Am. J. Psychiatr. **154**(2), 173–177 (1997)
10. Cohen, S., Kamarck, T., Mermelstein, R.: A global measure of perceived stress. J. Health Soc. Behav. **24**, 385–396 (1983)
11. Malik, M., Bigger, J.T., Camm, A.J., Kleiger, R.E., Malliani, A., Moss, A.J., Schwartz, P.J.: Heart rate variability standards of measurement, physiological interpretation, and clinical use. Eur. Heart J. **17**(3), 354–381 (1996)
12. Sun, F.T., Kuo, C., Cheng, H.T., Buthpitiya, S., Collins, P., Griss, M.: Activity-aware mental stress detection using physiological sensors. In: Gris, M., Yang, G. (eds.) Mobile Computing, Applications, and Services. Lecture Notes of the Institute for Computer Sciences, Social Informatics and Telecommunications Engineering, vol. 76, pp. 211–230. Springer, Heidelberg (2012)
13. Everly, G.S., Lating, J.M.: The anatomy and physiology of the human stress response. In: A Clinical Guide to the Treatment of the Human Stress Response, pp. 17–51. Springer, Heidelberg (2013)
14. Plarre, K., Raij, A., Hossain, S.M., Ali, A.A., Nakajima, M., al' Absi, M., Ertin, E., Kamarck, T., Kumar, S., Scott, M., Siewiorek, D., Smailagic, A., Wittmers, Jr., L.E.: Continuous inference of psychological stress from sensory measurements collected in the natural environment. In: 2011 10th International Conference on Information Processing in Sensor Networks (IPSN), pp. 97–108. IEEE (2011)
15. de Santos Sierra, A., Ávila, C.S., Casanova, J.G., del Pozo, G.B.: Real-time stress detection by means of physiological signals. Group of Biometrics, Biosignals and Security Universidad Politécnica de Madrid, Spain, pp. 24–44 (2011)

16. Alamudun, F., Choi, J., Gutierrez-Osuna, R., Khan, H., Ahmed, B.: Removal of subject-dependent and activity-dependent variation in physiological measures of stress. In: 2012 6th International Conference on Pervasive Computing Technologies for Healthcare (PervasiveHealth), pp. 115–122. IEEE (2012)

17. Bakker, J., Pechenizkiy, M., Sidorova, N.: What's your current stress level? Detection of stress patterns from GSR sensor data. In: 2011 IEEE 11th International Conference on Data Mining Workshops (ICDMW), pp. 573–580. IEEE (2011)

18. Choi, J., Ahmed, B., Gutierrez-Osuna, R.: Development and evaluation of an ambulatory stress monitor based on wearable sensors. IEEE Trans. Inf. Technol. Biomed. 16(2), 279–286 (2012)

19. Dechmeroswski, S., Winslow, B., Chadderdon, G., Schmidt-Daly, T.N., Jones, D.: Classifying stress in a mobile environment. In: Interservice Training, Simulation, and Education Conference (I/ITSEC) (2014)

20. Slater, M.: A note on presence terminology. Presence-Connect 3, 1–5 (2003)

21. Meehan, M.: Physiological reaction as an objective measure of presence in virtual environments. Doctoral Dissertation, University of North Carolina at Chapel Hill (2001)

22. Wiederhold, B.K., Jang, D.P., Kaneda, M., Cabral, I., Lurie, Y., May, T., Kim, I.Y., Wiederhold, M.D., Kim, S.I.: An investigation into physiological responses in virtual environments: an objective measurement of presence. In: Riva, G., Galimberti, C. (eds.) Towards CyberPsychology: Mind, Cognitions and Society in the Internet Age. IOS Press, Amsterdam (2001)

23. Stanney, K.M., Schmorrow, D.D., Johnston, M., Fuchs, S., Jones, D., Hale, K.S., Ahmad, A., Young, P.: Augmented cognition: an overview. Rev. Hum. Fact. Ergon. 5(1), 195–224 (2009)

24. Driskell, J., Johnston, J.: Stress exposure training. In: Cannon-Bowers, J.A., Salas, E. (eds.) Making Decisions Under Stress: Implications for Individual and Team Training, pp. 191–217. American Psychological Association, Washington, DC (1998)

25. Scherer, K., Shorr, A., Johnstone, T.: Appraisal Process in Emotion: Theory, Methods, Research. Oxford University Press, Canary (2001)

26. Hardy, M., Wiebe, E.N., Grafsgaard, J.F., Boyer, K.E., Lester, J.C.: Physiological responses to events during training use of skin conductance to inform future adaptive learning systems. In: Proceedings of the Human Factors and Ergonomics Society Annual Meeting, pp. 2101–2105 (2013)

27. Sottilare, R.A., Gilbert, S.: Considerations for adaptive tutoring within serious games: authoring cognitive models and game interfaces. Presentation at the authoring simulation and game-based intelligent tutoring workshop at the fifteenth conference on artificial intelligence in education, Auckland (2011)

28. Joëls, M.: Corticosteroid effects in the brain: U-shape it. Trends Pharmacol. Sci. 27, 244–250 (2006)

29. Diamond, D.M., Campbell, A.M., Park, C.R., Halonen, J., Zoladz, P.R.: The temporal dynamics model of emotional memory processing: a synthesis on the neurobiological basis of stress-induced amnesia, flashbulb and traumatic memories, and the Yerkes-Dodson law. Neural Plast. 2007, 1–33 (2007)

30. Smeets, T., Giesbrecht, T., Jelicic, M., Merckelbach, H.: Context-dependent enhancement of declarative memory performance following acute psychosocial stress. Biol. Psychol. 76, 116–123 (2007)

31. Andreano, J.M., Cahill, L.: Glucocorticoid release and memory consolidation in men and women. Psychol. Sci. 17, 466–470 (2006)

32. Beckner, V.E., Tiucker, D.M., Delville, Y., Mohr, D.C.: Stress facilitates consolidation of verbal memory for a film but does not affect memory retrieval. Behav. Neurosci. **120**, 518–527 (2006)
33. Schwabe, L., Wolf, O.T.: The context counts: congruent learning and testing environments prevent memory retrieval impairment following stress. Cogn. Affect. Behav. Neurosci. **9**, 229–236 (2009)
34. Guenzel, F.M., Wolf, O.T., Schwabe, L.: Stress disrupts response memory retrieval. Psychoneuroendocrinology **38**(8), 1460–1465 (2013)
35. Schmidt, P.I., Rosga, K., Schatto, C., et al.: Stress reduces the incorporation of misinformation into an established memory. Learn. Mem. **21**, 744–747 (2014)
36. Schwabe, L., Worlf, O.T.: Stress impairs the reconsolidation of autobiographical memories. Neurobiol. Learn. Mem. **94**, 153–157 (2010)

Alternate Rubric for Performance Assessment of Infantry Soldier Skills Training

Douglas Maxwell[1(✉)], Jonathan Stevens[2], and Crystal Maraj[2]

[1] U.S. Army Research Laboratory, Orlando, FL, USA
douglas.maxwell3.civ@mail.mil
[2] University of Central Florida, Orlando, FL, USA
jonathan.stevens@knights.ucf.edu, cmaraj@ist.ucf.edu

Abstract. Gauging the impact of simulation-based training (SBT) technology has been straightforward in the past when applied to domains such as pilot training and ground vehicle operator training. In the dismounted infantry soldier skills domain, the low hanging fruit for effective use of (SBT) are weapons and equipment operations training. However, the complexities of the operational environment are often too difficult to replicate in current virtual environments to represent an accurate or effective training for the skills requiring identification of enemy activity or reacting to enemy contact. This paper discusses the need for an alternate method of performance assessment when comparing traditional training means to SBT.

Keywords: Simulation based training · Infantry soldier training · Rubric · Return on investment

1 Introduction

In early 2013, a research team composed of personnel from the U.S. Army Research Laboratory and the University of Central Florida performed a data collection activity with the Florida Army National Guard's 2/124th Regiment Apache Company. The data collection activity focused on individual and team performance of soldiers performing room clearing exercises. In this experiment, a company of soldiers were divided into two groups, where the control group only was provided training using a traditional classroom method and the experimental group was provided training that included a game-based simulator. Subject matter experts (SMEs) were tasked with assigning a pass/fail rating to each soldier and fire team. The research team did not wish to interfere with the method of assessment used by the SMEs, as the guidance for this is given in training support packages provided by the U.S. Army Training and Doctrine Command. Analysis of this categorical data proved to be problematic and yielded results that could only indicate differences in soldier performance, but not by how much. In essence, it was only possible to determine if the virtual training treatment had an effect.

Since mid-2014, the research team has been conducting studies using large numbers of soldiers to determine how effective virtual training methods are in comparison to traditional training methods for dismounted infantry soldier skills in the Warrior Leader Course (WLC) at the Florida National Guard's 211th Regional Training

D.D. Schmorrow and C.M. Fidopiastis (Eds.): AC 2016, Part II, LNAI 9744, pp. 34–45, 2016.
DOI: 10.1007/978-3-319-39952-2_4

Institute. The ARL/UCF team worked with the WLC course managers to incorporate lessons learned from the previous experiment to create a new assessment methodology for collecting more meaningful data. A new rubric was jointly developed and used during data collection activities. This paper discusses the rationale for incorporating new ideas that enhance the development of the performance rubric. The rubric allows for a more in-depth understanding of the required tasks. Instead of using the traditional assessment "GO or NO-GO" ratings for the task evaluation, the revised rubric incorporates each major task and list all related subtask activities. Modifying the rubric not only allows for clarification of each major task but also assess whether the subtasks were successfully accomplished. In addition to discussing the performance rubric, this paper also integrates sample performance data collected from 20 squads of soldiers and demonstrates the value of the revised rubric to the data analysis.

2 Background

The United States Army has invested significant funding dedicated to the use of virtual environments (VEs) for training infantry soldier skills. There is a pervasive attitude in the acquisition community that a simulation-based training (SBT) system's graphics quality are the strongest indicators of utility and training quality. Very little data exists to quantify the return on investment (ROI) provided by these training systems (Bell et al. 2008). There is also a lack of formal methodologies for the identification of where in the training cycle these technologies belong as well as which training tasks they should be applied (Kincaid et al. 2003; Salas et al. 2003). The United States Government Accountability Office issued a report in August of 2013 which calls for better assessment of performance and accounting of costs to accurately assess SBT systems throughout the United States Army and Marine Corps (Pickup 2013). As a result of limited empirical data supporting training effectiveness using VEs (Haque and Srinivasan 2006), there is little guidance for the program manager's to follow in the decision-making process. This leaves the requirements generation team and the acquisition process to attempt to simulate the training provided by traditional means using VEs. There is too much leeway in the interpretation of this replication and lack of empirically driven data to make informed decisions.

To further complicate matters, the lack of formal requirements and performance measurement methodologies has led to a fracturing of the training space within the United States military that utilizes game-based virtual environments (GBVE). Although, there is a GBVE training system listed as the program of record called Virtual Battlespace, it is limited for specialized training needs of some organizations. Pockets of innovation and product development in recent years have resulted in numerous training systems specializing in different utilization such as education (McLennan 2012) and military applications (Buede et al. 2013).

The United States Army requires a mechanism for properly assessing the performance of infantry soldiers who have been trained using virtual simulations in order to establish statistically significant differences (if any) for comparisons to traditional training methods. This research initiative was conducted through Cooperative Agreements (CA) #W911NF-14-0012 and #W911NF-15-0004 between the United States

Army Research Laboratory and the University of Central Florida. These CAs were created to facilitate the investigation of training effectiveness of operationally relevant tasks in a VE as compared to traditional classroom and live training. The desired outcome of this work is to establish a methodology for quantitatively defining the training effectiveness differences between traditional and virtual methods, and acquiring data through field experimentation to apply the methodology.

A literature review has revealed a lack of knowledge surrounding the efficacy of the practical application of virtual world technology for infantry soldier training, specifically ground combat skills training such as room clearing and reaction to contact (Lackey et al. 2014). Due to the current subjective nature of gauging training effectiveness of VEs, it is difficult to calculate a ROI. Lastly, it is difficult to determine comparisons of knowledge transfer between traditional and virtual training activities for ground combat skills.

Whether it is labeled *virtual world technology*, *GBVEs*, or *VEs*, the technology is becoming ubiquitous in the lives of infantry soldiers. However, it is unclear as to where in the ground combat skills training cycle this technology is applied most effectively. The literature is terse in identifying the appropriate tasks the technology is most suitable for training. Further, the assessment methodology is not standardized across the combat skills training cycle and is often assessed through subjective means.

3 Infantry Soldiers Skills Assessment

Minimal empirical evidence exists regarding the effectiveness of game-based and virtual world SBT (Whitney et al. 2014; Sotomayor and Proctor 2009), especially at the collective echelon. While some virtual training has been empirically proven to be effective in the transfer of skills to the live environment (Blow 2012; Hays et al. 1992), this has been primarily demonstrated for platform-centric training, such as aviation and vehicle-type training. However, platform-based training is restricted to low-density specialties in the United States Army; the vast majority of soldiers do not require this type of training and are not tethered to a platform. In contrast, all soldiers are required to be proficient in basic infantry skills, yet minimal SBT capabilities exist to support this training need and are rarely examined for efficacy. Therefore, this study's primary objective was to examine the training efficacy of SBT for infantry skills.

Training effectiveness evaluations are generally subjective in nature, making it difficult to ascertain whether or not training technology, methods and/or approaches are effective. The literature indicates that some of the primary challenges to effective, collective training in simulation are the lack of clear performance measures (Seibert et al. 2011) as well as a lack of comprehension of the simulation's capabilities by the unit trainers (Seibert et al. 2012). Thus, technology is only part of the analysis; the selection of the proper instructional strategy is equally as critical to whether or not training is effective (Salas et al. 1999).

Current approaches to measuring training effectiveness remain primarily subjective in nature (Wong et al. 2012; Sotomayor and Proctor 2009; Beal and Christ 2004; Kunche et al. 2011), employing techniques such as questionnaires, knowledge review and evaluation of training by trainees or SME observers. These means of assessment offer insight into trainees and trainers' perceptions of training environments, but reporting might be influenced by factors other than those directly attributed to the training itself. Therefore, a secondary goal of this study was the creation of a rubric that minimizes subjectivity in performance assessment, while not increasing raters' over-head, in order to determine whether game-based simulation and virtual world simulation-based training is truly effective or not. Objective evaluation of performance is critical in order for the Army to design, create and implement the next generation of simulation-based trainers for infantry-centric skills training.

3.1   Pilot: Assessment of Room Clearing Task Performance

The ARL research team worked with the 2/124th Florida Army National Guard to design a training event that coincided with data collection activities. The data collection event represent the presentation of a single ground training task to the unit. The training condition chosen for this study is a room clearing task that requires a fire team composed of four soldiers to enter and search a room. The participants are assessed both at the individual performance level as well as group performance level.

For this data collection event, two training conditions were selected for the soldiers. The first condition represented the control group and was composed of traditional classroom and slide presentation of the procedures described by FM 3-21.8, Field Manual for the Infantry Rifle Platoon and Squad (U.S. Army Training and Doctrine Command 2007) for room clearing (Fig. 1). The experimental condition comprised of training materials presented to the soldiers using a prototype virtual training simulator,

Fig. 1. 2/124th classroom training site

called the Military Open Simulator Enterprise Strategy (MOSES) (Ortiz and Maxwell 2016). MOSES was used to provide a virtual training arena utilizing practice task scenarios (Fig. 2) (Maraj et al. 2015).

Room clearing exercises represent one of the most common tasks performed by an infantry soldier, and is considered to be of the most dangerous tasks to complete. Although this is a collective task, each of the individual positions in the task is assessed independently. This allows for both an individual performance assessment and a collective team assessment.

On the day of the experiment, 64 soldiers were divided into two groups, 32 soldiers each and placed into groups of four to compose 8 fire teams. All of the soldiers were assembled and provided with a briefing to explain the intent of the experimentation. Each soldier signed a consent form agreeing to participate in the study. Due to the nature of the experimental design and utilizing a targeted population, the ARL/UCF team required two formal review processes. One process occurred through the UCF Institutional Review Board (IRB) and another through ARL IRB before data collection efforts began for the two groups.

One group received virtual training while the second group received the traditional training. After training, all soldiers were asked to perform a live room clearing exercise

Fig. 2. 2/124th virtual training site

during which time the SMEs assessed their performance according to the rubric. Although the task of clearing a room is performed as a collective effort, each position in the team is unique and can be assessed individually. The assessment is provided using a "GO or NO-GO" rating, which indicated whether the soldier completed their task to the SME's satisfaction.

The SMEs rated the performance of 64 individuals and 16 fire teams by following a 4 step rubric (Fig. 3). Table 1 shows the tasks and assessments for collective performance. Step one of the rubric (entry phase) was to assess the speed of entry, removal of self from the entry area, follow the path of least resistance and flow of movement. Step two (eliminate threat phase) was to maintain correct sector of fire throughout the flow. Step three (position of dominance) was to assess the soldier's ability to move to the correct position of dominance for their position in the entry team and for the team leader to announce "CLEAR." Step four (Consolidation and Reorganization) is to assess the team's ability to report ammunition, casualty, and equipment status (ACE report).

The data collected from this event provided enough information to determine the performance effect of different training conditions of individual soldiers. In this case, the independent variable is the training condition and the performance assessment is the

Table 1. Rubric for collective performance assessment for 2/124th FLANG Leesburg trial

Task	Assessment
Step 1. Entry phase	Go/No-Go
Step 2. Eliminate threat phase	Go/No-Go
Step 3. Position of dominance phase	Go/No-Go
Step 4. Consolidation and reorganization	Go/No-Go

Fig. 3. 2/124th live assessment activity

dependent variable. The use of a "GO/NO-GO" performance metric limited the data analysis to simply determining dependence of the variables to each other. This categorical data lent itself to Chi-Square analysis and could indicate whether differences between the two training conditions were significant. However, this data could not be used to determine by how much the performance differences between the two training conditions. The ROI of the virtual treatment could not be established using this method.

3.2 Warrior Leader Course: Assessment of Dismounted Infantry Soldier Skills

The Florida Army National Guard's 211th Regional Training Institute, located at Camp Blanding, incorporates the Warrior Leader Course (WLC) as part of its training curriculum. This leadership course is designed to teach squad leadership skills to the infantry soldier (Association of the United States Army 2010), specifically the squad leader position.

The course managers, or Small Group Leaders (SGLs), worked closely with the ARL/UCF research team to examine the WLC to determine how to create a comparison study similar to the one described in Sect. 3.1. An examination of the course revealed that it would be possible to use a between-treatments experimental design to compare a traditional training treatment to a virtual training treatment.

Table 2 shows the original evaluation rubric used in the course for team performance evaluations. In order to gather the data from the WLC, it was necessary to make adjustments to the rubric so that a more meaningful comparison could be made between the control and virtual training treatment. As with the room clearing tasks from the 2/124th, the WLC training also relied on a "Go/No-Go" performance evaluation metric.

Table 2. Original rubric for collective performance assessment for 211th FLANG RTI pilot

Task	Assessment
1. React to indirect fire while dismounted	Go/No-Go
2. React to improvised explosive device	Go/No-Go
3. React to near ambush	Go/No-Go
4. React to far ambush	Go/No-Go

This research focus seeks to determine applicability of specific infantry soldier skills against different training treatments. The current rubric indicates differences between the training treatments, but a new rubric is required to provide a comparison of how much one treatment differed from another. Each major training task was divided into subtasks and the assessment performed utilized a four point Likert scale (Garland 1991). A four point Likert scale provides an opportunity to make a choice by eliminating the midpoint responses. This research expands the rating categories from two (i.e., GO/NO-GO) to four (i.e., needs improvement, adequate, successful, and excels) which enables the research team, as well as the course cadre, to gain greater insight into whether or not the preceding training condition had an effect on trainee performance.

Coded categorical data can be treated as numerical and lends itself to deeper analysis if the optimal number of categories are employed. For this study, four categories of rated performance were created through a questionnaire and used in order to not overload cadre rating requirements (i.e. performing the actual evaluations); while providing the research team with quantifiable data for analysis. Further, subjectivity in evaluation was reduced by decomposing the training tasks to the subtask level, thereby allowing the cadre to increase their objectivity ratings of the performance evaluation at each atomic step. Table 3 shows the adjusted rubric the ARL/UCF team provided to the SGLs for use in their final squad performance evaluations.

Table 3. Revised Rubric for Task 1

Task	Assessment			
	Needs improvement	Adequate	Successful	Excels
1. React to indirect fire while dismounted				
1.1 Shout "incoming" in a loud, recognizable voice				
1.2 React to the Instruction of the leader and look for guidance				
1.3 Seek nearest cover				
1.4 Assess situation				
1.5 Report situation to leader				
1.6 Continue mission				

The period of instruction (POI) for this course is 20 days. For days 1–17, the soldiers receive the same classroom-based training including PowerPoint slides and SME instruction. Typically, day 18 is reserved for practical exercises with a four hour block allocated for scenario-based training. The practical exercises consists of "walk-throughs," where the four major tasks are posed to the soldiers and they are given the opportunity to practice responding to the task. The 211th RTI uses the United States Army's Virtual Battlespace 3 (VBS3) simulation platform for training. On days 19 and 20, a formal assessment of the squad's performance is evaluated during an on-site situational training exercise (STX).

For this experiment, an adjustment was made to the POI such that the class was separated into two groups and provided with different walkthrough training treatments. This control group represented a traditional method of providing practical instruction. The practical instruction comprised of sending the control group into the near-by wooded areas where an instructor provides guided instruction during the practical exercises (Fig. 4.). Alternatively, the experimental group received the training treatment in a computer lab using the VBS3 suite (Fig. 5.) The VBS3 scenarios were developed by onsite contractors who replicated the STX lanes the soldiers would encounter the following day during their performance evaluations.

Fig. 4. Warrior leader course control group in traditional "walkthrough" treatment

On day 18 of the POI, all soldiers enrolled in the WLC were assembled and provided a brief describing the experiment. The soldiers were given the opportunity to ask questions pertaining to the experiment before signing consent forms. The UCF/ARL IRB reviewed the consent form to ensure the study had minimal risk to the soldiers. After the soldiers signed the consent forms, they completed a series of pre-experimental questionnaires.

Fig. 5. Warrior leader class using virtual battlespaces 3 (VBS3)

Following the walkthroughs on day 18, the two treatment groups assembled at the STX lanes (on day 19) to participate in the live simulation that evaluated the performance of the training tasks (Fig. 6.). The SGLs assessed the squads (or groups) according to a new rubric in real-time. This evaluation process was repeated for nine WLC class rotations, starting in April 2015 and ending in December of 2015. A total of 23 squads were evaluated and over 250 soldiers provided questionnaire input. Twenty squads followed the experimental protocols explicitly, yielding data for 10 squads exposed to the control treatment and 10 squads with the virtual treatment. By applying the new rubric, a large number of data points were generated allowing the team to apply parametric statistics to the survey data and calculate analysis of variables on the squad performance data. Implementation of the new rubric was instrumental for gathering expanded data points to calculate comparisons between the two treatment groups.

Fig. 6. Live performance assessment in the situation training exercise (STX) lanes

4 Discussion

The purpose of this study was to initiate an examination and analysis of the training effectiveness of game-based and virtual world simulation as it applies to infantry-centric skills training. The selection of infantry-centric skills for analysis represents a novel approach, as most SBT for the United States Army is affiliated with a particular platform, such as a helicopter or tank. However, the large majority of soldiers have no requirement to be proficient with this type of equipment; in contrast *all* soldiers must be proficient in basic infantry skills. Therefore, it is authors hope that this longitudinal study provides the Army with meaningful data to create effective, next-generation simulation-based trainers that are applicable to more than just niche specialties.

Removing the implicit subjectivity of training effectiveness evaluations is an ambitious goal, which may or may not be achieved. The creation of a rubric that reduces subjectivity in performance assessment, through the use of multiple categories on a four-point Likert scale with training tasks decomposed to the subtask level, will hopefully contribute to and improve the quality and accuracy of SBT efficacy evaluations. This is a critical first step to determine whether game-based simulation and virtual world SBT are truly effective. Future papers will expand on SBT as an effectiveness tool for training soldiers on basic infantry skills.

Acknowledgements. The U. S. Army Research Laboratory and the University of Central Florida research team would like to express our profound gratitude to the dedicated men and women of the 2/124th and 211th without whom this work could not have been performed. We thank you for your service to our country.

References

Association of the United States Army: Preparing for Warrior Leader course (WLC). Arlington, Virginia, United States of America (2010). http://www.ausa.org/RESOURCES/NCO/TRAINING/CAREERADVANCEMENT/PREPARINGFORSCHOOL/Pages/PreparingforWarriorLeadercourse(WLC).aspx. Accessed 1 Feb 2016

Beal, S., Christ, R.: Training effectiveness evaluation of the full spectrum command game (No. ARI-TR-1140). Army Research Institute for the Behavioral and Social Sciences, Fort Benning, GA (2004)

Bell, B.S., Kanar, A.M., Kozlowski, S.W.: Current issues and future directions in simulation-based training. CAHRS Working Paper Series, 492 (2008)

Blow, C.: Flight School in the Virtual Environment. United States Army Command and General Staff College Fort Leavenworth, Kansas (2012)

Buede, D., Maxwell, D., McCarter, B.: Filling the need for intelligent, adaptive non-player characters. In: Proceedings of the Interservice/Industry Training, Simulation, and Education Conference (I/ITSEC), Orlando, FL (2013)

Garland, R.: The mid-point on a rating scale: is it desirable. Mark. Bull. 2(1), 66–70 (1991)

Haque, S., Srinivasan, S.: A meta-analysis of the training effectiveness of virtual reality surgical simulators. IEEE Trans. Inf. Technol. Biomed. 10, 51–58 (2006)

Hays, R., Jacobs, J., Carolyn, P., Salas, E.: Flight simulator training effectiveness: a meta-analysis. Mil. Psychol. 4, 63–74 (1992)

Kincaid, J.P., Hamilton, R., Tarr, R., Sangani, H.: Simulation in Education and Training, pp. 437–456. Springer, US (2003)

Kunche, A., Puli, R.K., Guniganti, S., Puli, D.: Analysis and evaluation of training effectiveness. Hum. Resour. Manag. Res. 1(1), 1–7 (2011)

Lackey, S., Salcedo, J., Matthews, G., Maxwell, D.: Virtual world room clearing: a study in training effectiveness. In: Interservice/Industry Training, Simulation and Education Conference (I/ITSEC), Orlando, Florida (2014)

Maraj, C., Lackey, S., Badillo-Urquiola, K., Ogreten, S., Maxwell, D.: Empirically derived recommendations for training novices using virtual worlds. In: Interservice/Industry Training, Simulation and Education Conference (I/ITSEC), Orlando, pp. 1–8 (2015)

McLennan, K.: Interactivity, engagement, and increased learning outcomes in 3D virtual world educational simulations. In: Proceedings of the World Conference on Educational Multimedia, Hypermedia and Telecommunications, p. 843. AACE, Chesapeake, VA (2012)

Ortiz, E., Maxwell, D.: Military Open Simulator Enterprise Strategy (MOSES) (2016). Retrieved from Military Metaverse: http://militarymetaverse.org/

Pickup, S.: ARMY AND MARINE Better Performance and Cost Data Needed to More Fully Assess Efforts. United States Government Accountability Office, Washington, D.C. (2013). http://www.gao.gov/assets/660/657115.pdf

Salas, E., Fowlkes, J., Stout, R., Milanovich, D., Prince, C.: Does CRM training improve teamwork skills in the cockpit?: two evaluation studies. Hum. Fact. J. Hum. Fact. Ergon. Soc. **41**, 326–343 (1999)

Salas, E., Milham, L.M., Bowers, C.A.: Training evaluation in the military: misconception, opportunities, and challenges. Mil. Psychol. **15**(1), 3–16 (2003)

Seibert, M., Diedrich, F., Ayers, J., Dean, C., Zeidman, T., Bink, M., Stewart, J.: Addressing Army Aviation Collective Training Challenges with Simulators and Simulations Capabilities. Aptima, Woburn (2012)

Seibert, M., Diedrich, F., Stewart, J., Bink, M., Zeidman, T.: Developing Performance Measures for Army Aviation Collective Training. Army Research Institute, Fort Benning (2011)

Sotomayor, T., Proctor, M.: Assessing combat medic knowledge and transfer effects resulting from alternative training treatments. J. Defense Model. Simul. Appl. Methodol. Technol. **6**, 121–134 (2009)

U.S. Army Training and Doctrine Command: FM 3–21.8 The Infantry Rifle Platoon and Squad. Washington, D.C. (2007). http://armypubs.army.mil/doctrine/DR_pubs/dr_a/pdf/fm3_21x8. pdf

Whitney, S., Tempby, P., Stephens, A.: A review of the effectiveness of game-based training for dismounted soldiers. J. Defense Model. Simul. 319–328 (2014)

Wong, J., Nguyen A, Ogren, L.: Serious Game and Virtual World Training: Instrumentation and Assessment. Naval Undersea Warfare Center, Newport, RI (2012)

Leveraging Interoperable Data to Improve Training Effectiveness Using the Experience API (XAPI)

Jennifer Murphy[1]([✉]), Francis Hannigan[1], Michael Hruska[2], Ashley Medford[2], and Gabriel Diaz[2]

[1] Quantum Improvements Consulting, Orlando, FL, USA
{jennifer.murphy,fhannigan}@quantumimprovements.net
[2] Problem Solutions, Johnstown, PA, USA
{mike,amedford,gdiaz}@problemsolutions.net

Abstract. This paper discusses our research efforts aimed at improving the training effectiveness and efficiency of the U.S. Army's gunnery and rifle marksmanship curriculum. Soldier assessments, typically in the form of final qualifications scores, are insufficient to conduct experimental comparisons required to evaluate training effectiveness. More importantly, this level of performance assessment does not speak to the root cause of the errors soldiers make during training. Using the Experience API (xAPI) specification, learning experiences are represented in terms of activity statements and can be used to track learning that happens both inside and outside of the classroom, enabling the development of robust, persistent student models. Importantly, xAPI data are interoperable across training systems, allowing a student's performance to be tracked across multiple platforms. Our research demonstrates the utility of xAPI to improve the effectiveness of Army simulation-based training through improved performance assessment capabilities.

Keywords: Adaptive learning systems · Experience API · Data interoperability · Training effectiveness evaluation

1 Introduction

Throughout military history, simulation has been used to train warfighting skills. The benefits of simulation include the ability to provide a controlled, safe environment to experiment at a relatively low cost. Simulation enables warfighters to experience high fidelity replications of operational settings prior to combat, which reduces the risk to lives and equipment. Unlike live operations, in simulated environments events can be replayed, paused, and customized, providing the opportunity for tailoring learning experiences to the individual or unit. Despite its clear benefits, quantifying the benefit of simulation-based training remains a challenge. Recently, the Government Accountability Office [1] critiqued the U.S. Army and the Marine Corps for insufficiently assessing the effectiveness of their simulation-based training systems. In response to this report as well as broader budgetary limitations, there has been a renewed interest in training effectiveness assessments (TEA) by the Department of Defense, and the Army in particular.

© Springer International Publishing Switzerland 2016
D.D. Schmorrow and C.M. Fidopiastis (Eds.): AC 2016, Part II, LNAI 9744, pp. 46–54, 2016.
DOI: 10.1007/978-3-319-39952-2_5

The value of training technology is typically conceptualized in one of two ways, depending on the rationale behind the evaluation. TEA focuses on the learner, and the extent to which he or she develops and applies new skills as a result of the training. When applied to new technologies, training effectiveness is usually evaluated through comparison to existing solutions or to live training. If learning outcomes are similar or improved relative to the standard, the training is considered effective. Another approach to evaluating training systems involves determining their cost effectiveness. As one of the primary benefits of simulation is reduced training costs, the purpose of these analyses is to demonstrate the extent to which a simulator can produce comparable learning outcomes to more expensive solutions. Variables of interest often include material costs, time to train, instructor hours, transportation costs, and increased safety. While TEA is centered on the trainee and often disregards cost considerations, cost effectiveness analysis (CEA) assumes similar learning outcomes and instead focuses on training resources. However, to fully address the value of training systems, both training and cost effectiveness should be considered. In other words, these systems should be evaluated in terms of training efficiency.

The concept of evaluating training efficiency is not new, but performing such an analysis has proven prohibitively challenging. Fletcher and Chatelier [2] described the goal of combining assessments of training and cost effectiveness for military training and identified barriers to conducting such an analysis. Training outcomes are difficult to quantify in financial terms. Additionally, modeling the cost element structure associated with developing, delivering and sustaining military training is in itself very complex [3]. Despite this, the Department of Defense does evaluate the cost of implementing any technology prior to a procurement. On the other hand, TEA is rarely conducted, and if so, it is typically not conducted well. Improving the TEA process, then, would go a long way toward improving our understanding of the true value of simulation-based training.

Why is TEA conducted so rarely? Evaluating military simulation as an effective means of instruction is not a new problem, and best practices for conducting TEA have been well-documented [4, 5]. Despite ample evidence to the contrary [6], an attitude that simply replicating the operational environment to the highest fidelity possible is sufficient to guarantee effective training persists in the military community. While the U.S. Defense laboratories are funded to conduct training research, acquiring troop support and equipment for data collection is consistently difficult. A more challenging issue, however, is a lack of objective, valid measures of warfighter performance during training events. Typically, performance is assessed either subjectively by an instructor or through a single qualification score at the end of a training event. These data are typically insufficient to conduct the experimental comparisons required to evaluate training effectiveness. More importantly, this level of performance assessment does not speak to the root cause of errors warfighters may make during training.

What is needed is a methodology to develop objective measures and metrics of warfighter performance within simulator systems. These metrics could be generated using the data simulators currently use to drive the training curriculum they provide. Currently, these metrics are not calculated, largely because training systems developers are not required to do so. In addition, there is no guidance for these developers with regard to how to identify the appropriate metrics for use in these systems.

In this paper, we describe ongoing research efforts aimed at improving Army training effectiveness through the use of interoperable performance data. This work focuses on two critical warfighting domains: crew gunnery and basic rifle marksmanship. Using the Experience API (xAPI) as a means of standardizing performance data, we demonstrate the extent to which TEA can be improved. Importantly, our research also speaks to the larger challenge of assessing training efficiency through performance assessment.

1.1 Assessing the Effectiveness of Simulation-Based Training

Training effectiveness is usually thought of as the extent to which learners gain an understanding of a content domain as a result of a training intervention. As such, TEA has historically used assessments of learner knowledge as criteria. One enduring model for conducting these evaluations is Donald Kirkpatrick's Four Levels [7]. Using this approach, training effectiveness is evaluated based on four criteria, or levels. Level 1, "Reaction," focuses on the extent to which trainees enjoy the learning experience, which is usually assessed by a questionnaire at the end of the training. At Level 2, "Learning," effectiveness is conceptualized as a change in knowledge gained, skills acquired, or attitudes changed as a result of the intervention. Level 3, "Behavior," refers to the extent to which the training event influences subsequent actions. This is usually operationalized as an assessment of learner performance on the job by a third party, such as a supervisor or peer. Finally, the fourth level, "Results," describes the overall impact of a training intervention on the organization as a whole. In a corporate setting, Level 4 is often assessed in terms of a company's productivity or profitability. Defining the value of a training event on this level is challenging, and is rarely achieved. The benefits to an organization are not immediately evident, and determining them requires a long-term assessment strategy. Further, isolating the effects of a single intervention in the context of larger organizational shifts that naturally happen over time is difficult.

Although Kirkpatrick's Four Levels were designed to address the effectiveness of training in a civilian corporate context, this approach has been widely adopted to assess military training. Morrison and Hammon [4] and Simpson and Oser [5] advocate this framework as a basis for designing TEA for simulation-based training in particular. While this approach is certainly appropriate, its application to military training technology comes with unique challenges. A primary limitation is the feasibility of conducting Level 3 and 4 assessments. Typically, simulation is one component of a training continuum spanning introductory didactic instruction, hands-on exercises increasing in levels of complexity, and cumulating in a live exercise and qualification event. In this context, a Level 3 evaluation would involve assessing the extent to which simulator performance transfers to subsequent, higher fidelity training events. While the opportunity for this assessment exists, an individual warfighter's performance is not typically tracked across training events, and often final qualification scores are the only persistent record of the training experience. Level 4 evaluations are rare in any setting, but in a military context, "Results" translates to the effectiveness of a unit during combat operations. Opportunities to assess these events are rare, and the complexities of the battlefield make definitive assessments of the impact of one training event nearly impossible. Examples of successful Level 4 evaluations of military training have involved air-to-air combat outcomes [8] and bombing accuracy [9]. However, the outcomes of ground operations are much more difficult to evaluate. As a result, most evaluations of simulation-based training are limited to Level 1 and 2. While impressions of training and retained knowledge are important, the true value of training is the ability to apply what is learned in an operational setting.

Ultimately, the success of achieving Level 3 and 4 evaluations is dependent upon the ability to assess the extent to which knowledge and skills gained during training transfer to higher fidelity, if not live, environments. Historically, collecting assessments of performance across a variety of training platforms has proven prohibitively difficult. However, recent developments in learning technology have supported the capture and analysis of more granular performance data. The rise of mobile technology and ubiquitous wireless data access have enabled both training and assessment anytime and anyplace. Improvements in low-cost wearable sensor technology have made unobtrusive assessments of a learner's location, physiological state, and activity level a possibility. Advances in machine learning have facilitated the interpretation of these data, and the ability to store massive amounts of data in a cost-effective way without reducing processing speed has made "big data" a reality. As a result of these recent advances, the data exist to inform real-time performance measurement in nearly any environment. A remaining challenge involves standardizing these data for use across multiple platforms. To address the need for performance data standardization, the Experience API (xAPI) was developed.

1.2   The Experience API and Data Interoperability

xAPI is a data specification developed by the Advanced Distributed Learning (ADL) Co-Lab as a means of tracking learning experiences across a wide variety of technology platforms. Although other data standards, such as High Level Architecture (HLA) and Distributed Interactive Simulation (DIS), are used in the context of training technology, xAPI is the only one designed specifically to capture and share human performance data. Using xAPI, learning experiences are represented in terms of statements in the format "Actor – Verb – Object" (e.g., "Chad read *Twilight*"), with the option of including additional contextual information and results. Performance data in xAPI format are stored in a Learning Record Store (LRS), which serves as a mechanism for multiple training and analysis systems to store and access these statements through a centralized point.

The primary benefit of using the xAPI specification is the ability it affords to store human performance data from multiple sources in a single, intuitive format. Because of its flexibility, xAPI enables the capture of a wide variety of learning experiences, both inside and outside the classroom. This data interoperability allows a much broader assessment capability than was previously possible. In terms of TEA, there are a number of implications. xAPI supports the development of robust, persistent learner models in training systems. As a result, tracking performance across multiple training events is possible. Importantly, all types of experiences can be represented in xAPI format, including events that occur completely outside of a training environment. Whereas Level

3 and Level 4 evaluations were previously limited in terms of reliable access to operational performance data, xAPI enables objective assessment of skill transfer to a higher fidelity or live scenario.

In addition to enabling more robust TEA, interoperable performance data support advanced training methodologies that have been shown to improve the efficiency of simulation-based training. Persistent models of learner performance enable the adapting of training content to the individual based on their performance in previous training events. These data allow for the predictive modeling of training outcomes, which can be used to prescribe a training curriculum based on existing knowledge, skills, and abilities.

Our research demonstrates the utility of xAPI to improve the effectiveness of Army simulation-based training through improved performance assessment capabilities. Below, we describe efforts to investigate the extent to which the effectiveness of an unstabilized crew gunnery simulator was improved by adapting training using interoperable data from an individual gunnery simulator. In addition, we address our research into the extent to which these data could be used to improve the overall efficiency of the Army training process by addressing the needs of multiple stakeholders in the marksmanship training community.

2   Adapting Training Using Interoperable Performance Data

In 2011, the Army's Training and Doctrine Command (TRADOC) published the Army Learning Concept for 2015 [10], a document outlining a vision for modernizing Army training. This new Army Learning Model (ALM) called for increasing the role of emerging technology as a way of improving the quality of soldier training while reducing costs. In particular, the ALM identified adaptive training technology as a means of efficiently tailoring learning experiences to the individual warfighter. Despite this guidance, adaptive training has still not been widely adopted by the Army. One reason for this is the expense associated with developing adaptive training systems, and research efforts such as the Army Research Laboratory's Generalized Intelligent Framework for Tutoring (GIFT) have focused on reducing these costs by improving the reusability of adaptive training content. However, a more significant barrier to the implementation of adaptive training is a lack of clear data showing the benefits of these systems. In their review of adaptive training technologies, Durlach and Ray [11] call for additional research to quantify the improvements in effectiveness expected from adaptive training.

A challenge in conducting TEA of adaptive training technologies is the need to provide a non-adaptive system as a standard for comparison. Typically, military training systems are developed to meet a specific requirement, and developing an additional adaptive or non-adaptive version for research purposes is prohibitively expensive. Under our current research effort, our team has been fortunate enough to have the ability to conduct such a comparison. Raydon Corporation's Unstabilized Gunnery Trainers (UGT) are simulators that support the training of Army gunnery crews. These trainers provide training on the individual level to gunners as well as gunnery crews in accordance with Army gunnery standards. Warfighters first learn gunnery basics, including how to maneuver the weapon, how to respond to commands, and how to quickly acquire and destroy targets in the individual trainer. In this simulator, the gunner interacts with a virtual crew and engages targets in a number of scenarios under a variety of conditions (e.g. day/night, stationary/moving) per the relevant Army training manuals (TC 3-20.31). This trainer is unique in that instead of progressing the warfighter through the entire training tables, the curriculum is adapted in real time based on the performance of the gunner. As the gunner progresses through the tables, subsequent scenarios are automatically selected based on the score the gunner receives. (The specific details of how the training is adapted are documented in Long et al. [12, 13].)

After the gunner completes individual training, he or she progresses to a crew simulator in which a live crew composed of the gunner, a commander, and driver, trains together to complete the gunnery tables required for qualification. Similar to the individual trainer, the crew is required to master target engagement in a variety of positions and conditions prior to graduating to a simulation of the live qualification exercise. The training is facilitated by an instructor, who scores the crew's performance. (Again, specifics are described in [12, 13].)

For research purposes, an experimental crew curriculum was developed that adapted the crew's course of instruction based on the performance of the gunner during individual training. Specifically, the crew's training was accelerated based on the tasks and conditions in which the gunner demonstrated proficiency. This adaptation was made possible by leveraging the xAPI specification as a means of communicating performance data across simulators. Our task was to determine the extent to which using this adaptive training curriculum would increase the efficiency of the training process. To that end, we compared the performance of a group of participants who completed the crew training with no adaptation to a group who completed the experimental curriculum, which was tailored to their previous performance in the individual trainer. Our participants were a sample of Reserve Officers' Training Corps (ROTC) cadets from a local university. Performance was defined as the crew's final qualification score and the time required to complete the training.

The results of this experiment showed that while both groups performed exceptionally well, the adaptive group completed the training in nearly 40 % less time than the non-adaptive control. These findings speak directly to the current limitations of most TEA conducted with military simulations. If our evaluation had simply focused on comparing learning outcomes as most TEA do, the finding that both experimental and control groups performed well above standard would suggest no benefit to the adaptive curriculum. However, by assessing the time required to complete the training, our findings speak more to training efficiency. Further, because the manpower and material resources needed to conduct training using these simulators are knowable quantities, the resulting cost savings to the Army could easily be calculated.

An important caveat to this point is the finding that using these simulators, nearly all crews achieved a "distinguished" rating. While this speaks to the effectiveness of the training, it begs the question of whether the existing Army guidance on gunnery training could be further streamlined. While the goal of all Army training is to produce highly proficient soldiers, it would be worthwhile to investigate the extent to which training requirements could be reduced before a decrement in performance is noticed in order to maximize the efficiency of this training requirement.

3   Improving Training Efficiency with Interoperable Performance Data

Our research shows the utility of interoperable performance data to facilitate the evaluation of training technologies. While TEA is critical in demonstrating the value of training systems, what it does not capture is the broader context in which these technologies are used. Simulation-based training is rarely used alone, and is typically conducted as part of a curriculum involving introductory, didactic instruction followed by increasingly complex, hands-on practice. The Army refers to this process as "crawl-walk-run," and simulation is often used as part of the "crawl" or "walk" phases of soldier training. In order to determine the true value of a training system, the extent to which it maximizes the efficiency of the entire training process should be considered. Our ongoing research efforts aim to determine a methodology and system for using human performance data to evaluate and improve the overall efficiency of the Army basic rifle marksmanship process.

Army rifle marksmanship is a skill every soldier must acquire during Basic Combat Training. Thousands of soldiers every year complete the basic rifle marksmanship curriculum, which involves classroom familiarization with marksmanship fundamentals, ballistics, and weapon care, simulation-based training on grouping and zeroing, and honing skills on live ranges. The management of this process requires extensive coordination between many groups of stakeholders, including drill sergeants, training developers, range control personnel, resource managers, and simulator operators. Each of these groups require specific data to accomplish their responsibilities. However, these data are often stove-piped in different databases, and coordination is difficult. As a result, precious training time is often wasted, drill instructors are overwhelmed, and soldiers are not receiving an optimal training experience. If access to performance data throughout the entire training process was improved, the marksmanship training process could be much more efficient.

A first step in conducting this research was the identification of the limitations of the current training process, which was carried out through a user needs analysis with representatives of the marksmanship training community at Fort Benning. Our team conducted interviews and focus groups with drill instructors, instructors from the Marksmanship Master Trainer Course and the 194th Armor Brigade, and training developers from the Individual and Systems Training Division of the Department of Training Development. Additionally, we consulted resource managers associated with marksmanship training, including managers from the Simulations Training Division, Range Control Operations personnel, and the Maneuver Center of Excellence's Ammunitions Manager. Finally, we discussed the extent to which improved access to marksmanship data could support research goals with Research Psychologists from the Army Research Institute's Fort Benning Research Unit. These discussions resulted in an understanding of the extent to which soldier marksmanship performance is currently being assessed, the challenges associated with delivering marksmanship training, and opportunities for improving the training process.

Our findings showed that while basic rifle marksmanship training takes place over the course of approximately two weeks, objective measures of soldier performance are typically not captured nor maintained with the exception of a final qualification score. However, many opportunities for assessing performance over the course of training exist. If performance was assessed more frequently, the Army could realize many benefits. Tailoring training to the individual soldier would be possible, maximizing the potential of each soldier. More accurate estimates of soldier needs for simulation hours, ammunition, and range time could be produced. The effectiveness of the training curriculum could be evaluated, and experimentation with new training systems could easily be conducted.

Discussions with marksmanship instructors informed the most common and critical issues soldiers have when learning to shoot. The issues reported described various cognitive, psychomotor, and affective components of marksmanship performance. Based on these discussions, we developed prototype measures of these components for implementation. The cognitive measures include assessments of soldier knowledge and aptitude. Measures of the marksmanship fundamentals, vision, and handedness address the psychomotor components of the domain. Affective measures include perceived stress, grit, conscientiousness, and self-efficacy. Our future research will validate these measures with a sample of soldiers undergoing marksmanship training.

In order to provide access to these data across the marksmanship training community, our team designed a system for tracking trainee performance across multiple instances of Army basic rifle marksmanship training, across a variety of training technologies using the xAPI standard. The system enables (1) a historical view of trainee or unit proficiency, (2) a live view of performance, and (3) macro and micro adaptation.

4   Conclusions

Our research speaks to the extent to which human performance data can be used to improve the TEA process. At a broader lever, our aim is to not only demonstrate the extent to which training systems provide learning experiences to trainees, but to address the efficiency of the training process. To do this, the extent to which training systems provide benefit above and beyond existing solutions should be evaluated with an appreciation for the costs associated with delivering training. As our gunnery simulator research shows, systems can provide comparable learning outcomes with very different costs associated with implementing them. In addition, our research suggests performance data can be used to not only assess the efficiency of the training process, but to improve it through addressing the needs of the broader training community.

References

1. U.S. Government Accountability Office. Army and Marine Corps Training: Better Performance and Cost Data Needed to More Fully Assess Simulation-Based EFforts. U.S. Government Accountability Office, Washington (2013)
2. Fletcher, J.D., Chatelier, P.R.: An overview of military training. Institute of Defense Analysis Document D-2514. Institute of Defense Analysis, Alexandria, VA (2000)
3. Knapp, M. I., Orlansky, J.: A cost element structure for defense training. Institute of Defense Analysis Document P-1709. Institute of Defense Analysis, Alexandria, VA (1983)

4. Morrison, J. E., Hammon, C.: On measuring the effectiveness of large-scale training simulations. Institute of Defense Analysis Document P-3570. Institute of Defense Analysis, Alexandria, VA (2000)

5. Simpson, H., Oser, R.L.: Evaluating large-scale training simulations. Mil. Psychol. **15**(1), 25–40 (2003)

6. Salas, E., Bowers, C.A., Rhodenizer, L.: It's not how much you have but how you use it: toward a rational use of simulation to support aviation training. Int. J. Aviat. Psychol. **8**(3), 197–208 (1998)

7. Kirkpatrick, D.L.: Techniques for evaluating training programs. Training Dev. J. **33**(6), 78–92 (1979)

8. Hammond, C., Horowitz, S.A.: Flying hours and aircrew performance (IDA Paper P-2347). Institute for Defense Analyses, Alexandria, VA (1990)

9. Cavaluzzo, L.C.: OPTEMPO and training effectiveness (Professional Paper 427). Center for Naval Analyses, Alexandria, VA (1984)

10. U.S. Department of the Army. The U.S. Army Learning Concept for 2015. TRADOC Pam 525-8-2. Department of the Army, Washington, DC (2011)

11. Durlach, P.J., Ray, J.M.: Designing adaptive instructional environments: insights from empirical evidence (Technical report 1297) (2011). http://www.adlnet.gov/wp-content/uploads/2011/11/TR-1297.pdf

12. Long, R., Murphy, J., Newton, C., Hruska, M., Medford, A., Kilcullen, T., Harvey Jr., R.: Adapting gunnery training using the experience API. In: Proceedings of the Interservice/Industry Training, Simulation, and Education Conference (I/ITSEC) (2015)

13. Long, R. Murphy, J., Ruprecht, C., Medford, A., Diaz, G., Kilcullen, T., Harvey Jr., R.: Evaluating adaptive training for teams using the experience API. In: Proceedings of the MODSIM World Conference (2016)

Practical Requirements for ITS Authoring Tools from a User Experience Perspective

Scott Ososky[✉]

U.S. Army Research Laboratory (ARL), Orlando, FL, USA
Scott.J.Ososky.ctr@mail.mil

Abstract. Intelligent Tutoring Systems (ITS) are not yet widely implemented in learning, despite the general prevalence of digital resources in educational and training environments. ITS have been demonstrated to be effective for learners, but ITS development is not yet efficient for authors. Creating an ITS requires time, resources, and multidisciplinary skills. *Authoring tools* are intended to reduce the time and skill required to create an ITS, but the current state of those tools is categorized as a series of design tradeoffs between functionality, generalizability, and usability. In practice, the former two factors matter little if potential authors disregard the ITS in favor of other solutions. In this sense, *authors*, not learners, are the primary users of an ITS; the user experience of authors is critical to greater ITS adoption at an organizational level. With those challenges in mind, ongoing work and lessons learned on the design of authoring tools are described for a specific ITS platform, the Generalized Framework for Intelligent Tutoring (GIFT). User-centered design considerations are examined through the lens of authors' goals, mental models for authoring, and the definition of authoring sub-roles. Recommendations for authoring tool design and future research directions for design research in authoring tools are discussed.

Keywords: Intelligent tutoring systems · Adaptive tutoring · Authoring tools · User-centered design · User experience · Mental models · Design research

1 Introduction

Intelligent Tutoring Systems (ITS), or adaptive tutors, are learning systems that have the ability to collect data about a learner, including assessments, attributes, and states, in order to tailor content to that learner's needs. These systems have been demonstrated to be more effective than many other types of instruction, approaching the effectiveness of one-to-one human tutoring [1]. However, ITS are not yet widely implemented in educational [2, 3] or military [4] environments, despite the prevalence of general digital resources in learning environments. One contributing factor to the slow adoption of ITS is the lack of accessible authoring tools that can meet the needs of modern training and educational institutions. There has been an extensive body of research on the engineering and development of authoring tools, but there is a considerable lack of literature related to user experiences and user goals associated with authoring tools. Thus, the current

© Springer International Publishing Switzerland 2016
D.D. Schmorrow and C.M. Fidopiastis (Eds.): AC 2016, Part II, LNAI 9744, pp. 55–66, 2016.
DOI: 10.1007/978-3-319-39952-2_6

work takes a user-centered approach to authoring tool design and user acceptance. End-user needs are also discussed in the context of identifying requirements for and focusing engineering efforts in authoring tools. First, an overview of ITS as well as learning and training environments is provided.

1.1   Intelligent Tutoring Systems

ITS, which are also referred to as adaptive tutors, have been described as "computer-based learning systems which attempt to adapt to the needs of learners" (p. 350) [5], or a computer system that customizes instruction and/or feedback to learners [6]. Intelligent tutoring systems are modular with four primary components: a learner/student model, a pedagogical/instructional model, a domain knowledge model, and a user interface/communications model. Each of those components exchanges data with one another, either directly or indirectly. Unlike traditional computer based training, ITS capture and process data about the learner, in order to tailor instruction toward individual learners' needs. In addition to performance and behavioral learner modeling, ITS can support the affective and motivational needs of the learner as well [4, 7].

The educational and training potential within ITS is underscored by one inherent problem, succinctly described by Murray, "Intelligent Tutoring Systems are highly complex educational software applications used to produce highly complex software applications" [8]. Despite decades of research and development, barriers to greater ITS adoption from an authoring perspective include high development costs, limited reuse of tutors, and the multidisciplinary skills required to build a robust tutor [9, 10]. Thus, by focusing on the needs of those that develop and manage adaptive training content, the ITS community can begin to address some of the barriers to greater adoption, both within the classroom and beyond.

1.2   Technology in the Classroom

A recent report from the Bill and Melinda Gates foundation describes the current state of educational technology in the classroom: Although 93 % of participating teachers use some form of digital resources in their instructional plans, more time is spent without digital tools than with them for independent practice, for assessment, and for individual tutoring [2]. Further, 58 % of teachers found digital tools to be effective, but gaps in these tools were reported to exist in all subject areas and grades. For instance, only 33 % of teachers believed that digital tools could be useful in remediation. ITS have the inherent capabilities to support all of those activities.

So why would a teacher select some other instructional method over using an ITS? The report provided some additional clues: When selecting instructional resources, teachers place the most emphasis on cost-effectiveness, ease of integration with their current methods and materials, and the ability of the tool to help teachers tailor instruction toward student needs. Additionally, organizational commitment to technology usage varies wildly, leaving many teachers (31 %) to acquire digital tools and manage the data produced by digital tools on their own [2]. Ultimately, most classroom time is still spent on whole-classroom instruction, despite the availability of digital tools.

Barriers to incorporating ITS (and digital tools, in general) are further compounded for classrooms in developing countries with respect to availability of hardware, infrastructure, and appropriate instructional content [11].

1.3 Tutoring Beyond the Classroom and in Military Domains

Considerations for ITS in developing countries may seem ancillary to tutor authoring concerns, given general availability of internet, electricity, and data connections for the ubiquitous devices in developed nations. However, those barriers which inhibit the use of digital tools in developing world classrooms are not unlike the challenges associated with learning in the field, particularly military training for and in operational environments (sometimes referred to as tutoring in-the-wild).

The Army, for instance, requires training solutions that are cost-effective, readily available and easily accessible. Current Army training needs include leadership, long-term learning, and operational adaptability under conditions of uncertainty and complexity [12]. To that end, there are cases in which training at a desktop computer is not practical, such as training for psychomotor tasks and field work. Further, Soldiers need to be able to train anywhere, at any time, and for a variety of operational constraints. Those constraints (whether simulated for training purposes or actual constrains imposed by the setting) include environments that are noisy, lack a data connection, and may be GPS-denied; a land navigation is one such task in which field training with an ITS is challenging [13]. Soldiers sensory attention and gear configuration in a hemorrhage control training task, for example, may prohibit tactile interaction with a digital tutor [14]. Similar lists of constraints may be identified for other physical and field-based tasks in non-military domains as well.

Finally, ITS (or adaptive tutoring) in military domains is also limited due to the complexity and ill-defined nature of military tasks. For instance, there are many aspects to peacekeeping operations in foreign environments, where the structure of knowledge is not declarative, there are no clear right or wrong solutions, and the quality of those solutions are likely to change based on specific situational factors [4]. Task complexity and ill-defined tasks are challenges to ITS adoption in the classroom and the field, in military applications and elsewhere (e.g., a tutor for jazz piano, or theatrical improvisation).

2 Authoring Tools: From Usability to User Experiences

The previous section paints a broad picture of the potential for ITS in educational and training settings along with real-world factors that inhibit increased ITS use. Greater use of adaptive tutoring in training and education ultimately requires the trust and confidence of training and educational stakeholders. Students and learners might be considered stakeholders, but they typically consume the courses developed within an ITS. Thus, the stakeholders of current interest are course creators, data managers, and facilitators. Teachers, instructional designers, and subject matter experts may fill one or more of these roles; therefore the needs of these users are paramount in designing sub-systems and tools that foster trust and confidence in ITS. Authoring tools for ITS do not directly address all of the needs of those groups, but authoring tools influence and are influenced by every other aspect of the ITS, including the tutor-user interface, pedagogical engines, domain models, and data management dashboards.

Much has been written on the topic of theory- and engineering-based efforts to develop authoring tools that provide to potential authors the functions necessary to create tutors without computer science or instructional design knowledge [15–18]. Murray, specifically, has published numerous works on authoring tools over the past two decades. His work includes analysis of the problem (or opportunity) in which design tradeoffs are made in authoring tools between usability, depth, and flexibility [19, 20]. In summary, increasing the power of the authoring tools (i.e., depth), the applicability of the tools to different domains and problem spaces (i.e., flexibility), or the usability of the tools themselves (i.e., learnability, productivity), comes at a cost to one or both of the other two [3].

The current discussion does not endeavor to duplicate the effort of those prior works, rather to extend and build upon the dialogue on tradeoffs in two very important ways from the perspective of user experience (UX) research and practice.

2.1 Authoring Tools and the Reality of Alternatives

First, it is imperative to start thinking about ITS and Authoring Tools from a product perspective if the ITS community truly wants to have a user base that extends far beyond its respective ITS research communities. Even if monetization is not part of an ITS project plan, the non-learner users of an ITS must be thought of and treated like customers. For instance, any time teachers, subject matter experts, or instructional designers interact with a channel associated with an ITS product (e.g., software, website, documentation), those users' experiences should be ones in which they feel confident and positive about using the associated authoring tools. Further, regardless of users' skill levels, developers should aspire to create experiences that make users feel smart when using their authoring tools. Consider, for example, how patient and tolerant a potential user might be with a set of authoring tools, before giving up completely. As the idiom states, you only have one chance to make a first impression.

Taking a product perspective allows ITS development teams to consider the reality of alternatives. There are currently a handful of ITS systems in the public domain, which are a subset of available digital tools in general, in addition to tools already available in the analog space. Simply put, a potential user of an ITS can consider many alternatives whose functionality and learning-benefit may vary wildly in comparison to a specific ITS. However, if a textbook, digital tool, other ITS, field manual, job-aid, etc. is perceived by a potential author to be *good enough*, the usability-depth-flexibility challenge becomes something of a moot issue. In some cases, a decision to not use an ITS may result in a potential author choosing to do *nothing at all,* focusing their time elsewhere. Recall, the reasons why ITS have not been more widely adopted in the first sections of this paper. Marketing might contribute to the problem of ITS adoption, but marketing is outside the scope of this discussion. While superficially similar, marketing is *selling*, user experience is *serving* [21].

This is not to say that the depth and flexibility of the product are not important; of course they are. Great experiences can quickly sour if there is no substance to the product. Rather, the emphasis on UX complements Murray's notion that subject matter experts (i.e., potential authors) should be involved in the ongoing development of authoring tools [3, 10]. Identifying user goals, user expectations, and the issues that users encounter provides a path to creating *authoring tools right*, in addition to the *right authoring tools*. Furthermore, the overall user experience associated with ITS and its authoring tools need to not just be *as good* as whatever a potential ITS user is doing now, but it has to be *better* in order to justify switching to a new method of training or educating. This applies to the actual author as well as their associated organizational stakeholders. In that sense, the concept of the positive user experience covers all types of authoring systems along the usability-depth-flexibility continuum.

2.2 Complex Authoring Tools Can Be Usable

Second, UX design can help the ITS community to rethink the problem of trading authoring tool depth or flexibility for usability. Murray operationalized usability for ITS Authoring Tools as *learnability* (how easy is it to learn a system) and *productivity* (how efficiently a tutor can be authored) [3]. In order to rethink the usability tradeoff, inspiration can be found within the similarly complex domain of game design and their associated game development tools.

Like intelligent tutors, games come in many shapes and sizes, with various levels of depth and flexibility. With respect to learnability, the barrier to game design previously limited the user-base to those with computer programming experience; today, freely available development tools and game engines provide the foundation for designers of all skill levels to start learning to create their own games (again, of varying scope and complexity). The powerful, flexible Unity and Unreal game development tools, respectively, are available at no cost, whose learnability is broadly supported by user-driven communities. The popular Minecraft game is an example of using a simple tool to teach students about a variety of subjects including programming fundamentals [22]. There are also genre-specific game development tools including Super Mario Maker and RPG Maker, for 2D-platform and role-playing games, respectively.

Similarly, the potential for what an ITS could be is still evolving, which creates a moving target for authoring tool design [19]. There will continue to be a variety of ITS platforms with authoring tools of varying levels of depth and flexibility corresponding to the needs of various learning environments. Along the depth/flexibility continuum, the key is providing authoring tools with a comprehensive approach to learnability including forums, examples, tutorial videos, and web-documentation, in addition to usable tools. In this way, a novice author that uses simple authoring tools to create a simple tutor can gain the knowledge and confidence to use complex authoring tools to create a complex tutor in the future, apply skills to a different authoring platform, or perhaps develop an entirely new type of tutor, not yet imagined.

With respect to productivity, current user experience research in game development tools seeks to increase the efficiency of even the most complex development tools, for example, by reducing the time to complete specific tasks, helping the user to organize information, and reducing the potential for user error [23]. These are usability improvements that do not come at the cost of depth and flexibility; rather research effort improves development tools by identifying user goals, understanding human mental models of specific tasks, and adjusting interface elements in order to help developers to accomplish their tasks in a more efficient way. Similar efforts are needed to increase the efficiency of ITS authoring tools, without changing the power of the existing system. The power of specific authoring tools can also scale with automation and templates. In this way, simple and complex authoring tools become part of the same system, giving the author the flexibility to discover and explore advanced authoring functions, when desired (see [10] for an authoring tool design case study).

In thinking about the design of authoring tools, the ITS community should endeavor to separate usability from the depth and flexibility tradeoff. Next, the notion of usability should be expanded to a comprehensive user experience for authoring tools, which considers every point of interaction between the system and the potential user. This approach applies to authoring tools that have both limited and wide application, as well as tools that exist today and ones not yet conceived. Because user trust is slowly gained, and easily lost, the needs of potential authors and organizational stakeholders should be at the center of any authoring tool design plan. If it seems difficult to justify allocating resources to the UX of authoring tools, consider the cost of *not* doing this work with respect to the user base and overall success of the ITS platform.

3   Practical UX Requirements for Authoring Tools

The current work concludes with some practical examples of in-progress user experience efforts for a specific ITS platform, the Generalized Intelligent Framework for Tutoring (GIFT). GIFT is described as "an empirically-based, service-oriented framework of tools, methods, and standards to make it easier to author computer-based tutoring systems (CBTS), manage instruction and assess the effect of CBTS, components and methodologies" [4]. Simultaneously, GIFT is an open-source research project and public-facing application. GIFT is currently under development and includes a number of technologies, features, tools, and methods intended to support a variety of users including instructional designers, authors, instructors, researchers, and learners.

While the UX requirements described below are framed in the context of GIFT-based research, the requirements can be adapted to other ITS authoring tools. Finally, this list is not intended to be comprehensive. Instead, the examples in the following sections serve to illuminate UX concerns and generate dialog for improving authoring tools to the benefit of current and future adaptive tutor authors and associated organizations.

3.1   Comprehensive Help and Documentation

GIFT has seen numerous improvements to its authoring tools and overall authoring workflow. In the absence of formal tools, GIFT courses were created by editing eXtensible markup language (XML) files. The first formal authoring tools allowed for indirect manipulation of the XML files through desktop software. Currently, web-based applications are being developed that provide a more menu-based approach to creating courses. While the underlying structure of the GIFT architecture has not changed dramatically, the end-user authoring experience has seen significant change. In order to provide a consistent experience with the web-application, the GIFT team is working to transition the support documentation to an online, web-based format, which can be rapidly updated along with the application.

ITS Documentation and help files must (first exist, and then) keep pace with authoring tool development. Creating this material may be one of the last tasks in a development effort, but documentation will be one of the first elements that an ITS author will seek when encountering an issue. Therefore documentation warrants considerable attention. Documentation should be up to date, searchable, and internally cross-referenced. Help (in the form of descriptions, hints, and tips) should be easily accessible within the interface at the point-of-need. Help and documentation should serve to support authors' knowledge and confidence, as well as prevent them from getting *lost* in authoring tool interfaces.

3.2   Beyond Documentation: Demonstrations and Social Channels

ITS authoring tools should contain example courses to inspect and modify. These examples should be highly polished (both visually and functionally) in order to make a positive first impression on users. To the extent that is practical, supplementary documentation should reference these examples in order to ground the authors' knowledge in a tangible work. Complementary to that, ITS support should extend beyond software tools into social media, which might include tutorial videos, conversations in forums, and interactions with users via social channels. Some of the topics to discuss in these channels are obvious: What is [product name]? What do I do now/first? Or, what is a tutor and how is one created? Topics for other tutorials and discussions can be generated from user research, as well as through internal discussion within the interdisciplinary development team. Finally, opening channels for conversation will help authors to connect one another, and hopefully form a community around which a user base can grow and improve together.

GIFT, for example, has forums in which users can quickly connect with key members of the development team. Additionally, the GIFT authoring tools contain a number of courses that demonstrate technical functionality. These courses can also be viewed within the authoring tools to get a sense of how those courses were created. However, much of the burden is on the author to discovering how all of the systems work together, and it is not immediately clear how these examples would apply to authors' original course creations. The GIFT team is currently working to develop additional example courses, as well as provide additional support through interactions in forums and via tutorial videos in order to support knowledge development.

3.3   Authoring for Non-traditional Learning Environments

When designing a tutor, authors must consider their learners and the environments in which they will interact with the tutor. Thus, authoring system design must also consider the learning contexts for which authors will need appropriate tools in order to properly configure a *tutor-user interface*. For example, authoring systems may need visual styling options in order to simultaneously support PC, tablet, and mobile displays, respectively. Where text input may be appropriate for PC learning, voice input may be required for tutoring on a mobile device in a field environment. Further outside-the-box thinking might consider tutoring with wearable displays such as smart watches, smart glasses, or augmented reality headsets in which novel methods are needed to communicate across the tutor-user interface. Other considerations include designing courses for limited power (processing or battery, respectively) capacity as well as supporting downloadable courses to use in a temporarily offline state.

Multiple lines of GIFT research and development are addressing mobile, offline, and field tutoring, respectively. The GIFT Cloud web-application provides the first steps toward browser-based compatibility with mobile and tablet systems. The PC-based GIFT Local supports offline use, with a server-based implementation in planning for secure network environments. Finally, distinct research efforts are examining non-traditional displays, such as sand-tables [24] and smart-glasses [13, 14], in order to define software and hardware requirements supporting tutoring *in-the-wild* for military tasks in operational settings. These efforts, in turn, continue to define requirements for new authoring tools including, for example, situated GIFT authoring within an external software application.

3.4   Collaboration, Sharing, and Authoring Roles

Part of a comprehensive user experience is understanding how actual users might use an ITS in a real-world environment. Given the skills involved in creating a tutor (e.g., computer science, instructional design, and subject matter expertise) it is reasonable to anticipate that *teams of authors*, instead of individual authors, will be creating adaptive tutors. These teams might be centrally located or geographically distributed. They may be working on the same course at the same time or multiple courses simultaneously. As such, ITS authoring tools will need to have features supporting, for instance, collaborative editing, change tracking, approval, and version control. Additionally, user roles will be necessary to support project management structures within the organization using the tools. Authoring roles can benefit specialized authors as well; for example, the tools and default view available to a subject matter expert should be different than those of an instructional designer.

GIFT, specifically, is research-driven. Thus, GIFT has a particular need to support experimental research, in addition to collaborative authoring. To that end, additional tools have been created in order to facilitate experimentation in topics related to adaptive tutoring. While those tools have no direct impact on the usability, depth, and flexibility of the authoring tools, the research tools complement the authoring tools in a way that provides functionality that meets needs of a subset of end-users. Specialized interfaces allow researchers to create research studies from existing courses, with specialized access links, and participant data reporting interfaces. The GIFT team continues to gather information about how authors might want to utilize GIFT, and consider this input for UX and feature improvements in subsequent platform updates.

3.5   Mental Models for ITS and Authoring Tools: The Elephant in the Room

Finally, Murray [19] explained that authoring tools should help users build accurate mental models of the ITS building blocks, configurations, and workflow afforded by the authoring tool. This is inherently difficult, because ITS are evolving, and each ITS will differ in some ways from others. However, mental model theory can provide some guidance with respect to approaching this interaction problem en route to an *accurate* mental model. Rouse and Morris [25] described mental models as "mechanisms whereby humans are able to generate descriptions of purpose and form, explanations of system functioning and observed system states, and predictions of future states" (p. 7). Mental models influence users' expectations regarding a system's functionality and guide user interaction behavior [26]. An individual's mental model regarding a particular system is influenced by past experiences and perceived similarity of other systems to the target system. Further, human mental models do not need to be complete or even accurate to be applied to a specific system interaction [27].

To that end, there are a number of approaches for designing authoring tools with human mental models in mind. For instance, in the absence of a mental model for ITS authoring, users will attempt to leverage a known model of another system, and test assumptions about the authoring tools, based on that model. The mental model that a user selects can be influenced by the look and feel of the authoring tool. For instance, a mental model of PowerPoint may be suggested by stacking course elements along the left side of the UI, with the design space occupying a larger right-side area. The use of metaphors and existing mental models can be useful in acclimating new users to a system. However, the usefulness of that approach has limits; and in order to leverage a metaphor it is generally necessary to also understand the user's mental model of the metaphor system (e.g., what they know about PowerPoint). The goal of this approach is that, over time, users will exhaust the metaphor model and develop a distinct mental model of the target authoring system.

An alternative approach leverages general and specific mental models in helping new users to understand ITS authoring tools. Generally, there are some basic concepts and components that are common to ITS (e.g., learner model, pedagogical model, domain knowledge, tutor-user interface). However, the specific manner in which these components are operationalized will differ with each ITS, and therefore within each authoring system. In order to address the learnability of a specific authoring system, it may beneficial to first establish the general mental model of an ITS with potential authors. Then, potential authors can use this generalized mental model to develop a specific model of a particular ITS and associated authoring tools. In this way, authors would be better prepared to move between novice and expert tools within the same authoring system, or apply their knowledge to other authoring systems, with a stronger baseline mental model for adapting to those new experiences.

GIFT, specifically, has a variety of general (theory-based) and specific (applied) scholarly publications located on the web-based portal located at www.gifttutoring.org in order to support current and potential users in their development of system mental models. Additionally, GIFT has seen significant improvements to the authoring interface with the alpha release of the web-based GIFT Cloud application. Current efforts are examining the use of familiar interface elements to potentially evoke system metaphors and increase the learnability of GIFT. Potential authoring design interfaces being considered include lists and hierarchical structures, as well as object-oriented structures such as flow charts and discrete-event models.

4 Discussion

Intelligent tutoring systems have the potential to revolutionize how, when, and where learners can interact with instructional content. Though, despite decades of research and development in ITS, they are not yet widely used outside of research and development settings. Significant barriers to the greater adoption of ITS in educational and training contexts include the steep learning curve and high resources required to create adaptive tutors. Authoring tools can reduce these barriers and make ITS more accessible to both novice and expert adaptive tutor authors. While authoring tools continue to evolve in depth and flexibility, it is necessary to expand the concept of tool usability toward a comprehensive end-to-end user experience with respect to actual users interacting with ITS authoring products in real-world contexts.

Interactions with ITS authoring tools should build trust and confidence in their users, and authors should feel smart when interacting with authoring tools. Authors should be able to view high-quality example courses showcasing the power and/or flexibility of an ITS, and then use authoring tools to examine and deconstruct those examples. Authoring tools should provide capabilities that allow novice users to create tutors, while providing discoverable advanced functions that help novice users become experts. Further, simple authoring tools for simple tutors create opportunities for potential users to get interested in tutor authoring. Forums, social media, and video tutorials are recommended to grow community of practice around the authoring tools, and encourage interaction among members and ITS developers, respectively.

Designing the user experience of authoring tools is not an effort that should come at the cost of theory and platform development; it should be an integral part of the development plan from the outset of an ITS project. By considering the needs, goals, and mental models of potential end-users, system developers create a path to building the right authoring tools, while building authoring tools right. In order to gain greater adoption in educational and training communities, ITS and authoring tool end-user experiences must not just be as good as digital and analog tool alternatives, they must inspire trust and confidence in order to switch from alternatives, they must be better.

Acknowledgments. The author would like to thank Deeja Cruz for her helpful review and critique of this manuscript. Research was sponsored by the Army Research Laboratory and was accomplished under Cooperative Agreement Number W911NF-12-2-0019. The views and conclusions contained in this document are those of the authors and should not be interpreted as representing the official policies, either expressed or implied, of the Army Research Laboratory or the U.S. Government. The U.S. Government is authorized to reproduce and distribute reprints for Government purposes notwithstanding and copyright notation herein.

References

1. VanLehn, K.: The relative effectiveness of human tutoring, intelligent tutoring systems and other tutoring systems. Educ. Psychol. **46**, 197–221 (2011)
2. Bill & Melinda Gates Foundation: Teachers know best: What educators want from digital instructional tools 2.0 (2015). http://collegeready.gatesfoundation.org/2015/12/what-educators-want-from-digital-tools-2-0/
3. Murray, T.: Design tradeoffs in usability and power for advanced educational software authoring tools. Educ. Technol. **44**, 10–16 (2004)
4. Sottilare, R.A., Graesser, A.C., Hu, X., Holden, H.: Design Recommendations for Intelligent Tutoring Systems. Learner Modeling, vol. 1. U.S. Army Research Laboratory, Orlando (2013)
5. Self, J.: The defining characteristics of intelligent tutoring systems research. Int. J. Artif. Intell. Educ. (IJAIED) **10**, 350–364 (1998)
6. Psotka, J., Massey, L.D., Mutter, S.A.: Intelligent Tutoring Systems: Lessons Learned. Psychology Press, Hillsdale (1988)
7. Beck, J., Stern, M., Haugsjaa, E.: Applications of AI in education. Crossroads **3**, 11–15 (1996)
8. Murray, T.: Coordinating the complexity of tools, tasks, and users: on theory-based approaches to authoring tool usability. Int. J. Artif. Intell. Educ. **26**(1), 37–71 (2016)
9. Picard, R.: Building an affective learning companion. Keynote Address at the 8th International Conference on Intelligent Tutoring Systems (2006). http://www.its2006.org/ITS_keynote/ITS2006_01.pdf
10. Murray, T., Woolf, B., Marshall, D.: Lessons learned from authoring for inquiry learning: a tale of authoring tool evolution. In: Lester, J.C., Vicari, R.M., Paraguaçu, F. (eds.) ITS 2004. LNCS, vol. 3220, pp. 197–206. Springer, Heidelberg (2004)
11. Nye, B.D.: Intelligent tutoring systems by and for the developing world: a review of trends and approaches for educational technology in a global context. Int. J. Artif. Intell. Educ. **25**, 177–203 (2014)
12. U.S. Army Training and Doctrine Command: The United States Army Learning Concept for 2015, Fort Monroe, VA (2011)
13. Sottilare, R.A., LaViola, J.: Extending intelligent tutoring beyond the desktop to the psychomotor domain. In: Interservice/Industry Training Simulation & Education Conference, Orlando, FL, December 2015
14. Sottilare, R., Hackett, M., Pike, W., LaViola, J.: Adaptive instruction for medical training in the psychomotor domain. In: Cohn, J., Fitzhugh, D., Freeman, H. (eds.) Special Issue: Modeling and Simulation Technologies to Enhance and Optimize the DoD's Medical Readiness and Response Capabilities of the Journal for Defense Modeling & Simulation (JDMS) (2016, in review)
15. Olsen, J.K., Belenky, D.M., Aleven, V., Rummel, N.: Intelligent tutoring systems for collaborative learning: enhancements to authoring tools. In: Lane, H., Yacef, K., Mostow, J., Pavlik, P. (eds.) AIED 2013. LNCS, vol. 7926, pp. 900–903. Springer, Heidelberg (2013)
16. Aleven, V., Sewall, J.: Hands-on introduction to creating intelligent tutoring systems without programming using the cognitive tutor authoring tools (CTAT). In: Proceedings of the 9th International Conference of the Learning Sciences, vol. 2, pp. 511–512. International Society of the Learning Sciences (2010)
17. Suraweera, P., Mitrovic, A., Martin, B.: Widening the knowledge acquisition bottleneck for constraint-based tutors. Int. J. Artif. Intell. Educ. (IJAIED) **20**, 137–173 (2010)
18. Mitrovic, A., Martin, B., Suraweera, P., Zakharov, K., Milik, N., Holland, J., McGuigan, N.: ASPIRE: an authoring system and deployment environment for constraint-based tutors. Int. J. Artif. Intell. Educ. **19**, 155–188 (2009)

19. Murray, T.: Theory-based authoring tool design: considering the complexity of tasks and mental models. In: Sottilare, R.A., Graesser, A.C., Hu, X., Brawner, K. (eds.) Design Recommendations for Intelligent Tutoring Systems. Authoring Tools and Expert Modeling Techniques, vol. 3, pp. 9–29. U.S. Army Research Laboratory, Orlando (2014)
20. Murray, T.: Having it all, maybe: design tradeoffs in ITS authoring tools. In: Frasson, C., Gauthier, G., Lesgold, A. (eds.) ITS 1996. LNCS, vol. 1086, pp. 93–101. Springer, Heidelberg (1996)
21. Fraco, A.: UX vs. Marketing: Can these opposites attract? Agency Post. HubSpot (2014). http://blog.hubspot.com/agency/ux-vs-marketing-opposites-attract
22. Kastrenakes, J.: Microsoft announces Minecraft: Education Edition for schools. The Verge (2016). http://www.theverge.com/2016/1/19/10788994/minecraft-education-edition-announced-microsoft
23. Lightbown, D.: Designing the User Experience of Game Development Tools. CRC Press, Boca Raton (2015)
24. Boyce, M.W., Amburn, C.R., Sottilare, R.A., Goldberg, B.S., Moss, J.D.: The Effect of Topography on Learning Military Tactics. Department of Defense Human Factors and Engineering Technical Advisory Group, Orlando (2015)
25. Rouse, W.B., Morris, N.M.: On looking into the black box: prospects and limits in the search for mental models. Psychol. Bull. **100**, 349 (1986)
26. Ososky, S.: Influence of Task-Role Mental Models on Human Interpretation of Robot Motion Behavior. University of Central Florida, Orlando (2013)
27. Norman, D.A.: Cognitive engineering. In: Norman, D.A., Draper, S.W. (eds.) User Centered System Design: New Perspectives on Human-Computer Interaction, pp. 31–61. Lawrence Erlbaum Associates, Hillsdale (1986)

Making Sense of Cognitive Performance in Small Unit Training

William A. Ross[1(✉)], Joan H. Johnston[2], Dawn Riddle[3],
CDR Henry Phillips[3], Lisa Townsend[3], and Laura Milham[3]

[1] Cognitive Performance Group Orlando, Orlando, FL, USA
bill@cognitiveperformancegroup.com
[2] ARL-HRED Advanced Training and Simulation Division Orlando,
Orlando, FL, USA
joan.h.johnston.civ@mail.mil
[3] Naval Air Warfare Center Training Systems Division Orlando,
Orlando, FL, USA
{dawn.riddle,henry.phillips,lisa.townsend,
laura.milham}@navy.mil

Abstract. The goal of the Squad Overmatch (SOvM) for Tactical Combat Casualty Care (TC3) study was to introduce and assess an integrated training approach (ITA) for producing adaptable, high performing infantry squads. The challenge is to create the conditions and encode learning experiences for re-use in combat situations. Effective performance embedded in force-on-force actions are unscripted and required unpacking to understand and use as performance feedback. This paper describes the development of a prototype team performance observation tool developed to support the assessment of mission critical tasks during the simulation and live training phases of the ITA. The tool was constructed based on tactical use cases developed with subject matter experts. Discrete TC3 tasks were defined so that observers could recognize and record squad member performance, and that could be traceable to understanding underlying cognitions of team members during an after action review. Lessons learned on usability and reliability of the tool are discussed.

Keywords: Infantry squad · Decision making · Sense making · Observation rubric · Human dimension · Measurement

1 Introduction

In a complex world, infantry squads must be prepared to recognize patterns, make accurate predictions, select workable courses of action (COAs), and adapt to uncertainty [6]. Squad behaviors are context-driven and shaped by the experience of decision making, using pattern recognition and predictions to select courses of action. Conditions that produce problems that reward adaptive thinkers with success based on accurate predictions and timely decision making are a challenge to simulate for training. In dynamically complex contexts like the battlefield, effective performance embedded in force-on-force actions are unscripted and required unpacking to understand and use as performance feedback.

© Springer International Publishing Switzerland 2016
D.D. Schmorrow and C.M. Fidopiastis (Eds.): AC 2016, Part II, LNAI 9744, pp. 67–75, 2016.
DOI: 10.1007/978-3-319-39952-2_7

While military training developers have adopted many adult learning strategies and instructional technologies, virtual training simulations and live training have not filled the measurement gap. Traditional, easy to produce measures like killer-victim scoreboards fall far short of explaining how cognitive complexity was mastered by the most skilled practitioners of infantry tactics. The challenge for small unit trainers is making sense of human performance and then measuring the collective performance as training takes place in both virtual- and live training systems. In other words, understanding performance of high performing teams requires more than checking the box that Warrior Leader-, collective- or individual tasks have been performed [5]. Of greater importance to the trainee in the context of the infantry squad is the ability to benchmark team performance in order to focus and adapt training for performance improvements and developing accurate shared mental models. Direct measures of cognitive performance are inconsistent because outcome measures alone cannot be traced directly to decision skills.

The purpose of this paper is to describe the development and application of a prototype observation tool and observer training rubric that was developed to address this problem. The tool development was a key effort in a series of Squad Overmatch (SOvM) studies focusing on whether an integrated training approach (ITA) of instruction, simulation, and live training, could effectively demonstrate methods, tools, and strategies for improving team performance and creating resilience among squad members [1]. An observation rubric was developed as a set of guidelines and procedures for providing observable evidence of the type of behaviors and thinking skills that expert teams use to continually improve; and it was tested during the most recent SOvM 2015 study that focused on Tactical Combat Casualty Care (TC3).

2 Approach

We adopted the Simulation-Based Training (SBT) method as an organizing framework for designing and constructing the SOvM TC3 observation tool. SBT was developed and validated to create an instructionally sound, organizing framework for designing and delivering effective team training [2, 3]. It is effective because it provides an adaptive training approach - through seven linked elements - that use performance results from training exercises to tailor future exercises that accelerate development of skills.

The cycle begins with identifying competencies (knowledge and skills) and the associated learning objectives (LOs) based on the military mission essential task lists. Then, specific instructional strategies are derived from the LOs so that skill development is optimized. Training strategies enable defining the training simulation scripts and scenario events. Events are scripted into a scenario that will allow for performing the targeted skills. Diagnostic performance measures are developed and used to determine if the LOs have been mastered. Once diagnoses are defined, a structured after action review (AAR) can be constructed and delivered so there is a basis on which to improve in subsequent scenarios. To close the loop, performance information must be incorporated into future training sessions to ensure new training objectives build on what has already been learned.

SBT will be effective if the measures used during training exercises can be employed to diagnose learning and performance for the AARs, and are used for determining future training objectives in order to adapt training to learning requirements. Next, we describe the development of the prototype team performance assessment rubric and lessons learned following the SOVM TC3 demonstration conducted in October and November 2015.

3 TC3 Mission Tasks

We leveraged the existing research products from the SOvM 2014 demonstration to focus on the TC3 mission task components for 2015 [1, 5]. Working with TC3 Subject Matter Experts (SMEs) we focused on the combined challenges of handling both the tactical *and* casualty care responsibilities. The key TC3 mission tasks were determined to be:

- Integrate Medical Planning with Tactical Plans
- Provide Care Under Fire (while in contact or kill zone)
- Perform Tactical Field Care (once area has been secured)
- Manage Casualty Evacuation (priority of care/treatment)

Use cases were then developed for each of the major mission task areas; examples for Care Under Fire (CUF) and Tactical Field Care (TFC) are detailed below.

3.1 Care Under Fire

The Squad is conducting combat operations and has taken casualties. During the direct fire engagement, the casualty is reported. The wounded individual informs the Squad Leader of who is injured, the nature of the injury, whether the wounded individual is capable of Shooting, Moving, Communicating (staying in the fight), what treatment is required, and who must perform the treatment. The casualty is moved to safety or covered position where treatment is performed. When any of these elements of casualty information are missing, medical decisions are delayed. Tasks common to CUF are:

- Squad Leader receives a report of a casualty
- Squad achieves fire superiority and continues the mission
- Squad Leader decides how to act based on information in the casualty report.
- Treatment is based on information displayed on the Combat Casualty Card
- Treatment is begun in a covered (safe) area until the area is secure
- Treatment priorities are followed in accordance with SOP
- Treatment is appropriate for the wound type
- Combat casualty card is prepared and maintained as treatment progresses
- Squad Leader submits contact/casualty report to Platoon
- Squad identifies and secures a Casualty Collection Point based on situation

3.2   Tactical Field Care

The Squad is conducting combat operations and has taken casualties. They have achieved control over the situation. A Casualty Collection Point has been established in a secure area, where the Medic/Corpsman can manage the treatment. He determines the treatment needs and allocates resources to provide the necessary care. He organizes the CCP based on the casualty markings and wound type, to facilitate effective treatment and efficient transport to an evacuation point. He maintains contact with the Squad Leader and keeps him informed on the status of injuries. He recommends evacuation actions based on his awareness of the medical situation at the CCP. The Squad Leader allocates resources and prioritizes support of the CCP. If evacuation is necessary, he prepares/ submits the 9-line report. He keeps the Platoon aware of the situation in his area. Tasks common to TFC are:

- Squad Leader receives a report of a casualty
- Squad achieves fire superiority and continues the mission
- Squad Leader decides how to act based on information in the casualty report
- Treatment is based on information displayed on the Combat Casualty Card
- Treatment is begun in a covered area until the area is secure
- Treatment priorities are followed in accordance with TC3 standard operating procedures
- Treatment is appropriate for the wound type
- A combat casualty card is prepared and maintained as treatment progresses
- Squad Leader submits contact/casualty report to Platoon
- Squad identifies and secures a Casualty Collection Point based on situation

4   Competencies and Learning Objectives

Listed below are the key TC3 competencies (knowledge and skills) and learning objectives that were developed and verified with SMEs based on the use case analyses. Advanced Situation Awareness (ASA) and Resilience and Performance Enhancement (RPE) had been identified under the SOvM 2014 study; and we then added Team Development and Learning to the competency requirements for SOvM TC3.

Tactical Combat Casualty Care - while maintaining a tactical mission focus, manage combat casualties and provide the right treatment, by the right person, at the right time, to reduce the death by wound rate and facilitate evacuation to the appropriate medical treatment facility.

Advanced Situational Awareness - gain time or stand-off for disrupting or preventing an attack by detecting hostile indicators and anomalies and comparing them to a baseline of normality consisting of patterns of human behavior and environmental factors; this includes accurate assessment of enemy intentions or risks by using perceptual actions (orienting on target, observing patterns, interpreting patterns), selecting courses of action, and reporting actionable information.

Resilience and Performance Enhancement - monitor and maintain individual resilience by self-monitoring and regulating physical and cognitive resources in order to balance individual energy and attention resources when encountering operational stressors.

Team Development and Learning - exchange information, communicate clearly, support and backup team members, use initiative, provide guidance and priorities, and employ guided team self-correction during AARs to improve learning effective team performance behaviors.

5 Event-Based Scenarios and Measures

Based on SOvM 2014, the SOvM TC3 curriculum was implemented in three stages and modalities: knowledge acquisition in the classroom, skill acquisition and practice in virtual simulation-based training, and skill application in live, simulation enhanced training exercises. In each modality, a standard approach was used to frame the instruction based on learning objectives, guided learning, and checks on learning. This instructional design created a foundation for learning, scaffolding for skill development, and coaching for continual improvement. As the participants progressed through each stage, the aim was to produce near-term transfer that would support achievement at the next stage.

Event-based scenarios and the performance observation rubrics were developed from the use cases. A task sequence was constructed within each use case that was aligned with the doctrinal norm and based on SME inputs. In this manner we created a set of performance indicators that we reasonably expected would occur. The same story narrative and critical events were used in both the simulation and live training scenarios.

Using one of the live scenarios as an example, Table 1 shows how each of the competencies was linked to key chronological events and tasks in the scenario. Our goal was to present sufficient opportunities for squads to demonstrate performance in each of the four competency areas over the course of the scenario, which lasted about 45 min. In this scenario we generated a total of 97 instances for the 5 key events.

Table 1. Chronological scenario events, tasks and instances of key competencies

Chronological scenario events/tasks	Instances of expected actions tied to competencies				Total instances
	TC3	ASA	RPE	TD	
1. Planning and troop leading procedures (TLP)	1	6	2	10	19
2. Surveillance and reporting from an observation post	——	8	2	9	19
3. Key leader engagement (2 events)	2	8	5	10	25
4. Respond to sniper attack and care under fire	5	5	3	5	18
5. Tactical field care (once area has been secured)	5	5	2	4	16

Next we developed the observation measurement rubric based on the complete lists of expected behaviors derived for each of the events in the two simulation and two live training scenarios. The intent was to determine what task behaviors could be observed and whether they could be reliably assessed by multiple observers.

For each scenario, a short description of each event was presented on a single page. For example, Event 4 – Respond to Sniper Attack And Care Under Fire – requires the squad to react to sniper fire and respond to a civilian casualty while on patrol. Two women (roleplayers) plead with the squad for medical assistance which should cause the Squad to stop. A sniper (shots are heard) begins engaging the squad with effective direct fire, initiating "Respond to Sniper Attack." One of the females is shot and falls to the ground, and this should cause the squad to attempt to render aid, initiating "Care Under Fire." Then a squad member receives a gunshot wound to the arm, which requires treatment. The Squad should take cover, returning fire and maneuvering against the sniper as its immediate response. There is no follow-on attack by the Sniper.

Table 2. Instances of expected squad behaviors

TC3 (5)	ASA (5)	RPE (3)	TD (5)
During care under fire, moved the casualty from effective enemy fire to a safe area	Cover is provided for SL as females are meeting with the squad asking for assistance	Squad members accepted that they cannot prevent every friendly casualty, they focused on "What's Important Now" and resumed their mission focus	Squad members exchanged information about the location of the sniper as they used suppressive fire and maneuver to neutralize the threat
Initial treatment to control bleeding Chest seal on female; tourniquet on Soldier	Suppressive fires resulted in sniper withdrawing from his firing position	Squad members used deliberate breathing to deal with the threat posed by snipers	Squad members communicated details clearly
Medic/Corpsman monitored the situation to be tactically aware	Squad exploited site where the shot was fired to collect additional information	Squad member used buddy talk to help members overcome the close call and resume the mission	Squad members exchanged information to maintain the momentum of their response to the sniper
Treatment for the gunshot wound provided by using a first aid kit	Squad assessed and reported atmospherics for indications of a threat to others		Squad Leader submitted a report to Platoon as soon as he understood the situation
Casualty card completed and casualty status reported to Medic/Corpsman to main-tain situation awareness while the area is being secured	Squad used their optics to scan the area for threats		Squad Leader communicated with others including the Medic about the wounded civilian's medical needs

Then, the behavioral indicators were listed in columns for raters to look for during the event. For example, above are listed the 18 instances of expected behaviors that should be triggered in the squad from Event 4 in Table 2. TC3 had five indicators, ASA had five indicators, RPE had three indicators, and TD had five indicators.

The rubric in total consisted of 40 pages of data collection sheets. Table 3 presents an example of how the Team Development behaviors for Event 4 were presented as an observer checklist. A checkmark is placed next to the behavior if it was observed during the scenario.

Table 3. Observer checklist for team development behaviors

Event 4 - Team development checklist	✓
• Exchanged information about the location of the sniper as they used suppressive fire and maneuver to neutralize the threat	
• Clearly communicated details about sniper location	
• Exchanged information in response to sniper	
• Squad Leader submitted a report to Platoon	
• Squad Leader communicated with others including the Medic/Corpsman about the wounded civilian's medical needs	

6   Lessons Learned

Three criteria for an effective rubric were prescribed by the SOvM research team: the content and criteria must be valid; the rubric must be usable; and the rubric must result in reliable data collection. If these criteria were met, the study results would show that critical incidents were observable and the team performance could be assessed by trained data collectors.

Therefore, several weeks before the SOvM TC3 demonstration, a team of six experienced researchers were assembled for one-day rubric training. They possessed knowledge of the curriculum, had participated in observer training, and understood the training design. The training session was conducted to develop an understanding of how the tool would be used. Then the tool was tested during the SOvM TC3 demonstration over a 5 week period in October and November 2015 with four USA and three USMC squads.

During the two virtual simulation-based training scenarios, observers listened to squad member communications over headsets and in the simulation room, and were able to observe the squad member movements in the virtual world on a "god's eye" view computer monitor. During the two live training scenarios, some observers listened to the squad member communications in a control room facility and observed a live feed of video and audio of the environment as the squad moved through it. Other observers were co-located with the squad and walked with the squad through the exercise at a safe distance. Observers used the checklist when they heard or saw squad members performing the indicated behaviors for each scenario event.

6.1   Content

Responses from observers led us to conclude that the use cases were sufficiently clear and complete to support the data collection requirement. Each use case was based on a tactical event. However, depending on the experience level of the Squad and their interpretations of various tactical cues, it was never possible to completely track performance as it was defined in the use case. For future studies we will update the content and structure of the rubric as we improve the prototype. Use cases will be adapted to a checklist sheet similar to the TARGET methodology [4] developed to increase the reliability of observing and counting instances of the behaviors during training and as part of the team AARs that follow.

6.2   Usability

Usability issues interfered with the ability to pinpoint squad performance and assign an accurate or consistent checkmark. We found data collectors experienced difficulty keeping up with the pace of the scenarios. The layout and form of the rubric use cases tended to interfere with the direct observation and recording of reliable data. This was an inevitable outcome based on the complexity of the scenarios, size of the squad, and size and structure of the rubric. Each Observer adapted and found alternative ways to capture the performance indicators that suggested learning had taken place. This included concept maps, field notes, transcripts of voice communications, and checklists of key events. To improve its usability and the functionality necessary for efficiently navigating through the tool and reducing workload when it is critical for the observer to attend to the squad performance, we will implement the rubric on a tablet. The tablet will initially store data and accumulate results for off-line data analysis. We intend to develop a set of Behaviorally Anchored Rating Scales (BARS) that are aligned with the key performance areas. These BARS include a feature for "tagging" weighted performance indicators within each BARS and generating a rating for use by analysts.

6.3   Reliability

We also learned that the researcher's qualifications were not sufficient for using the rubric to observe squad tactical performance during virtual or live training. Data collection was hampered by a lack of understanding of the tactical behaviors being demonstrated by the squads. A more rigorous training and preparation period for data collectors/non-participant observers is needed. This would include interactive multi-media training solutions that would provide researchers and data collectors an opportunity to test the rubric using videos and observations of live and virtual training. Aligning data collectors with specific teams that make up the squad, i.e., the Squad Leader and Medic/Corpsman and individual the infantry fire teams is expected to reduce workload and increase reliability.

7 Conclusion

Infantry squad training is a "wicked" problem. Small unit training has assumed greater importance because operations in a complex world demand agile, adaptive thinkers who must make critical decisions under pressure. Training that focuses on tactical outcomes misses the point of developing the underlying critical cognitive skills. The SOvM TC3 research exposed a gap in current training that affects the development of high performing teams. The SBT approach enabled us to systematically develop and demonstrate linkages between mission tasks, competencies, learning objectives, instructional strategies, scenarios, and a prototype team performance observation tool. The rapid development and testing of the prototype observation rubric enabled researchers to determine how to link task performance with cognitive skills such as decision making and problem solving. Lessons learned enabled us to chart a path forward for a more valid and reliable automated, transition-ready data collection tool.

Acknowledgments. The authors express their appreciation to the Defense Medical Research and Development Program through Joint Program Committee 1 (JPC-1: Medical Training and Health Information Services) for sponsoring and funding this critical effort.

References

1. Brimstin, J., Higgs, A., Wolf, R.: Stress exposure training for the dismounted squad: the human dimension. In: Interservice/Industry Training, Simulation, and Education Conference [CD-ROM], Orlando, FL (2015)
2. Cannon-Bowers, J., Bowers, C.: Training support technologies. In: Nicholson, D., Schmorrow, D., Cohn, J. (eds.) The PSI Handbook of Virtual Environments for Training and Education: Developments for the Military and Beyond. VE Components and Training Technologies, vol. 2, pp. 263–269. Praeger, Westport, CT (2009)
3. Cannon-Bowers, J.A., Burns, J.J., Salas, E., Pruitt, J.S.: Advanced technology in scenario-based training. In: Cannon-Bowers, J.A., Salas, E. (eds.) Making Decisions Under Stress: Implications for Individual and Team Training, pp. 365–374. APA, Washington, DC (1998)
4. Fowlkes, J.E., Lane, N.E., Salas, E., Franz, T., Oser, R.: Improving the measurement of team performance: the TARGETS methodology. Mil. Psychol. **6**(1), 47–61 (1994)
5. Johnston, J.H., Napier, S., Ross, W.A.: Adapting immersive training environments to develop squad resilience skills. In: Schmorrow, D.D., Fidopiastis, C.M. (eds.) AC 2015. LNCS, vol. 9183, pp. 616–627. Springer, Heidelberg (2015)
6. U.S. Army Training and Doctrine Command: TRADOC Pam. 525-3-1, The Army Operating Concept, Win in a Complex World 2020-2040. Ft. Eustis, VA (2014)

Considerations for Immersive Learning in Intelligent Tutoring Systems

Anne M. Sinatra[✉]

U.S. Army Research Laboratory, Orlando, FL, USA
anne.m.sinatra.civ@mail.mil

Abstract. Research has examined the benefits and retractors of immersing the learner in an environment. Immersive computer-based training environments are costly to construct and may not always lead to significant learning or transfer benefits over other methods. The current paper presents a brief review of presence and immersion research in computer-based learning and adaptive tutoring. The Generalized Intelligent Framework for Tutoring (GIFT) is an open source domain-independent framework for creating intelligent tutoring systems (ITS). GIFT offers flexibility, and can be interfaced with training applications ranging from highly immersive computer-based learning environments (e.g., TC3Sim, VBS2) to less immersive mediums such as PowerPoint. The capabilities of GIFT that can be used to create immersive adaptive tutoring are discussed. Additionally, the use of GIFT to run and generate experimental studies to examine the impact of immersion is highlighted. Finally, recommendations are given on how to provide more opportunities to integrate immersive environments into GIFT.

Keywords: Immersion · Intelligent tutoring systems · Generalized Intelligent Framework for Tutoring · Presence

1 Introduction

Presence and immersion are concepts that are tightly coupled together in the literature [1, 2]. In many cases the terms have been used interchangeably to represent similar concepts [1]. Presence has been defined as "the subjective experience of being in one place or environment, even when one is physically situated in another" [2, p. 225]. Therefore, presence is the overall feeling that an individual has of being somewhere different than they are based on what they are experiencing. Immersion has been defined in the literature as "a psychological state characterized by perceiving oneself to be enveloped by, included in, and interacting with an environment that provides a continuous stream of stimuli and experiences" [2, p. 227]. McMahan [1] clarified immersion as being when an individual feels highly engaged in or "caught up in" an environment or story, and the positive feelings towards the environment. Further, McMahan distinguished presence from immersion, as presence is a term that tends to be applied to virtual reality and virtual environments [1].

As technology continues to rapidly improve, opportunities to encourage feelings of immersion in both virtual and physical environments have become more frequent.

© Springer International Publishing Switzerland 2016
D.D. Schmorrow and C.M. Fidopiastis (Eds.): AC 2016, Part II, LNAI 9744, pp. 76–84, 2016.
DOI: 10.1007/978-3-319-39952-2_8

Feelings of immersion and presence are often goals of different entertainment mediums such as videogames, movies, and theme parks. Videogames have become increasingly more interactive with not only more visually realistic environments, but also more realistic motion based user input methods as seen in the Nintendo Wii, Kinect and Playstation Move [3]. In an effort to encourage consumers to see movies in theaters, the film industry have moved in a similar direction by releasing movies that are in 3D and IMAX 3D to give the audience the impression that they are in the action instead of watching it. Additionally, DBOX has specially designed seats in select theaters that move or shake depending on what is happening on the screen. Rather than just relying on the film's story to draw viewers in, these 3D and tactile elements provide additional sensory cues to further enhance feelings of being in the action as opposed to watching it. Theme parks have also moved toward including 3D in their rides, to further enhance the experience. While the "land" structure of theme parks such as Disney's Magic Kingdom and Disneyland are not a relatively new idea (i.e. Fantasyland, Tomorrowland, Frontierland, etc.), there has recently been a trend toward new highly themed and conceptually tied together "lands" that make the visitor feel like they have walked into a movie such as *Harry Potter* or *Avatar* by seamlessly recreating places that have only existed in film or books. The goal of lands is not only to provide an attraction, but also an experience where the guest feels that they are transported to a different, often fictional, place. Immersion can occur in the multisensory mediums described, however, getting highly involved in a book or movie and putting oneself in the place of a character is a form of immersion as well [2]. The current strategies of 3D and large format screens, and being able to walk into a fictional place like Hogwarts Castle at a theme park are examples of approaches that are currently being used to foster these feelings of identification with characters and immersion.

There are individual differences and characteristics of individuals which may make them more or less likely to become involved with a virtual environment or other medium. Scales such as Witmer and Singer's Presence Questionnaire [2] and the ITC-Sense of Presence Inventory [4] have been developed in order to measure and quantify these feelings of presence. Immersion and presence are goals of all the previously described entertainment mediums. However, all of these examples are of mediums that are trying to create a sense of immersion and presence that are primarily aimed at entertainment. Many times these immersive videogames, rides, and movies get positive reviews and feedback from consumers, which results in a continued push towards using these methods. In general people tend to like systems that offer more realism and fidelity, however, this may ultimately be more distracting to the task than helpful [5]. As videogames and virtual environments have become more prevalent, they have been harnessed for learning and training purposes. The assumption that is often made is that because something is more immersive it will lead to better outcomes in training and transfer to real world tasks. Immersion has been found to have positive impacts on learning due to encouragement of situated learning, and simulating the real world [6], however, it may not be the case for every domain. Training transfer may not occur from all videogames and virtual environments, and research is needed to continue examining the interactions and impacts of presence and immersion on outcomes [7]. While immersive virtual environments and videogames may provide opportunities to learn and practice skills they may not always include pedagogy. Intelligent tutoring systems (ITS) can be combined with these environments and games to improve learning outcomes, and to foster research into the influence of these environments on training transfer/learning.

2   Considerations for Immersive Learning and Tutoring

Immersive learning environments can include established videogames or virtual environments in which learners are taught to perform a task. Learners may interact with these while looking at a computer screen and typing their inputs; or they may wear a head mounted display, or look at another visual display. Rather than simply using a keyboard, the user input method may be by motion (i.e. Kinect), voice command, or game controller. Using these varying displays and input methods may impact how immersed the individual learner feels in the environment [8].

Immersive environments are designed to engage learners in their story and the action that is being performed. By adding tutoring and feedback components to these environments it requires providing instruction and feedback. However, sometimes it can be distracting for feedback to be provided to the learner while engaging with the environment. If the gameplay is stopped to provide video or auditory feedback it may take the learner out of the experience. Also, it is important for the feedback to be salient enough for the learner to understand it. Therefore, careful consideration should be given to the method in which feedback is given, how frequently it is given, and how disruptive it should be to engaging in the environment [9, 10].

It is important for there to be a match between the learning environment and the material that is being taught [8]. It has been found that using head mounted displays while engaging with a learning environment about science and botany did not lead to positive training or transfer effects [11]. However, a head mounted display may not have been the ideal environment to teach that specific material in. Another topic that may lend itself to the display method may have had differing results. For instance, land navigation has been suggested as a relevant domain that could be used for adaptive tutoring with smart glasses [12], however, teaching algebra using smart glasses may not be as beneficial. Therefore, it is important for the match between the domain and delivery method to be examined.

There may be individual differences in learners in regard to how likely they are to become involved or immersed in an environment [2]. Additionally, while the assumption is generally made that more detail or fidelity in an environment will lead to better learning outcomes, it is not necessarily true [5]. If extra non-relevant details are included it may actually lead to distraction from the important information. This distraction has been referred to as the seductive details effect, and has been found in both assessments after viewing text based, and multimedia based training/videos [13, 14]. Therefore, it is important to consider how much detail to provide and to make sure that it enhances the focus of the tutoring rather than distracting from it.

3 Intelligent Tutoring Systems and Immersive Learning

Intelligent tutoring systems and adaptive training provide excellent opportunities for both instructors and students. Materials can be presented to students, and the computer-based system can then react and adjust the student's path based on their specific characteristics, answers to questions, and performance in assessments. Instructors have the flexibility to decide what material they would like to teach and create alternate paths that can help provide remediation on material that students are not necessarily grasping. Additionally, the performance of a student in one lesson can generally be stored and applied to their future interactions with the learning system. ITS result in highly adaptable learning content that is tied to the specific learner's strengths, weaknesses, and needs. ITS instruction can assist in improving learner outcomes [15, 16]. While benefits of training in immersive environments alone are not always clear, integrating these environments with an ITS could help improve learning outcomes.

3.1 Challenges of Creating Immersive Tutoring in an ITS

Even though ITS have benefits, there are still challenges to instructors who want to use them, specifically in applied domains that have virtual environment training associated with them. In general, ITS often take a great deal of time to author, as their multiple paths result in the need for more content, and carefully selected rules to send students down those specific remediation paths based on performance. [17]. Additionally, due to the time it takes to create the materials and structure of an ITS they tend to be tightly linked to the subject matter or domain that they were designed for, as opposed to flexible and reusable. Finally, creating an ITS can be very expensive due to the amount of time that it takes to author it, as well as the expertise that is often needed: subject matter expert, instructional designer, computer programmer, etc. [17].

While some tutors engage with students through simple questions/answers, and more traditional assessments, it is also possible to create tutoring/feedback that is incorporated into interactive and immersive computer-based environments. In many cases to create ITS instruction, a course instructor will need to know the subject that they want to teach, have an established videogame or virtual environment, and will need to be adept at computer programming in order to successfully design the tutor. If the instructor does not have the computer programming expertise to integrate their environment, then they will need a computer programmer to do the initial integration, which could be costly. Therefore, creating an adaptive tutor with immersive content could be cost prohibitive, and difficult.

3.2 The Generalized Intelligent Framework for Tutoring (GIFT)

Many of the challenges of creating adaptive tutoring can be lessened by using a domain-independent framework that is designed for reusability. The Generalized Intelligent Framework for Tutoring (GIFT) is a free, open-source, domain independent framework for creating ITS that has been developed in order to increase the usability of ITS components, reduce the expertise level needed to author an ITS, and reduce the time it takes to create an ITS [17]. GIFT can be used by instructors and subject matter experts (SMEs) to author adaptive tutoring. At the current time, GIFT is available in two forms: downloadable (from https://www.gifttutoring.org) and cloud based (GIFT Virtual Open Campus, https://cloud.gifttutoring.org). Adaptive tutoring can be created with both versions, and student data can be extracted by instructors in order to monitor a student's learning and progress.

One of the larger challenges of creating immersive training in an adaptive tutoring system is the need to integrate the training application/environment with the tutor. GIFT includes a number of modules that traditionally exist in ITS: learner module, pedagogical module, domain module, sensor module, and a gateway module [18]. The gateway module serves as the bridge between GIFT and external training applications. Messages can be sent between the external game and GIFT through this gateway module. This allows for a consistent method of integration of different environments with the GIFT system. While integrating a virtual environment or training application with GIFT may initially appear challenging, GIFT includes a Developers Guide (in the GIFT help files/documentation) to assist in the process. While it is unlikely that an instructor themselves will be conducting the initial integration, the guide will help streamline the process for the individual that does, reducing the amount of time required.

Once the integration has occurred, the course instructor will have the opportunity to author adaptive feedback that links directly to the actions that occur within the immersive environment/game. This feedback is authored by creating a Domain Knowledge File (DKF) using the GIFT Authoring Tool. See Fig. 1 for an example of a DKF in the GIFT Authoring Tool. There are three levels or states of performance that a learner can have: above expectation, at expectation, and below expectation. When selected actions or inactions occur in the environment, it can trigger a move from one of these states to the next, which then subsequently triggers authored feedback. The DKF interfaces with the training environment, and feedback can be provided through the game itself or through a feedback bar on the left side of the screen that is graphically separate from the environment.

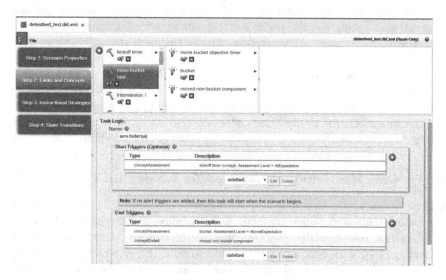

Fig. 1. Screenshot of DKF authoring in the GIFT Authoring Tool

GIFT will track the learner's state and follow the authored instructions to provide specific adjustments and feedback based on actions in the environment. Additionally, GIFT is integrated with PowerPoint, which can be used by instructors to enhance their courses with lesson materials or create interactive material using Visual Basic for Applications.

All of the components of the desired course are put together using the GIFT Authoring Tool. DKFs can be accessed, created and edited with this tool. Additionally the flow of the course is determined by the author by adding different elements including instructions, surveys, training applications, and after action reviews. See Fig. 2 for a screenshot of course authoring in the GIFT Authoring Tool.

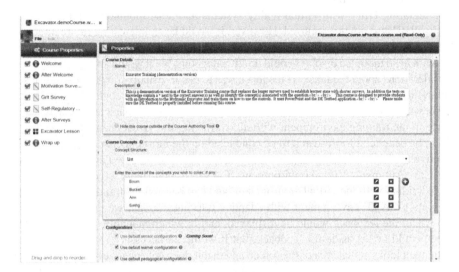

Fig. 2. Screenshot of course authoring in GIFT. Components of the course and their order are listed on the left side of the screen.

There are two highly immersive games/environments that are currently integrated with GIFT: the military based training game, Virtual Battlespace (VBS2 and VBS3) and the medical game, TC3Sim (VMedic). VMedic can be downloaded for free from GIFT-tutoring.org, and is used to run the *Explicit Feedback within Game-Based Training-1* and *Explicit Feedback within Game-Based Training-4* courses in the desktop version of GIFT. These courses demonstrate an integration between an immersive game and GIFT. The development of these courses and the associated experiment has been documented in the literature [19, 20]. Additionally, an interactive excavator training course which uses an XBOX controller can be accessed in both the cloud and desktop versions of GIFT. The authored components of these courses (Course Files, DKFs, etc.) are also of interest to individuals who wish to use GIFT as they provide working examples of the technical files associated with GIFT, which can then be used as a basis for future course and experiment development. Further, instructors may be able to use these integrated virtual environments to create new GIFT courses without needing to engage in integrating an entirely new training environment with GIFT.

3.3 Considerations and Future Directions for Immersive Learning in GIFT

At current time, the immersive virtual environments that GIFT has primarily been integrated with have been computer-based games that are intended to be interacted with on a stationary computer. However, GIFT has been integrated with the psychomotor domain of adaptive marksmanship training, which provides feedback based on actions that individuals physically take as opposed to keyboard input [21, 22]. Initial work and idea generation has also begun toward moving GIFT to the "wild", such that learners can receive feedback through mobile devices, smart glasses, and smart watches instead of at a stationary computer [12, 23].

Integrating GIFT with virtual reality systems and head mounted displays such as Oculus RIFT has not yet occurred. However, it would be an interesting future direction that would be beneficial to examining immersive training. Providing tutoring in conjunction with head mounted displays could be advantageous, but it would also lead to specific considerations about feedback. If feedback was to occur visually it would require space within the display, and may distract from the training. Feedback could be provided by audio, which could assist in feelings of immersion or presence that a learner may experience in the training environment without overtaxing the visual channel. However, it would be beneficial for research to be conducted on the most effective ways to provide adaptive feedback when training is occurring using a head mounted display. Additionally, Cave Automatic Virtual Environments (CAVE) provide large screens that surround the individual with the virtual environment, and can be used for training. Similarly, to integrate a CAVE environment with adaptive tutoring, thought would need to be put into where the feedback would be displayed, and in which modality. A portion of the screen could be set aside for feedback, but it would be necessary to confirm that the participant looks at that area of the screen and that it does not negatively impact feelings of immersion. As the area that visual feedback is displayed on would be very different in both of these instances (head mounted display and CAVE) it may be helpful to have a tool that would allow authors to select where their visual feedback will be located and superimpose it upon the image screen size that they expect their learners to view. Templates for standard size screens could be provided. This would help for course planning purposes, and also can help course authors to see any initial problems that may come up with their configuration.

It would be helpful for authors to have very clear options and precise control over the modality that feedback is presented in. Some authors may want a character present with text, others may want a character present that speaks with no text, and others may just want text without a character taking up screen space. Providing clear flexibility and options within the authoring process will be beneficial to facilitating the feedback presentation. Additionally, it would be helpful for the course author to have a scenario preview before finalizing their course, such that they can see how their authored feedback is presented in the virtual environment without needing to validate their entire course.

As more research is needed into the impacts of presence and immersion on learning, GIFT could also be used to conduct studies. GIFT offers flexibility in the presentation of materials and has assessment capabilities that would be useful to conducting this type of research. Measures of presence and immersion can be given to learners who engage with GIFT through use of it's Survey Authoring System (SAS). One or more questionnaires such as Witmer and Singer's Presence Inventory [2] or the ITC-Sense of Presence Inventory [4] could be entered into the GIFT's SAS and presented to the learner. Further, scores on the scale could be stored for the individual, and if desired, adaptation to the course could occur based on answers that are provided by the learner. These surveys could be automatically presented to the user before or after entering the training environment or completing gameplay.

4 Conclusions

Game based learning and immersive training environments can provide highly engaging educational environments for learners. However, often times there could be a benefit from integrating the learning environment with intelligent tutoring such that learners can get real time adaptive feedback. GIFT provides an opportunity to integrate a virtual environment with training, while aiming to reduce the time and effort that it would traditionally take to do so. GIFT could be used to conduct immersion and presence research, or it can be used by instructors who wish to provide an adaptive tutoring component to their game based training. GIFT has begun branching out into different tasks and modes of input/feedback that would be advantageous to use with virtual environments. Those who choose to integrate ITS and immersive training, need to give consideration to a number of features of their training including display and input methods, learner characteristics, and how/where feedback will be provided. Due to GIFT's flexibility, it can be a used for future research to further examine the influence of presence and immersion on ITS learning outcomes in varying domains.

References

1. McMahan, A.: Immersion, engagement and presence. Video Game Theory Reader **67**, 67–86 (2003)
2. Witmer, B.G., Singer, M.J.: Measuring presence in virtual environments: a presence questionnaire. Presence: Teleoper. Virtual Environ. **7**(3), 225–240 (1998)
3. Greenwald, W.: Kinect vs. PlayStation Move vs. Wii: Motion-Control Showdown. PC Magazine, 6 November 2010. http://www.pcmag.com/article2/0,2817,2372244,00.asp
4. Lessiter, J., Freeman, J., Keogh, E., Davidoff, J.: Across-media presence questionnaire: the ITC-sense of presence inventory. Presence **10**(3), 282–297 (2001)
5. Andre, A.D., Wickens, C.D.: When users want what's not best for them. Ergon. Des. Q. Hum. Fact. Appl. **3**(4), 10–14 (1995)
6. Dede, C.: Immersive interfaces for engagement and learning. Science **323**(5910), 66–69 (2009)
7. Alexander, A.L., Brunye, T., Sidman, J., Weil, S.A.: From gaming to training: a review of studies on fidelity, immersion, presence, and buy-in and their effects on transfer in PC-based simulations and games. DARWARS Training Impact Group **5**, 1–14 (2005)
8. Mantovani, F.: 12 VR learning: potential and challenges for the use of 3D environments in education and training. Towards Cyberpsychol.: Mind Cogn. Soc. Internet Age **2**, 207–225 (2001)

9. Kickmeier-Rust, M.D., Albert, D.: Micro-adaptivity: protecting immersion in didactically adaptive digital educational games. J. Comput. Assist. Learn. **26**(2), 95–105 (2010)
10. Kickmeier-Rust, M.D., Hockemeyer, C., Albert, D., Augustin, T.: Micro adaptive, non-invasive knowledge assessment in educational games. In: 2nd IEEE International Conference on Digital Games and Intelligent Toys Based Education, pp. 135–137. IEEE (2008)
11. Moreno, R., Mayer, R.E.: Learning science in virtual reality multimedia environments: role of methods and media. J. Educ. Psychol. **94**(3), 598–610 (2002)
12. Sottilare, R.A., LaViola, J.: Extending intelligent tutoring beyond the desktop to the psychomotor domain. In: Proceedings of Interservice/Industry Training, Simulation, and Education Conference (I/ITSEC) (2015)
13. Harp, S.F., Mayer, R.E.: How seductive details do their damage: a theory of cognitive interest in science learning. J. Educ. Psychol. **90**(3), 414–434 (1998)
14. Mayer, R.E., Heiser, J., Lonn, S.: Cognitive constraints on multimedia learning: when presenting more material results in less understanding. J. Educ. Psychol. **93**(1), 187–198 (2001)
15. Anderson, J.R., Corbett, A.T., Koedinger, K.R., Pelletier, R.: Cognitive tutors: lessons learned. J. Learn. Sci. **4**, 167–207 (1995)
16. VanLehn, K., Lynch, C., Schulze, K., Shapiro, J.A., Shelby, R., Taylor, L., et al.: The Andes physics tutoring system: lessons learned. Int. J. Artif. Intell. Educ. **15**(3), 147–204 (2005)
17. Sottilare, R.A., Brawner, K.W., Goldberg, B.S., Holden, H.K.: The Generalized Intelligent Framework for Tutoring (GIFT) (2012). https://gifttutoring.org/documents/31
18. Sottilare, R.A., Graesser, A.C., Hu, X., Holden, H.: Preface. In: Design Recommendations for Intelligent Tutoring Systems: Volume 1, Learner Modeling, pp. ii–xiii (2013)
19. Goldberg, B., Cannon-Bowers, J.: Experimentation with the generalized intelligent framework for tutoring (GIFT): a testbed use case. In: AIED 2013 Workshops Proceedings, volume 7, pp. 27–36 (2013)
20. Goldberg, B., Cannon-Bowers, J.: Feedback source modality effects on training outcomes in a serious game: pedagogical agents make a difference. Comput. Hum. Behav. **52**, 1–11 (2015)
21. Goldberg, B., Amburn, C., Brawner, K., Westphal, M.: Developing models of expert performance for support in an adaptive marksmanship trainer. In: Proceedings of the Interservice/Industry Training, Simulation, and Education Conference (I/ITSEC) (2014)
22. Goldberg, B., Amburn, C.: The application of GIFT in a psychomotor domain of instruction: a marksmanship use case. In: Generalized Intelligent Framework for Tutoring (GIFT) Users Symposium (GIFTSym3), pp. 115–124 (2015)
23. Sottilare, R.A.: Augmented cognition on the run: considerations for the design and authoring of mobile tutoring systems. In: Schmorrow, D.D., Fidopiastis, C.M. (eds.) AC 2015. LNCS, vol. 9183, pp. 683–689. Springer, Heidelberg (2015)

Elements of Adaptive Instruction for Training and Education

Robert A. Sottilare and Michael W. Boyce[✉]

U.S. Army Research Laboratory, Orlando, FL, USA
{Robert.A.Sottilare.civ,Michael.W.Boyce.ctr}@mail.mil

Abstract. This paper discusses critical elements of adaptive instruction in support of training and education. Modeling and assessing learners and teams, optimizing adaptive instructional methods, applying domain modeling outside of traditional training and educational domains, automating authoring processes, and assessing the learning effect of instruction are among the challenges reviewed.

Keywords: Adaptive instruction · Intelligent tutoring systems · Learner modeling · Domain modeling · Authoring tools · Learning effect

1 Introduction

The goal of adaptive instruction is to tailor learning experiences to the capabilities and needs of each individual learner or team. Adaptive instructional systems, also known as intelligent tutoring systems (ITSs) alter their decisions, behaviors, and actions based on their recognition of changing states/traits of the learner or changing conditions in the environment [1]. These changes are usually managed by software-based agents who use machine learning techniques (i.e. Markov Decision Processes (MDPs), k-Nearest Neighbor, Support Vector Machines) to optimize their responses (decisions and actions) [2, 3]. Adaptive instruction usually results in increased authoring requirements, some of which may not be completely defined at the outset, to support tailored learning experiences for the wide variety of learner states and traits. The following research goals are on the critical path of making adaptive instruction practical and affordable:

- Understand and model the states and traits of individual learners and teams
- Tailor adaptive instructional methods to optimize learning, performance, retention of knowledge and skill, and transfer of learning to other domains
- Understand and model domains beyond those traditional well-defined intelligent tutoring system (ITS) domains (e.g., mathematics and physics)
- Develop replicable processes to assess the appropriateness of models beyond leveraging subject matter experts
- Investigate and develop methods to automate authoring processes and thereby reduce the time and skill needed to develop ITSs
- Investigate and develop methods to assess learning effect and thereby provide a mechanism with which to continuously improve adaptive instruction

© Springer International Publishing Switzerland 2016
D.D. Schmorrow and C.M. Fidopiastis (Eds.): AC 2016, Part II, LNAI 9744, pp. 85–89, 2016.
DOI: 10.1007/978-3-319-39952-2_9

2   Modeling Individual Learners and Teams

The more the tutor understands about the learning habits, capabilities, and needs of the learner, the more efficient and effective that tutor will be in guiding learning experiences. Lepper et al. [4] identified the characteristics of an expert human tutor in their INSPIRE (intelligent, nurturant, Socratic, progressive, indirect, reflective and encouraging) model. The characteristics in this model were further explored in Lepper and Woolverton's [5] study of highly effective tutors with the goal of developing best tutoring practices. Expert tutors are such that they have subject matter knowledge and understanding the appropriate teaching strategies for the types of problems at hand. Capturing the traits and interpreting the states of the learner is a key to modeling the learner's habits, capabilities and needs, and thereby critical to selecting the most effective learning strategies. Lepper and Woolverton found that highly skilled tutors manage two primary processes related to learning: engagement and motivation.

While there are several challenges in modeling individual learners and teams to support the goal of adaptive instruction, four areas of research are noteworthy: techniques to model individuals and teams (i.e. how to identify differences affecting learning and performance); use of big data to support domain competency modeling of the learner; providing training at the point-of-need (i.e. tutoring anyplace and any time also known as "in the wild"); and the use of artificial intelligence (AI) techniques to support learner state classification (i.e. Bayesian Classifiers, Markov Decision Processes) [6].

Each of these four areas of research prompts associated questions. What learner states and traits are needed for our learner model? What measurements are needed to assess domain competency? What methods are available to capture data when the training is provided at the point-of-need? What methods can be used to classify learner states based on captured data (Fig. 1)?

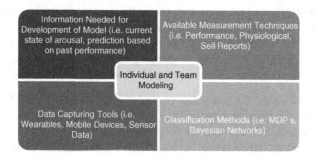

Fig. 1. Open questions related to individual and team modeling

3   Tailoring Adaptive Instructional Methods

The goal of adaptive instruction is to tailor training and educational experiences to match the learning capabilities and needs of each individual, and thereby reduce the amount of instruction required to reach a minimum level of competence in a given domain [7].

By evaluating the states and traits of the learner in real-time, ITSs can select an optimal strategy or plan for action (e.g., prompt the user for additional information) and thereby select an optimal tactic or tutor action (e.g., ask a specific question based on where the user is in the instruction). In the Generalized Intelligent Framework for Tutoring (GIFT), an open-source architecture for authoring, delivering, and evaluating ITSs [8], instructional decisions are driven by two processes: Merrill's component display theory [9], and the learning effect model (LEM) [10].

There are several challenges associated with tailoring adaptive instruction, but five areas of research are noteworthy: determining the type and frequency of guidance and feedback provided by the tutor; understanding the effect of social dynamics in instruction; understanding the effect of metacognitive processes on self-regulated learning; optimizing the selection of instructional tactics; and the effect of personalization (occupational and non-cognitive factors) on learning, retention, and motivation [11].

4   Modeling Non-traditional Domains

Today, ITSs primarily represent well-defined, process-oriented domains which include mathematics and physics. The primary goal for domain modeling is to be able represent the diversity of domains in training and education. This means expanding assessment methods to allow measurement of key moderators of learning for a variety of tasks and conditions, and well beyond common desktop training and education applications.

Again, there are several areas which provide challenges, but we have selected four that align with our primary goal: representing and understanding the influence of domain attributes; reducing the time, cost, and skill required to author and deliver complex instruction; improving the interoperability of domain models; and extending adaptive instruction to include fuzzy domains [12].

5   Automating Authoring Processes

Authoring or development costs are the most significant element in determining the affordability of adaptive instruction. The return on investment is clearer for high density courses where there are many students, but much less so for courses with lower density. Processes are needed to make authoring affordable regardless of density [13]. Beyond affordability, improved authoring experiences can make adaptive instruction more enticing and engaging to the community, and thereby increase use and buy-in of ITSs.

Another major goal is to reduce the time and skill needed to author adaptive instruction so tailored instructional solutions can be available to the masses at an affordable cost, and so people with domain knowledge (but lacking programming skills and instruction design knowledge) can author them. Identifying candidate authoring tasks for automation can reduce the time users spend manually generating tutors and reduce the skill required to author ITSs.

There are five major challenges in automating authoring processes are: describing mental models and defining interaction paradigms for authoring (i.e., different mental models exist for different user groups, which alter how the system is used); identifying candidate processes for automated authoring (i.e., taking those well defined tasks and automating them to reduce workload); extending authoring capabilities to support integration with existing training and educational systems; and enabling collaborative authoring to match skills with authoring tasks [13]. If these challenges are met, then authoring has the opportunity to be less focused around the system itself, and more concentrated on the user and paths to getting the authoring task completed.

6   Assessing Learning Effect

The major challenges in assessing effect during adaptive instructional events include the development of accurate assessment methods for measuring: learning, performance, retention potential, and transfer potential; the wide spectrum of task domains (e.g., cognitive, affective, physical, social); the varying spectrum of kinetic tasks (i.e., from static to limited kinetic to full kinetic) [7].

7   Next Steps

Each version of GIFT has been focused on improving the interoperability of ITS components, capturing best instructional practices, and developing tools and methods to reduce the time and skill needed to author adaptive instruction. Future versions of GIFT are targeted to capture the results of training and educational research with the goal of bringing the state-of-the-art concepts to the state-of-practice. Of particular emphasis is the understanding and development of shared mental models to support adaptive instruction for teams [14, 15].

Acknowledgments. This research was sponsored by the U.S. Army Research Laboratory. The views and conclusions contained in this document are those of the authors and should not be interpreted as representing the official policies, either expressed or implied, of the Army Research Laboratory or the U.S. Government. The U.S. Government is authorized to reproduce and distribute reprints for Government purposes notwithstanding and copyright notation herein.

References

1. Oppermann, R.: Adaptive User Support. Lawrence Erlbaum, Hillsdale (1994)
2. Sottilare, R.: Making a case for machine perception of trainee affect to aid learning and performance in embedded virtual simulations. In: NATO Research Workshop (HFM-RWS-169) on Human Dimensions in Embedded Virtual Simulations, Orlando, Florida, October 2009
3. Sottilare, R., Roessingh, J.: Exploring the application of intelligent agents in embedded virtual simulations (EVS). In: Final Report of the NATO Human Factors and Medicine Panel – Research Task Group (HFM-RTG-165) on Human Effectiveness in Embedded Virtual Simulation. NATO Research and Technology Office (2012)

4. Lepper, M.R., Drake, M., O'Donnell-Johnson, T.M.: Scaffolding techniques of expert human tutors. In: Hogan, K., Pressley, M. (eds.) Scaffolding Student Learning: Instructional Approaches and Issues, pp. 108–144. Brookline Books, New York (1997)
5. Lepper, M., Woolverton, M.: The wisdom of practice: lessons learned from the study of highly effective tutors. In: Aronson, J. (ed.) Improving Academic Achievement: Impact of Psychological Factors on Education, pp. 135–158. Academic Press, New York (2002)
6. Goodwin, G., Johnston, J., Sottilare, R., Brawner, K., Sinatra, A., Graesser, A.: Individual Learner and Team Modeling for Adaptive Training and Education in Support of the US Army Learning Model: Research Outline. Army Research Laboratory (ARL-SR-0336), September 2015
7. Sottilare, R., Sinatra, A., Boyce, M., Graesser, A.: Domain Modeling for Adaptive Training and Education in Support of the US Army Learning Model: Research Outline. Army Research Laboratory (ARL-SR-0325), June 2015
8. Sottilare, R.A., Brawner, K.W., Goldberg, B.S., Holden, H.K.: The Generalized Intelligent Framework for Tutoring (GIFT). U.S. Army Research Laboratory – Human Research and Engineering Directorate (ARL-HRED), Orlando (2012)
9. Merrill, M.D.: The Descriptive Component Display Theory. Educational Technology Publications, Englewood Cliffs (1994)
10. Sottilare, R., Ragusa, C., Hoffman, M., Goldberg, B.: Characterizing an adaptive tutoring learning effect chain for individual and team tutoring. In: Proceedings of the Interservice/Industry Training Simulation and Education Conference, Orlando, Florida, December 2013
11. Goldberg, B., Sinatra, A., Sottilare, R., Moss, J., Graesser, A.: Instructional Management for Adaptive Training and Education in Support of the US Army Learning Model: Research Outline. Army Research Laboratory (ARL-SR-0345), November 2015
12. Fletcher, J., Sottilare, R.: Cost analysis for training and educational systems. In: Sottilare, R., Graesser, A., Hu, X., Goldberg, B. (eds.) Design Recommendations for Intelligent Tutoring Systems: Volume 2 - Instructional Management. Army Research Laboratory, Orlando (2014). ISBN 978-0-9893923-2-7
13. Ososky, S., Sottilare, R., Brawner, K., Long, R., Graesser, A.: Authoring Tools and Methods for Adaptive Training and Education in Support of the US Army Learning Model: Research Outline. Army Research Laboratory (ARL-SR-0339), October 2015
14. Johnston, J., Goodwin, G., Moss, J., Sottilare, R., Ososky, S., Cruz, D., Graesser, A.: Effectiveness Evaluation Tools and Methods for Adaptive Training and Education in Support of the US Army Learning Model—Research Outline. Army Research Laboratory (ARL-SR-0333), September 2015
15. Fletcher, J.D., Sottilare, R.: Shared mental models of cognition for intelligent tutoring of teams. In: Sottilare, R., Graesser, A., Hu, X., Holden, H. (eds.) Design Recommendations for Intelligent Tutoring Systems: Volume 1- Learner Modeling. Army Research Laboratory, Orlando (2013). ISBN 978-0-9893923-0-3

Adaptive Instruction for Individual Learners Within the Generalized Intelligent Framework for Tutoring (GIFT)

Robert A. Sottilare[✉]

U.S. Army Research Laboratory, Orlando, FL, USA
Robert.A.Sottilare.civ@mail.mil

Abstract. This paper discusses tools and methods which are needed to support adaptive instruction for individual learners within the Generalized Intelligent Framework for Tutoring (GIFT), an open source architecture for authoring, adapting instruction, and evaluating intelligent tutoring systems. Specifically, this paper reviews the learning effect model (LEM) which drives adaptive instruction within GIFT-based tutors. The original LEM was developed in 2012 and has been enhanced over time to represent a full range of function encompassing both the learner's and the tutor's interactions and decisions. This paper proposes a set of 10 functions to enhance the scope and functionality of the LEM and to extend it to be a career-long model of adaptive instruction and competency.

Keywords: Adaptive instruction · Intelligent tutoring systems · Learning effect model

1 Introduction

Adaptive instruction is a critical concept in the partnership between self-regulated learners and computer-based intelligent tutoring systems (ITSs). Adaptive systems demonstrate intelligence by altering their behaviors and actions based on their recognition of changing conditions in either the user or the environment [1]. This change is usually managed by software-based agents who use artificial intelligence techniques to guide their decisions and actions [2, 3].

The ability of ITSs to enhance self-regulated learning (SRL) habits is an ongoing challenge in the ITS development community. Self-regulated learners develop skills to allow them to persist in pursuit of learning goals in the face of adversity. Question asking, hypothesis testing skills, and reflection are examples of good SRL attributes. To foster the development of these SRL attributes, the adaptive ITS must allow interaction with the learner to influence ITS courses of action. This is the basis of the learning effect model (LEM) [4] used to drive adaptive instruction in GIFT [5] today.

The original LEM [6] examined the relationship between the learner's data (measures of behavior, physiology, and the learner's input and interaction), the learner's states (informed by the learner's data) and the strategies/tactics (plans and actions) available to and selected by the ITS, but other processes are also important to

© Springer International Publishing Switzerland 2016
D.D. Schmorrow and C.M. Fidopiastis (Eds.): AC 2016, Part II, LNAI 9744, pp. 90–96, 2016.
DOI: 10.1007/978-3-319-39952-2_10

extending the LEM to be a long term model of instruction. In other words, it is desirable for the model of instruction to extend beyond a single lesson and to be a career-long model of instruction and competency. If we were to develop a user interface (UI) to support interaction between the learner and the tutor, this UI might include some of the functions shown in Fig. 1 below. These functions are shown without respect to their order or the relationship between these functions and represent brainstorming of representative functions for our UI.

Fig. 1. Functions in an adaptive user interface

Learning objectives define the learning and performance end-state after training/education. Concepts, the basis of GIFT's instructional model, break down learning objectives into measurable elements. Learning events define the tasks or experiences needed to expose the learner to all the concepts identified in our learning objectives. Other critical elements of this UI are the conditions under which the tasks will be conducted during training and how they will be measured. Finally, the UI must determine how the tutor will respond to learner actions and changes in the instructional environment to optimize learning and performance.

So, what is missing from this model? As noted earlier, the functions in Fig. 1 are shown without respect to their sequencing, inputs or outputs. To develop a more comprehensive UI and to understand the effect of these functions on learning and performance, we must understand the ontology or relationship of these functions [6].

2 Functions of a Learning Effect Model

The latest version of the LEM is shown in Fig. 2. Note that both learning and performance are essential measures in the LEM, but learning is the key measure to determining acquisition of knowledge and skill, and transfer of skills to new experiences. Performance is a behavioral indicator of the learner's ability to apply skills to new experiences and tasks of increasing complexity over time.

Each of the ten functions shown in the figure and are discussed below in terms of their functional description, relationships to other functions (e.g., inputs and outputs), and their impact or effect on learning and performance.

2.1 Function 1: Identifying Required Knowledge and Skills

Whether the learner is interacting with a human tutor or an ITS, a key first step is to identify what knowledge and skills the learner should acquire over time. The complexity of skills and the time needed to reach a level of competency in a particular domain should

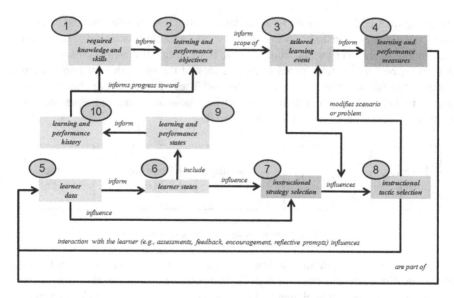

Fig. 2. 10 functions in an adaptive instructional platform for individual learners

be considered. Domain knowledge and skills along with minimum standards are usually determined at the organizational level to support organizational competencies and goals. Input to this function includes the learning and performance history of the learner (see Function 10) which is compared to the required knowledge and skills to identify the output of this function: learning gaps.

2.2 Function 2: Developing and Maintaining Learning and Performance Objectives

Learning gaps from Function 1, identifying required knowledge and skills, are used to determine learning and performance objectives for future learning events which are tailored for each individual learner. Learning and performance objectives act as a roadmap. Once we have identified where we want to go on the map, we can begin figuring out how to get to our destinations by using objectives to inform the scope and complexity of a series of tailored learning events.

2.3 Function 3: Crafting a Tailored Learning Event

Learning and performance objectives developed in Function 2 are used to identify a set of experiences (problems or scenarios) which can impart knowledge and develop/exercise skills. The tailored learning event represents what was called "context" in previous versions of the LEM, and influences the selection of specific actions or tactics by the tutor as discussed in Function 8. The tailored learning event also aids in identifying learning and performance measures.

2.4 Function 4: Identifying Learning and Performance Measures

Based on the tailored learning event, we must identify learning and performance measures which are used to compare the knowledge acquisition, skill acquisition, and performance during the tailored learning events to an expert model (highest standard) or standards of minimum performance. Measures are part of a larger dataset which we identify as learner data.

2.5 Function 5: Capturing Learner Data

The learning and performance measures are usually captured via sensors which monitor learner behaviors or via learner responses to assessments, but learner data includes more than just learning and performance data. Learner data may also include behavioral and physiological data captured by sensors, but unrelated to learning or performance measures. Learner data may also include achievement data or other trait data (e.g., preferences, interests, or values) which may be used to inform the learner's states and the selection of an instruction strategy.

2.6 Function 6: Classifying Learner States

As noted above, learner data is used to classify learner states. Methods for classifying learner states vary and the types of learner states include cognitive, affective, and physical states which may moderate learning and performance. Cognitive states include, but are not limited to learning and performance states, engagement, and comprehension. Affective states include personality, mood, motivation, and emotions. Physical states include speed, accuracy, and stamina. As with learner data, learner states are also used to influence instructional strategy selection.

2.7 Function 7: Optimizing Instructional Strategies

In the LEM, instructional strategies are plans for action by the tutor based only on the states and traits of the learner. In other words, the selection of an instructional strategy is independent of the instructional context, domain or learning event. It's all about the learner. Examples of an instructional strategy include prompting the learner for more information, asking the learner to reflect on a recent learning event, asking the learner a question, providing feedback to the learner, or changing the challenge level or complexity of a problem or scenario to match the learner's changing capabilities. The instructional strategy narrows the options for selection and implementation of specific instructional tactics.

2.8 Function 8: Optimizing Instructional Tactics

Now that the selection of instructional strategy has been determined by the tutor, the selection of an appropriate action or instructional tactic can begin. General options for instructional tactics fall into two categories: interaction with the learner or interaction with the learning environment. Examples of these align with the examples provided in Function 7 (optimizing instructional strategies) and simplified interactions between the learner, the learning environment, and the tutor are illustrated in Fig. 3.

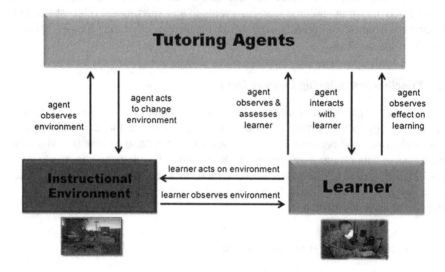

Fig. 3. Interaction between the tutor, the learner and the instructional environment

If the instructional strategy selection was to "ask the learner to reflect on recent learning event", GIFT considers "context" in selecting an appropriate tactic. Context includes consideration for where they are in the learning event described in Function 3. More deeply, it also includes consideration for what quadrant (rule, example, recall, practice) of Merrill's Component Display Theory [7] is under instruction. Function 9: Measuring Learning and Performance States.

It should also be noted that the implementation of an instructional tactic may also influence the learner (see Function 5) and affect their cognitive, affective, or physical measures and thereby their associated states. For example, a tactic involving an increase to the challenge level of a scenario might surprise the learner and increase their mental workload resulting in physiological changes.

2.9 Function 9: Tracking Learning and Performance States in Real-Time

An important subset of classifying learner states (Function 6) is the process of tracking changes to learning (knowledge and skill acquisition) and the performance of tasks which are indicators of learning. As with other transient learner states (e.g., affect), learning and performance are informed by learner data (Function 5) which include learning and performance measures identified as part of Function 4. In GIFT, achievement or mastery of concepts are recorded in a long-term learner model via experience application program interface (xAPI) statements of achievement [8]. Achievements can be defined at various levels of granularity (e.g., course completion, concept mastery, or assignment completion). Over time, changes to learning and performance states indicate trends which form the basis for a long-term learn model of learning and performance discussed in Function 10.

2.10   Function 10: Logging Learning and Performance History

In Function 9, we periodically assess the progress of the learner toward learning and performance objectives and at a more granular level their progress in mastering specific concepts and performing specific tasks under a set of conditions to a specific standard (e.g., passing = 70 % correct). If we track learning and performance over time, we see trends including progress of the learner compared to standards, norms, or other learners. We may also be able to classify the domain competency of the learner relative to an upcoming training or educational experience. This can be used to identify tailored learning and performance objectives (Function 2) for an individual learner relative to the required knowledge and skills (Function 1) for a given training or educational domain.

3   Next Steps

To date, both instructional strategies and tactics within GIFT are based on decision trees and have largely been developed based on best instructional practices identified in the literature. To a large degree many of the best practices implemented are domain-independent and the literature does not cover all of the conditions which might be encountered by the learner during an adaptive instructional event.

Experimentation is needed to identify domain-specific tactics and domain-independent strategies which deal with uncertainty related to classification of learner states in order to optimize learning and performance in real-time during instructional events. Ideally, some type of machine learning algorithm which provides reinforced learning over time will allow GIFT to tailor and optimize learning with each individual learner it encounters. Software-based agents are needed to monitor the status of the 10 LEM functions described in this paper and to develop appropriate policies to govern tutor actions with the goal of optimizing learning and performance.

Finally, an enhanced LEM must be developed to support team tutoring or adaptive instruction for collaborative learning, team development, and cooperative, interdependent tasks.

Acknowledgments. This research was sponsored by the U.S. Army Research Laboratory. The views and conclusions contained in this document are those of the authors and should not be interpreted as representing the official policies, either expressed or implied, of the Army Research Laboratory or the U.S. Government. The U.S. Government is authorized to reproduce and distribute reprints for Government purposes notwithstanding and copyright notation herein.

References

1. Oppermann, R.: Adaptive User Support. Lawrence Erlbaum, Hillsdale (1994)
2. Sottilare, R.: Making a case for machine perception of trainee affect to aid learning and performance in embedded virtual simulations. In: NATO Research Workshop (HFM-RWS-169) on Human Dimensions in Embedded Virtual Simulations, Orlando, Florida, October 2009
3. Sottilare, R., Roessingh, J.: Exploring the application of intelligent agents in embedded virtual simulations (EVS). In: Final Report of the NATO Human Factors and Medicine Panel – Research Task Group (HFM-RTG-165) on Human Effectiveness in Embedded Virtual Simulation. NATO Research and Technology Office (2012)
4. Sottilare, R.: Fundamentals of adaptive intelligent tutoring systems for self-regulated learning. In: Proceedings of the Interservice/Industry Training Simulation and Education Conference, Orlando, Florida, December 2014
5. Sottilare, R.A., Brawner, K.W., Goldberg, B.S., Holden, H.K.: The Generalized Intelligent Framework for Tutoring (GIFT). U.S. Army Research Laboratory – Human Research and Engineering Directorate (ARL-HRED), Orlando (2012)
6. Sottilare, R.: Considerations in the development of an ontology for a generalized intelligent framework for tutoring. In: Proceedings of the I3M Conference International Defense and Homeland Security Simulation Workshop, Vienna, Austria, September 2012
7. Merrill, M.D.: The Descriptive Component Display Theory. Educational Technology Publications, Englewood Cliffs (1994)
8. Advanced Distributed Learning Initiative. "xAPI Architecture Overview" (2012). http://adlnet.gov/adl-research/performance-tracking-analysis/experience-api/xapi-architecture-overview/. Accessed 11 Dec 2015

Applying Augmented Cognition to Flip-Flop Methodology

Jan Stelovsky[1]([✉]), Randall K. Minas[2], Umida Stelovska[3], and John Wu[3]

[1] Department of Information and Computer Sciences, University of Hawaii at Manoa,
2550 Campus Road, Honolulu, HI 96822, USA
janst@hawaii.edu

[2] Shidler College of Business, University of Hawaii at Manoa, 2404 Maile Way,
Honolulu, HI 96822, USA
rminas@hawaii.edu

[3] parWinr, Inc., 415 Oakmead Parkway, Sunnyvale, CA 94085, USA
{umida,johnwu}@parwinr.com

Abstract. The Flip-Flop instructional methodology involves students in creating quizzes synchronized with video recordings of lectures. While students create questions, which involves generating right and wrong answers, feedback for the answers, hints and links leading to relevant resources, they get deeply involved with the content presented in the lecture screencasts. We propose to conduct a wide range of experiments testing the effectiveness of this approach – from simple surveys, evaluations of time spent creating quizzes and assessment of their quality to extensive longitudinal studies of the students' emotional responses and cognitive load using a electroencephalography (EEG), electrodermal activity (EDA), heart rate variability (HRV) and facial electromyography (EMG).

Keywords: Instructional methods · Inverted classroom · Educational technology · Augmented cognition · Cognitive neuroscience · Psychophysiological methods

1 Introduction

The Flip-Flop instructional methodology is designed to augment the currently increasingly popular teaching concepts that rely on students learning from video recordings of lectures posted online. Inverted or flipped classroom and learning based on MOOCs (Massive Open Online Classes) are prime examples of such educational strategies. Our Flip-Flop method requires the students to construct quizzes that are synchronized with the screencast of the lecture. In essence, Flip-Flop offers a structured approach to the "Learning by Teaching" concept and supports it with several online tools that facilitate creating quizzes, taking quizzes, administrative chores such as scheduling and creating quiz templates. Moreover, our Flip-Flop tools support instructors in evaluation of the quizzes and provide them with a plethora of data that can be used for grading and to ascertain the effectiveness of a students' learning. In addition, peer evaluation is also an integral component of the Flip-Flop method.

Since Flip-Flop quizzes are tightly interconnected with the lecture videos, students do not just listen to a lecture, but are virtually guaranteed to interact with its content - either while making a quiz from one of its segments, or by taking a quiz from the other

© Springer International Publishing Switzerland 2016
D.D. Schmorrow and C.M. Fidopiastis (Eds.): AC 2016, Part II, LNAI 9744, pp. 97–106, 2016.
DOI: 10.1007/978-3-319-39952-2_11

segments of the screencast that were created by one of their peers. In particular, creating a quiz is an intrinsically creative endeavor that the vast majority of students have never attempted before. Studies devoted to this uncharted creative activity promise to deliver fundamental insights into students' emotion and cognitive load, which can provide deep insight into how deeply the information is being processed, the creativity used to create the quizzes, and the effectiveness of the method.

2   Theoretical Background Flip-Flop

At the core of the Flip-Flop methodology is the concept of making and taking quizzes synchronized with video recordings of lectures in order to deepen the students' understanding of the subject presented in the screencast. On the technology side, this basic strategy is supported by several online tools.

Taking a quiz is straightforward: As the screenshot in Fig. 1 shows, while the students view at the lecture video on the left hand side of the screen, tasks are displayed to the right. A smiley face confirms that a correct choice has been selected at which point a feedback may provide additional information. Similarly, a crying face indicates an incorrect answer. When student selects the hint button, the video stops playing and a short hint text appears. The hint can be accompanied by link to a web page with related information.

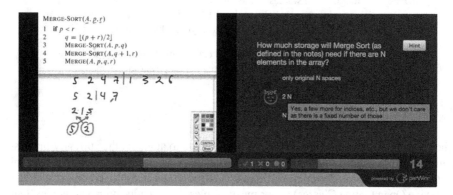

Fig. 1. Taking a quiz: selecting a correct choice displays a feedback that offers additional information.

But the Flip-Flop methodology goes beyond simply taking a quiz prepared by the instructor: Using the online quiz authoring tool depicted in Fig. 2, students create quiz tasks synchronized with video lectures. When students need to formulate a multiple choice task related to a segment of the video they need to view the segment, understand what the lecturer is presenting within this particular segment and then formulate a related question with numerous possible answers. In addition to entering the question and answers as text and/or image, the Flip-Flop authoring tool supports entering a feedback for each of the correct and incorrect choices, adding a hint text and creating a link button with a web address (URL) that leads to an external online document that offers additional information that may help solve the task. Students are encouraged to formulate feedbacks that point to reasoning why the correct choice is incorrect and what is the likely misconception that leads to answer incorrectly. The screenshot in Fig. 1 shows, for instance, a feedback that explains why the chosen answer is the correct one.

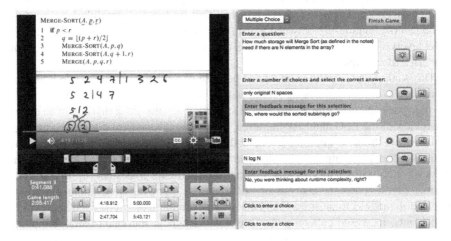

Fig. 2. Creating a quiz: multiple-choice task synchronized with a segment of video and entries for hint text, hint link label, hint link URL, and for choice feedback.

Peer evaluation is another essential component of Flip-Flop. Students are asked to have several poll questions at the end of each quiz. These survey questions allow the quiz author's peers to judge the quality of the questions, the answers, the feedbacks as well as the hints and the resources accessed via the hint links.

The Flip-Flop technology incorporates two other online support tools. The scheduling tool offers extensive support for the students as well as for the instructor: it can be used assign students to groups, it provides the quiz author with an initial quiz template and notifies the other members of the other members in the group once a quiz is ready.

The Instructor Support Tool allows the instructor to view all the quizzes students created and add to the database their evaluation of all the components of a quiz – questions, answers, feedbacks, etc. This data together with the students' peer evaluations may constitute a valuable component of grading.

2.1   Creativity and Cognitive Load Measured by EEG

When developing hypotheses for this study, it was first necessary to deconstruct the cognitive processes associated with the study task—a text-based creation of a quiz with feedback using a novel tool. Students will creatively generate quiz questions with feedback using this tool. In this study we will use EEG and psychophysiological measures. EEG is a psychophysiological measurement of post-synaptic electrical potentials on the surface of the scalp [1]. Electrodes are placed on specific locations of the scalp which collect the summation of synchronized activity from underlying pyramidal neurons lying near the surface of the cortex. The measure at each electrode location is then compared to a reference electrode located elsewhere on the scalp [2]. The recorded oscillations of brain activity at each electrode are complex waveforms that can be decomposed into simple waveforms of different periodicity at varying amplitudes. EEG researchers often are interested in five frequency bands: delta (<4 Hz), theta (4–8 Hz), alpha (8–13 Hz), beta (13–20 Hz), and gamma (>20) [2]. In this study we focus on the alpha band because of the inverse relationship between alpha frequency amplitude and attention, wherein lower levels of alpha represent higher levels of cognitive processing. This phenomenon is referred to as "alpha blocking" [3–5].

This study focuses on the alpha band because of a plethora of findings relating the alpha wave to creative processes. At this point it is important to delineate different creative processes and their effects on cortical activation and the alpha rhythm. In an extensive review of the EEG and ERP literature, Dietrich and Kanso [6] discuss the findings of many EEG studies examining divergent thinking, artistic creativity and insight. There findings indicate that much of the divergent thinking literature findings relating to the alpha wave is contradictory, but the findings on insight are consistent [6]. In one study of creativity, a coherence analysis of EEG data (i.e., showing correlations of activity among different electrode sites) found that when examining the alpha band in groups of participants, increased coherence is observed throughout the alpha band, exhibiting intra- and interhemispherical long-distance coherences [7] and, more specifically higher levels of alpha in response to creative tasks, such as alternate uses tasks [8, 9]. Other creativity findings have shown increases in alpha power being associated with creativity (both divergent thinking and artistic) [10]. In the realm of divergent thinking, findings have indicated that disinhibition (increases in power within frequency bands) corresponds to increased creativity [11]. Another line of EEG research has found that increases in the alpha rhythm in the frontal cortices during creative ideation [12]. However, these findings note an intriguing nuance. Increases in the alpha rhythm are found only during internally oriented attention that is characterized by the absence of bottom-up stimulation [12]. When creative generation is externally-directed, however, decreases in alpha power have been observed [12]. In the context of Flip-Flop creative generation it is important to note that external stimulation is occurring as the individual interacts with the quiz design tool to generate quiz ideas.

One consistent finding in the EEG creativity literature deals with insight. Insight refers to acquisition of a new understanding of the problem situation after repeated attempts to solve the problem [13]. Studies have shown that creative insight problem solving requires less working memory than other problem solving [14]. Research on insight using EEG has found consistently a decrease in alpha power in frontal, temporal and parietal sites [6]. Idea generation is process that links two or more separate concepts in working memory to produce a new idea [15]. There are two different processes to this linking, search and insight, with search being a more methodical process and insight being more creative [16, 17]. Methodical thinking is commonly associated with activation of the frontal cortex [18, 19]. Creativity and insight have been studied in a variety of contexts using EEG [6]. Findings on insight have been fairly consistent, with several EEG studies finding decreases in alpha power in the frontal cortices to be connected to insight [20–22]. In generating a quiz question within the Flip-Flop environment, it is expected that the students will generate insightful thinking.

In addition to creativity, the current research will examine the cognitive load of the students while they generate quiz questions in the Flip-Flop environment. Working memory plays a central role in cognition and cognitive load [23]. It encapsulates both what many consider "short-term memory" and attention. Therefore, working memory is pivotal for both information processing and decision making, responsible for encoding information from the environment and retrieving information from long-term memory in order to make sense of it [23–25]. A useful computer analogy for understanding working memory is that it represents the brain's RAM, storing of information currently undergoing processing but limited in its capacity [26]. Working memory is located in the frontal areas of cortex, namely Dorsolateral Prefrontal Cortex (DLPFC) [27]. Changes in activity in the DLPFC can indicate changes in working memory load and attention [18, 28]. In EEG, attenuation of the alpha rhythm over DLPFC indicates increases in working memory load [29]. Better performance has been found as a result of increased activity in this region [30]. Initially using the Flip-Flop tool to generate quiz questions should result in increased levels of cognitive load. However, as the student becomes used to the generative process and the tool, it is expected the cognitive load required to generate quizzes will decrease, despite an increase in the difficulty of the questions they are generating.

3   Method

3.1   Experimental Context and Participants

The "Algorithms" course is a key course at Department of Information and Computer Sciences at University of Hawaii - it is the prerequisite for most of the senior level courses and no student will be able to graduate without passing it with a satisfactory grade. The majority of the students consider this course to be the most demanding course in the curriculum.

This course has been taught in the inverted classroom fashion for the last five semesters. The lectures consist of 72 screencasts, mostly 15–20 min long. The students have to view typically 3 or 4 screencasts at home before they come to a classroom session. There are two such classroom sessions per week. Every screencast set is accompanied by a web page with detailed notes and the students are encouraged to view these notes while watching the videos. During the classroom session the students first take a paper quiz, and then solve class problems that practice the topics presented in the corresponding set of screencasts.

The Flip-Flop method is being applied in a pilot fashion in the "Algorithms" course during the current semester. Preliminary results indicate that while student are concerned about the extra time needed to make and take the quizzes, they are more than willing to take on these chores to gain bonus points. Moreover, the quality of the quiz tasks seems to have improved considerably within only a couple of weeks.

The Flip-Flop method will be applied systematically in the aforementioned "Algorithms" course in the upcoming Fall 2016 semester. We expect that 20 to 30 students will enroll in each of the two sections. After an initial introductory classroom session the students will complete a 'warm-up' exercise where they will make a quiz from a YouTube video of their choice. Based on our experience from current pilot course, the students a likely to choose a topic related to their hobbies, favorite sports, movie trailers, music videos, etc.

In subsequent weeks, both course sections will be subdivided into groups of up to four students. The Flip-Flop scheduling app will then subdivide each screencast into four segments and assign each student one of the segments to make a quiz from. This tool also allows the student author to download a template that she can then upload within the quiz authoring tool to define a set of default multiple-choice tasks as well as the set of peer evaluation poll questions asked at the end of the quiz. Since the default length of each task is one minute, most screencasts are 15 to 20 min long and each is subdivided among four authors, the template typically defines 4 to 5 tasks. This template greatly simplifies the menial chores of defining the components of a task – question, answers, feedbacks, hints and links to online resources - as well as of synchronizing the tasks with the video segments.

Once the author has created the quiz, she can use this app to send an email to the other three the students in the group announcing that the quiz is ready and they can take it. Note that this way every student creates one quiz and takes three other quizzes from a screencast. As a consequence the quizzes she makes or takes cover the entire length of this video.

We plan to 'flip-flop' alternate set of screencasts for each of the sections. I.e., suppose that the classroom sessions will be scheduled for Monday and Wednesday for both sections – then the first section will make and take the quizzes from screencasts for the Monday's session and the other section from screencasts for the Wednesday's session. In other words, the sections will use Flip-Flop for different sets of screencasts. Since the paper quizzes as well as the problems on midterms and final exam will be identical for both sections and will be closely related to the topics of the individual screencasts, we will be able to contrast the student's performance on problems where they either created or took a quiz with the problems related to screencast that they only needed to watch. Our hypothesis is that they will receive significantly more points on problems related to their 'flip-flop' topics.

To be able to assess the quality of the quizzes students created, our instructor support tool will integrate evaluation facilities that will allow a rater to give points to all of the individual components of a task: the questions, answers, answer feedbacks, hints and links to related resources. Our hypothesis is that the ratings for all the task components will be significantly better towards the end of the semester.

Furthermore, we plan to augment the quiz authoring software to collect data while the author is creating a quiz. Obviously, it will be interesting to investigate the time needed to create the entire quiz. Moreover, the times needed to create a question, to come up with the correct and incorrect answers, and to formulate a hint will be collected. Our hypothesis is that despite the fact that the course topics are more difficult towards the end of the semester, all these times will become gradually improve, and at the end of the semester they will be significantly shorter than at the beginning of the semester.

Our intuition as instructors lets us believe that creating an incorrect answer is more difficult that creating the correct answer – after all, an incorrect answer should be neither partially correct nor obviously wrong. Furthermore, a good task should have several incorrect choices so that guessing the right choice is less likely and coming up with yet another 'good' incorrect answer seems to be increasingly difficult. The analysis of the quiz-making data will show us whether this hypothesis is correct.

In addition to the above data analysis we will let the students fill out a survey questionnaire asking for their assessment of the Flip-Flop method at the beginning, after the second week, and at the end of the semester. Our hypothesis is that they will be initially inclined to give rather positive feedback given that they could freely choose the subject of the warm-up exercise. We expect, however, that the students will be much more critical once they had to make a few quizzes based on the actual course screencasts. (After all, taking quizzes and in particular making quizzes takes time). Finally, their assessment at the end of semester is likely to be more positive as quiz-making and - taking becomes merely another routine.

3.2   Neurophysiological and Psychophysiological Measurement of Flip-Flop

Our dependent variables are cortical alpha wave activity, autonomic arousal, and emotional valence. These are operationalized using neurological and psychophysiological measures. EEG measures will be collected using a 14-channel headset (Emotiv Systems, San Francisco, CA, USA) with electrodes dispersed over the scalp along the 10–20 system [31] (see Fig. 1). The electrodes connect with the scalp surface via felt pads saturated in saline solution. The reference electrodes are located at P3 and P4 over the inferior, posterior parietal lobule [31]. All other channels were measured in relation to the electrical activity present at these locations, sampled at 128 Hz. Impedances were verified and data collected using Emotiv TestBench Software Version 1.5.0.3, which export into comma-delimited format for subsequent analysis (Fig. 3).

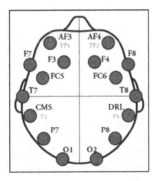

Fig. 3. Position of the electrodes on the EEG headset with labels along the 10–20 system

Autonomic arousal will be operationalized as skin conductance level measured with disposable electrodes filled with electrically neutral gel and adhered planar surface of the foot. A Biopac MP150 system will be used to collect the skin conductance data at

1000 Hz. Emotional valence will be operationalized as the relative activation of the corrugator supercilli muscle group (facial EMG). Corrugator EMG will be measured using a pair of mini (4 mm) reusable AG/AGCL electrodes filled with electrolyte gel placed above the subject's left eye after dead skin cells has been removed by a skin prep pad containing rubbing alcohol and pumice. The bipolar corrugator measures were collected using the Biopac MP150 system with high pass filters set at 8 Hz. The full wave signal was rectified and then contour integrated online at a time constant of 100 ms, and then sampled at 1000 Hz by the Biopac MP150 system.

4   Future Directions

The empirical examination of the Flip-Flop tool opens many doors in the educational arena. First, the neurophysiological and psychophysiological correlates of using this method in the classroom will be elucidated. There are many different ways individuals learn and much research in psychology has examined it. However, using EEG and psychophysiology in such an applied setting can provide insight into how to better engage students in the process of learning. Tying these to behavioral outcomes (i.e., surveys and instructor evaluations) will provide invaluable feedback in how to develop tools that help facilitate learning. Furthermore, the use of the tools from cognitive neuroscience could spawn a new area of research that can be used in a variety of academic settings to evaluate pedagogical tools and their outcomes. We refer to this future research area as "NeuroEDU." NeuroEDU utilizes the tools of cognitive neuro-science (EEG, fMRI, fNIRS, etc) to understand and facilitate the development or improvement of pedagogical methods or tools. Our study will provide the first longitu-dinal investigation of a developed tool that ties both neurophysiology and psychophysi-ology to course outcomes. Future NeuroEDU research can examine the effectiveness of Flip-Flop and other emerging educational methodologies for different age groups – in particular at high-school and elementary school level –, different subject areas – such as social sciences and arts – as well as in different educational settings – for instance in commercial training courses.

References

1. Gibbs, F.A., Gibbs, E.L.: Atlas of Electroencephalography. F.A. Gibbs, Boston City Hospital, Oxford (1941)
2. Harmon-Jones, F., Peterson, C.K.: Electroencephalographic methods in social and personality psychology. In: Harmon-Jones, E., Beer, J.S. (eds.) Methods and Social Neuroscience, pp. 170–197. The Guilford Press, New York (2009)
3. Andreassi, J.L.: Psychophysiology: Human Behavior & Physiological Response, 5th edn. Lawrence Erlbaum Associates, Mahwah (2007)
4. Potter, R.F., Bolls, P.D.: Psychophysiological Measurement and Meaning: Cognitive and Emotional Processing of Media. Routledge, New York (2011)
5. Minas, R.K., Potter, R.F., Dennis, A.R., Bartelt, V., Bae, S.: Putting on the thinking cap: using neurois to understand information processing biases in virtual teams. J. Manag. Inf. Syst. **30**, 49–82 (2014)

6. Dietrich, A., Kanso, R.: A review of EEG, erp, and neuroimaging studies of creativity and insight. Psychol. Bull. **136**, 822–848 (2010)

7. Petsche, H.: Approaches to verbal, visual and musical creativity by EEG coherence analysis. Int. J. Psychophysiol. **24**, 145–159 (1996)

8. Fink, A., Schwab, D., Papousek, I.: Sensitivity of EEG upper alpha activity to cognitive and affective creativity interventions. Int. J. Psychophysiol. **82**, 233–239 (2011)

9. Martindale, C., Hasenfus, N.: EEG differences as a function of creativity, stage of the creative process, and effort to be original. Biol. Psychol. **6**, 157–167 (1978)

10. Fink, A., Neubauer, A.C.: EEG alpha oscillations during the performance of verbal creativity tasks: differential effects of sex and verbal intelligence. Int. J. Psychophysiol. **62**, 46–53 (2006)

11. Radel, R., Davranche, K., Fournier, M., Dietrich, A.: The role of (dis) inhibition in creativity: decreased inhibition improves idea generation. Cognition **134**, 110–120 (2015)

12. Fink, A., Benedek, M.: EEG alpha power and creative ideation. Neurosci. Biobehav. Rev. **44**, 111–123 (2014)

13. Mumford, M.D., Whetzel, D.L.: Insight, creativity, and cognition: on Sternberg and Davidson's the nature of insight. Creativity Res. J. **9**, 103 (1996)

14. Lavric, A., Forstmeier, S., Rippon, G.: Differences in working memory involvement in analytical and creative tasks: an ERP study. NeuroReport **11**, 1613–1618 (2000)

15. Nijstad, B.A., Stroebe, D.: How the group affects the mind: a cognitive model of idea generation in groups. Pers. Soc. Psychol. Rev. **10**, 186–213 (2006)

16. Ericsson, K.A., Simon, H.A.: Protocol Analysis. MIT Press, Cambridge (1993)

17. Bowden, E.M., Jung-Beeman, M., Fleck, J., Kounios, J.: New approaches to demystifying insight. Trends Cogn. Sci. **9**, 322–328 (2005)

18. Wager, T.D., Jonides, J., Reading, S.: Neuroimaging studies of shifting attention: a meta-analysis. NeuroImage **22**, 1679–1693 (2004)

19. Amodio, D.M., Frith, C.D.: Meeting of minds: the medial frontal cortex and social cognition. Nat. Rev. Neurosci. **7**, 268–277 (2006, print)

20. Kounios, J., Fleck, J.I., Green, D.L., Payne, L., Stevenson, J.L., Bowden, E.M., Jung-Beeman, M.: The origins of insight in resting-state brain activity. Neuropsychologia **46**, 281–291 (2008)

21. Kounios, J., Frymiare, J.L., Bowden, E.M., Fleck, J.I., Subramaniam, K., Parrish, T.B., Jung-Beeman, M.: The prepared mind: neural activity prior to problem presentation predicts subsequent solution by sudden insight. Psychol. Sci. **17**, 882–890 (2006)

22. Sandkühler, S., Bhattacharya, J.: Deconstructing insight: EEG correlates of insightful problem solving. PLoS ONE **3**, e1459 (2008)

23. Baddeley, A.: Working Memory. Science **255**, 556–559 (1992)

24. Conway, A.R.A., Engle, R.W.: Working memory and retrieval: a resource-dependent inhibition model. J. Exp. Psychol.: Gen. **123**, 354–373 (1994)

25. Welsh, M.C., Satterlee-Cartmell, T., Stine, M.: Towers of Hanoi and London: contribution of working memory and inhibition to performance. Brain Cogn. **41**, 231–242 (1999)

26. D'Esposito, M.: From cognitive to neural models of working memory. Philo. Trans. Roy. Soc. B: Biol. Sci. **362**, 761–772 (2007)

27. D'Esposito, M., Detre, J.A., Alsop, D.C., Shin, R.K., Atlas, S., Grossman, M.: The neural basis of the central executive system of working memory. Nature **378**, 279–281 (1995)

28. Curtis, C.E., D'Esposito, M.: Persistent activity in the prefrontal cortex during working memory. Trends Cogn. Sci. **7**, 415–423 (2003)

29. Gevins, A., Smith, M.E., McEvoy, L., Yu, D.: High-resolution EEG mapping of cortical activation related to working memory: effects of task difficulty, type of processing, and practice. Cereb. Cortex **7**, 374–385 (1997)
30. Hoptman, M.J., Davidson, R.J.: Baseline EEG asymmetries and performance on neuropsychological tasks. Neuropsychologia **36**, 1343–1353 (1998)
31. Herwig, U., Satrapi, P., Schönfeldt-Lecuona, C.: Using the international 10–20 EEG system for positioning of transcranial magnetic stimulation. Brain Topogr. **16**, 95–99 (2003)
32. Newmann, F.M.: Student Engagement and Achievement in American Secondary Schools. ERIC (1992)
33. Andreassi, J.L., Filipovic, S.R.: Psychophysiology: Human Behavior and Physiological Response. Elsevier, Philadelphia (2001)
34. Crosby, M.E., Auernheimer, B., Aschwanden, C., Ikehara, C.: Physiological data feedback for application in distance education. Presented at the Proceedings of the 2001 Workshop on Perceptive User Interfaces, Orlando, Florida, USA (2001)
35. Vick, R.M., Ikehara, C.S.: Methodological issues of real time data acquisition from multiple sources of physiological data. In: Proceedings of the 36th Annual Hawaii International Conference on System Sciences, p. 7 (2003)
36. Ikehara, C., Crosby, M.E.: A real-time cognitive load in educational multimedia. In: Proceedings of the 2003 World Conference on Educational Multimedia, Hypermedia & Telecommunications, Honolulu, HI (2003)
37. Colmenarez, A.J., Xiong, Z., Huang, T.S.: Facial Analysis from Continuous Video with Applications to Human-Computer Interface, vol. 2. Springer Science & Business Media, Heidelberg (2006)
38. Busso, C., Deng, Z., Yildirim, S., Bulut, M., Lee, C.M., Kazemzadeh, A., Lee, S., Neumann, U., Narayanan, S.: Analysis of emotion recognition using facial expressions, speech and multimodal information. Presented at the Proceedings of the 6th International Conference on Multimodal Interfaces, State College, PA, USA (2004)

Real Time Assessment of Cognitive State: Research and Implementation Challenges

Michael C. Trumbo[1(✉)], Mikaela L. Armenta[1], Michael J. Haass[1], Karin M. Butler[1], Aaron P. Jones[2], and Charles S.H. Robinson[2]

[1] Sandia National Laboratories, Albuquerque, USA
{mctrumb,mlarmen,mjhaass,kbutle}@sandia.gov
[2] University of New Mexico, Albuquerque, USA
{aaronjones,charob}@unm.edu

Abstract. Inferring the cognitive state of an individual in real time during task performance allows for implementation of corrective measures prior to the occurrence of an error. Current technology allows for real time cognitive state assessment based on objective physiological data though techniques such as neuroimaging and eye tracking. Although early results indicate effective construction of classifiers that distinguish between cognitive states in real time is a possibility in some settings, implementation of these classifiers into real world settings poses a number of challenges. Cognitive states of interest must be sufficiently distinct to allow for continuous discrimination in the operational environment using technology that is currently available as well as practical to implement.

Keywords: Cognitive state · Real time · Eye tracking · Attention

1   Introduction

The link between the mind and the brain makes it possible to use objective physiological signals to infer the mental state of an individual. Decoding of mental states, however, is currently limited with regard to both precision and efficiency. In a typical scenario, data is collected over many trials that occur under varying conditions designed to elicit distinct cognitive states, then the aggregate data is subjected to statistical analyses in order to determine if discrimination between cognitive states is possible based on physiological data associated with each task condition (see [1] for review). This approach increases statistical sensitivity by virtue of including a large number of samples in the analysis, but it does not allow for cognitive state inference on a trial-by-trial basis, thereby limiting efficiency.

Construction of a classifier capable of real time cognitive state inference is desirable in a number of contexts as it allows for implementation of adjustments that prevent errors or enhance performance while a task is ongoing. For instance, assessment of cognitive state in real time may prove valuable in determining if a driver is distracted or engaged in the driving task [2], in providing feedback with regard to emotional state and cognitive load of operators [3], in classifying an individual as alert or fatigued during visual search [4], and in detecting deception allowing for adjustment of questioning [5]. Researchers

© Springer International Publishing Switzerland 2016
D.D. Schmorrow and C.M. Fidopiastis (Eds.): AC 2016, Part II, LNAI 9744, pp. 107–119, 2016.
DOI: 10.1007/978-3-319-39952-2_12

have used a number of technologies to accomplish real time cognitive state assessment, often by using neuroimaging data such as electroencephalogram (EEG; [6]), functional magnetic resonance imaging (fMRI; [7]), or functional near-infrared spectroscopy (fNIRS; [8]), as well as physiological data such as galvanic skin response (GSR) and heart rate [9]. Such technologies, however, have several limitations. For instance, MRI equipment is expensive, immobile, noisy, necessitates a shielded room, and requires participants to lie perfectly still during scanning, making it infeasible to implement in most job contexts. EEG, fNIRS, GSR, and heart rate monitoring all require an individual to wear equipment that limits mobility and may become uncomfortable over time, making these methods ill-suited for data collection over long durations of time, such as a regular workday of 8 h [10].

Eye tracking technology uses video recordings from cameras which may be unobtrusively placed in nearly any environment to quantify eye phenomena such as pupil size, eye fixations, eye movements, and blinks [11]. The temporal resolution of these recordings is on the order of milliseconds, allowing for discrimination between cognitive states in real time using these eye metrics [4]. While the notion that eyes are the window to the soul may be debatable, eye metrics are thought to reflect brain activity, thereby acting as a window to cognitive processes [12–14]. Brain state information may be less susceptible to conscious or unconscious countermeasures than indirect metrics such as blood pressure, respiration, and GSR [15], thereby making incorporation of brain state information particularly valuable as a relatively clean source of data reflecting the mental state of an individual.

Broadly speaking, the human visual system may be divided into two modes of attentional processing: ambient and focal. During ambient processing attention is allocated broadly across the visual field. This type of processing is subserved by a dorsal neural pathway in the brain dedicated to determining where in space objects exist and how to interact with them. During focal processing attention is allocated to a region of the visual field defined by an object. Focal attention is associated with a ventral neural pathway concerned with object identification [16]. These distinct brain processes manifest in the amplitude and duration of the saccadic eye movements that occur between fixations (a relative stillness in eye position lasting from tens of milliseconds to several seconds and largely considered indicative of attention to the given position), may be categorized as related to ambient or focal processing based on the amplitude and duration of saccades, or the quick motions of the eye from one fixation to another, prior and subsequent to the fixation [11, 17]. Thus, for an individual engaged in a task with a visual component it is possible to monitor the balance between ambient and focal attention in real time. Eye tracking is therefore efficient, as its temporal resolution is conducive to real time monitoring, as well as relatively precise, in that it enables classification depth beyond a coarse inference of whether or not an individual is allocating attentional resources to a task by further allowing determination of type of attentional resources allocated.

Often, visual search follows a coarse-to-fine strategy in which initial search is dominated by ambient processing characterized by long saccades and short fixations in order to acquire the gist of a scene, followed by focal search characterized by short saccades and long fixations for purposes of object recognition; essentially exploration followed by inspection [18]. There are, however, exceptions – for instance free viewing of natural scenes such as land or cityscapes in the absence of a task or goal is characterized by dominant focal attention, both over time and immediately following stimulus onset [17]. Thus, it is important to consider how task demands influence search patterns [19]. Real-time assessment of the balance between ambient and focal attention may be a valuable predictor of performance in a variety of domains, enabling implementation of mitigation measures prior to a critical incident. For instance, drivers have demonstrated selective impairment in response to side tasks depending on if the ancillary task required ambient or focal processing [20], while level of stress [21] and mood [22] bias the amount of time spent in each processing mode. Thus, real-time assessment of visual processing that allows for discrimination between focal and ambient processing may allow performance predication as well as inference of cognitive state.

One method of visualizing the dynamic interplay between ambient and focal attention is to compute the K-Coefficient by standardizing the current fixation duration and the subsequent saccade amplitude and taking the difference between them, with positive ordinates indicating focal processing at the fixation and negative indicating ambient processing [23]. In the current work, we applied this method to two categories of task-oriented viewings of natural scenes. For the first category of images, we gave participants the task of determining either the profession portrayed in a photograph or the season during which the photograph was taken. For the second category, we asked participants either to count the number of vehicles in an image or to count the number of floors in the tallest building in the image. Eye movements were recorded during image search, and fixations were subsequently categorized as ambient or focal using the K-Coefficient algorithm. The results from this analysis are used to underscore obstacles to real time cognitive state assessment.

2   Method

Participants. Forty-one participants (Males = 22; Age: Mean = 26.97, SD = 11.53, Range = 17–65 years), employees, interns, staff, and contractors of Sandia National Laboratories, participated in this study. Three did not provide the requisite demographic information. Technical issues led to loss of data in two instances, reducing usable data to n = 39 (Males = 20; Age: Mean = 27.14, SD = 11.69, Range = 17–65 years). Participants were paid their hourly wage for participation in the study.

Stimuli. Photos, 13 in all, were divided into two categories: (1) five with cars and buildings (CB) and (2) eight that we have termed 'Seasons, Professions' (SP), photographs of people in various roles ranging from that of an early 20th century factory assembly line to policemen.

Visual Search Task. Participants completed a still image search task in which they were directed to answer a given question based on what they discerned from various photographs. The task was created and presented with EyePresentation, visual stimulus presentation software developed at Sandia National Laboratories. Stimuli were presented at a resolution of 1280 × 1024 on a Dell 1901FP LCD Monitor (38 cm x 30 cm). Before viewing the photos, participants were presented with a slide that asked questions similar to a Yarbus task [24]. Questions on instruction slides pertaining to CB images included "How many vehicles can you see?" or "How many stories does the tallest building have?" while questions preceding SP images were "In what season was this photo taken?" and "What job or profession is portrayed in the photo?" While all participants saw all images, questions were counterbalanced by condition (CB and SP). After viewing an instruction slide, participants viewed a fixation cross for 1 s. A fixation cross preceded all instruction, image stimulus and response slides. All participants viewed the photographs in the same order, but two orders of questions were used such that across participants both questions were asked for each image. For instance, in the SP condition both groups saw a photo of an early twentieth century assembly line, however one group (n = 18) was asked "What job or profession is portrayed in the photo?" and the other (n = 21) responded to, "In what season was this photo taken?" Our other condition (CB) featured city and landscapes in which participants were asked either "How many stories are in the tallest building?" or "How many vehicles are there?" When prepared to answer the question, participants pressed the space bar on a keyboard. The image was replaced by the fixation cross and followed by a response slide.

Each phase of the trial was self-paced. Participants pressed the space bar on a keyboard to progress to the next phase when they understood the question, obtained an answer, and had verbalized their answer for the experimenter. There was, however, a ceiling of 45 s for instruction, image stimulus and response slide viewing. Most participants proceeded through the task before reaching this. See Fig. 1 for visualization of the task progression.

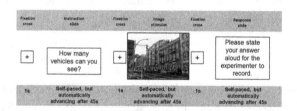

Fig. 1. Timeline of each trial, using vehicle counting as an example. The progression from instructions to image stimulus to response was self-paced, within a 45 s time window for each portion of the trial. Image source: CC0 Public Domain, https://pixabay.com/en/berlin-germany-urban-buildings-103154/.

Procedure. After being informed of their rights as research participants and providing informed consent, participants completed a demographic questionnaire providing information on age, sex, and experience with visual imagery work such as photography and other forms of imagery. Participants were then seated in a 148 cm long × 102 cm wide (58 in. x 40in.) 'SE 2000' soundproof, dark room manufactured by Whisper Room Sound Isolation Enclosures at a viewing distance of 54–92 cm from the computer monitor. The door was propped open to enable verbal communication between the participant and experimenter. The open door allowed ambient light to enter the room and the amount varied between participants. Although we did not take light measurements, typical illumination ranges from 1 lx in a very dim room to a typical value of

90 lx in a work or living space [25]. Prior research indicates that illumination in the range of 0 to 1000 lx does not significantly affect accuracy or precision of eye tracking data [26].

We collected eye tracking data using EyeWorks Suite (v. 3.12.5395.30517) on a DELL Precision T3600 using Windows 7 operating system on an Intel Xeon CPU E5-1603 0 @ 2.80 GHz with 8 GB of RAM. All stimuli were presented at a resolution of 1280 × 1024 on a DELL 19" LCD monitor. We utilized a 60 Hz FOVIO eye-tracker manufactured by Seeing Machines and verified calibration through a five-point calibration procedure in EyeWorks Record prior to the task. Calibration was considered sufficient if the dot following the eye movement trajectory was sustained (indicating that the eye movement monitor was not losing tracking) and if the calibration dot was accurate (falling on the calibration check targets at the center and corners of the screen when the participant was instructed to look at them, with inaccuracy of up to one centimeter for the upper two corner targets). The eye-tracker was located between 9.5 cm and 8 cm beneath the bottom of the viewing screen. Following calibration, participants completed the task as described above, and in Fig. 1.

After completing this task, the FOVIO was recalibrated before moving on to a Smooth Pursuit task. As this task is not pertinent to this article, it is not discussed further but is described in [27]. Upon completion of this task, the experimental portion of the study was complete and subjects discussed the study with the experimenter before leaving. From consent to debriefing, the study duration spanned roughly 45 min.

3 Results

Fixations were classified as relating to ambient or focal attention using the K-Coefficient [23], which was calculated for each fixation using the difference between the standardized values (z-scores) of the duration of the current fixation (di) and subsequent saccade amplitude (ai + 1), as such:

$$K_i = \frac{d_i - \mu_d}{\sigma_d} - \frac{a_{i+1} - \mu_a}{\sigma_a}, \quad i \in [1, n-1] \tag{1}$$

In this equation, μ_d and σ_d represent the mean and standard deviation, respectively, of the fixation duration while μ_a and σ_a represent the mean and standard deviation, respectively, of the saccade amplitude, computed over all n fixations. Positive values therefore represent a relatively long fixation followed by a relatively short saccade, indicative of focal attention for that fixation. Conversely, negative values represent a relatively short fixation followed by a relatively long saccade, indicative of a state of ambient attention for that fixation. Similar to prior research [17], scanpaths with less than four total fixations were excluded from analyses. In addition, the first fixation for a given trial was removed from analysis to compensate for the effect of the fixation cross which biases first fixations toward the center of the screen.

In order to evaluate potential differences between conditions with regard to ambient and focal attention, a RM ANOVA was conducted, with two levels of fixation type (ambient vs. focal) and four levels of condition (cars vs. buildings vs. seasons vs. professions).

All pairwise comparisons were planned, and thus no alpha correction was applied. This analysis revealed an attention x condition interaction, ($F(3,36) = 2.930, p = 0.047$), as well as a main effect of attention ($F(1,38) = 8.946, p = 0.005$) and a main effect of condition ($F(3,36) = 8.325, p < 0.001$). Follow-up pairwise comparisons indicate a greater number of focal vs. ambient fixations (mean difference .617, $p = 0.005$) and that more fixations (collapsed across attention type) occurred in the buildings vs. cars condition (mean difference 4.438, $p < 0.001$), in the buildings vs. professions condition (mean difference 3.651, $p < 0.001$), in the seasons vs. cars condition (mean difference 3.511, $p < 0.001$), and in the seasons vs. professions condition (mean difference 2.727, $p < 0.001$).

Additionally, there was a simple effect of condition within ambient attention ($F(3,36) = 6.774, p < 0.001$) and a simple effect of condition within focal attention ($F(3,36) = 9.460, p < 0.001$). Follow-up pairwise comparisons indicate a greater number of ambient fixations in the buildings vs. cars condition (mean difference 3.628, $p < .001$), in the buildings vs. professions condition (mean difference 2.934, p = 0.003), in the seasons vs. cars condition (mean difference 3.325, $p < .001$), and in the seasons vs. professions condition (mean difference 2.630, $p < 0.001$). Additional pairwise comparisons indicate a greater number of focal fixations in the buildings vs. cars condition (mean difference 5.248, $p < 0.001$), in the buildings vs. professions condition (mean difference 4.368, $p < 0.001$), in the seasons vs. cars condition (mean difference 3.697, $p < 0.001$), and in the seasons vs. professions condition (mean difference 2.816, p = 0.002).

These pairwise comparisons indicate similar findings for both focal and ambient fixation types (more of both types for buildings vs. cars and vs. professions, and more of both type for seasons vs. cars and vs. professions). In order to determine if these findings may be an artifact of differential search times between conditions (given the nature of the task involved self-terminated search up to a ceiling of 45 s) we conducted a number of pairwise comparisons evaluating the effect of condition on search time, collapsed across attention. These comparisons revealed a greater amount of time (in seconds) was spent searching in the buildings vs. cars condition (mean difference 1.445, $p = 0.004$), in the buildings vs. seasons condition (mean difference 1.541, $p < 0.001$), in the buildings vs. professions condition (mean difference 2.215, $p < 0.001$), and in the seasons vs. professions condition (mean difference .674, $p = 0.021$; see Fig. 2). As these differences closely mapped onto the findings for number of fixations, we re-ran the previous analysis with total search time within the appropriate condition(s) as a covariate. With this control in place, the difference in number of focal or ambient fixations between conditions was no longer significant for any comparisons between conditions (all $ps > .05$).

Due to the overall differences in search times between conditions, and based on previously identified visual processing periods, we divided data into early, middle, and late search periods, as in [28]. The early search period corresponds to the first 1.5 s of scene viewing, the middle to 1.5–3.0 s, and the late 3.0–4.5 s. Early visual search phases are thought to be driven largely by bottom-up visual features (e.g., color, edges, luminance, motion) while during later stages top-down influences (e.g., task goals, motivations, strategies) are thought to dominate [29]. Therefore, we investigated the possibility that bottom-up and top-down search contributions would shift across these search

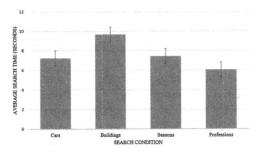

Fig. 2. Average search time in seconds broken down by search condition. Note that overall differences in search time between conditions account for differences between conditions in number of ambient and focal fixations.

periods, reflected in a difference in number of ambient or focal fixations over time. Collapsed by condition, there were no significant differences in number of ambient or focal fixations between time periods (all $ps > 0.05$; see Fig. 3), though the trend of more focal relative to ambient attention over time is consistent with previous literature [28].

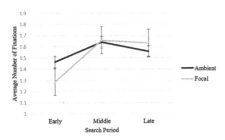

Fig. 3. Average number of fixations by search period and attention type, collapsed across condition.

Additional planned pairwise comparisons were conducted in order to investigate a potential effect of time within each condition and attention type. These pairwise comparisons revealed a significant difference within ambient attention for the buildings condition, such that the middle search period contained more fixations than the late search period (mean difference .494, $p = 0.013$) and for the professions condition such that the middle search period contained more ambient fixations than the early search period (mean difference .342, $p = 0.031$). Within focal attention, for the buildings condition more fixations occurred within the middle search period than the late search period (mean difference .414, $p = 0.018$), and more within the late search compared to the early search period (mean difference .523, $p = 0.003$). For the seasons condition, more focal fixations occurred within the middle than the early search period (mean difference .560, $p < 0.001$) and more focal fixations occurred within the late vs. early search period (mean difference .517, $p < 0.001$). For the professions condition, more focal fixations occurred within the middle vs. early search period (mean difference .431, $p = 0.002$) and within the late vs. early search period (mean difference .520, $p < .001$).

We also calculated planned pairwise comparisons between conditions within early, middle, and late search periods in order to determine if there was a difference within any search period for the different search conditions. These analyses revealed no significant differences in ambient fixations within the early search period (all $ps > 0.05$), but a significant difference in focal fixations within the early search period such that there were more focal fixations in the cars condition vs. the professions condition (mean difference .325, $p = 0.041$). Within the middle search period there was a difference in ambient fixations, with more fixations in the seasons condition vs. the cars condition (mean difference .678, $p = 0.008$) and more in the profession condition than the cars condition (mean difference .580, $p = 0.021$). There were no differences for focal fixations in the middle search period (all $ps > 0.05$). In the late search period, there were differences in number of ambient fixations, with more occurring in the seasons vs. cars condition (mean difference .555, $p = .005$), more in the seasons vs. buildings condition (mean difference .739, $p < 0.001$), more in the professions vs. cars condition (mean difference .434, $p = 0.04$), and more in the professions vs. buildings condition (mean difference .618, $p = 0.01$).

4   Discussion

Eye tracking represents a non-invasive method of collecting data that may be implemented in many research and job contexts without interfering with task performance, and is therefore a technology worth pursuing in the realm of real-time assessment. There are, however, a number of challenges to overcome with regard to both research and practical implementations. The preliminary results of the current study indicate the ability to discriminate between ambient and focal attention states and differentiation by task. We found that when search time is self-terminated there were differences in the average time spent searching between image conditions; notably, participants spent more time searching in the buildings condition than in the other search conditions. Controlling for this difference in average search time rendered differences in overall number of ambient and focal fixations between conditions non-significant. Dividing search time into early, middle, and late search periods, however, revealed several differences between conditions with regard to ambient and focal attention within a given search period. Notably, differences between conditions within ambient were limited to middle and late search periods, while differences within focal were limited to early search. Within conditions, we found evidence for an effect of time within attention type. For the seasons and professions conditions, there tended to be more ambient fixations in the middle search period relative to the early, while for the buildings condition there were more ambient fixations in the middle vs. late search period. For focal attention, there were significantly more fixations in the middle and late search periods vs. the early search period for the buildings, seasons, and professions conditions.

Focal attention is thought to be driven by bottom-up stimulus characteristics to a greater degree than ambient attention when participants are free-viewing natural scenes [17], and is associated with top-down processing later on in visual search when knowledge and expectations guide a detailed inspection of a particular image feature [17, 29].

The current task was goal-directed, standing in contrast to previous research that has characterized attentional states under free viewing conditions [17]. Giving participants a search goal prior to the onset of each image, as in the current research, may impact the time course of focal attention associated with top-down, goal-directed behavior. While this seemed to be the case for the cars condition, in all other conditions there was a greater number focal fixations in middle and late search periods relative to early search. This is consistent with prior research suggesting dominance of focal attention over time [28], and collapsing across conditions suggests an overall pattern of a shift toward focal attention as search time increases in goal-direct visual search (see Fig. 3). It is important to note that in the current study search time was self-terminated by participants, with a ceiling of 45 s. This potentially leaves substantial time following the "late" visual processing period cutoff of 4.5 s. We found a main effect of attention type such that across the entirety of the search period there were significantly more focal fixations than ambient fixations, but given the time span of the search it may be useful to use a finer analysis with regard to time. For instance, it is possible in some search conditions participants cycle through periods of ambient and focal domination as they move between areas of interest. This shifting cycle may be different between search conditions or over time, making it a potential valuable contribution to a classifier. Additionally, this may help determine if visual processing periods of the durations used in this and prior work are appropriate for self-terminated search which may substantially exceed 4.5 s.

For the cars and buildings conditions, participants were explicitly directed to locate targets (cars or buildings) and count them. In the seasons and professions condition, we asked participants to look at an image and make a judgement based on the evidence they were able to gather from cues within the image. It may be that this type of judgement requires more ambient processing as one develops a 'gist' of the situation. This is supported by a greater number of ambient fixations during the late search period in both the seasons and professions conditions relative to the cars and buildings conditions, suggesting persistence of ambient attention for conditions involving judgement based on image cues. Additionally, image stimuli in the cars and buildings conditions did not include any human beings, while the seasons and professions conditions contained human beings in each image, which are highly salient to attentional and visual processing [30].

Ecological Validity. The current research demonstrates that tasks under the same general domain (e.g., visual search) may elicit different patterns of cognitive states, contingent on such factors as specific stimuli content and task goals. Therefore, when attempting to generalize laboratory research to an operational environment, it is critical that the laboratory circumstances closely mimic those of the environment of interest. Often, real time cognitive state classifiers are built under laboratory conditions of strict control, using tasks specifically designed to elicit drastically different cognitive states in a binary fashion (e.g., alert vs. fatigued; anxious vs. relaxed) thereby maximizing the likelihood of building a successful classifier [1, 4]. Establishing that a classifier is effective under these ideal conditions is a valuable feasibility step. Real-world jobs, however, do not often embody the same method of utilizing extremely different task conditions for purposes of identifying distinct cognitive states based on physiological metrics.

Instead, they may elicit many overlapping cognitive states on a continuum not present in laboratory conditions [1]. In addition, real-world environments may introduce obstacles to data quality not present in a laboratory, such as substantial participant movement and sources of electrical interference that may dictate the types of technologies available for data collection [10]. Therefore, research geared toward application within a particular environment should attempt to mimic the environment of planned deployment as closely as possible.

Classifier Construction. Building a classifier capable of discriminating between cognitive states in real time invites a number of challenging decisions. One such decision is which data to collect and use. For instance, eye tracking offers the ability to collect several data streams in parallel, including eye movement metrics, pupil size, and blinks, all of which have been demonstrated to relate to cognitive state [4]. Previous research using eye tracking data suggests that a classifier constructed implementing all of these data streams significantly outperforms classifiers built using only one data stream [4]. In the current study, ambient fixations resulted in discrimination between certain search conditions within middle and late search periods, while number of focal fixations allowed discrimination during the early search period, suggesting value in tracking both types of fixations. It is therefore important to determine acceptable margins of error weighed against additional costs in terms of computational resources. In a similar vein, it may be true that each data stream allows discriminability between different cognitive states. For instance, blinks may provide critical information when discriminating between an alert vs. a fatigued state, while eye movement metrics may be particularly valuable in discriminating between different types of attention within an alert state, and pupil size may be the best indicator of cognitive load [11]. Thus, multiple data streams may allow for varying levels of cognitive state classification that are particularly well suited to performance prediction at different task stages. It is also worth noting that search time differed between conditions, with average search time in the buildings condition exceeding that of the other conditions. In many operational environments, visual search is self-terminated by the operator (e.g., airport bag screening, radar analysis); if different conditions allow classification of goal state, incorporating search time into a classifier may prove valuable.

An additional consideration is the type of classifier to use. Both linear and nonlinear models are available, and evidence suggests either may be effective [4]. Success, however, may interact with the time interval of data fed into each model. Nonlinear models were found to outperform linear models in two out of three cases when a 1 s interval was used, while linear models performed based when a 10 s interval was used [4]. It is worth noting that model performance varied between individuals such that one model did not exhibit superior performance across all individuals within any given condition. Likewise, an analysis of relative contribution of data streams (i.e., eye movements, blinks, pupil size) revealed that no single metric was a better predictor of cognitive state than the other metrics across all individuals for a given task. Therefore, individual calibration may be necessary when attempting to maximize the accuracy of a classifier.

Indeed, individual differences may affect classifier performance in a number of ways. For instance, eye tracking data quality may vary as a function of age, sex, ethnicity, and disease state [26, 31], cultural variation has been found to influence patterns of visual scene inspection [32], and older adults may exhibit different viewing patterns than younger adults [33]. In addition to differences between individuals, substantial variability may occur within an individual or an individual's environment over time. For instance, adjustments in ambient light intensity and sound, use of caffeine or nicotine, and eye makeup all influence the quality of eye tracking [34]. Controlling for these factors can be a particular challenge if eye tracking is to be implemented under necessarily changing environmental circumstances, such as during driving. A number of studies have indicated that classifiers trained and tested using physiological data obtained over a single session are capable of discriminating between cognitive states [4, 17, 35–37], but classifier accuracy may deteriorate over time due to these individual and environmental changes [38]. Training a new classifier is time consuming, so one compromise is to adjust the classifier at regular intervals using a small amount of newly collected data. For a task involving complex multitasking, an additional 2.5–7 min of data per level of task difficulty was found to significantly enhance classifier accuracy for the remainder of the day, though this improvement was attenuated when extending classifier use for an additional day without incorporating additional training data [38]. Therefore, it may be useful to consider applying additional training data on at least a daily basis in order to account for individual and environmental changes over time.

5   Conclusion

Several technologies offer the possibility of assessing cognitive state in real time using objective physiological data, allowing for online adjustment of task demands to avoid costly errors. There are a number of conditions that must be met for successful implementation of a real time cognitive assessment system in a job setting. The task performed must elicit cognitive states which are discriminable using technology that is practical within the job setting, these cognitive states must map onto performance in a meaningful way, and the classifier must account for differences both between and within individuals and environments. Current eye tracking technology makes this a feasible endeavor within certain contexts, yet there are a number of critical considerations to be cognizant of when attempting translation from a laboratory to an operational environment.

Acknowledgements. We wish to acknowledge James D. Morrow of Sandia National Laboratories, Albuquerque New Mexico for creating the software used in our study to display the visual stimuli and record subject responses.

Sandia National Laboratories is a multi-program laboratory managed and operated by Sandia Corporation, a wholly owned subsidiary of Lockheed Martin Corporation, for the U.S. Department of Energy's National Nuclear Security Administration under contract DE-AC04-94AL85000.

References

1. Haynes, J., Rees, G.: Decoding mental states from brain activity in humans. Nat. Rev. Neurosci. **7**(7), 523–534 (2006)
2. Liang, Y., et al.: Real-time detection of driver cognitive distraction using support vector machines. IEEE Trans. Intell. Trans. Syst. **8**(2), 340–350 (2007)
3. Neerincx, M.A., Harbers, M., Lim, D., van der Tas, V.: Automatic feedback on cognitive load and emotional state of traffic controllers. In: Harris, D. (ed.) EPCE 2014. LNCS, vol. 8532, pp. 42–49. Springer, Heidelberg (2014)
4. Marshall, S.P.: Identifying cognitive state from eye metrics. Aviat. Space Environ. Med. **78**(1), B165–B175 (2007)
5. deCharms, R.: Applications of real-time fMRI. Nat. Rev. Neurosci. **9**(9), 720–729 (2008)
6. Parra, L., et al.: Response error correction-a demonstration of improved human-machine performance using real-time EEG monitoring. IEEE Trans. Neural Syst. Rehabil. Eng. **11**(2), 173–177 (2003)
7. Cox, D., Savoy, R.: Functional magnetic resonance imaging (fMRI) "brain reading": detecting and classifying distributed patterns of fMRI activity in human visual cortex. NeuroImage **19**(2), 261–270 (2003)
8. Snow, M.P., Barker, R.A., O'Neill, K.R., Offer, B.W., Edwards, R.E.: Augmented cognition in a prototype uninhabited combat air vehicle operator console. In: Foundations of Augmented Cognition. 2nd edn., pp. 279–288 (2006)
9. Ikehara, C.S., Crosby, M.E.: Assessing cognitive load with physiological sensors. In: Proceedings of the 38th Annual HICSS 2005, p. 295a, January 2005
10. Palmer, E.D., Kobus, D.A.: The future of augmented cognition systems in education and training. In: Schmorrow, D.D., Reeves, L.M. (eds.) HCII 2007 and FAC 2007. LNCS (LNAI), vol. 4565, pp. 373–379. Springer, Heidelberg (2007)
11. Holmqvist, K., et al.: Eye Tracking. OUP Oxford, Oxford (2011)
12. Beatty, J., Lucero-Wagoner, B.: The pupillary system. Handb. Psychophysiol. **2**, 142–162 (2000)
13. Carlson-Radvansky, L.: Memory for relational information across eye movements. Percept. Psychophys. **61**(5), 919–934 (1999)
14. Stern, J., et al.: The endogenous eyeblink. Psychophysiology **21**(1), 22–33 (1984)
15. Farwell, L.A., Smith, S.S.: Using brain MERMER testing to detect knowledge despite efforts to conceal. J. Forensic Sci. **46**(1), 135–143 (2001)
16. Oliva, A., Schyns, P.G.: Diagnostic colors mediate scene recognition. Cogn. Psychol. **41**(2), 176–210 (2000)
17. Follet, B., et al.: New insights into ambient and focal visual fixations using an automatic classification algorithm. i-Perception **2**(6), 592–610 (2011)
18. Unema, P., et al.: Time course of information processing during scene perception: the relationship between saccade amplitude and fixation duration. Vis. Cogn. **12**(3), 473–494 (2005)
19. Scinto, L., et al.: Cognitive strategies for visual search. Acta Psychol. **62**(3), 263–292 (1986)
20. Lenneman, J.K., Lenneman, J., Cassavaugh, N., Backs, R.: Differential effects of focal and ambient visual processing demands on driving performance. In: Proceedings of the Fifth International Driving Symposium on Human Factors in Driver Assessment, Training, and Vehicle Design, vol. 5, pp. 306–312. University of Iowa Public Policy Center (2009)
21. Leibowitz, H.W., Shupert, C.L., Post, R.B.: The two modes of visual processing: implications for spatial orientation. In: PVHD, NASA Conference Publication, vol. 2306, pp. 41–44, March 1983

22. Biele, C., Kopacz, A., Krejtz, K.: Shall we care about the user's feelings? Influence of affect and engagement on visual attention. In: Proceedings of the International Conference on Multimedia, Interaction, Design and Innovation, p. 7. ACM, June 2013

23. Duchowski, A.T. Krejtz, K.: Visualizing dynamic ambient/focal attention with coefficient K. In: Proceedings of the First Workshop on ETVIS, Chicago, IL, October 2015

24. Yarbus, A.: Eye Movements and Vision. pp. 171–211. Plenum Press, New York (1967)

25. Chang, A., et al.: The human circadian system adapts to prior photic history. J. Physiol. **589**(5), 1095–1102 (2011)

26. Blignaut, P., Wium, D.: Eye-tracking data quality as affected by ethnicity and experimental design. Behav. Res. **46**(1), 67–80 (2013)

27. Haass, M.J., Matzen, L.E., Butler, K.M., Armenta, M.: A new method for categorizing scanpaths from eye tracking data. In: ETRA 2016, April 2016

28. Pannasch, S., Velichkovsky, B.: Distractor effect and saccade amplitudes: further evidence on different modes of processing in free exploration of visual images. Vis. Cogn. **17**(6–7), 1109–1131 (2009)

29. Parkhurst, D., et al.: Modeling the role of salience in the allocation of overt visual attention. Vis. Res. **42**(1), 107–123 (2002)

30. Judd, T., Ehinger, K., Durand, F., Torralba, A.: Learning to predict where humans look. In: 2009 IEEE 12th International Conference on Computer Vision, pp. 2106–2113. IEEE September 2009

31. Kuechenmeister, C.: Eye tracking in relation to age, sex, and illness. Arch. Gen. Psychiatry **34**(5), 578 (1977)

32. Chua, H.F., Boland, J.E., Nisbett, R.E.: Cultural variation in eye movements during scene perception. Proc. Nat. Acad. Sci. U.S.A. **102**(35), 12629–12633 (2005)

33. Romano Bergstrom, J.C., Olmsted-Hawala, E.L., Jans, M.E.: Age-related differences in eye tracking and usability performance: website usability for older adults. Int. J. Hum.-Comput. Inter. **29**(8), 541–548 (2013)

34. O'Brien, S.: Eye tracking in translation process research: methodological challenges and solutions. Methodol. Technol. Innov. Transl. Process. Res. **38**, 251–266 (2009)

35. Berka, C., et al.: Real-Time analysis of EEG indexes of alertness, cognition, and memory acquired with a wireless EEG headset. Int. J. Hum.-Comput. Inter. **17**(2), 151–170 (2004)

36. Freeman, F., et al.: Evaluation of an adaptive automation system using three EEG indices with a visual tracking task. Biol. Psychol. **50**(1), 61–76 (1999)

37. Gevins, A., et al.: Monitoring working memory load during computer-based tasks with EEG pattern recognition methods. Hum. Factors **40**(1), 79–91 (1998)

38. Christensen, J., et al.: The effects of day-to-day variability of physiological data on operator functional state classification. NeuroImage **59**(1), 57–63 (2012)

How Novices Read Source Code
in Introductory Courses on Programming:
An Eye-Tracking Experiment

Leelakrishna Yenigalla[1], Vinayak Sinha[1], Bonita Sharif[1(✉)],
and Martha Crosby[2]

[1] Youngstown State University, Youngstown, OH 44555, USA
{lkyenigalla, vsinha}@student.ysu.edu, bsharif@ysu.edu
[2] University of Hawaii at Mānoa, Honolulu, HI 96822, USA
crosby@hawaii.edu

Abstract. We present an empirical study using eye tracking equipment to understand how novices read source code in the context of two introductory programming classes. Our main goal is to begin to understand how novices read source code and to determine if we see any improvement in program comprehension as the course progresses. The results indicate that novices put in more effort and had more difficulty reading source code as they progress through the course. However, they are able to partially comprehend code at a later point in the course. The relationship between fixation counts and durations is linear but shows more clusters later in the course, indicating groups of students that learned at the same pace. The results also show that we did not see any significant shift in learning (indicated by the eye tracking metrics) during the course, indicating that there might be more than one course that needs to be taken over the course of a few years to realize the significance of the shift. We call for more studies over a student's undergraduate years to further learn about this shift.

Keywords: Eye tracking study · Program comprehension · Novices

1 Introduction

Programming involves both reading and writing source code [1]. Present computing education focuses on teaching how to write code, by taking reading skills for granted. Code reading which is also an important part of program comprehension is rarely considered [2]. If we understand how novices read source code, and what difficulty they face during initial learning, we can design better instruction tools, and educational environments. In this paper, we present an empirical study using eye tracking equipment to understand how novices read source code in the context of two introductory programming classes. Our main goal is to begin to understand how novices read code and determine any improvements in program comprehension as the course progresses. We use an eye tracker in the study as it is known that visual attention triggers mental processes in order to comprehend and solve a given task and effort put visually is directly linked to the cognitive effort [3]. A fixation is when the eye stabilizes on a

© Springer International Publishing Switzerland 2016
D.D. Schmorrow and C.M. Fidopiastis (Eds.): AC 2016, Part II, LNAI 9744, pp. 120–131, 2016.
DOI: 10.1007/978-3-319-39952-2_13

particular location for a particular duration. Saccades are quick movements between eye fixations. A *scan path* is a directed path formed by saccades between fixations. According to eye tracking literature, processing of visual information occurs during fixations but no processing occurs during saccades [4, 5].

The main contribution of this paper is an eye tracking empirical study that assesses how students, in particular novices read source code during a semester. Data collection was done using two methods: online questionnaires and an eye tracker (hardware and software). The ultimate goal is to develop better teaching strategies specifically targeted to novices and how they learn. To achieve this long-term goal, we first need to conduct several studies to determine individual behavior and determine if any differences exist before we can generalize this process. In this paper, we seek to answer the following research questions.

- RQ1: What progress do novices make as they go through a programming course?
- RQ2: Can we determine the difference in novice accuracy and progress using eye tracking data?
- RQ3: What are the similarities and differences in eye gaze between different tasks as time progresses in a course setting?

The paper is organized as follows. We give a brief description of related work in Sect. 2 followed by details on the experimental setup in Sect. 3. Section 4 presents observations and results. We present a discussion of the results in Sect. 5 followed by conclusions with ideas for future work.

2 Related Work

Busjahn and Schulte [1] conduct a study to find the importance of code reading and comprehension in teaching programming. They interviewed instructors to determine the importance of code reading in five categories: conceptualization, occurrences, and effects of successful code reading, challenges for learners, as well as approaches to facilitate code reading. The results tend to show that code reading is connected to comprehending programs and algorithms.

Sharif et al. study the impact of identifier style (i.e., camel case or underscore) on code reading and comprehension using an eye-tracker [6, 7]. They find camel case to be an overall better choice for comprehension. Sharafi et al. [8] extended this work and conducted an eye tracking study to determine if gender impacts the effort, time, and ability to recall identifiers.

Turner et al. [9] conducted a comparison study between C++ and Python source code to assess effect of programming language on student comprehension. They found no statistical difference between C++ and Python with respect to accuracy and time, but there is a significant difference between C++ and Python for fixation rate on buggy lines of code for find bug tasks.

Crosby et al. studied the effect of beacons on program comprehension and stated that beacons may be in the eye of the beholder [10]. Fan noted similar results on a study done in 2010 affirming results that suggest beacon identification is in the eyes of the beholder but noticed that the presence of comments does have an effect on code reading [11].

Hansen et al. looked into factors that made code hard to understand [12]. It was conducted online and used variants of Python source code to determine difficulty. The study was conducted on a wide range of subjects with varied programming experience. Their results led to a better understanding that experience helps when programmers believe that there may be errors but can actually hinder their ability when they haven't been trained for specific cases. Their results also showed that vertical whitespace was a factor in grouping sections of related statements together.

Busjahn et al. [13] talk about the relevance of eye tracking in computer education. In more recent work, Busjahn et al. [14] look into how source code reading differs from reading natural language and find that there is indeed a significant statistical difference.

3 The Study

An overview of the experiment is shown in Table 1. In order to understand the progression of the novice's understanding, we decided to conduct the experiment in two phases. The first phase was held in September 2014 and the second phase was held in November 2014. Different material was covered in class before each phase was conducted. The novice was instructed to read the code snippets shown to them and answer a comprehension question. They were also asked about the level of difficulty and their confidence level of answering the questions related to the code snippets.

The main dependent variables we want to determine that might be affected by the two phases are the accuracy, time, fixation count, and fixation duration.

Table 1. Experiment overview

Goal	To understand how novices read source code
Main factor	Time between testing: Phase 1 and Phase 2
Dependent variables	Accuracy, time, fixation count, fixation duration
Secondary factor	Class (Group1, Group2)

3.1 Hypotheses

Based on the research questions presented above, four detailed null hypotheses on each of the four dependent variables are given below.

H_a: There is no significant difference in accuracy between Phase 1 and Phase 2.
H_t: There is no significant difference in time between Phase 1 and Phase 2.
H_{fc}: There is no significant difference in fixation counts between Phase 1 and Phase 2.
H_{fd}: There is no significant difference in fixation durations between Phase 1 and Phase 2.

Alternative Hypotheses: There is a significant difference in accuracy, time, fixation count, and fixation duration when it comes to the two phases. Thus it is expected that if some improvement in learning occurs then there will be large differences between Phase 1 and Phase 2.

3.2   Participants

We recruited students from two classes in Fall 2014 at Youngstown State University (YSU). The first class was an object oriented beginner programming class and the second class was the server-side class on web development. We refer to the OOP class as Group 1 and the Server side class as Group 2 throughout the rest of the paper. There were 11 and 10 students in the OOP class and the server side class respectively. The syllabus for the OOP class was observed during the creation of the tasks. We asked our participants to self-assess their skills in a pre-questionnaire. Even though Group 2 had students with slightly more experience than Group 1, they were still novices. Figure 1 shows demographics of participants.

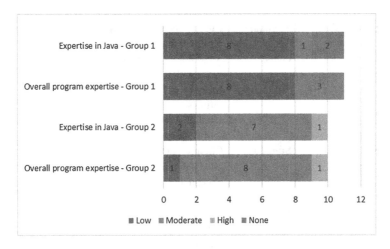

Fig. 1. Java expertise in both groups (Color figure online)

3.3   Tasks

We designed the tasks for both the phases of the study based on what the novices covered in the class syllabus for OOP in Group 1. In Phase 1, the tasks involved the following topics: array of strings, static keyword, random, substring, and static class methods. In Phase 2, the tasks involved topics such as GUI and events, exception handling, validation and OO inheritance and polymorphism. See Table 2 for an overview of the tasks used in the study. The complete set of study questions and programs including all background questions and post questionnaires can be found at http://seresl.csis.ysu.edu/HCII2016.

This study had six stimuli (programs) in each phase. The first phase had two tasks: "What is the output?" and "Give a summary". In the second phase we restricted the task to only giving a summary. There were easy, medium, and difficult programs with varying length to test different scenarios. In Phase 2, a program that was conceptually similar to a program is Phase 1 was also used to see if it was easier to comprehend after a couple of months. The *Primes* program was compared with *CheckString* from phase 2 in the difficult category, *StringProcessingDemo* was compared with *TextClass* and *Count* was compared with *PrintPattern*. They are shown in bold in Table 2.

Table 2. Overview of tasks and programs used in the study

Program name	Task	Overview of the program	Difficulty level	Phase 1	Phase 2
StringCheck	Output	String comparison	Easy	X	
Primes	**Summary**	**Finds all primes <=n**	**Difficult**	**X**	
TestPassArray	Output	Swapping array elements	Medium	X	
StringProcessingDemo	**Summary**	**Change part of a string**	**Easy**	**X**	
Rectangle	Output	Area of a rectangle	Difficult	X	
Count	**Summary**	**Number of times a letter occur in a string**	**Medium**	**X**	
TextClass	**Summary**	**Change part of a string**	**Easy**		**X**
TestingCircle	Summary	Exception handling	Medium		X
CheckString	**Summary**	**Check if string input is a palindrome**	**Difficult**		**X**
DoSomething	Summary	Selection sort	Easy		X
PrintPattern	**Summary**	**Prints three rows of stars in triangle**	**Medium**		**X**
KeyboardPanel	Summary	Draws a letter and moves it using arrow keys	Difficult		X

3.4 Data Collection and Apparatus

All subjects answered the six tasks in each phase via an online questionnaire presented as a Google Form. Each question was timed and the subjects' eyes were tracked. The subjects had to type the answer in the space provided in the online forms after they finished each task. We obtained IRB training and approval before we began this study.

The Tobii X60 eye tracker was used in this study. It is a 60 Hz video-based binocular remote eye tracker that does not require the user to wear any head gear. It generates 60 samples of eye data per second. The average accuracy for the Tobii eye tracker is 0.5 degrees which averages to about 15 pixels. The eye tracker compensates for head movement during the study. The study was conducted on a 24 in. monitor with screen resolution set at 1920 * 1080. The eye gaze data includes timestamps, gaze positions, fixations and their durations, pupil sizes, and validity codes. In this study, we only analyze fixations and their durations.

4 Study Results

We now present the results and seek to provide answers to our research questions posed in the Introduction. Since our data is not normal and we have a small sample size, we use non-parametric measures to determine significance using the Wilcoxon paired test with alpha set at 0.05 that determines significance with a 5 % error and 95 % confidence.

4.1 Accuracy and Time

Each of the twelve programs were anonymously scored by the first author as fully correct, partially correct, or completely incorrect where partially correct got a rating of 0.5 and fully correct got a score of 1. With respect to correctness in Group 1, Wilcoxon test shows that Phase 1 total accuracy was significantly less accurate than Phase 2

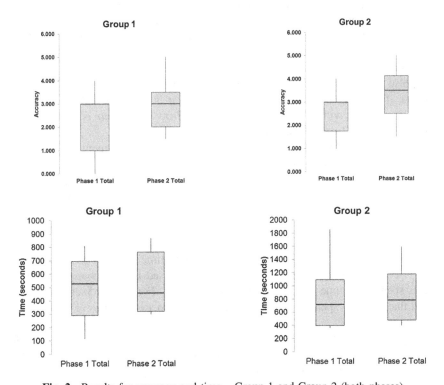

Fig. 2. Results for accuracy and time – Group 1 and Group 2 (both phases)

($p = 0.045$). In Group 2, Wilcoxon test also shows that Phase 1 total accuracy was significant less than Phase 2 ($p = 0.010$). We see that in Group 1, novices were more accurate in Phase 2 compared to Phase 1. They were also able to partially give answers to the programs in the second phase. Refer to Fig. 2 for the descriptive statistics.

With respect to time, there was no significant difference between Phase 1 and Phase 2 in terms of overall time of both groups. However we did find a significant difference between the following programs (Refer to Table 2 for more information on the tasks).

- *Count* and *PrintPattern* ($p = 0.012$) – Medium difficulty
- *StringProcessingDemo* and TextClass ($p = 0.049$) – Easy difficulty

where the program task in Phase 2 took longer to solve.

We notice that the *StringCheck* program that was the easiest was done in the least amount of time with not much variation between the subjects. The *Primes* and the *Count* programs were at the difficult and medium level of difficulty respectively. We notice that there is a much larger variation among the students for the harder programs that involve more programming constructs. In Phase 2, we found that the easy program *TextClass* took subjects longer to solve than its comparable counterpart in Phase 1 (i.e. *StringCheck*). We could speculate that this is because the novices start to focus more at the code and genuinely try to understand it. We notice this similar trend for Group 2 for the easy programs (i.e. *StringCheck* and *TextClass*). Group 2 took longer for almost all the tasks since they were more experienced than Group 1 and put in the effort to understand the programs to produce a reasonably correct answer. We also wanted to determine if there is any correlation between time and accuracy. We find that with increased amount of time, we see higher accuracy. In Phase 2, we again notice a step shift for two sets of students indicating that they might have learned in a similar fashion throughout the course.

We also compare programs that are similar in concept in Phase 1 and Phase 2 to determine if learning improved. The program *Count* is matched with *PrintPattern*, *Primes* is matched with *CheckString*, and *StringProcessingDemo* is matched with *TextClass* in Phase 1 and Phase 2 respectively.

Group 1 - We find that in the case of *Count* and *PrintPattern*, many of the students could not get the program correct in Phase 1 but many of them got *PrintPattern* partially correct in Phase 2. Comparison between *Primes* and *CheckString* shows that half of the total students of Group 1 showed partial improvement in accuracy solving *Checkstring* in Phase 2, hence there is no big difference in accuracy. When we compare *StringProcessingDemo* with *Textclass*, we noticed that three novices answered better in the second phase and four novices answered with the same level of accuracy (correct) in both phases. In terms of time, novices spent more time on the *Count* program in Phase 1. For *Primes* and *CheckString*, this was reversed because a majority of the students spent more time on *CheckString* from Phase 2. For the third set of programs we find that students spent more time reading *StringProcessingDemo* of Phase 1 than *TextClass* of Phase 2.

Group 2 - Between *Count* and *PrintPattern*, we found a huge jump in accuracy for *PrintPattern* in Phase 2. For the second set, four students had the same level of accuracy. Two of them answered better in the second phase with two answering incorrectly in the second phase. In terms of time, we see that half of the students spent more time reading *Count* of Phase 1 compared to *PrintPattern* of Phase 2. For *Primes* vs. *CheckString*, four students took longer for *Primes* (Phase 1) than *CheckString* in Phase 2. Six students took longer for the *StringProcessingDemo* in Phase 1 than the program in Phase 2. This could indicate higher cognitive load.

4.2   Fixation Counts and Fixation Durations

Before we calculate fixation counts and durations we need to define areas of interest (AOIs) for which to collect them in. In this study, an AOI comprises each line of source code. The number of AOIs are equivalent to the number of lines in the program. We do not count any eye gazes that fall outside these lines i.e., blank space. In this paper, we only focus on the total lines AOI and not on an individual line-level analysis. The Wilcoxon test did not report any significant results for fixation counts or fixation durations between phases. In Phase 1, the highest fixation counts were on *Primes*, and the *Count* program. In Phase 2, *TestingCircle* and the *DoSomething* programs were the hardest for the participants. Only one participant got the *DoSomething* program correct in Group 1. None of the students got the *DoSomething* program correct in Group 2. The same trend is observed in the fixation counts in Group 2 for Phase 1 and Phase 2. See Fig. 3 for fixation counts in Group 1 for both phases.

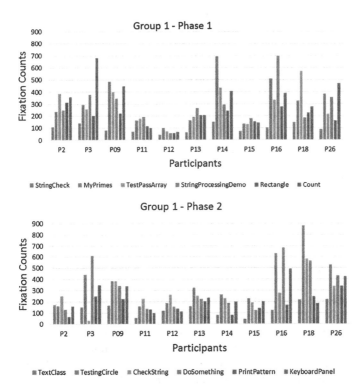

Fig. 3. Fixation counts for Group 1 (both phases) (Color figure online)

See Fig. 4 for fixation durations for Group 1. We have provided the fixation duration figures for Group 2 on the supplementary website listed in Sect. 3.3. In Group 1, the fixation durations were higher for *Primes* and *Count* programs in Phase 1. In Phase 2, *TestingCircle* and *DoSomething* had the highest fixation durations and the most variability between subjects. This indicates that not all the students were learning the concepts at the same rate. The standard deviation of the distribution for these programs was larger than the others.

In Group 2, for Phase 1, we find the most fixation durations on the *Primes* and *StringProcessingDemo* programs. In Phase 2, *TestingCircle* was the most difficult program since it had the highest number of mean fixation durations. This indicates higher cognitive load which is clearly harder for the novices to understand. Regressions (fixating over the same lines over and over) is also noticed for these programs.

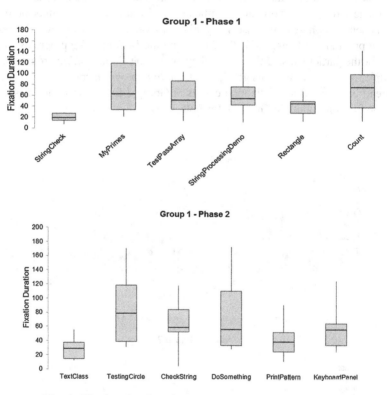

Fig. 4. Fixation durations for Group 1 – Phase 1 and Phase 2

We now discuss any relationship, if one exists, between the two dependent variables: fixation count and fixation duration. We notice that as the fixation count increases the fixation duration also increases in a linear fashion. In Phase 2, the relationship is more clustered indicating groups of students that learned at the same pace. We can clearly see three clusters in Fig. 5. The slope of both these graphs (Phase 1 (not shown) and Phase 2) is not the same indicating that in Phase 2 novices took the study more seriously taking longer time to accurately answer the questions.

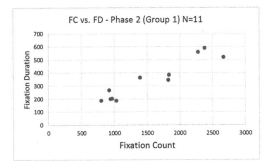

Fig. 5. Fixation count vs. fixation duration for Group 1 – Phase 2

4.3 Threats to Validity

We discuss how we minimize the main threats to validity in our study. The research participants did not know about the hypotheses used in the research. They only knew that they would participate in helping us understand how code is read and summarized. During the study, there was minimal contact between the experimenter and the participants. The experimenter did not interact or direct the participants to complete the questions in one way or another. We used the Wilcoxon paired test since we were comparing the same subject across Phase 1 and Phase 2. We used non-parametric measures due to our low sample size and non-normality of the data.

We tested this in only two classes at YSU. More tests need to be done to generalize the findings presented here. It is possible that there could have been some syllabus deviations in the classes that was unknown to experimenters which might have caused comprehension problems, however, after interviewing the students, this did not seem to be the case. They were exposed to all the ideas tested. Group 2 students were made aware of the topics that were covered in the object oriented class (Group 1).

In the first phase, we asked the subjects two types of tasks: determine the output and summarize the program. In the second phase, we only asked the subjects to summarize the programs. This could affect the results as well. We found that the summary included the output as a subset i.e., most students state the output of the program in the summary.

5 Discussion

We did not observe much progress in the novices in Group 1 however, there was a tendency to partially understand what the program is about. It is possible that one course is not enough to have a student master the concepts in Java. Ideally, we would want to follow a novice until they graduate to determine when the change in their mental model occurs. In one of the programs with a ternary operator, a novice was having a hard time understanding it as evidenced by many fixations and regressions on that line. We also noticed that novices tend to read source code like reading natural language text as pointed out in [14]. They do it in a linear sequential fashion.

We now revisit our hypotheses as presented in Sect. 3.1. Based on the results presented in Sect. 4, we are able to reject H_a as we do see higher accuracy in Phase 2 tasks. With respect to H_t when we take into account all the tasks together and compare Phase 1 and Phase 2 as a whole, we are not able to reject this hypothesis. We also did not find any significant differences between fixation counts and durations between Phase 1 and Phase 2. We are unable to reject H_{fc} and H_{fd}. Some possible explanations could be that the differences are more fine-grained and much more individualized to the specific student. A more fine-grained analysis across and between lines in the programs might produce a different result. We have left this as a future exercise.

6 Conclusions and Future Work

How does a novice read and comprehend code? In order to start to answer this question, we conducted a semester long experiment to determine if students learn the concepts presented during the semester. We ran the study in two phases with a 7-week separation between phases. We hypothesize that the students will be more accurate and spend less time on programs that they are familiar with when compared with other new and unfamiliar ones. We found that in both groups (classes) the novices were significantly less accurate in Phase 1 than Phase 2 but there was no significant difference in terms of time. In fact, more time was spent in Phase 2 to produce a correct answer. This came as a surprise at first but on second thought, we believe students were trying hard to understand code and put in more effort even though they clearly found the tasks difficult. Group 2 (still novices) had a slightly higher expertise in Java performed slightly better but not significantly. Also, in Phase 2 they were partially able to tell what the program did whereas in Phase 1 they bluntly stated that they did not know what the program's output was or how to summarize the program.

In the future, we plan on conducting a line by line analysis of the programs to identify patterns of lines that the novices looked at most and least. This will give us some idea on which parts of the program they looked at the most and had the hardest time with. A look at the transitions between beacons and chunks in the programs will also be beneficial since it has been shown that experts tend to chunk things together. For example, many of the novices did not realize one of the programs shown in Phase 2 was a sorting program. They were not able to chunk yet, however if we analyze their line-level transitions, it might provide a better indication of how they comprehend the loops involved in the sort. We also plan to continue this research by conducting this study at a much lower level such as CS0 or CS1 so we have a different aspect of how students learn when they are exposed to no programming language whatsoever. Finally, we believe one way to determine when a novice student is on their way to becoming an expert (i.e., mastering concepts), is to follow a small sample of students across their undergraduate study sampling eye movements on relevant tasks. Such a study will help us study progression as it occurs and then perhaps we could say that a shift in a student's mental model has occurred.

Acknowledgements. We thank all the students for their time and participation in this study. Many thanks to Teresa Busjahn for providing inspiration for some tasks in the study.

References

1. Busjahn, T., Schulte, C.: The use of code reading in teaching programming. In: Proceedings of the 13th Koli Calling International Conference on Computing Education Research, New York, NY, USA, pp. 3–11 (2013)
2. Busjahn, T., Schulte, C., Busjahn, A.: Analysis of code reading to gain more insight in program comprehension. In: Proceedings of the 11th Koli Calling International Conference on Computing Education Research, New York, NY, USA, pp. 1–9 (2011)
3. Just, M.A., Carpenter, P.A.: A theory of reading: from eye fixations to comprehension. Psychol. Rev. **87**(4), 329–354 (1980)
4. Rayner, K.: Eye movements in reading and information processing: 20 years of research. Psychol. Bull. **124**(3), 372–422 (1998)
5. Duchowski, A.T.: Eye Tracking Methodology: Theory and Practice. Springer-Verlag New York Inc., Secaucus (2007)
6. Binkley, D., Davis, M., Lawrie, D., Maletic, J.I., Morrell, C., Sharif, B.: The impact of identifier style on effort and comprehension. Empir. Softw. Eng. **18**(2), 219–276 (2012)
7. Sharif, B., Maletic, J.I.: An eye tracking study on camelCase and under_score Identifier styles. In: 2010 IEEE 18th International Conference on Program Comprehension, pp. 196–205 (2010)
8. Sharafi, Z., Soh, Z., Gueheneuc, Y.-G., Antoniol, G.: Women and men - different but equal: on the impact of identifier style on source code reading. In: 2012 IEEE 20th International Conference on Program Comprehension, ICPC, pp. 27–36 (2012)
9. Turner, R., Falcone, M., Sharif, B., Lazar, A.: An eye-tracking study assessing the comprehension of C++ and Python source code. In: Proceedings of the Symposium on Eye Tracking Research and Applications, New York, NY, USA, pp. 231–234 (2014)
10. Crosby, M.E., Scholtz, J., Wiedenbeck, S.: The roles beacons play in comprehension for novice and expert programmers. In: 14th Workshop of the Psychology of Programming Interest Group, pp. 58–73 (2002)
11. Fan, Q.: The effects of beacons, comments, and tasks on program comprehension process in software maintenance. Ph.D. Dissertation, University of Maryland at Baltimore County, Catonsville, MD, USA (2010)
12. Hansen, M.E., Goldstone, R.L., Lumsdaine, A.: What makes code hard to understand? CoRR, vol. abs/1304.5257 (2013)
13. Busjahn, T., Schulte, C., Sharif, B., Simon, Begel, A., Hansen, M., Bednarik, R., Orlov, P., Ihantola, P., Shchekotova, G., Antropova, M.: Eye tracking in computing education. In: Proceedings of the Tenth Annual Conference on International Computing Education Research, New York, NY, USA, pp. 3–10 (2014)
14. Busjahn, T., Bednarik, R., Begel, A., Crosby, M., Paterson, J., Schulte, C., Sharif, B., Tamm, S.: Eye movements in code reading: relaxing the linear order. In: International Conference on Program Comprehension, pp. 255–265 (2015)

Human Cognition and Behavior in Complex Tasks and Environments

Implementing User-Centered Methods and Virtual Reality to Rapidly Prototype Augmented Reality Tools for Firefighters

Tess Bailie[1,2(✉)], Jim Martin[1,2], Zachary Aman[1], Ryan Brill[1], and Alan Herman[1]

[1] Human-Computer Interaction Institute, Computer Science, Carnegie Mellon University,
Pittsburgh, USA
zackyuaman@gmail.com, brill.ryan@gmail.com, alanhp@gmail.com
[2] Draper, Cambridge, USA
{tbailie,jmartin}@draper.com

Abstract. Designing and testing products for high-risk emergencies is a challenging task, especially due to the inhibitive cost of building testing environments that recreate the psychological pressures of the field. The chaotic nature of emergency environments makes gathering accurate data amidst the chaos of such environments difficult, while ethical and practical considerations limit prototype deployment in potentially life-threatening situations. These environments pose serious risk to physical and mental well-being. This paper provides a case study to examine the benefits and drawbacks of a Virtual Reality (VR) environment to test prototypes of a tool for firefighters. The VR simulated environment out performs a physical simulation because it is cheaper and safer, generates more reliable data, and provides greater control and flexibility of prototypes, allowing designers to test prototypes more rapidly than in a physical environment. This paper summarizes a 9-month Draper-sponsored capstone project with 5 HCII students.

Keywords: Virtual reality · Augmented cognition · Rapid prototyping · Human centered design · Contextual design

1 Introduction

Firefighters face immense stress and physical trauma when responding to a call. Physical dangers include burns, extreme heat, high noise levels, smoke inhalation, heavy equipment, and building collapse. Active structure fires are disorienting, largely unknown, and highly dangerous. Firefighters enter a building with less than 15 min of air in their tank and the knowledge that, in the right conditions, a fire can spread faster than they can put it out. In these harsh conditions, the radios that firefighters rely on for communication often fall behind their pace of work as the scene demands increasingly more of their attention and they cease to have a hand free to operate their radio mouthpiece. Systems deployed in these environments need to be adequately vetted prior to testing in working fires and must be fully accepted and trusted by firefighters in order to be adopted into use.

© Springer International Publishing Switzerland 2016
D.D. Schmorrow and C.M. Fidopiastis (Eds.): AC 2016, Part II, LNAI 9744, pp. 135–144, 2016.
DOI: 10.1007/978-3-319-39952-2_14

The research group used the Human-Centered process to research and design a tool to enhance communication for firefighters on-scene. This process optimizes the traditional development process by bringing a "fail-fast" mentality to support rapid prototyping. Rather than focusing on fully developing a single idea to high fidelity, the human-centered design process makes rapid progress on multiple ideas toward a viable product by quickly eliminating flawed concepts. This is especially important for systems performing in dangerous scenarios, where failure in a single dimension can be enough to render a product useless.

This paper presents a case study involving the design and testing of multi-modal feedback supporting spatial orientation and task completion. Specifically, the project focused on supporting the situational awareness of firefighters within a burning building. Situational awareness is defined as each firefighter's general awareness of the past and current physical location of themselves and other actors on the scene. By focusing on the specific context of victim search and rescue within a multi-story building, the team built a case-specific model using Unity3D to simulate a burning building. This model provided a platform to quickly prototype and measure the efficacy of feedback methods across the visual, auditory, and haptic channels. Furthermore, the system housing this model was mobile, enabling researchers to go test prototypes with first responders to ensure solutions could realistically fit into the rescue workflow.

2   Design Constraints of Target Environment

Research revealed emergency responders operate in three tiers: oversight or management, supply and personnel coordination, and frontline response. This project focused on the front-line responders. Thirty-one interviews were conducted with police officers, firefighters and EMS responders. The driving insights from research were as follows: Firstly, the limitations of radio tend to block useful information and can actually increase the cognitive load on users as radio channels get busy. Secondly, as responders use the radio with less frequency, their current understanding of the factors in the scene, get synced up less frequently and communication breakdowns compound. This is a critical flaw, since teamwork and communication is crucial to mission success and maintenance personal well-being in these situations. Finally, the nature of fire response is extremely time-sensitive; depending on conditions, fires can double in size anywhere from every few minutes to every few seconds.

During work shifts, responders must be on constant alert. If there is an emergency, they have to leave within minutes to the scene. Responders operate in small team when on the response site; firefighters are always on shift with a team of four. Responders develop close ties to their teammates. This closeness is often essential in a response scenario where being in sync with each others' actions is elemental to coordinated responses. Experience working with one another increases each team member's ability to understand and predict the actions of other members (Fig. 1).

Rayner, K.: Eye movements in reading and information processing: 20 years of research. Psychol. Bull. **124**(3), 372 (1998)

Rayner, K., Chace, K.H., Slattery, T.J., Ashby, J.: Eye movements as reflections of comprehension processes in reading. Sci. Stud. Read. **10**(3), 241–255 (2006)

Reid, G.B., Nygren, T.E.: The subjective workload assessment technique: a scaling procedure for measuring mental workload. Adv. Psychol. **52**, 185–218 (1988)

Tsai, M.-J., Hou, H.-T., Lai, M.-L., Liu, W.-Y., Yang, F.-Y.: Visual attention for solving multiple-choice science problem: an eye-tracking analysis. Comput. Educ. **58**(1), 375–385 (2012)

Tsang, P.S., Velazquez, V.L.: Diagnosticity and multidimensional subjective workload ratings. Ergonomics **39**(3), 358–381 (1996)

van Gog, T., Scheiter, K.: Eye tracking as a tool to study and enhance multimedia learning. Learn. Instr. **20**(2), 95–99 (2010)

Yarbus, A.: Eye Movements and Vision. Plenum Press, New York (1967)

Exploring the Hybrid Space

Theoretical Framework Applying Cognitive Science in Military Cyberspace Operations

Øyvind Jøsok[1(✉)], Benjamin J. Knox[1], Kirsi Helkala[1], Ricardo G. Lugo[2],
Stefan Sütterlin[2], and Paul Ward[3]

[1] Norwegian Defence, Cyber Academy, Lillehammer, Norway
ojosok@cyfor.mil.no, {f-bknox,khelkala}@mil.no
[2] Department of Psychology, Lillehammer University College, Lillehammer, Norway
{Ricardo.Lugo,Stefan.Sutterlin}@hil.no
[3] The Applied Cognition & Cognitive Engineering (AC2E) Research Group,
University of Huddersfield, Manchester, UK
P.Ward@hud.ac.uk

Abstract. Operations in cyberspace are enabled by a digitized battlefield. The ability to control operations in cyberspace has become a central goal for defence forces. As a result, terms like cyber power, cyberspace operations and cyber deterrence have begun to emerge in military literature in an effort to describe and highlight the importance of related activities. Future military personnel, in all branches, will encounter the raised complexity of joint military operations with cyber as the key enabler. The constant change and complexity raises the demands for the structure and content of education and training. This interdisciplinary contribution discusses the need for a better understanding of the relationships between cyberspace and the physical domain, the cognitive challenges this represents, and proposes a theoretical framework - the Hybrid Space - allowing for the application of psychological concepts in assessment, training and action.

Keywords: Cyberspace · Physical domain · Cyber-physical system · Cyber security · Socio-technical system · Hybrid space · Human factors

1 Introduction

"The future commander needs to be as focused on cyber as on other environmental factors" [1]. This statement summarizes the current dilemma of contradictory task profiles and cognitive demands for military personnel, which result in challenges that present themselves across the social, physical and cyber domains. The complexity of cognitive work associated with human-technological interaction with multiple interdependent, interconnected and networked environments is compounded [2], as these human and technological agents consequently bring their own assets and goals (e.g., informational, social, physical, cyber [3–5]) into the operating and decision making space. Moreover, activity in this space is further complicated or complexified as each agent needs to secure their own assets, in order to maintain freedom of movement [17].

© Springer International Publishing Switzerland 2016
D.D. Schmorrow and C.M. Fidopiastis (Eds.): AC 2016, Part II, LNAI 9744, pp. 178–188, 2016.
DOI: 10.1007/978-3-319-39952-2_18

Examining asset protection from a security perspective is important to ensure security is not compromised, all assets need to be protected from current and future threats, both internal and external to the system. Simultaneously, vulnerabilities inherent within the entire socio-technical system (STS) have to be managed [5]. According to Whitman and Mattord [3] an asset is a protected organizational resource. Therefore, prioritizing these resources is achieved by weighting assets based on values ranging from: criticality, profitability, replacement or protection expenses, and embarrassment or loss of liability factor if the asset is revealed [3]. Assets and their vulnerabilities are interconnected. If an asset is lost, this loss has an effect on other assets and their vulnerabilities.

Expanded digitization and global network coverage [6] will connect people and physical infrastructure to cyberspace and to other physical entities via cyberspace. In turn, this will reveal novel and unforeseen connected vulnerabilities that requires human cognition to self-regulate and transform[1]. Several authors have identified a lack of understanding regarding how the connectivity of agents has negative consequences for decision making and action, especially relating to third party infrastructure [8]. We argue that today's decision makers have to acknowledge and understand how to prioritize multiple assets based on known and unknown vulnerabilities and risks. Achieving this level of understanding within a contradictory and hybrid landscape requires cognitive flexibility to control the multiple situational dynamics that can occur simultaneously between assets in the physical domain, the social domain and cyberspace.

In a military context, these hybrid conditions create challenges for efficient decision making as final responsibility lies with ranking officers whose past experience and current practice, including key command and control activities such as sensemaking and decision making, are rooted in and influenced by factors in the physical domain [7, 8]. Despite their affinity for the physical over cyber media, increasingly, officer understanding and decision making is being guided by information perceived, interpreted, evaluated and communicated to them by lower ranking, and often younger, officers who operate comfortably in this domain [10]. Agents equipped with the necessary capabilities to translate phenomena originating in cyberspace into the physical domain can potentially provide the crucial knowledge bridge required to influence far reaching military and political decision making.

The conjunction of age, rank and experience reveals a didactic shift in command responsibility and decision making. This can be addressed through better understanding of competencies or better definitions of competencies. The arrival of 'cyber' has revealed evidence that suggests more understanding of skill-sets and agile leadership [12] can contribute to defining human competencies as requisites for performance in contemporary military operations.

Huge investments have been made to develop and implement state-of-the-art technologies across sectors to improve human efficiency. Digitization has increased

---

[1] Kegan and Lahey [2] define the self-transforming mind as: "able to step back and reflect on the limits of our own ideology or personal authority; see that any one system or self-organization is in some way partial or incomplete; be friendlier toward contradiction and opposites; seek to hold on to multiple systems rather than projecting all but one onto the other" [2, p. 17].

information flow and interdependability of technological systems [13]. Efforts to leverage human performance have been answered by new technologies [15], yet the results seem only to increase cognitive demand [14, 16]. The cognitive workload placed on humans in this context exceed those in most common contexts [14]. Making the right decisions in Computer Network Operations (CNO) has added value given the potential for unknown or unintended consequences [17].

Several authors argued that there is a current lack of understanding of the human factors necessary to operate effectively, safely and securely in this complex space [9, 11, 18, 19]. This is revealed through the inability to adequately integrate CNO into contemporary military operations [17, 20], a pressing need for cyber related study materials at all command levels [8, 21], and insufficient career structures for cyber personnel [22]. The Hybrid Space approach acknowledges these factors as points of departure for continuing research that integrates situational dynamics in cyberspace and the physical domain, with individual cognitive skill-sets, psychological determinants of action and communicative aspects, within a merging socio-technical and cyber-physical system.

2   The Hybrid Space Framework

The Hybrid Space (Fig. 1) frames the interconnection between cyberspace and the physical domain, whilst simultaneously demonstrating the tension between tactical and strategic goals in decision making and action (compression of command-levels) in a future operating environment context. Individual domain specific competencies, experience and rank determine performance levels and behaviours in a organisational and institutional landscape that necessitate the integration, or at least complementary juxtaposition, of cyber and physical domains (henceforth, hybrid). Understanding the processes and actions required to enhance and accelerate these capabilities may hold the key to releasing the tension between command levels when attempting to project military power.

This framework acknowledges the Cyber-Physical System (CPS) and the effects of automation through cyber-based technological operations on the physical world. CPS research has been predominantly focused on the left side (Fig. 2a) of the horizontal axis and has been defined as "...the close interaction of computing systems and physical objects..." [24, p. 3]. With some exceptions (e.g., [37]), research in the area of STS - defined as; "...taking both social factors and technological factors into consideration" [25, p. 720] - resides primarily on the right of our horizontal axis (Fig. 2b). Going forward, we view the field of STS research exploring how people will cope and perform in a digitizing society.

In a pre-cyber landscape, the vertical axis has divided doctrine into three levels; tactical, operational and strategic [23]. The intent of the vertical axis in the Hybrid Space framework is to transfer conventional knowledge of military command levels and situate this doctrine into a present day context. This novel approach is representative of today's digitized context; where cyber pervades all aspects of military planning and leadership [23]. Cyber is shaping how traditional command levels are responding. It has resulted in the compression of command levels [10] as a means of adaptation for coping and

Hybrid Space

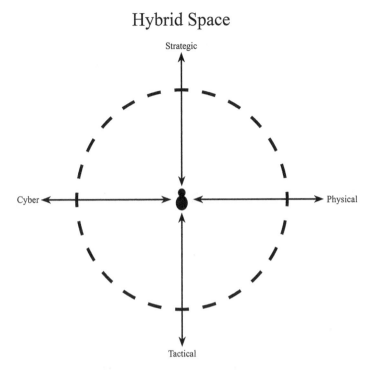

Fig. 1. The hybrid space framework

performance. In turn, bisecting the vertical axis with the horizontal axis reveals a convergence of complexity. The purpose of the Hybrid Space is to open the space for exploration in competencies, human behavior and cognitive processes [19] that occur, or need to occur, in and around this point of convergence.

Viewing this complex terrain through the lense of the Hybrid Space - where human and macrocognitive factors play a significant role [19] - can serve to bridge the expertise gap between cyberspace and the physical domain. Cyberspace operations merge in-depth tactical knowledge with strategic appreciation, which can create tension at different command levels as it challenges traditional military doctrine, education models and cultures [8, 16]. Inconsistencies in tactical and strategic operations across organizations result in difficulties in collaborative sensemaking with respect to core aspects of defining cyber and, as such, present significant barriers for CPS and STS interoperability [8]. Establishing clarity in this Hybrid Space is needed, not only to ensure effective intra and inter-organisational communication, cooperation and coordination, but to ensure national and international asset security.

2.1 Horizontal Axis

As indicated, the horizontal axis shown in Fig. 2 of the Hybrid Space framework acknowledges earlier research in CPS and STS. CPS research acknowledges the

Hybrid Space

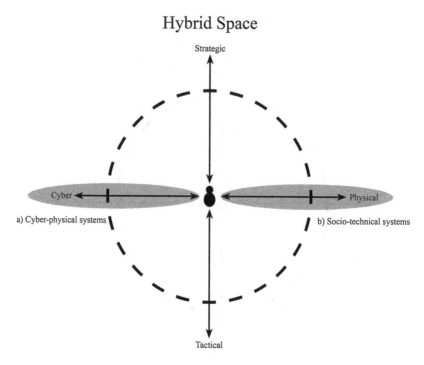

Fig. 2. The hybrid space framework in relation to CPS: "…the close interaction of computing systems and physical objects…" [24, p. 3] and STS: "…taking both social factors and technological factors into consideration" [25, p. 720].

integration of the cyber domain with the physical world [26, 27], but current frameworks describing CPS and cyber attack categorization are mostly technology-centric and tend to neglect the human factor [9, 19]. On the other hand, STS situates a human in the center and is composed of social, management and technical subsystems [28], but in most research conducted to date, STS has not fully embraced the role of cyberspace, as the technical subsystem only provides the necessary functions to meet the roles of the human [28]. We argue that including all environmental factors solely in an additive manner does not satisfy the level of complexity facing individuals and teams operating within these overlapping fields.

In the Hybrid Space framework, we extend the notion of STS to include cyber operations as well as the coordinating operations that result from its integration. As a result, the cognitive work in which humans engage, and the systems themselves, are increasingly complex [14]. Work is highly interactive and comprised of humans, agents and artifacts. Information may be novel, deceptive, and/or limited, and is typically distributed across space and time; Tactical goals (i.e., how to deal with a specific new threat) are frequently ill-defined, and there is often a need for conflict resolution between strategic goals (e.g., protect against a known state threat actor) and lower-order goals that are both dynamic and emergent. Much of this requires significant preparation, planning and replanning, as well as a considerable degree of domain-specific skill (such as situation assessment, sensemaking, and decision making skills within STS and CPS). A key feature is the requirement for proficiency at handling novelty, so that humans can adapt on the fly to changing demands. To complicate matters further, the stakes are almost always high, and uncertainty, time-constraints and stress are seldom absent. Moreover, tactics and strategy that dictate how work should unfold are typically constrained by broader professional, organizational, and institutional practice and policy [29]. The macrocognitive demand characteristics placed on young personnel when operating in the Hybrid Space exceeds those in most common contexts. Making the right decisions in the Hybrid Space has added value given the potential for unknown or unintended consequences [30].

The horizontal axis in the Hybrid Space model acknowledges the simultaneous presence and incongruent needs of cyberspace and the physical domain. Attacks in cyberspace do not differ from conventional attacks insofar as they generate effects beyond the intended domain of interest [9, 17]. However, they do differ in the way that consequences might be unintended or hidden, revealed in unconventional timeframes or affect third party interests. This incongruency necessitates a range of skill sets including highly developed technical skills (e.g., coding, programming, analysis, etc.), considerable macrocognitive skills (perception, interpretation, evaluation) and effective interpersonal and psychological skills (perspective taking, communicative skills, for instance to convey mission impact information to a commander). This axis highlights the need for a new category of personnel with a wide variety of social and technical expertise [1, 8, 11, 17, 20].

2.2 Vertical Axis

The vertical trajectory of the Hybrid Space framework visualizes the compression of command levels whilst simultaneously recognizing the institutional need to maintain such structures. The compression of command levels has been widely recognized in contemporary military doctrines and goes by the acronym of the Strategic Corporal [10]. Tactical decisions made by military personnel must take into account the strategic realities that used to be purview of the higher levels in the chain of command [10], as the distinction between tactical and strategic impact is becoming increasingly blurry [10]. In a CNO context, these decisions and actions performed by an operator, can have geopolitical consequences.

Lemay and colleagues [10] give a variety of plausible situations where a cyber operator is forced to decide and act on Advanced Persistent Threat (APT) incidents that may affect the strategic scope of the organization. Cyber operations are marked by unconventional timeframes (ranging from years to seconds in a both a future and historical timeline) that result in cognitive complexity and pressure when attempting to avoid negative consequences. Thus, a high level commander can easily miss out on decisions affecting the strategic goal due to his/her relatively distant placement on the Hybrid Space's horizontal axis. Consequently, strategic sensemaking and decision-making can suffer. When this is combined with concerns relating to adversary intent and attribution [10] young personnel need to understand the strategic picture in order to communicate events and respond accurately to uncertainty. This requires a model of leadership that is mature, agile and appropriate to context [8]. Lamay et al. [10] conclude that in this new context, the strict division between tactical and strategic personnel cannot hold as it potentially constrains and prevents leadership of cyber operators. They elaborate that it is unlikely that a manager with an IT background will keep up with technology development, and technical personnel spending all their time updating themselves, might lose track of the bigger picture. Having one supervisor for every cyber operator is not an answer, and given the time constraint and time available to make decisions [10] it narrows down the possible pathways ahead. As Lemay et al. [10] argue; enhanced training, understanding the commander's intent and decentralized decision making have been brought forward as possible solutions. However, this process will require instruction and training methods followed by evaluation to determine whether or not decentralized decision-making generally works.

So for now, incident handlers are strategic agents, often without being aware of it [10], and often without their operational and strategic levels of command being aware of it. If the current gap of technological skills and knowledge between managers/commanders and technical personnel [10] is viewed upon in the Hybrid Space framework, the implications for leadership training that can leverage mastery of the 'understand function' [1] through cognitive-technical and cognitive-psychological competencies becomes evident.

To the best of our knowledge, the Hybrid Space conceptualization is the first to fully acknowledge that investing in new technologies - to leverage human performance [31, 32] - has not accounted for what people view as important and given them strategies for organizing that information. The Hybrid Space acknowledges specific features that appear through a shift in contemporary military leadership. As knowledge agents (human and technical) are required to 'lead' commanders and senior military planners who experience heightened anxiety as their perceived self-efficacy and control beliefs are threatened due to the ambiguity and asynchronous nature of the digital battlefield [8].

The Hybrid Space framework simultaneously stresses how human agents are required to move between tactical and strategic considerations to master the understand function [1] and operate effectively within the complexity of merging CPS and STS landscapes. The Hybrid Space explains a novel state of being and opens up space for critical research that can guide practices capable of facilitating the necessary learning pathways for human performance in digitization.

3 Metacognition and Navigation Within the Hybrid Space

As command levels compress and systems converge, operating within the Hybrid Space requires agents take conscious control of assets and responsibility for improving their cognitive flexibility to move freely. This cognitive process builds on the Generation Y learning paradigm of perception, emotional involvement, intuitive and experience based practice [11, 33]; whilst also complimenting current pedagogical trends where learners are encouraged to develop their cognitive and metacognitive skills, as pathways to better performance and self-insight [35]. For military personnel, this learning process facilitates mastery of the future operating environment whilst also implying the need for systematic and autonomous application of adaptive reflection [36] to build self-regulatory processes and self-efficacy. Agents who are capable of mirroring the dynamism [34] of the complex developing Hybrid Space landscape, will demonstrate leadership qualities founded upon the power of knowledge-based abstractions, rather than being constrained by institutional norms of military command experience or rank. This cyber leadership 'art' chances that current military norms and solutions relating to command, control and understanding of leadership models, only present barriers and limit expectations [8].

Human factors focuses on the "fit" between the user, system, and the situational demands in a hybrid space between cyber and physical domain. The Hybrid Space model defines military personnel as located at the interface between CPS and STS and that both systems incorporate the human "in the loop". Events in the cyberspace, as perceived by the human agent, have not only direct effects on decisions made in the physical domain, but also influence human decision-making via indirect psychological effects. In a similar vein, circumstances in the physical domain can affect the interaction with and thus events within the cyberspace. Reacting adequately to constantly changing environmental needs requires efficient navigation within the Hybrid Space, i.e., between cyber- and physical domain (horizontal axis) as well as monitoring one's relationship towards current tactical and strategic goals and demands (vertical axis).

Metacognition refers to 'thinking about thinking' and includes the components knowledge of one's abilities, situational awareness, and behavioral regulation strategies [38]. Individuals with high metacognitive skills have more accurate and confident judgment of their own performance in relation to the demands and are better able to accurately describe their strengths, weaknesses, and their potential to improve. Thus, high metacognitive awareness of one's cognitive processes (planning, monitoring, evaluations) facilitates one's localisation within the Hybrid Space, a judgment on its appropriateness and initiation of change of cognition or action. As an example, individuals who recognize emotional impacts of events in one of the domains (e.g., a failure or sub-optimal performance in cyber) affecting their performance in the physical domain (e.g., distraction leading to impaired concentration and reduced physical or cognitive performance), can counter-regulate and apply emotion-regulation strategies.

An individual with a particular accurate judgment of his/her own performance level (high metacognitive awareness) will recognise a potential threat in cyberspace exceeding his/her technical abilities and consider to activate additional personal or technical resources in the physical domain. A person being aware that the outcomes of previous actions were taken under immense time pressure to serve short-term goals served primarily tactical purposes can readjust short-term goals earlier to put strategic goals back into the focus. The ability to be metacognitively aware of one's own performance without underestimation of own capacities or inappropriate over-confidence is considered a relatively stable personality trait that can be quantified and made subject to training and improvement. A crucial role for improvement of metacognitive skills is played by leaders, trainers, and all persons designing training and giving feedback.

As an example for the application of cognitive science in the Hybrid Space model serves the Recognition/Metacognition model [39] for tactical decision-making that involves the ability to recognize situations and supplement with processes of verification and optimal solution resolvement that is relevant to the Hybrid Space. The R/M approach identifies and outlines factors that can be trained to help deal with novel situations that may arise (see [39] for in-depth description). At the meta-recognition stage, agents will need to become aware of evidence-conclusion relationships, critically analyse the arguments that support a conclusion, correct any beliefs through external (collecting more data) and internal (attention shifting or regulating the recognitional process) actions, and quick testing the critical-analysis/correctional process. The meta-recognition component of the model provides information on the metacognitive factors so that it can monitor and evaluate the recognitional process to modify behavior efficiently. This process is dependent on expertise understanding of the Hybrid Space as well as an understanding of the physical demands and psychosocial processes needed (metacognitive skills) to function in it.

4   Future Research

Several authors suggest that cyber officers need a varied skill-set [10, 11]. We agree with these finding and see the Hybrid Space as a tool capable of framing the complex environment that both defines and reveals this skill-set. This is a framework that reflects the novel demands of the future operating environment.

The integration of cyber power into joint warfare presents a research gap that concerns more than just understanding CNO from a technological or human factors view. It requires us to understand the significance of these factors through their interdependency and the reciprocal processes that occur for functioning effectively in the Hybrid Space. At all operational levels agents can affect and are affected by abstraction levels of team and individual performance. Thus, by learning how to support performance in the Hybrid Space we hope to develop efficacy through multiple performance pathways. Research that embraces and leverages cross discipline collaboration is required to establish a pedagogic methodology concerning how to educate, train and accelerate the requisite skills that will enable responsible personnel to operate with superior cognition in the Hybrid Space.

This framework has the potential to reveal the cognitive and metacognitive processes required to conduct future military operations. By categorizing the relevant agents, prioritizing the critical assets and finding novel approaches to measuring adaptation can lead us to better understand the competencies, relationships and processes that occur in the Hybrid Space.

References

1. Ministry of Defence, United Kingdom: Future Trends Programme - Future Operating Environment 2035, 1st edn. First Published 14 December 2015. https://www.gov.uk/government/publications/future-operating-environment-2035
2. Kegan, R., Lahey, L.: Immunity to Change. Harvard Business School Publishing Corporation, Boston (2009)
3. Whitman, M., Mattord, H.: Principles of Information Security, 4th edn. Cengage Learning, Boston (2012)

4. NERC, Security Guideline for the Electricity Sector: Identifying Critical Cyber Assets (2015) http://www.nerc.com/docs/cip/sgwg/Critcal_Cyber_Asset_ID_V1_Final.pdf
5. von Solms, R., van Niekerk, J.: From information security to cyber security. Comput. Secur. **38**, 97–102 (2013)
6. Andrews, J., Buzzi, S., Choi, W., Hanly, S.V., Lozano, A., Soong, A.C.K., Zhang, C.J.: What will 5G be? IEEE J. Sel. Areas Commun. **32**(6), 23–44 (2014)
7. Trujillo, C.: The Limits of Cyberspace Deterrence. JFQ 74, 3rd Quarter 2014 (2014)
8. Tikk-Ringas, E., Kerttunen, M., Spirito, C.: Cyber Security as a Field of Military Education and Study. JFQ 74, 3rd Quarter 2014 (2014)
9. Mancuso, V.F., Strang, A.J., Funke, G.J., Finomore, V.S.: Human factors of cyber attacks: a framework for human-centered research. In: Proceedings of the Human Factors and Ergonomics Society 58th Annual Meeting – 2014, pp. 437–441 (2014)
10. Lamay, A., Leblanc, S., De Jesus, T.: Lessons form the strategic corporal - implications of cyber incident response. In: SIGMIS-CPR 2015, 4–6 June 2015. ACM, Newport Beach (2015). ISBN 978-1-4503-3557-7/15/06
11. Røyslien, H.: When the generation gap collides with military structure: the case of norwegian cyber officers. J. Mil. Strateg. Stud. **16**(3), 1065–1082 (2015)
12. Joiner, B., Josephs, S.: Leadership Agility, Five Levels of Mastery for Anticipating and Initiating Change. Wiley, San Francisco (2007)
13. Zanenga, P: Knowledge eyes, nature and emergence in society, culture, and economy. IEEE (2014). 978-1-4799-4735-5/14
14. Paterson, D.M.: Work domain analysis for network management revisited: infrastructure, teams and situation awareness. In: IEEE International Inter-Disciplinary Conference on Cognitive Methods in Situation Awareness and Decision Support (CogSIMA). IEEE (2014). 978-1-4799-3564-2/14
15. Sawilla, R.E., Wiemer, D.J.: Automated computer network defence technology demonstration project (ARMOUR TDP). IEEE (2011). 978-1-4577-1376-7/11
16. Zhong, C., Yen, J., Liu, P., Erbacher, R., Etoty, R., Garneau, C.: ARSCA: a computer tool for tracing the cognitive processes of cyber-attack analysis. In: IEEE International Inter-Disciplinary Conference on Cognitive Methods in Situation Awareness and Decision Support (CogSIMA) (2015). 978-1-4799-8015-4/15
17. Williams, B.T.: The joint force commander's guide to cyberspace operations. JFQ 73, 2nd Quarter 2014. Major General Brett T. Williams, USAF, is the Director of Operations, J3, for U.S. Cyber Command (2014)
18. Proctor, R.W. Chen, J.: The role of human factors/ergonomics in the science of security: decision making and action selection in cyberspace. Hum. Factors J. Hum. Factors Ergon. Soc. **57**(5), 721–727 (2015)
19. Gutzwiller, R.S., Fugate, S., Sawyer, B.D., Hancock, P.A.: The Human Factors of Cyber Network Defense. In: Proceedings of the Human Factors and Ergonomics Society Annual Meeting. vol. 59, no. 1, pp. 322–326. SAGE Publications, September 2015
20. Bonner, L.E.: Cyber Power in 21st Joint Warfare. JFQ 74, 3rd Quarter 2014. Lieutenant Colonel E. Lincoln Bonner III, USAF, is Director of Operations at the Space Operations Squadron Aerospace Data Facility–Colorado (2014)
21. NATO MC 0616: NATO Cyber Defence Education and Training Plan. 6th Draft MC 0616. NATO UNCLASSIFIED (2015)
22. Arnold, T., et al.: Towards A Career Path in Cyberspace Operations for Army Officers. J. Art. Aug. **18**(10), 37am (2014)
23. Dombrowski, P., Demchak, C.C.: Cyber war, cybered conflict, and the maritime domain. Naval War Coll. Rev. **67**(2), 70 (2014)

24. Hu, F.: Cyber-Physical Systems: Integrated Computing and Engineering Design. CRC Press, Boca Raton (2013)
25. Coghlan, D., Brydon-Miller, M. (eds.): The SAGE Encyclopedia of Action Research. Sage, London (2014)
26. Ahmed, S.H., Kim, G., Kim, D.: Cyber physical system: architecture, applications and research challenges. In: Wireless Days, 2013 IFIP. IEEE (2013). doi:10.1109/WD. 2013.6686528
27. Sanislav, T., Miclea, L.: Cyber-physical systems – concepts challenges and research areas. CEAI **14**(2), 28–33 (2012)
28. Troxler, P., Lauche, K.: Assessing Creating and Sustaining Knowledge Culture in Organisations (2014). http://www.academia.edu/1964062/Assessing_Creating_and_Sustaining_Knowledge_Culture_in_Organisations
29. Hoffman, R.R., Ward, P., Feltovich, P.J., DiBello, L., Fiore, S.M., Andrews, D.: Accelerated Expertise: Training for High Proficiency in a Complex World. Psychology Press, New York (2014). http://www.psypress.com/books/details/9781848726529
30. Farwell, J., Rohozinski, R.: The new reality of cyber war. Survival (00396338) **54**(4), 107–120 (2012). Academic Search Complete, EBSCOhost
31. Oltromani, A., Noam, B.-A., Cranor, L., Bauer, L., Christin, N.: General requirements of a hybrid-modeling framework for cyber security. In: Military Communications Conference (MILCOM). IEEE (2014)
32. Bennet, K.B.: Ecological interface design: military C2 and computer network defence. In: IEEE 2014 International Conference on Systems, Man, and Cybernetics, 5–8 October 2014, San Diego, CA, USA (2014)
33. Sookermany, AMcD: What is a skillful soldier? An epistemological foundation for understanding military skill acquisition in (post) modernized armed forces. Armed Forces Soc. **38**(4), 582–603 (2012)
34. Castells, M.: Information Technology, Globalization and Social Development. UNRISD Discussion Paper no. 114, Geneva, UNRI (1999)
35. Baas, D., Castelijns, J., Vermeulen, M., Martens, R., Segers, M.: The relation between assessment for learning and elementary students' cognitive and metacognitive strategy use. Br. J. Educ. Psychol. **85**(1), 33–46 (2015)
36. Hannah, S.T., Avolio, B.J.: Ready or not: how do we accelerate the developmental readiness of leaders? J. Organ. Behav. **31**(8), 1181–1187 (2010)
37. Woods, D.D., Hollnagel, E.: Joint Cognitive System: Patterns in Cognitive Systems Engineering. CRC Press, Boca Raton (2006)
38. Jacobs, J.E., Paris, S.G.: Children's metacognition about reading: Issues in definition, measurement, and instruction. Educ. Psychol. **22**, 255–278 (1978)
39. Cohen, M.S., Freeman, J.T., Thompson, B.: Critical thinking skills in tactical decision making: a model and a training strategy. In: Making Decisions Under Stress: Implications for Individual and Team Training, pp. 155–190 (1998)

Empirical Study of Secure Password Creation Habit

Chloe Chun-Wing Lo[(✉)]

Sirius 16, Hong Kong, China
chloewing.loll27@gmail.com

Abstract. The general public's understanding of "secure" passwords, and how they are generated is investigated. Habits that tend to foster the creation of more secure passwords are suggested. Empirical data collected by survey participants is shown to present solid evidence that "secure" passwords created by the participants who could recall them later contained substantial substrings of simpler password chosen earlier by the participants. In contrast, those who encounter difficulty in recalling the passwords are seen to have created complex passwords substantially different from simpler ones created earlier. Some user-coping methods for the complexity-memorability dilemma are addressed, Companies are urged to adopt a salting approach before encryption, and consider new hashing mechanisms to ensure the security of user passwords. Given the limitations of human memory, it is recommended that two-factor authentication be used.

Keywords: Password selection · Password strength · Password memorization

1 Introduction

Until now, password authentication has been the major strategy to restrict access to sensitive information and services, despite the availability of alternative methods. The resistance to change seems to stem from the potential for misuse of newer alternatives [1]. Therefore, password authentication is likely to remain the most commonly used authentication method for the near future. It is essential, therefore, to help internet users to come up behaviors that increase the likelihood that the passwords they select will meet the following criteria:

1. The password must be remembered by the user
2. The password should not contain any regular or predictable pattern which makes them more susceptible to brute-force attack

The first criterion is quite obvious in its necessity. If the user cannot remember the password, the user will not be able to access the information or service. (Additionally, passwords must not be stored in a manner that makes them accessible to unauthorized persons.) Therefore, the performance of password-based authentication is subject to the limitations imposed by human memory capacity. The second requirement above heavily relies on how dictionary attack works.

© Springer International Publishing Switzerland 2016
D.D. Schmorrow and C.M. Fidopiastis (Eds.): AC 2016, Part II, LNAI 9744, pp. 189–197, 2016.
DOI: 10.1007/978-3-319-39952-2_19

Dictionary attack, according to Internet Security Glossary Version 2 [2], is "an attack that uses a brute-force technique of successively trying all the words in some large, exhaustive list." In particular, using repeated substrings in passwords accelerates dictionary attack, facilitating the compromise of password security systems. The use of repeated substrings is a password security problem, since it reduces the size of the search space, and provides syntactic and semantic clues that can be exploited by an attacker.

Consequently, one way to address the password security problem is to require users to make up passwords that are as "random" as possible. In more technical terms, passwords having higher "entropy" are more less "predictable", and so, more secure.

This, of course, increases the challenge to human memory.

In psychological terms, "High entropy" can be translated to "low associative value". Associative value is the number of connection of a string to meaningful content made by a human being [3]. Most words one finds in a dictionary are considered to have high associative value, making them susceptible to dictionary attacks.

This sets up a dilemma between password strength and human memory: a password with higher entropy, which is more secure, has low associative value. This means those passwords are harder for human to remember [4]. Indeed, Yan et al. [5] had found empirical evidence for such intuitive phenomena, as they found that the participants who were given a randomly generated password needed to write the password down in order to memorize it.

One proposed underlying mechanism for such a trade-off in password strength and memory may lie behind the theory that human relies on phonological measures to commit information to memory. The current model of human's working memory suggested that it contains a phonological loop and a visual scratchpad [6], to which was later added an episodic buffer [7], enslaved to a central executive which regulates the attention.

The phonological loop provides a pathway to long-term memory formation by repeatedly rehearsing the information in one's own head. Strings of random characters, however, are often unpronounceable. This has been shown by Shallice, Warrington and McCarthy [8] to decrease their memorability.

Although this dilemma is well understood, it is not clear how the current internet users are adapting to the demand for ever-more-complex passwords. This study considers some user-coping mechanisms seen in collected data, as users' attempt to create "more secure" passwords.

It is here initially assumed that human's cope with the memory demand of more complex passwords by recycling and altering some simpler extant passwords (which, in any case, will not likely be "secure" either). That is, users attempt to remember their more secure passwords because they are embellished reiterations of simpler ones. It is crucial to recognize that this is not regarded by users as "reusing a password", yet poses an equivalent risk. For, the mere existence of substrings commonly present in simple passwords leaves hints for attackers; the full reuse is not necessary.

2 Method

2.1 Participants

Participants were invited from a global community of general users to participate in a demographic survey conducted on the internet. There were in total 149 completed sets of data. The data from the participants who were not able to recall their simple passwords were culled, since this level of incompleteness did not allow the computation of the necessary statistics. 93 sets of data remained available for analysis.

Among these 93 participants, 49 were male and 44 were female, with their age ranging from 16 to 66 and older, while a vast majority falls evenly within the range of 16–45. Most of them rated their computer literacy as "moderate" or "advanced" (Table 1).

Table 1. Demographic details of participants

Variable	Category	Total	Percentage
Gender	Male	49	52.7 %
	Female	44	47.3 %
Age	16–24	33	35.5 %
	25–35	23	24.7 %
	36–45	27	29.0 %
	46-55	0	0.0 % ·
	56–65	7	7.5 %
	66–older	3	3.2 %
Computer literacy	Basic	6	6.5 %
	Moderate	46	49.5 %
	Advanced	32	34.4 %
	Expert	9	9.7 %
Total participants		**93**	

2.2 Measure

The complexity of the passwords was measured by the double natural log of Kaspersky time-to-break score, a widely used commercial standard. The large range of the raw scores were not convenient for comparison, so the natural logarithm were taken twice to make the values readily commensurable.

The similarity between passwords was measured using Dice's Coefficient. Given two passwords, both bigrams and trigrams were counted for the calculation of Dice's Coefficient, according to the following equation:

$$s = \frac{2n_t}{n_x + n_y},\tag{1}$$

where n_t is the cardinality of the intersection of the bigrams or trigrams of the two passwords, and n_x and n_y are the cardinalities of the bigrams or trigrams of the simple password and the secure password, respectively. Dice's coefficient was chosen for its emphasizes on the existence of repeated substrings, which, as noted in the Introduction, is a major concern for password security.

2.3 Procedures

An electronic questionnaire was set up on the internet which required each participant to complete a survey. Respondents were not told that the purpose of the study was analysis of password selection strategies.

Before presentation of the survey, the participant was asked to create an account by filling in their email as the username, and providing a simple password. After the participants filled in their password, no matter how simple or secure the password was, the participants were prompted to revise their password and input one that is "more secure" (Fig. 1).

At the end of the survey, the participants were asked to recall their initial password, and their revised password (Fig. 2).

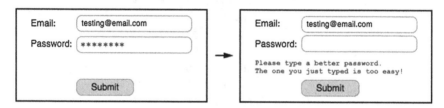

Fig. 1. A prompt for a more "secure" password after their first password

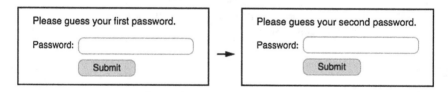

Fig. 2. A request to recall both passwords at the end of the survey

3 Result

First, a paired two-tailed t-test was conducted to compare the complexity of the simple passwords and the secure passwords. This was done to obtain an instance of a password the user believed was "more secure" than the initial one. The null hypothesis of the statistical comparison conducted was that there was no difference in the complexity of the simple password and revised password.

The result was that the revised passwords (M = 2.204, SD = 1.266) were significantly more complicated than the simple passwords (M = 0.830, SD = 1.627), $t(92) = 7.4796$, $p < 0.0001$.

An independent two-tailed t-test was conducted to find how similar the "secure" and simple passwords were between the group of participants who could successfully recall their more complicated passwords (72 of them) and those who could not (21 of them). The null hypothesis was that there was no difference in the similarity of the revised and simple passwords between these two groups of participants.

The result was that the revised passwords created by the participants who could recall them (n = 72, M = 0.324, SD = 0.389) were significantly more similar to their simple passwords, against those who failed to recall the revised passwords (n = 21, M = 0.119, SD = 0.233), t(55) = 2.9958, p = 0.0041.

The password similarity measure used Dice's Coefficient calculated from bigram counts. To measure substring reuse from the simple passwords by the "secure" passwords, a similar statistical analysis using Dice's Coefficient calculated from trigrams was also performed. A similar result was obtained: users who could recall their secure passwords (n = 72, M = 0.290, SD = 0.289) had selected "secure" passwords that were significantly more similar to their simple passwords, than users who failed to recall their revised passwords (n = 21, M = 0.090, SD = 0.198), t(65) = 3.2014, p = 0.0021.

4   Discussion

4.1   Findings

The collected data suggest that the major drawback of using passwords as the method of user authentication is that human memory capacity requires the user to choose a password that is similar to what they have been previously using. It is true that when a password gets longer, it is more difficult to crack using a brute-force approach. However, this is not the case if the attacker adopts a dictionary attack approach, especially if the attackers pre-treat the wordlist to consider the permutations of several shorter classic passwords.

This might mean that passwords users regard as "more secure" (which the data indicate are likely to contain substrings of "less secure" passwords) still carry the same security risk. Further, this problem might not be detected by the "password strength algorithm" hosted by a user's internet service. This follows from the fact that study participant's password embellishments increased the Kaspersky time-to-break score in an artificial way, leaving large substrings intact. The passwords that contain substrings of the simple passwords got a pass from the "complexity test", but the presence of repurposed substrings leaves the password authentication system susceptible to dictionary attacks.

This behavior is seen in the following examples extracted from the data:

The "secure" password in row 3 should not be any more secure than the simple one, yet the Kaspersky time-to-break score is much higher than the simple one from which it was created. This might mask the risk to dictionary attack it introduces.

4.2   Limitations

A large proportion of users decided to shift to a totally different password when prompted to enter a more secure one. There were indeed 45 out of 93 participants (48.4 %) who supplied a "secure" password having a similarity score of 0 (Dice's coefficient calculated using bigrams) with their simple password.

However, this in no way means that these passwords are any more secure than those found in Table 2. It is entirely possible (and we suspect probable) that these participants maintain a collection of different well-used passwords. This is one of the limitations of this study — other ready passwords that might be reused by participants were not known. This is left for future work, and will require more extensive and subtle data elicitation techniques.

Table 2. Example of Participants recycling their simple passwords

Simple password	Complexity score* for simple password	Secure password	Complexity score* for secure password
grapes	−1	gr@pejuice	1.839210505349484
police318	1.079918299522082	Pol318e	1.647303255736618
Delete a file	2.782182225673644	Delete a fileDelete a file	3.696182122985719
mnbvcxz	−1	mnbvcxzpoiuyt	1.566006629760012

The complexity is calculated by the double natural log of the Kaspersky time-to-break score.

It is emphasized that the level of similarity between the simple and "secure" passwords found during this study only constitute a lower bound. If other frequently used passwords are taken into consideration, the security risk is likely to be much higher than seen here, since internet users are known to reuse passwords across different platforms [9], and reuse usually 3 or less of them [10].

Another limitation is that Dice's Coefficient is not able to detect string patterns easily visible to humans, as shown in row 1 in Table 2. The revised password "gr@pejuice" will be deemed less similar to "grape" than "grapejuice" is due to the replaced character "a" by "@". This is a visual similarity and therefore only exists in human perception at the moment. Such similarity across passwords was not detected in this study. Another notable example will be changing "password" into "p455w0rd". Yet, this apparent randomness induced by substituting alphabets to visually similar characters does not necessarily make these password significantly more "secure".

The string morphs produced by character shape substitutions will not be present in a dictionary, but they are easily readable and pronounceable for a human being. Therefore, users might assume that such substitutions significantly strengthen security. However, this method is predictable, and does not produce combinatorial growth in the password search space. It is essentially a font variation. Attackers need only update their dictionary, rendering this strategy less effective than it appears.

The survey prompted for a more "secure" password without any explicit instruction on how the password should be made. This does not sufficiently reflect how the average internet users will react in real-life situation where the prompt for a more complex passwords usually comes with a list of criteria (e.g. at least 8 characters, include at least 1 digit, do not have 2 consecutive digits). This study provides no information on how they behave when the criteria for a strong password is difficult to meet. It is speculated that the users may respond by inputting even simpler passwords which is considered to be secure by the list of criteria but actually poses a higher security risk (e.g. "a1b2c3d4e5f6" if the prompt asks for no consecutive digits). More researches are needed to have a more accurate picture on how the users respond to the demand for a stronger password in real-life situation.

5   Recommendations

Since repeated substrings are the ultimate hint which makes gaming passwords effective, it is recommended that users implement an altered salting technique. Rather than simple salt concatenation, which does not solve the substring problem at all, users are advised to interleave the salt pattern being inserted at multiple points of the password. For example, let the salt string be $a_1a_2a_3...a_n$, and the string to be protected be given by $b_1b_2b_3...b_m$. We may combine them and form new string $a_1b_1a_2b_2a_3b_3...$ $a_nb_nb_{n+1}b_{n+2}...b_m$, encrypt this combined string and store this into the database. If a user has a username "AppleSeed" and password "macintosh", combine these two strings into "AmpapclienSteoesdh". This makes the string undetectable by dictionaries and, therefore, increases the password security while maintaining memorability.

On the industrial side, for online databases, it must be assumed that attackers will infer a *static* salting methodology. Therefore, enterprises should consider changing the way they combine the salt with the password, or even the hashing mechanism, depending on demographic information given by the account holder. This should be done in a way that introduces combinatorial complexity.

These approaches will reduce the unsustainable demand for increasingly complex passwords by allowing users to select simpler, more memorable passwords. Dynamic salting will also reduce the likelihood of many users having the same password, which can be used to defeat anonymization when an online database is compromised.

Completely forgoing the requirement for the selection of "secure" passwords is still not recommended. Although salting can reduce the likelihood of some attacks, it will not make the users' accounts less vulnerable to attack from people who can obtain their personal information (e.g., from social media).

If the users reuse substrings of their simple passwords when a more secure password is required in some contexts, there is increased risk that others in the user's social circle will guess the secure passwords from the other simple passwords the user is currently using. Therefore, there is still a need for users to select passwords that are not easy to guess, even by members of their intimate social circle. Consequently, education on the importance of password strength and password discretion is still necessary. It is essential that users understand that letting other people know even one of their passwords poses a risk to their other passwords. Of course, no technology can remedy misplaced trust.

Finally, it is recommended that enterprises adopt some form of two-party authentication where possible.

6   Conclusion

The effectiveness of password as a secure authentication process is not perfect, with poor password selection receiving most of the blame. The world has responded by requiring stronger passwords. We challenge the notion that asking the users to select stronger passwords solves the security problem. Password authentication relies upon human memory, and it is precisely this reliance that limits its effectiveness. How human memory works greatly restricts the level of security provided by passwords as an authentication method. This is clearly shown by how participants of this study tended to reuse substrings from their simple, less "secure" passwords to produce what they believed was a "secure" one.

There are, however, remedies to the security concern posed by weak passwords. The major drawback of weak passwords, besides being easy to guess, is that they make a database of encrypted passwords susceptible to dictionary attack. Using some altered salting technique or even variable hashing mechanisms mitigates the risk of dictionary attack.

The importance of educating the public about password strength is still of utmost importance, since none of the advanced salting techniques or hash mechanisms can fully protect passwords from being guessed by people in one's close social circle. The public must understand that people are prone to make up very similar passwords across platforms, and that this enables people in their circles to steal their account.

It is, therefore, best to incorporate additional authentication methods that are not memory intensive alongside passwords.

Acknowledgements. I would like to thank you Mr. Monte F. Hancock for the data, and his guidance and critical review to this paper. It would not be possible for me to conduct this research without his invitation and support. There will be no words which can exactly convey the heartfelt gratitude I would like to express for his trust (hopefully not misplaced) and confidence in me.

References

1. Furnell, S.M., Papadopoulos, I., Dowland, P.: A long-term trial of alternative user authentication technologies. Inf. Manag. Comput. Secur. **12**(2), 178–190 (2004)
2. Shirey, R.W.: Internet Security Glossary, Version 2 (2007). https://tools.ietf.org/html/rfc4949
3. Noble, C.E.: An analysis of meaning. Psychol. Rev. **59**(6), 421–430 (1952)
4. McGeoch, J.A.: The influence of associative value upon the difficulty of nonsense-syllable lists. Pedagog. Semin. J. Genet. Psychol. **37**, 421–426 (1930)

5. Yan, J., et al.: Password memorability and security: empirical results. Secur. Priv. IEEE **2**(5), 25–31 (2004)
6. Baddeley, A.: Working memory. Science **255**(5044), 556–559 (1992)
7. Baddeley, A.: Working memory: looking back and looking forward. Nat. Rev. Neurosci. **4**, 829–839 (2003)
8. Shallice, T., Warringtona, E.K., Mccarthy, R.: Reading without semantics. Q. J. Exp. Psychol. **35**(1), 111–138 (1983)
9. Bryant, K., Campbell, J.: User behaviours associated with password security and management. Aust. J. Inf. Syst. **14**(1), 81–100 (2006)
10. Gaw, S., Felten, E.W.: Password management strategies for online accounts. In: Proceedings of the Second Symposium on Usable Privacy and Security. ACM (2006)

Team Cognition as a Mechanism for Developing Collaborative and Proactive Decision Support in Remotely Piloted Aircraft Systems

Nathan J. McNeese$^{(\boxtimes)}$ and Nancy J. Cooke$^{(\boxtimes)}$

Arizona State University, Mesa, AZ, USA
{nmcneese,ncooke}@asu.edu

Abstract. Remotely piloted aircraft systems (RPAS) are steadily increasing in their presence and role in the Military's overall strategic operational picture. The benefits of RPAS are apparent, ranging from saving time, money, and lives. Yet, the utilization of RPAS is still very challenging in many different aspects. Teams have become a central focus of RPAS due to their many benefits. Yet, teamwork is challenging and the RPAS community must continue to attempt to understand how to support it. A specific aspect of teamwork that has proven over the years to be of paramount importance is *team cognition*. In this paper, we discuss how team cognition needs to be considered during the development of collaborative and proactive RPAS decision support. We highlight the concept of team cognition accounting for multiple perspectives, outline an integrative perspective of team cognition for the RPAS domain, and conclude by outlining multiple design objectives for utilizing team cognition as a mechanism for RPAS decision support.

Keywords: Remotely piloted aircraft systems · Teamwork · Team cognition · Collaboration · Decision support · System design

1 The Growing Importance of Teamwork Within RPAS

Over the past decade, multiple military entities have adapted their overall strategic operational picture from fighting wars with "boots on the ground" to a more technologically innovative means of utilizing Remotely Piloted Aircraft Systems (RPAS). RPAS allow the Military to conduct a wide range of activities ranging from intelligence gathering to real time operational weapons deployment. The increasing usage of RPAS has been steady, and in recent years has become a standard within multiple sectors of the Military.

The reasons for the increased presence of RPAS are abundant and often well documented. When compared to a traditional boots on the ground approach, the utilization of RPAS often saves, time, money, and lives [1]. For these reasons, we have seen the many successes owing directly to RPAS usage.

Yet, while RPAS have shown to be effective in many situations, there are still many research questions that need to be addressed. Historically speaking RPAS are relatively new. This relative newness has resulted in a myriad of challenging issues and problems throughout the growth of the platform. Specifically, in recent years, the RPAS domain

© Springer International Publishing Switzerland 2016
D.D. Schmorrow and C.M. Fidopiastis (Eds.): AC 2016, Part II, LNAI 9744, pp. 198–209, 2016.
DOI: 10.1007/978-3-319-39952-2_20

has become increasingly collaborative. Collaboration within and across multiple RPAS teams is a beneficial aspect of recent RPAS work but with it comes significant challenges. Communication and coordination challenges, a lack of team level situational awareness, and information overload are just a few of the many potential problems stemming from increased collaboration in RPAS.

Teams are a central and critical focus and function of RPAS operations, often directing multiple different components of the overall RPAS system. The specific operation of an RPAS is dependent on interdependent and heterogeneous roles within the teams working together to provide information critical to the deployment, flight, and operational needs of the mission. Not only are teams collaborating to operate the vehicle and carry out mission objectives, they are also collaborating within a larger set of teams who may or may not be working on a similar strategic goal. The RPAS domain is a system that consists of multiple sub-systems. Often, these sub-systems are teams, and if one team or even one individual fails to perform effectively, the entire system is jeopardized.

For these reasons, we must consider how to facilitate effective teamwork within the domain of RPAS. If we fail to promote, train, and apply effective teamwork principles, the pending results can be deadly. There is a science of teamwork that can be applied to enhance team performance and teamwork occurring within the specific context of RPAS. In general, across multiple domains of work, teamwork is viewed as beneficial as long as the team members understand how to work together in an efficient, accurate, and meaningful way. These assumptions are no different in the context of RPAS. Yet, in order to produce effective teamwork, multiple considerations must be made. A specific aspect of teamwork that has proven over the years to be of paramount importance is *team cognition*. Team cognition is cognition that occurs at the team level [2]. The development of team cognition occurs during real time team level interactions where team members share relevant teamwork and taskwork knowledge resulting in a shared understanding. Team cognition is typically associated with concepts such as shared mental models, interactive team cognition, situational awareness, and transactive memory. More than 20 years of team cognition research has demonstrated that the development of team cognition has the potential to improve team effectiveness [3].

The role of team cognition within the domain of RPAS needs to be further explored and articulated. We see team cognition as being applicable to many of the collaborative problems that RPAS is currently facing. By considering team cognition as a form of interaction, as we do within the theory of Interactive Team Cognition (ITC), we can begin to postulate how to better manifest and develop it through rich meaningful team level interactions. Teamwork within the context of RPAS must instill communication and coordination at the team level. Disparate interactions that occur at the individual level and are then abstracted up the chain of command do not represent effective teamwork and fail to allow for team cognition.

In addition to specifically outlining and highlighting how team cognition can be used for better collaborative RPAS work, we will also articulate the role of team cognition in collaborative and proactive decision support for RPAS. As RPAS have become more collaborative in nature, a myriad of collaborative technologies and tools have been developed to support the increased collaboration. These technologies have often been meet with inconclusive results, with many failing to actually support the most essential collaborative activities within the RPAS mission set. In addition, many of the decision support systems that are currently being utilized are dependent on individualistic notions. RPAS decision support systems should support the individual user, but also the team as a whole (through team level interactions).

Knowing the benefits and importance of team cognition, decision support systems need to account for the role of team cognition. Similarly, we need to develop collaborative technologies that support team cognition during RPAS activities. Yet, to develop these systems and technologies we need to know what design features and objectives are critical to team cognition within the domain of RPAS. Later in the paper, we outline specific affordances that should be built within RPAS decision support to better develop team cognition. First, we begin the paper by conceptually outlining team cognition.

2 Team Cognition Within the Context of RPAS

Team cognition has long been studied within the context of teamwork and team decision-making. As teams were identified as an important facet of society, scientific research investigating them became common. Through years of research, knowledge regarding the importance of a shared understanding of both team and task related issues were acknowledged. Initially, team cognition was viewed through the psychological viewpoint of input, processing, output, where teams were viewed as actual information processing units [4]. In this sense, team cognition was the result of each individuals' cognition as it was combined together. So, the input was each individuals' cognition, the processing was the aggregation of each individuals' cognition, and the output was often referred to as a shared mental model. As the concept of team cognition has grown, an alternative perspective has developed that has moved away from team cognition being the aggregation of individuals' cognition, and rather surmises that team cognition is the actual interaction that occurs at the team level. The theory of Interactive Team Cognition (ITC) [2] further postulates that the communication and coordination occurring amongst the team is team cognition.

As the concept of team cognition has grown, multiple other conceptual areas of interest have been studied within the corpus of team cognition. Concepts such as the shared mental model [5], team situational awareness [6], and transactive memory [7] have all been directly linked to team cognition. The concept of a shared mental model will further be explained in the next section, as it is the main outlet for the shared knowledge perspective of team cognition.

2.1 The Shared Knowledge Perspective of Team Cognition

As previously noted, team cognition was initially viewed as the aggregation of individual team members' cognition. Throughout the team's life span, relevant individual knowledge is shared amongst the team resulting in shared knowledge. To this day, the shared knowledge approach is held in high regard and often what people consider when team cognition is brought up.

The primary concept aligned with the shared knowledge perspective is shared mental models. The shared mental model concept stems from the mental model concept, an individual cognitive construct that helps to explain situations and environments. More specifically, Rouse and Morris [8: pg. 96], define a mental model as a *"mechanism whereby humans generate descriptions of system purpose and form, explanations of system functioning and observed system states, and predictions of future system states"*. As research on mental models expanded and teams become increasingly important, the mental model was extended to the team level, conceptualizing the *shared (or team)* mental model [9]. Shared mental models are defined as *"team members' shared understandings and mental representations of knowledge about key elements of the team's relevant environment"* [10, 11].

Initially, the shared mental model was articulated into multiple sub-models: *equipment, task, team interaction,* and *team* [12]. Each separate sub-model contained specific cognitive aspects of the overall shared mental model. Yet, these separate models brought forth unnecessary convolution, and they were eventually collapsed into a *taskwork* and *teamwork* model [13]. With this new delineation, the taskwork model encompasses much of the procedural aspects of the work the team conducts, whereas the teamwork model includes aspects of interpersonal relationship, emotion, and understanding who team members are beyond a taskwork perspective [14, 15].

In addition to being defined by the content of the model (taskwork and teamwork), shared mental models are associated by two properties: accuracy and similarity. Accuracy is defined by how close the shared mental model is to the real world, consisting of properties accurate to human behavior and complex environments [16]. Whereas, similarity is how close or similar a team members' knowledge structure is to an experts' structure [17]. Support for both accuracy and similarity have been empirically mixed in predicting an increase in team performance [5].

2.2 The Ecological Perspective of Team Cognition

Another perspective on team cognition follows from ecological psychology that positions much of cognition in the world [18, 19]. Interactive Team Cognition (ITC) [2] is one ecologically based theory of team cognition that holds that team cognition can be observed in the interactions among teammates. These interactions occur in the world and are therefore observable and are analogous to cognitive processing that occurs at the individual level, though not as observable. The think aloud procedure is, in fact, an attempt to reveal individual cognitive processes. Teams often communicate as part of their everyday work.

Positioning team cognition in the world not only makes it easier to observe, but also allows observation of dynamics in team cognition as opposed to a static knowledge structure. Another advantage of the ecological perspective is that the focus is on interaction which is inherently a team variable. Shared knowledge perspectives tend to measure team cognition at the level of the individual.

2.3   Relevant Team Cognition Work Within RPAS

The theory of Interactive Team Cognition (ITC) was developed through multiple empirical teamwork studies that occurred within the UAV-STE (Uninhibited Aerial Vehicle-Synthetic Task Environment) [20]. Below, we will briefly highlight some of the teamwork studies that have occurred within the UAV-STE.

The metric of experience has been studied within the UAV-STE setting. An experiment that brought both novice and experienced command and control teams into the lab found that the experienced teams performed better than the novice teams [21]. The interesting finding of this study is that teams that were experienced in command and control surpassed novice teams in performance but were not superior in regard to individual or shared knowledge. The performance differences between teams depended on how the team interacted.

Over multiple experiments in the UAV-STE, we have found that team skill acquisition (reflected by changes in a team performance score) follows the log-law of skill acquisition [18, 22, 23]. Essentially, as a team gains experience with the UAV-STE, their performance increases in a log-linear fashion. Team performance is typically associated with better communication and coordination, and not individual or shared knowledge. If shared knowledge does occur, it occurs early in the mission set.

In addition, the UAV-STE setting has shown the value of team training for retention and skill acquisition. Gorman et al. [24] compared three types of training, procedural (training followed a script), cross-training (team members given training of all roles-increased shared knowledge), and perturbation training (team presented with brief disruptions forcing adaptation) to better understand each training types impact on skill retention and transfer of cognitive skill. The findings indicate that the perturbation-trained teams performed better in missions that consisted of conditions requiring adaptation. In addition, the procedural trained teams were the least adaptive. Finally, the teams that were cross-trained failed to perform as the task became non-routine.

3   An Integrative Framework of Team Cognition Within RPAS

The shared knowledge perspective and ecological perspective on team cognition are both fundamentally important to defining team cognition. Yet, as identified in the previous section, most scholars subscribe to one or the other, with more adhering to the traditional shared knowledge approach. In this paper, we recommend that the ecological approach would be beneficial for the context of RPAS. The often fast-paced and dynamic tasks found within RPAS teams are better aligned to the theoretical positioning of the ecological approach. Yet, we also suggest that while utilizing the ecological approach, it would be most appropriate to also integrate and consider aspects of the shared knowledge approach. Although, we subscribe to the notion that team cognition is team level interaction, we also acknowledge that individual cognition is being shared, albeit through team interaction.

In the UAV-STE we started looking for evidence of shared mental models as relevant to performance. We found early on that taskwork and teamwork knowledge developed by Mission 1 and remained stable throughout the experiment, not further differentiating effective from ineffective teams. At the same time, we noticed that our various process measures (communication and coordination) continued to show improvement as performance improved. This general pattern of findings led to Interactive Team Cognition (ITC). The UAV-STE task is a command-and-control task as opposed to a knowledge building task and seems suited for ITC over shared mental models. We feel that the findings from the UAV-STE task are ecologically valid to real RPAS operations, hence why we recommend utilizing the ecological approach with aspects of shared knowledge being also integrated depending on the specific task.

4   Team Cognition as a Mechanism for Developing Collaborative and Proactive Decision Support in RPAS

The tasks of both AVOs (air vehicle operator) and sensor operators are becoming increasingly complex due to mission goals, but also due to collaborative responsibilities. It is simply not enough to individually perform the tasks of both jobs, rather collaboration consistent with high levels of both communication and coordination are needed. Not only must the UAV team steadily communicate amongst each other, but they often are forced to communicate with members outside the direct team to provide status updates. In response to increased collaborative efforts in this domain, the community has, in many instances, sought to develop decision support or aids that are oriented towards supporting collaborative work. This is certainly a step in right direction, but many of the collaborative decision support tools are not adequate to support the collaboration occurring within context. Much of these tools are not representative of supporting *real time* interaction via *multiple* team dynamics. In addition, decision support within RPAS takes on an individualistic flavor. The tool itself is often marketed as being collaborative, yet only provides specific support for the individual *within* the team, and rather not support of team level functions or interactions. In other words, collaborative and proactive decision support in RPAS should support the *team* at the true team level, and not the *team* as the sum of the addition of each individual's roles or actions.

Unfortunately, to this day, many decision support systems are developed with little direction from human factors. The classic tale of engineers developing a technology via their insular perspective of what they *think* is useful to the user is often still persistent in this context. Collaborative and proactive decision support systems represent a great deal of future potential, but if we ever want them to be useful to the real users, then we must continue to study the users, and in this context, the team. The teamwork that occurs during a RPAS mission is incredibly complex and it must be fully understood before we can attempt to develop support mechanisms for collaborative efforts.

One approach to attempting to help develop better collaborative and proactive RPAS decision support is to consider the theoretical distinctions of team cognition. The direct team members (AVO and sensor operator) need team cognition to effectively perform their jobs. We feel confident in saying that most RPAS decision support systems never consider the impact or benefits of team cognition. Taking into account the theory of Interactive Team Cognition, we should be able to design decision support systems, tools, and aids that allow for team level support via interaction and decision-making.

In many ways, current RPAS collaborative decision support systems take forth a shared knowledge approach of team cognition where the outputs of the system are simply an aggregate of individual team member information. This perspective to designing collaborative proactive decision support systems is simply lacking and has the potential to hinder real time teamwork. Below, we highlight specific objectives that should be considered when designing for bettering team cognition through collaborative and proactive decision support.

(1) *Support team interaction: communication & coordination*

Team level interaction is the heart of team cognition, and our eyes into observing it take place. Through interaction we are able to see teams communicate and coordinate in real time, which is team cognition. Knowing the importance of team interaction, decision support systems that are inherently focused on collaboration must support these associated activities. These systems should support both the individual's roles and tasks, but also team level activities. Support at the team level means that all members of the team are able to observe and interact with the support in real time.

Specific examples supporting team level interaction are providing communication and coordination mechanisms that are available to be used and observed by all team members at the same time. In order for decision support to truly occur at the team level and be proactive, the support itself must become embedded within the team. Conceptually, one could even think of the support as a team member where the team member has the ability to help with communication and coordination efforts. In fact, this is what our research team is currently exploring. In recent years, we have looked at the role of a synthetic agent as a proactive member of an RPAS team [25–27]. Our most recent experiment examined the conditions of *control, synthetic,* and *experimenter.* In the control condition we investigated team performance of a three person RPAS team working on typical RPAS task problems. In the synthetic condition, the role of the AVO was taken over by a fully autonomous ACT-R based synthetic agent. Finally, in the experimenter condition, a wizard of oz study was utilized where a human experimenter acted as a synthetic agent. In this condition, the experimenter attempted to push and pull information through communication and coordination at various moments during teamwork. Essentially this condition set out to show how an expert synthetic agent (or proactive decision support tool) could help improve RPAS team performance through aiding in team level interactions.

Moving forward, more collaborative and proactive decision support RPAS systems should consider features that help the team complete activities during team level interactions, and not just the integration of separate individual team activities.

(2) *Support individual and team work*

Designing for collaboration is tricky. The collaborative system must inherently afford the ability to collaborate in real time, but also allow for individual work to still be conducted in concert with team work. The give and take between collaborative and individual work in system design is even more important when one takes into account team cognition. As previously outlined, team cognition is dependent on team level interactions but individual cognition still plays a major role in articulating team level cognition. The implications of the relationship of team level interaction and individual cognition means that collaborative RPAS decision support systems must allow for both to simultaneously take place. From the perspective of system design and human computer interaction, this is a highly complex design due to multiple varying goals.

Historically when we have designed collaborative systems, the focus has been on collaboration with the perspective that each team member has separate tasks and the goal is to support those tasks and often abstract them to the team level. Moving forward, system design of collaborative and proactive RPAS support must support both team level interactions and also individual work and cognition. If we are to adequately help team members develop team cognition during RPAS operations, then we need systems that support team level interaction via specific team activities that are dependent on team wide communication and coordination mechanisms. Yet, we must be deft enough to also allow for the appropriate individual tasks to be supported within the larger collaborative system. If we push too much focus on collaboration of team level interactions, individual team members will not be able to complete the individual work that is important to the team's work, as well as not be able to develop the appropriate individual cognition that is relevant to team cognition.

(3) *Support team level awareness*

Much like interaction, awareness is fundamental to team cognition. If team level awareness is not present, then the ability for team cognition to be present is significantly lessened. Yet, much like designing for the correct balance of individual vs. team work, it is also difficult to achieve a design that provides the correct amount of team level awareness. Similar to the issues outlined in the previous section, the system should allow for the correct amount of individual awareness to be supported in the system, while also affording the development of team level awareness. Developing team level awareness through system capabilities is challenging for two reasons: (1) the system must understand how much team level awareness is necessary to help develop team cognition and thus hopefully improve team performance, and (2) the system must acknowledge how to maintain awareness without disrupting both individual and team level work. It is imperative that decision support understands *when* to bring light of information to the entire team. If decision support is constantly bringing forth information that is not timely or relevant, the team's performance can be harmed. Team level awareness is helpful to developing team cognition if and only if the correct amount of awareness is acquired through the teams. Too much or too little awareness is counterproductive to teamwork and team cognition.

(4) *Use visualizations appropriately*

Decision support is increasingly using data visualizations to aid in team level decision making. Although, these visualizations have the potential to be useful to team cognition, it is important that the visualization itself aids in team level interaction. Visualizations should be equally representative of important team level information and meaningful to all members on the team. Far too often, supposed team level visualizations are not equally helpful for the entire team, thus limiting team level understanding and cognition.

(5) *Designing for heterogeneous and interdependent team member*

A team is a special group of people who all have interdependent and heterogeneous roles. These differing roles directly feed into the importance of team cognition. If team cognition is present, then team members have a better understanding of the scope and importance of each team members' individual role and how it aligns with the overall team's goals.

Yet, these specialized roles present a challenge to developing collaborative and proactive decision support for RPAS teams. The support must account for an equal balancing act between supporting team level interactions through various communication and coordination mechanisms (as highlighted above) and also catering to the individual team member's specific role. Thus, the decision support needs to be flexible in providing and aiding team level functions and individualized role based functions. This balancing act must be delineated on a situation by situation basis, depending on the goals and context that the decision support is oriented to.

(6) *Account for cognitive load*

The tasks associated with RPAS teams are extremely complicated, requiring a great deal of individual and team level cognition. System design in this context must acknowledge the great deal of cognitive work required in RPAS. Systems should always account for cognitive load, but collaborative systems must pay closer attention to the additional cognitive load resulting from increased collaboration. Teamwork inherently brings forth a great deal of cognitive load as a result of having to manage both individual and team level work. The prevalence of too much cognitive load challenges the development of team cognition.

A human has limited cognitive bandwidth allowing them to process a certain amount of information within a specified amount of time. If that bandwidth is exceeded, performance drastically decreases. Unfortunately, many collaborative systems increase cognitive load through a myriad of unnecessary features. When RPAS collaborative systems are designed, they must not unnecessary stretch one's cognition- considering it is already stretched due to the dynamics of teamwork. Human factors analysis with the users must take place before, during, and after system development to fully understand what system features are necessary and actually help to aid team level interactions. If the system increases cognitive load through irrelevant and distracting features, individual team members will have trouble processing information, leading to team cognition not being present. The saying, "less is more" can be true in regard to designing for team cognition.

(7) *Different tasks require differing team cognition perspectives*

Although we have introduced an integrative perspective of team cognition within RPAS that incorporates aspects of both the shared knowledge and ecological perspectives, it is important to understand that specific tasks may be suited better for one task than others. For this reason, it is of paramount importance to fully understand the task and context that the decision support is being used for. Careful consideration and understanding of the specific RPAS mission goals and tasks need to be taken into account when considering how team cognition plays a role in developing collaborative and proactive decision support. For example, a task that is highly interactive and dynamic should take an ecological approach where the system pushes team level interaction and information. Yet, in contrast, a task that occurs over many weeks, might be better suited in utilizing a shared knowledge approach where information can be shared in a longitudinal manner. And, finally, there may be many tasks that need both perspectives, which is the purpose of the integrated perspective. A system of collaborative decision support can and should be oriented to the task and the appropriate perspective of team cognition.

5   Concluding Thoughts

There is no question that RPAS is becoming more reliant on teamwork and collaborative activities. As the prevalence of RPAS missions continues to increase we will also see an increase in teamwork. As a community, we must work to understand how teamwork occurs within this context. More specifically, we also need to understand how to support RPAS teams in their collaborative activities.

In this paper, we highlighted a critical aspect of teamwork, team cognition, that needs to be accounted for when we attempt to support RPAS teams. When collaborative and proactive decision support systems are developed, they should directly account for multiple perspectives of team cognition depending on the task. The presence and development of team cognition in RPAS teams has the potential to increase team effectiveness. As the community moves forward, we need more team cognition research within this context. This research will then help further inform and build on the recommendations outlined in this paper on how to use team cognition as a mechanism for bettering future RPAS decision support systems.

Acknowledgements. This research was partially supported by ONR Award N000141110844 (Program Managers: Marc Steinberg, Paul Bello). We would also like to thank Mustafa Demir for his insights during the conceptualization of this paper.

References

1. Connolly, P.: The Power Behind the Drone (2014). http://ethics.iit.edu/EEL/The%20power%20behind.pdf
2. Cooke, N.J., Gorman, J.C., Myers, C.W., Duran, J.L.: Interactive team cognition. Cogn. Sci. **37**(2), 255–285 (2013)
3. Salas, E., Cooke, N.J., Rosen, M.A.: On teams, teamwork, and team performance: discoveries and developments (cover story). Hum. Factors **50**(3), 540–547 (2008)
4. Hinsz, V.B., Tindale, R.S., Vollrath, D.A.: The emerging conceptualization of groups as information processors. Psychol. Bull. **121**(1), 43–64 (1997)
5. Mohammed, S., Ferzandi, L., Hamilton, K.: Metaphor no more: A 15-year review of the team mental model construct. J. Manag. **36**(4), 876–910 (2010)
6. Gorman, J.C., Cooke, N.J., Winner, J.L.: Measuring team situation awareness in decentralized command and control environments. Ergonomics **49**(12–13), 1312–1325 (2006)

7. Wegner, D.M.: Transactive memory: a contemporary analysis of the group mind. In: Mullen, B., Goethals, G.R. (eds.) Theories of Group Behavior, pp. 185–208. Springer, New York (1987)

8. Rouse, W.B., Morris, N.M.: On looking into the black box: prospects and limits in the search for mental models. Psychol. Bull. **100**(3), 349–363 (1986)

9. Cannon-Bowers, J.A., Salas, E., Converse, S.A.: Cognitive psychology and team training: training shared mental models and complex systems. Hum. Factors Soc. Bull. **33**(12), 1–4 (1990)

10. Klimoski, R., Mohammed, S.: Team mental model: construct or metaphor? J. Manag. **20**(2), 403–437 (1994)

11. Mohammed, S., Dumville, B.C.: Team mental models in a team knowledge framework: expanding theory and measurement across disciplinary boundaries. J. Organ. Behav. **22**(2), 89–106 (2001)

12. Cannon-Bowers, J., Salas, E., Converse, S.A.: Shared mental models in expert team decision making. In: Castellan, N.J. (ed.) Individual and Group Decision Making: Current Issues, pp. 221–244. Psychology Press (1993)

13. Mathieu, J.E., Heffner, T.S., Goodwin, G.F., Salas, E., Cannon-Bowers, J.A.: The influence of shared mental models on team process and performance. J. Appl. Psychol. **85**(2), 273–283 (2000)

14. McNeese, N.J., Reddy, M.C., Friedenberg, E.M.: Team mental models within collaborative information seeking. Presented at the Human Factors and Ergonomics Society, Chicago, IL, pp. 335–339 (2014)

15. McNeese, N.J., Reddy, M.C.: Articulating and understanding the development of a team mental model in a distributed medium. Proc. Hum. Factors Ergon. Soc. Annu. Meet. **59**(1), 240–244 (2015)

16. Edwards, B.D., Day, E.A., Arthur, W., Bell, S.T.: Relationships among team ability composition, team mental models, and team performance. J. Appl. Psychol. **91**(3), 727–736 (2006)

17. Hamilton, K.L.: The Effect of Team Training Strategies on Team Mental Model Formation and Team Performance Under Routine and Non-Routine Environmental Conditions. ProQuest LLC, Ann Arbor (2009)

18. Cooke, N.J., Gorman, J.C., Myers, C.W., Duran, J.L.: Theoretical underpinnings of interactive team cognition. In: Salas, E., Fiore, S.M., Letsky, M.P. (eds.) Theories of Team Cognition: Cross-Disciplinary Perspectives. Routledge, Taylor & Francis, New York (2011)

19. Gibson, J.J.: The Ecological Approach to Visual Perception, Classic edn. Psychology Press, Abingdon (1979)

20. Cooke, N.J., Shope, S.M.: Designing a synthetic task environment. In: Schiflett, L.R.E., Salas, E., Coovert, M.D. (eds.) Scaled Worlds: Development, Validation, and Application, pp. 263–278. Ashgate Publishing, Surrey, England (2004)

21. Cooke, N.J., Gorman, J.C., Duran, J.L., Taylor, A.R.: Team cognition in experienced command-and-control teams. J. Exp. Psychol. Appl. **13**(3), 146–157 (2007)

22. Cooke, N.J., Kiekel, P.A., Helm, E.E.: Measuring team knowledge during skill acquisition of a complex task. Int. J. Cogn. Ergon. **5**(3), 297–315 (2001)

23. Cooke, N.J., Shope, S.M., Kiekel, P.A.: Shared-knowledge and team performance: a cognitive engineering approach to measurement. Technical report for AFOSR F49620-98-1-0287 (2001)

24. Gorman, J.C., Cooke, N.J., Amazeen, P.G.: Training adaptive teams. Hum. Factors Ergon. **52**(2), 295–307 (2010)

25. Demir, M., McNeese, N.J.: The role of recognition primed decision making in human-automation (H-A) teaming. Presented at the International Conference on Naturalistic Decision Making 2015, McLean, VA (2015)
26. Demir, M., McNeese, N.J., Cooke, N.J., Ball, J.T., Myers, C., Freiman, M.: Synthetic teammate communication and coordination with humans. Proc. Hum. Factors Ergon. Soc. Annu. Meet. 59(1), 951–955 (2015)
27. Demir, M., McNeese, N.J., Cooke, N.J.: Team communication behaviors of human-automation teaming. In: Cognitive Methods in Situation Awareness and Decision Support (COGSIMA), San Diego, CA (2016)

Supporting Multi-objective Decision Making Within a Supervisory Control Environment

Ciara Sibley[1]([⊠]), Joseph Coyne[1], Gopi Vinod Avvari[2],
Manisha Mishra[2], and Krishna R. Pattipati[2]

[1] Naval Research Laboratory, Washington, DC, USA
{ciara.sibley, joseph.coyne}@nrl.navy.mil
[2] University of Connecticut, Storrs, CT, USA
{vinod, manisha.mishra, krishna}@engr.uconn.edu

Abstract. This paper discusses decision making challenges involved in the management of multiple unmanned vehicles within a dynamic mission environment. Given the increased likelihood of this new supervisory control paradigm, the authors developed the Supervisory Control Operations User Testbed (SCOUT). A brief overview of SCOUT will be provided, followed by a summary of initial research conducted within the testbed which demonstrates how eye tracking measurements can be utilized to assess workload and predict situation awareness. Subsequent discussion will address challenges associated with dynamic decision making under uncertainty, with respect to multiple asset allocation. Techniques for measuring the accuracy of these decisions as well as assessing operator risk throughout the mission will also be presented. The paper concludes with discussion of how these new decision making metrics can be used to drive decision aids and compares decision making performance and risk bias under varying levels of task load.

Keywords: Supervisory control · Decision making · Risk · Eye tracking · Situation awareness

1 Introduction

The future Unmanned Aerial Vehicle (UAV) operator will no longer directly control a single vehicle or its payload, but will instead manage a group of highly autonomous UAVs. Within this new supervisory role, the operator's primary responsibility will be one of determining how to allocate the UAVs to meet multiple mission requirements within a dynamic and uncertain environment. Implementing this new paradigm of UAV management requires an increase in autonomy as well as an understanding of how a human performs in this supervisory capacity. Since multi-objective decision making is a primary aspect of future UAV operations, conducting research within a realistic and complex testing environment which enables investigation of various decision support concepts and automation tools is critical to the successful implementation of supervisory control.

The first section of this paper will discuss the development of the Supervisory Control Operations User Testbed (SCOUT™), an experimental platform for investigating the

© Springer International Publishing Switzerland 2016
D.D. Schmorrow and C.M. Fidopiastis (Eds.): AC 2016, Part II, LNAI 9744, pp. 210–221, 2016.
DOI: 10.1007/978-3-319-39952-2_21

human performance challenges associated with supervisory control of multiple UAVs. The second section will highlight results from initial research conducted within SCOUT, addressing workload and situation awareness measurement techniques. The third section will discuss the development of a decision performance assessment algorithm as well as a new proposed approach for quantifying the difficulty of multi-objective asset allocation decisions within SCOUT. In addition, section three will present a method for providing an operator with customized decision support based upon the amount of risk he would like to take. The paper will conclude with a summary of future research that can be conducted within SCOUT, leveraging these new algorithms to enable mixed initiative decision support.

The Supervisory Control Operations User Testbed. The U.S. Naval Research Lab developed the Supervisory Control Operations User Testbed (SCOUT) to investigate future challenges that human operators will experience while managing missions involving multiple autonomous systems. SCOUT contains representative tasks that a future UAV supervisory controller will likely perform, assuming advancements in automation. The testing environment is also instrumented with physiological sensors, which are integrated with the SCOUT and user performance data, in order to gather a more complete understanding of a user's state, such as the operator's mental workload, or level of awareness (see Fig. 1). These constructs are inferred via proxy measures such as: an individual's pupil size, which is correlated with mental workload (e.g., [1]); eye gaze patterns, which can serve as indicators of situation awareness and attention allocation (e.g., [2]); and heart rate variability, which is inversely correlated with stress levels (e.g., [3]).

Fig. 1. SCOUT operator interacting with the testbed while eye tracking data is being collected

SCOUT operators engage in Intelligence Surveillance and Reconnaissance (ISR) missions in which they are responsible for mission planning as well as airspace management, updating UAV flight parameters, responding to communications and re-planning as new mission information is received. The operator's primary responsibility is to make decisions on how to dynamically allocate unmanned assets as is appropriate for achieving mission goals. Specifically, operators must decide where to send each of their three UAVs to search for targets of varying priority levels, uncertainty (with respect to intelligence information about location, which impacts time and ability to actually find targets), and deadlines. In addition, operators must respond to requests for information and commands via chat boxes, as well as monitor airspace, fuel levels and sensor feeds. In order to motivate users, SCOUT operators receive points for finding targets and for providing timely and accurate information to mission command, and they lose points for violating restricted airspace. All tasking is driven by pre-scripted scenario files, and event timing within the scenario can be used to increase or decrease the workload requirements of the operator.

2 Previous Research Within SCOUT

Human subject data collection was conducted within SCOUT with twenty volunteers. Each individual wore a Zephyr Bioharness, which recorded heart rate data, in addition to being calibrated on the SmartEye Pro system, which recorded eye gaze, pupil size and eyelid data. Prior to engaging with SCOUT, participants received approximately thirty minutes of training which consisted of viewing short videos, followed by interactive assessments to ensure a high level of comprehension. Following training, participants engaged in two SCOUT sessions. Each session was comprised of a planning phase, followed by three mission execution blocks. Participants were given up to ten minutes for the planning phase and when they were ready to continue, they began the mission.

Each mission execution session took approximately 18 min, which was comprised of three six minute blocks of varying difficulty (i.e. task load), but always started with a medium level of difficulty. Block difficulty was manipulated by the frequency of tasking (e.g., new target opportunities and chat requests/commands) and each session was counter-balanced such that half the participants received Session A first, while the other half received Session B first, as seen in Table 1. During the easy, medium and hard blocks, tasking was presented at a rate of every 75, 45 and 15 s, respectively. An example task may include chat requests to change the altitude on a UAV ("Increase altitude of UV-72 by 73") or relay information on a UAV ("Provide speed of UH-28"). Task frequency was systematically varied in order to observe the impact on human performance in addition to eye tracking and heart rate metrics.

Table 1. Sessions and Difficulty Blocks

	Planning Block	Block 1	Block 2	Block 3
Session A	Planning	Medium	Hard	Easy
Session B	Planning	Medium	Easy	Hard

Participants also experienced Situation Awareness (SA) freeze probes once per block. During these probes, everything on the SCOUT interface disappeared except for the map display, and the participant was instructed to recreate the position of the three UAVs and any active targets which were last present on the map. Additionally, participants were told to provide the current target each UAV was pursuing and how many points that target was worth. Lastly, they were asked whether the UAV would be able to complete its search within the next ten minutes. See Fig. 2 for a depiction of the SA probe.

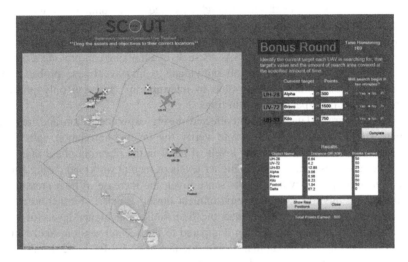

Fig. 2. Example SCOUT Situation Awareness freeze probe

The mission task performance measure of interest in this experiment (responses to tasking via chat) revealed increases in error and decreases in the percentage of tasks completed associated with increasing levels of task load [4, 5]. Following the same pattern, results on the SA probe showed increases in the error distance for map object placement (i.e., larger distances between where participants placed targets and UAVs and where they actually were) as a function of increases in block difficulty level. This same result was found to hold for the UAV-target pair accuracy on the SA probe, with decreases in performance on the hard condition compared to the easy one [6].

Results from this data collection also demonstrated how eye tracking and heart rate metrics align with performance metrics and can be used to infer a user's current cognitive state. Specifically, increases in participant's task load were associated with increases in the mean and maximum of participant's pupil size, derived over a six-minute block of data [4]. Additionally, pupil size standard deviation was statistically significant in differentiating the task load levels, and when a subset of the four top and four bottom performers were analyzed, the standard deviation of the bottom performers was much greater than the standard deviation of the top performers (see [4] for more details) for each task load level. This suggests that greater variability in pupil size values may reveal that a user is struggling with a task, while smaller fluctuations suggest greater task comprehension or mastery. This is consistent with research by

Ahern and Beatty [7], which demonstrated that students with lower scores on the scholastic aptitude test (SAT) exhibited greater pupillary dilation than those with higher scores, when given math problems.

Additional analysis conducted on the eye gaze data revealed that participants had significantly fewer fixations within the relevant display region, the map, one and two minutes prior to the SA probe during the high level of task load, compared to the low task load [8]. In addition, the fixation duration was significantly shorter during the high load level. Participants also exhibited smaller spread of fixations, or dispersion, one minute prior to the SA probe during the high task load level, compared to the low and medium levels [6]. These findings are significant since they correspond to SA performance data, demonstrating how fixation metrics calculated within the appropriate areas of interest can be predictive of SA. As such, eye tracking can provide a dynamic measure of SA without subjecting an individual to invasive freeze probes, which potentially add confounding effects (due to interruptions) and can only provide a measure of SA at that specific point in time.

Electrocardiogram data was also collected during experimentation and heart rate variability (HRV) data was analyzed to verify the inverse correlation with mental workload [3]. Results showed higher levels of HRV in the planning phase than in the first block of each session, indicating higher levels of mental workload during Block 1 than the planning phase, which makes sense given the increase in time pressure and dynamics of the mission execution environment during Block 1. Furthermore, HRV was greater in the second session than the first, indicating higher levels of mental workload in the first planning session compared to the second session, likely attributable to learning effects and familiarity with the task (See [9] for more details). HRV was not able to distinguish the differences in task load, however, during mission execution.

The various metrics discussed above can all be used in combination to help inform a user's state (i.e., workload, situation awareness) as they engage in a task. The authors have started to utilize machine learning methodologies to predict a SCOUT user's workload from 60 s chunks of eye tracking and performance data [10]. The objective is to identify when an operator is outside his or her optimal level of workload (e.g. overloaded) in order to know when to provide decision support, relief, or even additional tasking in the case of underload, to an operator and ultimately prevent errors.

3   Future Decision Making Research Within SCOUT

The primary task within SCOUT is the route planning task in which the operator develops a path plan for sending each of her three UAVs to find active targets, i.e., a plan that specifies the sequence of targets to search within their opportunity windows. Each of the UAVs are equipped with a sensor that actively searches for targets on the ground, but UAVs differ in capabilities, such that some are faster and have better sensor ranges than others, which facilitates more rapid location of targets. As this is a search task, the exact latitude and longitude of each target is uncertain and this area of uncertainty is represented on the main map with a white circle surrounding the target (as seen in Figs. 3 and 4). In determining the best plan, the operator must consider each

UAV's current position, velocity and sensor capabilities, and each target's value and location uncertainty, which is influenced by the target's search area size and deadline. A target can have a large search area, but long deadline, which enables a full search of the target area, or it could have a short deadline, which means that only a fraction of the target search area can be covered and the target may or may not be found.

The operator is tasked with developing an optimal plan that will maximize the cumulative value. Target values are only rewarded if a UAV finds the target, which occurs at a random point during the search, i.e., it could be located any time between 1 % or 99 % of the search. Furthermore, the operator's plan can include multiple targets for each vehicle, but the order in which the targets are visited influences how much of the search area can be covered before a target's deadline. This is comparable to developing a route plan for running errands of varying utility at multiple stores which have different operating hours and which will take variable amounts of time within the store to achieve one's objectives. In this respect, decisions must be made as to which items to prioritize, since not everything can be accomplished.

The scenarios within SCOUT are pre-scripted such that all the participants initially begin with the same decision making problem and receive new target opportunities and intelligence information at the same time during mission execution. However, every route decision an operator makes within SCOUT influences future decisions, that is, it is a dynamic decision making problem over a time horizon. As such, if two operators implement different initial plans, their UAVs will be moving in different directions and will thus be in different positions when new targets or updated target information occurs in the scenario. A specific vehicle's location could mean the difference between a new target being a better alternative than the existing plan or a poor choice. Initial studies conducted within SCOUT could determine if one operator's initial plan was superior to another's, based on expected utility theory, but had no way of assessing the operator's decision making quality as the scenario progressed since the two cumulative scores by the end of the mission were not comparable.

To address this shortcoming, NRL has been actively collaborating with the University of Connecticut to develop approaches to determine the optimal target sequence within SCOUT at every decision point for all operators [11]. The optimal solution is based upon a target's expected value. If a target was valued at 1000 points, but only 55 % of the area could be searched before its deadline, it would have an expected value of 550 points; however in SCOUT points are either awarded in full or not at all. Decision making within SCOUT is not a simple static process, but rather a continuous dynamic task, since plans need to be monitored and updated as new information becomes available. The computation of an optimal solution allows for the objective evaluation of the operator's decisions throughout the scenario by comparing the expected value and the time required to complete the operator's plan with a plan that maximizes the dynamically evolving expected value.

The route optimization algorithm may also afford a method of quantitatively evaluating the difficulty of different scenarios. The position of vehicles relative to targets makes the optimal plan for some scenarios "easier" than others. For example, within some scenarios, several UAV-target pairings can be eliminated simply based upon proximity and thus reduce the number of alternatives the operator is forced to choose from. Consider the scenarios in Figs. 3 and 4: the scenario depicted in Fig. 3

has the same target locations, point values and deadlines as the targets in Fig. 4, but the starting UAV locations are different: either clustered together or dispersed. Figure 4's Dispersed UAV scenario illustrates an example planning problem in which the operator can quickly eliminate potential vehicle-target assignments, since it would not make sense for an operator to consider sending a UAV to a target location far away when there are two within its close proximity.

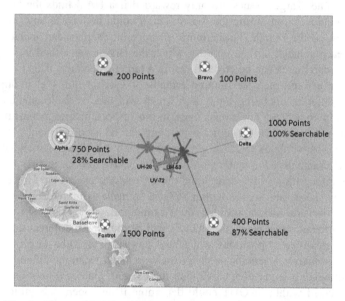

Fig. 3. Clustered UAV scenario with optimal route solutions displayed

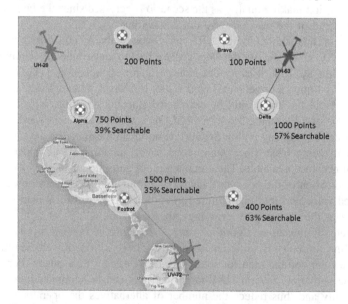

Fig. 4. Dispersed UAV scenario with optimal route solutions displayed

While the optimal route plan for the Dispersed UAV scenario in Fig. 4 yields the maximum reward of 1635 points, the 10th best plan yields only 1267 points and the standard deviation within the top 10 plans is 127 points. This scenario stands in contrast to the Clustered UAV scenario depicted in Fig. 3, in that there are fewer vehicle target-pairings that can be eliminated and the standard deviation within the top 10 plans is much less, at only 57 points (see Table 2 below). In this scenario, since multiple plans yield similar expected values, determining an ideal solution and comparing among various plan options should be qualitatively more difficult for the operator.

Table 2. Optimal plan scores, top 10 plan score averages and top 10 plan score standard deviations for Clustered and Dispered Scenarios

	Optimal Plan Score	10th Best Plan Score	Top 10 Plan's Score Average	Top 10 Plan's Score Stdev
Clustered UAV Scenario	1565	1391	1486	57
Dispersed UAV Scenario	1635	1267	1415	127

It is not definitive yet whether the variance among the top optimal scores can serve as a proxy for plan difficulty; however, the authors are developing a version of SCOUT in which the operator would only complete the route planning task across a range of different scenarios (planning blocks only, no mission execution). Comparing the amount of deviation of the top optimal plans with the time required to reach a decision should help determine if this type of metric can be applied in assessing the decision difficulty.

Accounting for Risk in Decision Making. When a SCOUT operator decides to prioritize one target over another, the operator is essentially making a choice that the potential reward and time requirements of one opportunity supersedes the other. These decisions made under uncertainty translate into the amount of risk an individual is willing to take. The optimal route solutions discussed above were computed using an expected utility function which is risk neutral. To explain, when applying expected utility theory, if we have a target worth 500 points and search 50 % of its possible searchable area, then the expected value of this target with this search is 250, assuming targets are uniformly distributed throughout the search areas and that search of the area is swept at a constant rate with respect to time. This is equivalent to:

$$E_t = V_t * (TD_t)/(TS_t), \text{ where} \tag{1}$$

t = target
E_t = expected value of target t
V_t = point value of target t
TD_t = time allocated to search before target t deadline
TS_t = time required to completely search target t

This equation fails to account for the human decision maker, however, who is not always perfectly rational and may desire to make riskier or more conservative (i.e., risk averse) decisions. For example, a conservative decision maker may feel uncomfortable pursuing a 500-point target, which only has a 50 % chance of being found (assuming 50 % of the target's area can be searched before the deadline). As such, this individual may mentally decrement the target value (say, to 180 points) and view it as being worth less than the expected value. This individual may, therefore, decide to pursue another target worth 200 points, which has a 100 % chance of being found, over this 500-point target, which is valued by the operator as 180. Conversely, an individual who is willing to make riskier decisions, may view the original uncertain target as being of higher worth than the expected value (say, 420 points) and therefore be more inclined to pursue this target, which only has a 50 % chance of being found, over a target which is valued at 350 points and has a 100 % certainty of being found.

In order to account for different risk thresholds which a SCOUT user is willing to accept, we propose a modified version of the expected utility function, which we call perceived value, which includes a parameterized risk threshold, R:

$$PV_t = V_t * \min((TD_t)/(TS_t * R), 1), \text{ where} \tag{2}$$

PV_t = perceived value of target t
R = risk threshold

Here, we see that when $R = 1$, the equation yields the same solution as the expected value; however, when $R > 1$ the perceived value decreases signifying a more conservative risk threshold, and when $R < 1$, the perceived value increases signifying a more liberal or risky threshold. R values less than 1.0 essentially represent the percentage of a search area that a decision maker would like to be able to search before the target deadline, or the amount of risk the user is willing to accept. R values greater than 1, on the other hand, serve the purpose of decrementing the value of a target which can only be partially searched (< 100 %) before deadline in order to represent a more conservative search approach. Also note the second half of the PV_t equation is bounded to a maximum of 1 in order to prevent PVs from becoming greater than the possible target value, since R values less than 1 can lead to $TD_t/(TS_t * R)$ greater than 1, which is not possible.

To demonstrate how this might support a decision maker, consider the following simple scenario in Table 3 in which a decision maker has the option to pursue only one of three different targets: Alpha, Beta or Charlie, each of which has a different point value and search area percentage which can be accomplished prior to its deadline. The three perceived value columns show the calculated values for different R values, which represent perceptions of a risk neutral, high risk and conservative pursuits. The highest value solution for each target is demarked with an asterisk; note how the ideal target to pursue varies depending on the R value utilized. This disparity demonstrates why it is important to provide users with mixed initiative planning tools, which enable them to impact the recommended decisions by providing customized weightings.

Reviewing Table 3, we see that if a decision maker employed a risk neutral strategy that Alpha is the optimal target to pursue; however, a high risk strategy would suggest

Table 3. Example scenario involving three targets with varying point values and uncertainty and their perceived values as a function of risk threshold

Target	Value	Percent Area Searchable by Deadline	Perceived Value (R = 1, Neutral)	Perceived Value (R = 0.2, Risky)	Perceived Value (R = 2.1, Conservative)
Alpha	750	50 %	375*	750	179
Beta	1500	15 %	225	1125*	107
Charlie	250	100 %	250	250	250*

Beta is actually a better gamble than Alpha. A conservative strategy, however, weights certainty as more important than the potential for more points, and, therefore, suggests Charlie as the best option. This ability to assess target options based upon different risk thresholds enables SCOUT operators to weigh the risks and benefits of various plans, given the context of the mission and its objectives. This tool is currently being integrated within SCOUT in order to provide the operator with a decision support route planning tool. User involvement is especially important in unmanned system applications since the human operator often has access to additional information that planning algorithms do not consider (e.g., intelligence briefs) which might impact how much risk is appropriate in different circumstances.

In addition to using different perceived values as weights to drive the optimal path plan options within a decision support tool, these perceived weights can also provide an additional tool for determining an operator's risk threshold based upon their decisions. This can be accomplished by applying different risk weightings to both the operator's plan and the optimal plan and comparing whether the operator's weighted plan value exceeds the value of an optimal risk neutral plan. If the operator's expected point total exceeds the risk neutral point total when a conservative weighting is applied, the operator's plan would be assumed to be more conservative than the risk neutral optimal plan. Conversely, if a risky weighting on the operator's plan exceeds the optimal plan's value this indicates the operator likely had a risky decision criterion. If the risk neutral plan exceeds the operator's plan with the different weights, this suggests that the operator may have selected a poor plan. While the perceived value formula above will likely be refined, it provides a powerful tool for investigating risk within a supervisory control task. This enables a number of research questions to be addressed such as how high and low workload impact an operator's decision making.

4 Summary

This paper reviewed previous research conducted within SCOUT, demonstrating the utility in collecting eye tracking and heart rate measurements within a realistic and complex supervisory control simulation. These findings are especially significant within the application domain of unmanned systems where system interaction can be limited and performance measures are difficult to acquire. These physiological metrics, in addition to performance and mission context information, can be utilized to inform predictions about whether a user will be able to successfully accomplish the mission, such that a user who has elevated pupil sizes, decreased HRV and reduced visual dispersion might be flagged as at risk and provided an alert. Furthermore, the cost of eye tracking technology continues to drop such that highly accurate low cost systems are now available and it is viable to instrument military work stations with eye tracking and heart rate sensors in order to apply research such as this to augment the effectiveness of US Warfighters.

The second section of the paper highlighted ongoing work to incorporate new route optimization and decision bias algorithms into SCOUT. One of the more important areas of research for supervisory control of UAVs is within planning and re-planning, which take place throughout the mission and is a multi-objective decision making problem. The incorporation of these new optimization algorithms allow for continuous assessment of both operator decisions and for providing decision support to suggest when new information (e.g., new target or updated intelligence) merits a change to the existing plan. The metrics provided by these new algorithms will enable future research investigating how varying levels of task load impact both decision quality as well as risk biases. Additionally these algorithms will help drive new decision support tools and research within SCOUT.

Ultimately SCOUT was created to represent the key characteristics of multi-objective decision making that is a critical part of the ISR UAV missions today, as well as demonstrate how those decisions will become increasingly complex when operators begin managing multiple vehicles in the future. The researches plan on making SCOUT freely available by the end of 2016 and encourage others to utilize SCOUT as a tool for their own research.

References

1. Hess, E.H., Polt, J.M.: Pupil size in relation to mental activity during simple problem-solving. Science **143**, 1190–1192 (1964)
2. Werneke, J., Vollrath, M.: What does the driver look at? The influence of intersection characteristics on attention allocation and driving behavior. Accid. Anal. Prev. **45**, 610–619 (2012)
3. Hjortskov, N., Rissén, D., Blangsted, A.K., Fallentin, N., Lundberg, U., Søgaard, K.: The effect of mental stress on heart rate variability and blood pressure during computer work. Eur. J. Appl. Physiol. **92**, 84–89 (2004)
4. Sibley, C., Coyne, J.T., Doddi, A., Jasper, P.: pupillary response as an indicator of processing demands within a supervisory control simulation environment. In: 18th International Symposium on Aviation Psychology, pp. 506–511. Wright State University (2015)
5. Mannaru, P., Balasingam, B., Pattipati, K.R., Sibley, C., Coyne, J.T.: Cognitive context detection in UAS operators using pupillary measurements. In: 2016 SPIE Defense + Commercial Sensing (in Press)
6. Coyne, J.T., Sibley, C., Monfort, S.S.: Using eye tracking measures as a correlate of situation awareness in an unmanned vehicle control task. In: Tsang, P., Vidulich, M., Flach, J. (eds.) Advances in Aviation Psychology II. Ashgate (in Press)

7. Ahern, S., Beatty, J.: Pupillary responses during information processing vary with scholastic aptitude test scores. Science **205**, 1289–1292 (1979)
8. Coyne, J.T., Sibley, C.: Impact of task load and gaze on situation awareness in unmanned aerial vehicle control. In: 18th International Symposium on Aviation Psychology, pp. 458–463. Wright State University (2015)
9. Jasper, P., Sibley, C., Coyne, J.T.: Using heart rate variability to assess mental workload in a command and control simulation of multiple unmanned aerial vehicles. In: 2016 Human Factors and Ergonomics Society Annual Meeting (in Press)
10. Monfort, S.S., Sibley, C., Coyne, J.T.: Using machine learning and real-time workload assessment to inform task allocation in a multiple UAV management simulation. In: 2016 SPIE Defense + Commercial Sensing (in Press)
11. Nadella, B.K., Avvari, G.V., Kumar, A., Mishra, M., Sidoti, D., Pattipati, K.R., Sibley, C., Coyne, J.T., Monfort, S.S.: Proactive Decision Support for Dynamic Assignment and Routing of Unmanned Aerial Systems. In: IEEE Aerospace Conference, Big Sky, Montana (2016)

Assessment of Expert Interaction with Multivariate Time Series 'Big Data'

Susan Stevens Adams[✉], Michael J. Haass, Laura E. Matzen, and Saskia King

Sandia National Laboratories, Albuquerque, USA
{smsteve,mjhaass,lematze,shking}@sandia.gov

Abstract. 'Big data' is a phrase that has gained much traction recently. It has been defined as 'a broad term for data sets so large or complex that traditional data processing applications are inadequate and there are challenges with analysis, searching and visualization' [1]. Many domains struggle with providing experts accurate visualizations of massive data sets so that the experts can understand and make decisions about the data e.g., [2, 3, 4, 5].

Abductive reasoning is the process of forming a conclusion that best explains observed facts and this type of reasoning plays an important role in process and product engineering. Throughout a production lifecycle, engineers will test subsystems for critical functions and use the test results to diagnose and improve production processes.

This paper describes a value-driven evaluation study [7] for expert analyst interactions with big data for a complex visual abductive reasoning task. Participants were asked to perform different tasks using a new tool, while eye tracking data of their interactions with the tool was collected. The participants were also asked to give their feedback and assessments regarding the usability of the tool. The results showed that the interactive nature of the new tool allowed the participants to gain new insights into their data sets, and all participants indicated that they would begin using the tool in its current state.

Keywords: Big data · Eye tracking · Evaluation study · Knowledge elicitation

1 Introduction

'Big data' is a phrase that has gained much traction recently. It has been defined as 'a broad term for data sets so large or complex that traditional data processing applications are inadequate and there are challenges with analysis, searching and visualization' [1]. Many domains struggle with providing experts accurate visualizations of massive data sets so that the experts can understand and make decisions about the data e.g., [2, 3, 4, 5]. One such domain includes tasks requiring abductive reasoning. Abductive reasoning is the process of forming a conclusion that best explains observed facts. This type of reasoning plays an important role in fields such as scientific research, economics and medicine. A common example of abductive reasoning is medical diagnosis. Given a set of symptoms, a doctor determines a diagnosis that best explains the combination of symptoms. Abductive reasoning is also important in process and product engineering. Throughout a

© Springer International Publishing Switzerland 2016
D.D. Schmorrow and C.M. Fidopiastis (Eds.): AC 2016, Part II, LNAI 9744, pp. 222–230, 2016.
DOI: 10.1007/978-3-319-39952-2_22

production lifecycle, engineers will test subsystems for critical functions and use the test results to diagnose and improve production processes.

This paper describes an evaluation study for expert analyst interactions with big data for a complex visual abductive reasoning task. The experts in our study use multivariate time series data to diagnose device performance throughout a production lifecycle and are tasked with determining whether there are failures or anomalies in these complex data sets. The current tools available to these analysts do not fully support interaction with this type of data. As such, our research team developed a new tool with the goal of allowing these analysts to explore, interact and better understand this 'big data' associated with task and their decision making process.

2   Visualization Evaluation with Experts

Visualization of data and information is growing in popularity and results in impressive images and pictures. But how well do these visualizations allow experts to perform their tasks and solve the problems they need to solve? Previous work has suggested that reviews with experts are a valuable way to evaluate visualizations [6]. As such, we performed an evaluation of the Dial-A-Cluster (DAC) tool using the analyst experts, and followed the recommended steps laid out by [6]. For example, we choose a set of experts who were most familiar with the analysis, had the experts work independently on the tasks and took copious notes.

We also resonated with the idea of value-driven evaluations [7]. This work argues that the value of a visualization goes beyond the ability to simply answer questions about the data (which is common is typical usability studies) but should provide a broader, more holistic, "bigger picture" understanding of the data set. The author explains that the value of a visualization includes the total time required to answer a variety of questions about the data, a visualization's ability to incite and discover insights or insightful questions about the data, a visualization's ability to convey overall essence or take-away sense of the data and a visualization's ability to generate confidence, knowledge and trust about the data [7]. Effective visualizations excel at presenting a set of heterogeneous data attributes in parallel, allowing a person to make inferences about the data set, allowing a person to gain a broad, total sense of a large data set beyond what can be gained from each individual data case, and allowing a person to learn and understand more than just the raw information contained within the data. The tool development and our expert evaluation study used a value-driven approach.

3   Analyst Task and Tool

The analysts in our study use complex, multivariate time series data to diagnose device performance throughout the production lifecycle. As we found in our previous work [8], these analysts made decisions by looking at trends across many different types of waveforms. The current analyst tool for analyzing these waveforms presents the waveforms one at a time, which does not allow the analyst to assess trends among the waveforms. As such, the team developed a new tool, termed Dial-a-Cluster (DAC), which allows the analysts to visualize and inspect multiple waveforms at a time as well as view other important metadata.

The DAC tool [9] uses multidimensional scaling to provide a visualization of the data points depending on distance measures provided for each time series. The analyst can interactively adjust (dial) the relative influence of each time series to change the visualization (and resulting clusters). Additional computations are provided which optimize the visualization according to metadata of interest and rank time series measurements according to their influence on analyst selected clusters. The tool was created to allow the analyst to pull in different types of information and to visualize many different waveforms at once. See [9] for a complete description of the DAC tool. Figure 1 displays the DAC interface.

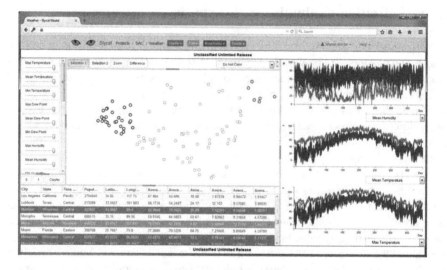

Fig. 1. Dial-a-Cluster interface

We performed a value-driven evaluation study of the DAC tool for complex, multivariate time series 'big data' with the expert analysts. We asked the participants to perform different tasks using the tool, while collecting eye tracking data of their interactions with the tool. We also collected their feedback and assessments regarding the usability of the tool.

4   Evaluation Study

4.1   Participants

Seven participants at Sandia National Laboratories volunteered to participate in our study. Six of the participants in the study were classified as experts; that is, they diagnosed device performance using the multivariate time series data as part of their daily job. These experts had an average of 10 years' experience performing this type of activity (range 5–14). One participant was categorized as a novice, with less than one year of experience in this domain.

4.2 Procedure

The participants completed the study individually. In the work domain studied, access to experts was limited due to their senior roles spanning multiple engineering teams; therefore usability sessions had to be as brief as possible, while still being thorough enough to acquire all data relevant to the work and the expert's reasoning processes. Many of the same participants from our first study (see [8]) participated in this usability study. If the participant had not previously participated, he/she first read through and signed the study consent form and asked any questions he/she had about the study.

The experimenter then calibrated the FaceLAB 5 Standard System Eye Tracker with two miniature digital cameras and one infrared illumination pod. Eye tracking was collected during both training and the actual study trials; the experimenters anticipated that eye tracking data during the training session would shed light on how the participants learned how to use the tool and could improve future training on the tool. The participants then received training on the DAC tool. The experimenter explained the functions of the DAC tool buttons and panes using weather data and walked through a series of practice tasks using the different buttons and capabilities of the tool. The participant was encouraged to ask questions throughout the training session and to experiment with the tool and the weather data. Training lasted about 20 min.

After the training session was over, the participant completed a series of trials using the tool. Each trial contained multivariate time series data from multiple device tests. For each trial, the experts were presented with 100 tests, 11 different waveforms and 14 columns of metadata. This was in stark comparison to the existing tool which displayed fewer than 10 tests, presented one waveform at a time and did not have metadata as readily accessible. The participant was asked to classify the data as anomalous or normal. If the participant indicated that any of the tests was anomalous, he/she was asked to indicate the type of anomaly. Eye tracking data and response times were recorded while the subject worked with the DAC tool for each trial. There were a total of ten trials that participants could complete, although no participant completed more than five trials during the time allotted for the experiment session. The participants completed the trials in the same order.

After the determination was made (and response time was collected) for each trial, participants were encouraged to explain their thought process to better understand how they reached their decision and to understand how they interacted with the tool to make their determination. Also, any comments made by the participants during the study trial were noted by the experimenters.

At the end of the study, participants completed a questionnaire assessing their satisfaction with the tool. Participants were asked what they liked best and least about the tool, to provide suggestions for improving the usefulness of the tool and whether they would actually use the tool to complete their regular analysis tasks.

5   Analysis and Results

The amount of time it took the participants to complete each trial varied widely. Two participants completed five trials during the experimental session, one completed four trials, two completed three trials, and two completed only two trials. The novice participant completed only two trials and did not identify any anomalous data in either trial. The more experienced participants identified several anomalies, averaging between one and four anomalies per trial. This difference in performance highlighted the interplay between domain expertise and tool usability and was informative to the team in terms of future tool training.

In general, the participants completed the trials more quickly as the experiment progressed and they became more familiar with the tool. The duration of each trial for each participant is shown in Fig. 2. The expert participants are labeled E1-E6 and the novice participant is N1. Some trials were more difficult than others in terms of how readily the anomalous data "popped out" in the DAC tool. On Trial 3, a relatively easy trial, most participants found the answer in less than five minutes. On Trial 4, a more difficult trial, the average response time was closer to ten minutes.

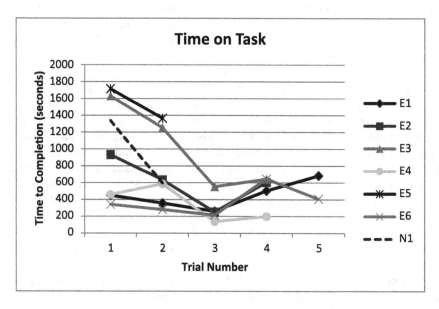

Fig. 2. Duration of each trial in seconds

Eye tracking data were analyzed using EyeWorks software, Eye Tracking Inc., Solana Beach, CA. The number of fixations per trial mirrored the time-on-task data, as shown in Fig. 3.

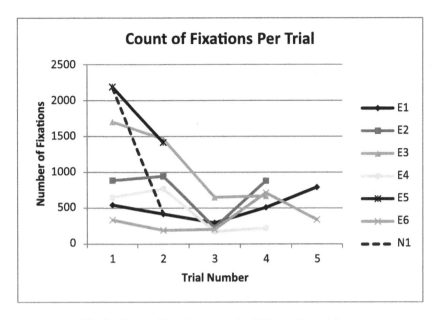

Fig. 3. Count of fixations on each trial for each participant

To analyze how the participants were using the DAC tool, the tool was divided into several regions of interest (ROIs), including the cluster pane, the graph pane, the slider pane, and the metadata pane. Figure 4 shows how the ROIs related to the DAC interface. The ROI analysis was conducted only for the first four trials, since few of the participants completed the fifth trial. On average, as the experiment progressed, participants spent more time viewing the cluster and graph panes and less time viewing the slider and metadata panes, as shown in Fig. 5. This pattern could indicate that as the participants became more comfortable with the tool, they spend more of their time focused on the data visualizations. Once the participants were familiar with the types of information in the slider and metadata panes, they would only need to consult that information when adjusting the way the data were displayed in the cluster panel or when investigating specific data points in the metadata.

We further subdivided the graph pane ROI to better understand how participants were using the data visualizations. The participants could display variables of their choice in the three graphs, or they could use a differencing tool that automatically set the graphs to show the variables that contributed most to the difference between two selections in the Cluster Pane. Early in the experiment, participants fixated on the top and middle graphs almost equally often. Surprisingly, as the experiment progressed, participant's average proportion of fixations increased for the middle graph, as shown in Fig. 6. This change could indicate that participants were developing strategies for how best to organize the information within the DAC tool in order to find the anomalies. A qualitative analysis of the participants' strategies, based on the observational notes taking during the sessions, indicated that most participants chose to display one key variable in the top graph. Their interactions with the cluster pane and the other

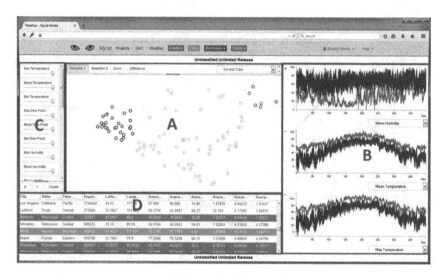

Fig. 4. Dial-a-Cluster interface divided into ROIs for the eye tracking analysis. **A** is the Cluster Pane, **B** is the Graph Pane, **C** is the Slider Pane, and **D** is the Metadata Pane.

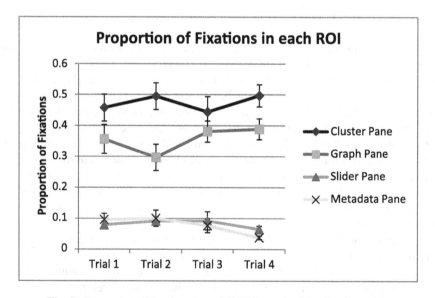

Fig. 5. Proportion of fixations in each ROI for each of the first four trials

graphs were largely focused on determining how other variables related to the variable of interest.

From a qualitative perspective, the participants responded positively to the tool. In their verbal and written assessments of the tool, they indicated that the interactivity and the linked visualizations were the key features that supported gaining insight into the data sets. Two of the participants (E5 and N1) revealed through their written feedback

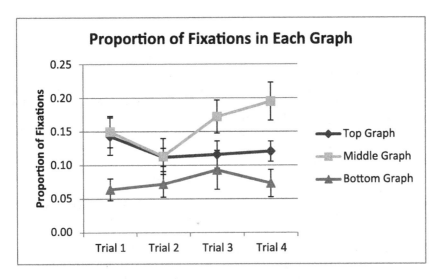

Fig. 6. Proportion of fixations in each graph within the Graph Pane ROI

that they viewed the information in the cluster pane as a correlation, rather than two-dimensional projection of multi-dimensional data. This misinterpretation may have slowed their analyses, as these were also the only two participants who completed only two trials during the experiment session. Identifying a potential source of confusion for future users of the DAC tool was a valuable outcome of the study.

In summary, this evaluation showed that users were readily able to adopt a new tool for performing abductive reasoning with large, complex data sets. The DAC tool provided users with a new way to view types of data that they work with frequently, allowing them to assess larger data sets and to perform new types of analyses in order to identify trends and outliers in the data. The interactive nature of the tool allowed the users to gain new insights into their data sets, and all seven participants indicated that they would begin using the tool in its current state. The value-driven evaluation approach, using multiple types of analysis (behavioral, eye tracking, and qualitative), pointed toward trends in how participants used the tool as they became familiar with it. It also revealed some of the strategies that participants adopted, as well as potential pitfalls where a misunderstanding of the data visualizations could lead to confusion. This information will be used to further refine and improve the DAC tool.

Acknowledgements. Sandia National Laboratories is a multi-program laboratory managed and operated by Sandia Corporation, a wholly owned subsidiary of Lockheed Martin Corporation, for the U.S. Department of Energy's National Nuclear Security Administration under contract DE-AC04-94AL85000. SAND NO. 2016-1724C. This work was funded by Laboratory Directed Research and Development (LDRD).

References

1. Wikipedia, Accessed on Dec 2015
2. Marx, V.: Biology: the big challenges of big data. Nature **498**, 255–260 (2013)
3. Ayhan, S., Pesce, J., Comitz, P., Sweet, D., Bliesner, S., Gerberick, G.: Predictive analytics with aviation big data. In: Integrated Communications, Navigation and Surveillance Conference (ICNS), pp. 1–13. IEEE (2013)
4. Fan, J., Han, F., Liu, H.: Challenges of big data analysis. Nat. Sci. Rev. **1**(2), 293–314 (2013)
5. Katal, A., Wazid, M., Goudar, R.H.: Big data: issues, challenges, tools and good practices. In: IEEE Sixth International Conference on Contemporary Computing (IC3), pp. 404–409 (2013)
6. Tory, M., Möller, T.: Evaluating visualizations: do expert reviews work? IEEE Comput. Graph. Appl. **25**(5), 8–11 (2005)
7. Stasko, J.: Value-driven evaluation of visualizations. In: Proceedings of the Fifth Workshop on Beyond Time and Errors: Novel Evaluation Methods for Visualization, pp. 46–53. ACM, November 2014
8. Haass, M.J., Matzen, L.E., Stevens-Adams, S.M., Roach, A.R.: Methodology for knowledge elicitation in visual abductive reasoning tasks. In: Schmorrow, D.D., Fidopiastis, C.M. (eds.) AC 2015. LNCS, vol. 9183, pp. 401–409. Springer, Heidelberg (2015)
9. Martin, S., Quach, T-T.: Interactive visualization of multivariate time series data. In: HCII 2016 Proceedings (2016)

Aircraft Pilot Intention Recognition for Advanced Cockpit Assistance Systems

Stefan Suck$^{(\boxtimes)}$ and Florian Fortmann

OFFIS Institute for Information Technology, Escherweg 2,
26121 Oldenburg, Germany
{stefan.suck,florian.fortmann}@offis.de

Abstract. Present aircraft are highly automated systems. In general, automation improved aviation safety significantly. However, automation exhibits itself in many forms of adverse behaviors related to human factors problems. A major finding is that insufficient support of partnership between the pilot crew and the aircraft automation can result in conflicting intentions. The European project A-PiMod (Applying Pilot Models for Safer Aircraft) addresses issues of conventional automation in the aviation domain. The overall objective of the project is to foster pilot crew-automation partnership on the basis of a novel architecture for cooperative automation. An essential part of the architecture is an intention recognition module. The intention recognition module employs a Hidden Markov Model (HMM) to infer the most probable current intention of the human pilots. The HMM is trained and evaluated with data containing interactions of human pilots with the aircraft cockpit systems. The data was obtained during experiments with human pilots in a flight simulator.

Keywords: Aircraft crew · Intention recognition · Markov Model

1 Introduction

Present aircraft are highly automated systems. In general, automation improved aviation safety significantly. However, automation exhibits itself in many forms of adverse behaviors, such as automation induced complacency [11], automation bias [14], decision making errors [15], lack of system knowledge and manual control skills [12], overconfidence [20], and vigilance issues [2]. A major finding is that insufficient support of partnership between the pilot crew and the aircraft automation can result in conflicting intentions. An example is the crash of China Airlines Flight 140 [18], where conflicting intentions of the human crew and the automation ended in a tragedy.

A recent research trend to overcome the problems of conventional automation is cooperative automation. The idea is that the human and the automation constitute a cooperative system in charge of the tasks of a jointly performed mission. Flemisch et al. [6] defined the term "cooperative" by key properties

© Springer International Publishing Switzerland 2016
D.D. Schmorrow and C.M. Fidopiastis (Eds.): AC 2016, Part II, LNAI 9744, pp. 231–240, 2016.
DOI: 10.1007/978-3-319-39952-2_23

such as sufficient skills to perception, cognition, action, interaction, conflict handling, internal and external compatibility, and balance between adaptivity and stability. In a cooperative automation system, humans and automation are considered as cognitive agents of a work system interacting with each other in order to achieve shared tasks. In this sense, humans and automation build a team. The task share in the human-automation team is the result of a negotiation process between the acting agents and depends on the availability and capacity utilization of resources.

The European project A-PiMod (Applying Pilot Models for Safer Aircraft) [1] addresses issues of conventional automation in the aviation domain. The overall objective of the project is to foster pilot crew-automation partnership on the basis of a novel architecture for cooperative automation. To improve the partnership between the pilots and the automation the project aims to develop a virtual crew member, which takes the position of classical aircraft automation. In the context of this project a pilot model is developed, which enables the virtual crew member to gain knowledge about the cognitive state of the human pilots. The cognitive state consists of different sub-states, which have been defined during the initial phase of the project, i.e., intentions, workload, and situation awareness. The sub-states are inferred in real-time based on data recorded during flight.

Figure 1 shows a simplified version of the A-PiMod architecture (see [8] for the holistic version). The focus of this version is on the intention inference module, and the connections of the pilot model to other selected A-PiMod modules. The Mission Level Situation Determination and the Human Machine Multimodal Interface (HMMI) deliver the real-time data from the flight simulator, data about the interactions with the cockpit systems, and the current flight phase. The Task Distribution module gives information about how pertinent flight tasks should be distributed between the human pilots and the automation in terms of risk and with regard to the abilities of the pilots and the automation. The Cockpit Level Risk Assessment continuously assesses the risk for all currently possible task distributions. The results of the intention recognition influence the Situation Awareness Assessment of the pilot model, the Cockpit Risk and eventually a new Task Distribution. The HMMI Interaction Manager adapts the output modality for certain information and the salience of certain displays and display elements in the cockpit. This adaption is also dependent on the pilot state.

In this paper, we describe the intention recognition module which is an important part of the pilot model of the A-PiMod architecture. It provides the virtual pilot with a sufficient understanding of the flight tasks the human pilots are carrying out. Understanding what the human pilots are doing allows the virtual pilot to make sense of the behaviors of the human pilots in context of the present situation, and allows to detect and to mitigate conflicting intentions. The intention recognition module employs a Hidden Markov Model (HMM) to infer the most probable current intention of the human pilots. The HMM is trained and evaluated with data containing interactions of human pilots with the aircraft cockpit systems. The data was obtained during experiments with human pilots in a flight simulator.

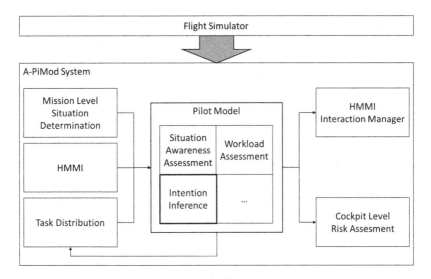

Fig. 1. Overview of the A-PiMod architecture with focus on the pilot model.

The paper is structured as follows: Sect. 2 provides an overview of aircraft pilot models and some applications of probabilistic behavior models. Section 3 explains our experimental setup and data collection approach. Section 4 describes the HMM used to recognize pilot intentions. Section 5 shows the evaluation results. Section 6 provides conclusions.

2   Related Work

There are already several approaches in the aviation domain to model human operators and their behavior. The Cognitive Architecture for Safety Critical Task Simulation (CASCaS) presented in [10] can be understood as a rule based approach of an operator model. CASCaS was applied in several projects among other things as aircraft pilot model which generates behavior and performs tasks similar to a human pilot. It is feasible for simulating human-machine interaction in highly dynamic environments. Contrary to our approach CASCaS is not probabilistic and generates actions and intentions of a pilot instead of monitoring the actions and inferring the associated intentions. Another approach is the adaptive pilot model of the Crew Assistant Military Aircraft (CAMA), which is described in [19]. This pilot model determines if deviations from a normative pilot model are real errors or are intended by the pilot. This approach is based on fuzzy rules and the focus is on manually flying of a military aircraft. So, interactions with the autopilot system of the aircraft are not considered. A probabilistic approach to model one part of the pilots behavior is presented in [7]. The author uses Hidden Markov Models to analyze the instrument scanning and attention switching behavior of aircraft pilots. In contrast to our approach eye-tracker data employed whereby our approach is based on physical interactions with, e.g., buttons. Additionally our focus is not on the scanning behavior but on the flight tasks.

In other domains, there are already some similar efforts. In [4] a probabilistic model for the behavior of an Unmanned Aerial Vehicle (UAV) operator is presented. The operator is not actually flying the UAV but has to identify and tag several objects in the live stream coming from the UAV. The author trains HMMs which are then used to infer on the behavior of the UAV operator and the currently performed task by monitoring their User Interface interactions.

In the automotive domain the recognition of driver intentions or driving maneuvers is an important aspect. In [5] an overview of several approaches is given, including approaches which employ probabilistic networks. For example, the authors of [13] use a hierarchical structure of Dynamic Bayesian Networks (DBN) as driver model, to generate driving actions from driving goals. It is also possible to use this approach to monitor the driver's actions to infer on the driving goals.

In the smart home domain an important technology to monitor a person's health is to detect and to track the currently performed Activities of Daily Living of the resident. In different approaches the activities are usually inferred from the observed interactions with tagged objects or areas. For example, the approaches presented in [9, 17] employ Hidden Markov Models to recognize interleaved activities of smart home residents.

3   Experiment

In order to collect the necessary data to train and validate our intention inference module we performed several experiments in the Generic Experimental Cockpit (GECO) of the German Aerospace Center (DLR) in Braunschweig. The GECO is a modular cockpit simulator with interchangeable flight-mechanical models to fit the needs of different applications. It provides a generic work environment, which is able to represent any of the state-of-the-art cockpits which are currently produced by the different aircraft manufacturers. With its several hardware and software modules it forms a fix-base experimental flight simulator with many features. Figure 2 shows a view of the GECO with an A320 layout and some additional installations which were used during the A-PiMod validation experiments.

The GECO is mainly used to perform simulations with human test subjects in the loop to evaluate new display and control concepts. In contrast to simulators designed for pilot training the GECO does not strive for the highest degree of realism for one particular type of aircraft. The major objective of the GECO is to provide maximum flexibility. Thus, it can meet different requirements in the fields of cockpit research regarding new systems with human-machine interfaces and new flight procedures.

We invited six professional aircraft crews to fly scenarios in the GECO. Each crew consisted of one captain and one fist officer. All these pilots were trained

Fig. 2. GECO flight simulator used for our experiments and the collection of data

and experienced in flying an Airbus A320 or a similar model. The scenarios were prepared primarily for the evaluation and the demonstration of the concepts of the A-PiMod project. For this reason the scenarios followed a "theater approach" but they did also fit our needs to gather the required data and to evaluate our intention inference module. Every scenario was constructed from a set of scenario elements and basically contained similar procedures. During each element the pilots had to perform some flight tasks. Each scenario had a duration of about 15 min and started in the descent flight phase. At this point the so called cruise phase is finished; the aircraft has left its travel altitude and is descending to approach an airport. For a better understanding, Fig. 3 illustrates the common order of the flight phases.

During one scenario the pilots first had to adapt the initially programmed flight route and after a while they had to divert to an alternative airport. Another scenario contained a missed approach. Meaning the aircraft was not in the correct configuration at a certain point of the approach to the airport. Therefore, the pilots were required to perform a Go-Around procedure to try a new approach. After the Go-Around procedure the pilots also had to adapt the programmed flight route.

While the pilots were flying the scenarios the data from the flight simulator and the different cockpit components were recorded continuously. This data contains all pilot interactions with the cockpit. Later on the data was annotated by an expert to mark the flight tasks.

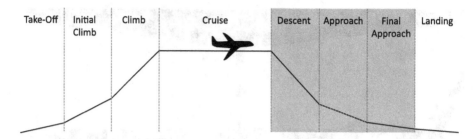

Fig. 3. Common order of the flight phases. The flight phases of the experiment are marked with a gray background.

4   Modeling Approach

The intentions of a pilot usually refer to the goals he is trying to achieve [3]. To accomplish a specific goal usually a more or less complex plan exists. Complex plans can be separated into sub-plans. This way the complex plans become the goals of their sub-plans. Flight tasks which occur in an aircraft cockpit also serve the achievement of a goal. The complexity of these tasks can reach from very basic activities like changing the altitude to more complex operations like performing a go-around procedure. Complex tasks can also be separated into sub-tasks and become the goals of their sub-task. Therefore, we interpret the intentions of a human pilot as the flight tasks he is currently performing. For the execution of a task a pilot has to show a specific behavior, which means he has to perform certain interactions with the cockpit systems. Thus, there is some set of actions which is typical for this task. These actions occur in a sequence and are directly observable, while the tasks cannot be observed directly. By monitoring the interactions it is possible to infer the currently performed flight task. However, some interactions can belong to one or more flight task. Theoretically flight tasks can also occur in an interleaved manner. This means the pilot interrupts one flight task, executes another task and then resumes the previously carried out flight task. In this paper we infer 8 basic flight tasks from observable interactions of pilots with the aircraft systems.

We use a 1st order Hidden Markov Model to infer the currently performed flight task from the observed interactions with the cockpit system. HMMs are used to describe dynamic probabilistic processes [16]. The model contains a set of different states $S = S_1, S_2, \ldots, S_N$ and a set of possible emissions $O = O_1, O_2, \ldots, O_M$ which both occur as a sequence. The states are not directly observable and are therefore usually called "hidden states". In a 1st order HMM the assumption is made that the current state at a certain point in time only depends on one previous state. So, the conditional probability of a certain state at the time t after a sequence of previous states can be simplified as shown in Eq. 1.

$$P(S_t|S_1, \ldots, S_{t-1}) = P(S_t|S_{t-1}) \tag{1}$$

Each state at a point in time generates an observable emission O_t. This observation depends only on the current state S_t and not on previous observations. Thus, the probability to make a certain observation at time t after a sequence of previous states an observation can be simplified as shown in Eq. 2.

$$P(O_t|O_1, \ldots, O_{t-1}, S_1, \ldots, S_t) = P(O_t|S_t) \tag{2}$$

For simplification it is assumed that at the start of the process at $t = 0$ the start state is $S_0 = 0$. The first transition from S_0 to S_1 then the first emission is O_1. The whole behavior of the HMM can be characterized with three probability matrices. The initial state probabilities $a_{0i} = P(S_1|S_0 = 0)$, the state transition probabilities $a_{ij} = P(S_t = j|S_{t-1} = i)$ and the emission probabilities $b_{jm} = P(O_t = m|S_{t-1} = j)$. The joint distribution of a sequence of observations $\mathbf{O} = O_1, O_2, \ldots, O_T$ and a sequence of states $\mathbf{S} = S_1, S_2, \ldots, S_T$ can then be written as Eq. 3.

$$P(\mathbf{S}, \mathbf{O}) = \prod_{t=1}^{T} P(S_t|S_{t-1})P(O_t|S_t) \tag{3}$$

In our context the flight tasks are the hidden states of the HMM since the task are not directly observable during run-time. For the training process the states are known since we are using annotated training data. The emissions are the observed interactions of the pilot with the cockpit systems. The initial state probability matrix is generated from the frequencies of the different flight tasks in the trainings data. The state transition probability matrix is generated from the frequencies of the flight task transitions in the trainings set. The emission probability matrix is generated from the frequencies of the combinations of flight tasks and interactions in the trainings set. For the calculation of the state transition probabilities and the emission probabilities Laplace smoothing is applied. Whereby $\#x_k$ denotes the counts of a state transition or the counts of an emission from a certain state and $\#X = \sum_{k=1}^{L} \#x_k$ is the count of all state transitions or emissions from a certain state in the training data. Then the smoothed estimated probability for this state transition or emission can then be written as Eq. 4.

$$\widehat{x}_k = \frac{\#x_k + 1}{\#X + L} \tag{4}$$

By doing so we avoid zero probabilities for flight task transitions which are possible but were not observed in the training data. The model would also be more robust against cases of a task execution which slightly differs from the standard procedure.

For our model we focus on 8 flight tasks. These are relevant for scenarios which were used during our simulator experiments mentioned in Sect. 3. The flight tasks are "monitor", "arm spoiler", "set flaps", "set thrust", "change speed", "change heading" "change altitude", and "set approach". The task "monitor" actually means that there is none of the other defined tasks ongoing. So, we assume the pilot is just monitoring the instruments. The monitored interactions with the cockpit systems are actions like pushing a button, turning a knob, or pulling a lever. For developing the intention recognition model, we used a knowledge engineering approach. We interviewed domain experts to gather knowledge about the relations between flight tasks and cockpit interactions, and certain context events which could be triggers for certain tasks. The parameters of the HMM are learned from manually annotated data. This data was obtained by recording the aircraft data and the interactions of professional pilots while they were flying the scenarios described in Sect. 3 in the GECO simulator with activated autopilot system.

5   Evaluation

For the evaluation the package *HMM* for the programming language *R* was used. The flight data which was recorded during our simulator experiments was split into a training set and a test set. The test set contains two of the eight recorded scenarios which were useful. Since our data consist of very long time series it would have been impractical to perform a cross-validation with random selection of test cases. For each data point in our test set the annotated task is compared to the task with the highest probability $P(S_t|O_{1:t})$ reported by our HMM. The model produces an error rate of 0.0069 on the test set. This means for 0.69 % of the cases in the test set the most probable tasks of the model does not match with the task given in the test set. Since our test data is strongly populated with the state 'monitor' we also calculated the error rate based only on the cases where the test data is not 'monitor'. For this configuration our model produces an error rate of 0.0039. The error rates and Fig. 4 show that the model expresses the data surprisingly well. This is due to the relative high degree of determinism which is currently present in the data and in the current set of flight tasks and interactions. Figure 4 also shows that the predicted task is detected somewhat after the start of the annotated. A possible reason is that the human annotator saw more than the just the bare interaction. He perceived the context and was also able to already see the pilot reaching for certain interfaces (Table 1).

Table 1. Confusion matrix of task predicted by the HMM and the actual task as marked in the data.

Predicted		monitor	arm.spl	set.flap	set.thrust	chg.spd	chg.hdg	chg.alt	set.appr
Actual	monitor	21308	0	0	0	0	0	2	0
	arm.spl	18	12	0	0	0	0	0	0
	set.flap	36	0	30	0	0	0	0	0
	set.thrust	27	0	0	64	0	0	0	0
	chg.spd	53	0	0	0	123	0	0	0
	chg.hdg	2	0	0	0	0	3	0	0
	chg.alt	8	0	0	0	0	0	28	0
	set.appr	5	0	0	0	0	0	0	0

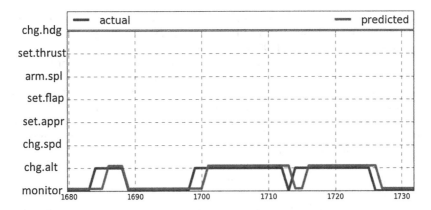

Fig. 4. Segment of the sequence of tasks detected by HMM and actual tasks as marked in the data

6 Conclusion

We presented a model to recognize the currently performed flight tasks of aircraft pilots by monitoring their interactions with the cockpit systems. The model uses a trained HMM which is integrated into the A-PiMod architecture as a part of the pilot model. The designated usage of the model is to receive new observations at a rate of 20 Hz during simulator flights and to infer $P(S_t|O_{1:t})$. The evaluation of our model showed that the model is able to detect our selected flight tasks in the flight phases 'descent', 'approach' and 'final approach' based on interactions with the cockpit systems. In the future we plan to detect more complex tasks with the model and eventually to add eye-tracker data and context information. This could result in a performance decrease compared to the current model but it makes the model more useful.

Acknowledgment. The A-PiMod project is funded by the European Commission Seventh Framework Programme (FP7/2007-2013) under contract number: 605141 Project A-PiMod. Thanks also to my colleague Mark Eilers for his advice during the creation of this work.

References

1. Applying pilot models for safer aircraft. http://www.apimod.eu
2. Caldwell, J.A.: Crew schedules, sleep deprivation, and aviation performance. Curr. Dir. Psychol. Sci. **21**(2), 85–89 (2012)
3. Cohen, P.R., Levesque, H.J.: Intention is choice with commitment. Artif. Intell. **42**, 213–261 (1990)
4. Donath, D.: Verhaltensanalyse der Beanspruchung des Operateurs in der Multi-UAV-Führung. Dissertation, Universität der Bundeswehr München (2012)

5. Doshi, A., Trivedi, M.M.: Tactical driver behavior prediction and intent inference: a review. In: 2011 14th International IEEE Conference on Intelligent Transportation Systems (ITSC), pp. 1892–1897. IEEE (2011)

6. Flemisch, F., Meier, S., Neuhöfer, J., Baltzer, M., Altendorf, E., Özyurt, E.: Kognitive und kooperative systeme in der fahrzeugführung: selektiver rückblick über die letzten dekaden und spekulation über die zukunft. Kognitive Systeme (2013)

7. Hayashi, M.: Hidden Markov Models for analysis of pilot instrument scanning and attention switching. Ph.D. thesis, Massachusetts Institute of Technology (2004)

8. Javaux, D., Fortmann, F., Möhlenbrink, C.: Adaptive human-automation cooperation: a general architecture for the cockpit and its application in the a-pimod project. In: 7th International Conference on Advanced Cognitive Technologies and Applications (COGNITIVE 2015). International Academy, Research, and Industry Association (IARIA) (2015)

9. Landwehr, N.: Modeling interleaved hidden processes. In: Cohen, W.W., McCallum, A., Roweis, S.T. (eds.) ICML. ACM International Conference Proceeding Series, vol. 307, pp. 520–527. ACM (2008)

10. Lüdtke, A., Weber, L., Osterloh, J.-P., Wortelen, B.: Modeling pilot and driver behavior for human error simulation. In: Duffy, V.G. (ed.) Digital Human Modeling, HCII 2009. LNCS, vol. 5620, pp. 403–412. Springer, Heidelberg (2009)

11. Manzey, D., Reichenbach, J., Onnasch, L.: Human performance consequences of automated decision aids: the impact of degree of automation and system experience. J. Cogn. Eng. Decis. Making **6**, 57–87 (2012)

12. McGee, J.P., Mavor, A.S., Wickens, C.D., et al.: Flight to the Future: Human Factors in Air Traffic Control. National Academies Press, Washington (1997)

13. Moebus, C., Eilers, M.: Prototyping smart assistance with bayesian autonomous driver models. In: Chong, N.Y., Mastrogiovanni, F. (eds.) Handbook of Research on Ambient Intelligence and Smart Environments: Trends and Perspectives, pp. 460–512. IGI Global, May 2011

14. Mosier, K.L., Skitka, L.J., Heers, S., Burdick, M.: Automation bias: decision making and performance in high-tech cockpits. Int. J. Aviat. Psychol. **8**(1), 47–63 (1998)

15. Orasanu, J., Martin, L., Davison, J.: Errors in Aviation Decision Making: Bad Decisions or Bad Luck? National Aeronautics and Space Administration, Ames Research Center (1998)

16. Rabiner, L.R.: A tutorial on hidden markov models and selected applications in speech recognition. Proc. IEEE **77**, 257–286 (1989)

17. Singla, G., Cook, D.J.: Interleaved activity recognition for smart home residents. In: Proceedings of the 5th International Conference on Intelligent Environments, IE 2009, Barcelona, Spain, pp. 145–152 (2009)

18. Sogame, H., Ladkin, P.: Aircraft accident investigation report 96-5. Japan: Ministry of transport (1996). http://sunnyday.mit.edu/accidents/nag-1.html

19. Strohal, M., Onken, R.: Intent and error recognition as part of a knowledge-based cockpit assistant. In: Proceedings of the SPIE, vol. 3390, pp. 287–299 (1998)

20. Wood, S.: Flight crew reliance on automation. CAA Paper 10 (2004)

Explaining a Virtual Worker's Job Performance: The Role of Psychological Distance

Ayoung Suh[⊠] and Christian Wagner

School of Creative Media and Department of Information Systems,
City University of Hong Kong, Kowloon Tong, Hong Kong
{ahysuh, c.wagner}@cityu.edu.hk

Abstract. Despite the shift in scholarly and managerial attention from the effects of objective distance to psychological distance between team members, the questions of how virtual worker psychological distance is formed and how it can be measured have not been fully answered. In search of answers, this study develops and tests a model that examines the antecedents and the consequence of psychological distance, drawing on construal level theory. The results reveal that psychological distance is a multi-dimensional construct consisting of responsiveness, subjective proximity, and accessibility. The results also demonstrate that the different dimensions of objective distance increase psychological distance in a nonlinear fashion; interaction between different dimensions of objective distance produces greater psychological distance than does their combination. Our findings contribute to the IS literature by conceptualizing psychological distance, showing that it can be directly modeled, and highlighting that it should be carefully managed to improve virtual workers' job performance.

Keywords: Virtual work · Construal level theory · Objective distance · Psychological distance · Job performance

1 Introduction

A long-standing tradition in virtual team (VT) literature is the adoption of the proximity perspective to identify the unique features of VTs and their impact on individual dynamics and group processes. Researchers have conceptualized multiple dimensions of "virtuality" (e.g., degrees of spatial, temporal, and cultural distances) to reflect the proximal characteristics of a VT and examine how virtuality influences individual variance in work outcomes. However, the empirical results have been inconsistent, with studies showing positive and negative relationships between proximity and work outcomes. Some studies found that the objective distance between individuals negatively influences communication quality, task performance, and knowledge sharing [2, 9]. In contrast, some studies have shown the positive influence of objective distance on work outcomes, such as decision quality, creativity, and job satisfaction [22, 34].

To resolve this inconsistency, scholars have recently called for research to address subjective representations of distance between VT members, instead focusing on objective distance measures [13, 28, 35, 36]. Trope et al. [31] have argued that

D.D. Schmorrow and C.M. Fidopiastis (Eds.): AC 2016, Part II, LNAI 9744, pp. 241–252, 2016.
DOI: 10.1007/978-3-319-39952-2_24

psychological distance is a factor that leads individuals to create higher level abstractions in the representation of target objects ("higher-level construals"). These higher-level construals disrupt and prevent information flow between virtual workers [36]. If psychological distance is an underlying mechanism that accounts for the representation of VT work and work outcomes, providing information technology (IT) functions to mitigate the objective distance may not be the most suitable approach. Instead, technological and managerial interventions should be focused on changing team members' perceptions of the subjective, psychological distance. Lesser psychological distance should lead to lower-level construals and more effective VT work. Yet despite the increased attention from research and practice, the operational conceptualization of psychological distance remains equivocal; research findings regarding its roles on work outcomes are inconsistent and often appear conflicting. To fill these gaps in understanding, this study addresses the following questions:

(1) How is the psychological distance between virtual workers formed?
(2) How does the psychological distance between virtual workers influence their job performance?

To answer these questions, drawing on construal level theory, this study conceptualizes psychological distance and then develops and tests a nomological network to explain the relationship between objective and subjective distance and job performance. By precisely disentangling the effects of different dimensions of objective distance on psychological distance, this study contributes to a more nuanced understanding of how virtual workers construct their perceptions of psychological distance, how it can be measured, and how it influences individual job performance in a VT.

2   Literature Review and Theory Development

2.1   Construal Level Theory

Construal level theory (CLT) explains how psychological distance influences the extent to which an individual's interpretation about objects or events is abstract or concrete [31, 32]. The general idea of CLT is that the more distant a target is from the individual, the more abstractly and less concretely it will be thought of, focusing more on abstract, holistic, and decontextualized features rather than specific details of information [17]. For example, a distant co-worker may be described as "Annie is clever" (more abstract), whereas a close one may be described as "Annie is able to spot any mistakes in our spreadsheets" (more concrete). Applying construal level theory, VT researchers posit that virtual workers' psychological distance perceptions determine their construal levels, which in turn affect their judgment and behavior, and enable or constrain their work outcomes. CLT thus challenges the conventional notion that objective distance causes difficulties in sharing a local context and developing a transactive memory (i.e., who knows what) [7]. CLT suggests that even if distant team members were provided with the contextual details normally associated with physical proximity, their subjective perception of the distance would still hinder them from focusing on the provided contextual detail, and thus they would still suffer from the same distance-related difficulties [31]. In other words, virtual workers difficulties, including knowledge sharing, can be explained based on the individual members' subjective perceptions about the distance between them (herein, psychological distance). In this sense, it has been argued that psychological distance is a direct factor that elicits high levels of construals that disrupt and prevents information flow between virtual workers [36].

2.2 Psychological Distance

Psychological distance refers to "an individual's perception of how close or how far another person is" [35, p. 983]. Tope and Liberman [32] define it as "a subjective experience that something is close to or far away from the self, here and now" (p. 440). In the VT literature, psychological distance is conceptualized as the extent to which a virtual worker feels he or she is distant from other VT members. Although objective distance and psychological distance are associated, researchers have acknowledged that the role of perceived psychological distance, which influences people's thoughts, feelings, and behavior, is independent of objective distance [33]. Accordingly, assessing a virtual worker's psychological distance is important for predicting his or her work outcomes.

Table 1. Operational definitions of psychological distance

Operational definition	References
Perceived ease with which VT members can be visited and the perceived effort required to get them in one place for a meeting. Perceived virtuality of communication (the use of virtual tools) and the perceived frequency of face-to-face meeting tools (Phone, email, teleconferencing, etc.)	[28]
The extent to which a virtual worker feels that most team members are reachable and they work directly in the vicinity	[18, 19]
A mental assessment, emotions and feelings of how distant a teammate seems.	[35]
The subjective experience that an event or object is close or far away from the self, here, and now. Sub-dimensions: (1) Social distance: The extent to which a social target is perceived as removed from oneself (2) Hypotheticality: The perceived probability that an event will happen or an object will exist, or its perceived similarity to the perceiver's reality (3) Temporal distance: The degree to which an object or event is perceived to take place in near versus distant future (or past) (4) Spatial distance: The perception that an object or event exists or takes place in nearby versus remote location	[3]
The extent to which an individual perceive to be close to one another spatially, temporally, and socially	[5, 23]

Nevertheless, as shown in Table 1, the operationalization of psychological distance is equivocal, which may cause inconsistent findings regarding the effects of psychological distance on job performance. Psychological distance was found to reduce individuals' willingness to collaborate in the future and to lower their beliefs about the efficacy of distance work [35]. In contrast, psychological distance also affected job performance positively, by increasing creativity and making people focus on essential task features [36]. Some studies found that moderate levels of psychological distance promote trust in information received from others [31]. The present lack of consensus and consistency between definitions necessitates the development and validation of an instrument that precisely captures psychological distance.

3 Research Model and Hypotheses

Drawing on CLT, we developed a model to explain how different dimensions of objective distance (spatial, temporal, and cultural) influence a virtual worker's psychological distance to other VT members and how this distance influences job performance. We outline the relations between objective distance, psychological distance, and job performance, as shown in Fig. 1.

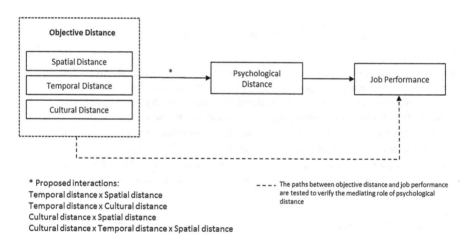

Fig. 1. Research model

3.1 Relationship between Objective and Psychological Distance

Objective distance has been widely considered as the most critical and important feature of VTs [6, 25]. Spatial distance refers to the extent to which a virtual worker is dispersed spatially from other members (e.g., different cities or countries), whereas temporal distance refers to the extent to which a virtual worker works in a different time zone from collaborators [10, 25]. Cultural distance is considered important in objective distance. In this study, cultural distance is operationalized as the extent to which a virtual worker works with other members of different nationalities [27]. Cultural distance has great potential to hinder effective interaction within a VT [1, 27].

Each dimension of objective distance can create psychological distance [7, 36], which may cause challenges in judgment and behavior within VTs and become a source of potential conflict. Fujita et al. [12] has recently suggested that because psychologically near events tend to be represented concretely and psychologically distant events tend to be represented abstractly, psychological distance should impede the processing of concrete event representations and facilitate the processing of abstract event representations. Hence, drawing on prior literature, we posit that each dimension of objective distance will influence psychological distance. Apart from a simple linear relationship between objective distance and psychological distance, we hypothesize that interaction effects exist between the dimensions of objective distance. This means that the combination of different objective distance dimensions may increase psychological distance in a non-additive way. Specifically, spatial distance can be overridden by synchronous communication technologies to a certain extent, but temporal distance is difficult to overcome [11, 30]. In particular, lags in feedback and asynchronous communication amplify the problems of mutual knowledge and common ground from which to work and share concerns [11], and these seriously reduce individuals' perceptions of copresence [13]. Researchers have also suggested that cultural differences interact with spatial distance to produce greater psychological distance than might be expected by the simple combination of the two dimensions of the objective distance [8].

Hypothesis 1: The different dimensions of objective distance interact in non-additive ways to increase psychological distance.

[H1a]: Temporal distance will positively moderate the relationship between spatial distance and psychological distance

[H1b]: Temporal distance will positively moderate the relationship between cultural distance and psychological distance

[H1c]: Cultural distance will positively moderate the relationship between spatial distance and psychological distance

[H1d]: Cultural distance will positively moderate the relationship between spatial and temporal distances and psychological distance

3.2 Psychological Distance and Job Performance

Construal-level theory [31] explains that people who perceive a high level of psychological distance from their remote partners are more likely to focus on high-level construals (the abstract and decontextualized features of objects) than on the low-level, detailed, and contextualized features of their remote team members' knowledge. Virtual workers thus tend to fail to share information about the local context, or if they share, other members may ignore the additional context. Studies have suggested that the failure of knowledge contextualization contributes to less effective knowledge utilization [7, 21], which negatively influences a virtual worker's job performance. Psychological distance also reduces psychological engagement [20]. People who are less psychologically engaged in their roles tend to show passive attitudes toward task performance.

Hypothesis 2:   Psychological distance will be negatively associated with job performance.

4   Methods

4.1   Data Collection

The proposed research model was tested with the collaboration of three multinational companies operating VTs across countries around the world. Executives of the target companies provided support for this research. With this support, we selected VTs where members worked separated by space (e.g., in different cities or countries), time (e.g., different time zones), or were of nationalities (to reflect cultural distance), thus meeting conventional definitions of a VT and providing variation across all dimensions of objective distance. Empirical data was collected by a series of surveys from 163 virtual workers employed across the VTs. The demographics of the respondents are summarized in Table 2.

Table 2. Demographic information of respondents

Item	Category	Frequency	Ratio
Gender	Male	107	65.6 %
	Female	56	34.4 %
Age	<30	22	7.4 %
	30 ∼ 40	81	49.7 %
	41 ∼ 50	70	42.9 %
Education	College	96	58.9 %
	Post graduate	52	31.9 %
	Above	15	9.2 %
Organizational tenure	<5	22	13.5 %
	5 ∼ 10	45	27.6 %
	11 ∼ 15	60	36.8 %
	16 ∼ 20	19	11.7 %
	>20	17	10.4 %

4.2   Measurement

Since the unit of analysis of this study was the individual, all of the research variables were measured at the individual level. We collected team rosters and information about every VT member's workplace, and nationality. Using this information, we measured the extent to which each virtual worker was dispersed in relation to others spatially, temporally, and culturally. A virtual workers' spatial distance was measured using the absolute number of air miles with other team members based on Hansen and Lovas [15]. Temporal distance was measured using time zone differences with other members following O'Leary and Cummings [25]. To compute cultural distance, we used nationality differences with other team members by drawing on Raab's research [27].

Job performance was measured by adapting items used by Mehra et al. [26]. We controlled for gender, age, and organizational tenure.

5   Analysis and Results

5.1   Measurement Model

An explorative factor analysis (EFA) was conducted to evaluate the construct validity of psychological distance. A principal axis factor analysis using the Direct Oblimin method was used for the test. We included measurement items proposed from previous studies, including Hoegl et al. [18], Wilson et al., [35], Lim et al. [23], and Siebdrat et al. [28] into the EFA. After we removed items with low factor loadings, the results of EFA revealed that psychological distance consisted of three sub-dimensions (responsiveness, subjective proximity, and accessibility). Table 3 shows the valid measurement items and the factor loadings corresponding to each item. Next, a confirmatory factor analysis (CFA) was used to validate the instrument. The standardized residuals between the individual instrument items ranged between -0.21 and 0.22, which was well with the recommended bounds for data quality.

The measurement model was assessed by examining its convergent and discrimi-

Table 3. EFA measurement model results

Items	Responsiveness	Subjective Proximity	Accessibility
-I feel our team responds to each other closely[R]	**.777**	.032	.180
-I feel I am interacting simultaneously with my team members[R]	**.742**	.129	.107
-Our team members give quick responses to my actions[R]	**.741**	.001	.148
-I feel isolated from other persons	.110	**.814**	.122
-When I think of another team member, he or she seems far away	.014	**.797**	.142
-Team members are located too far from one another to move the project along expeditiously	.311	**.701**	.059
-I feel it is difficult to get the team members together in one place for spontaneous meetings (e.g., for discussions and decisions)	.027	.315	**.780**
-Most members of my team work directly in the vicinity, so that they could visit each other without much effort[R]	.220	.067	**.774**
-I feel it is easy to visit most team members with whom I collaborate [R]	.295	.054	**.723**

[R] Reverse coded measures (i.e., higher scores on these items implies lower persistent labeling).

nant validity. To assess convergent validity, the composite reliability (CR) of each multi-item construct was examined. As shown in Tables 4, all CR values rang from 0.821 to 0.862. To assess discriminant validity, we examined the values for average variance extracted (AVE). For satisfactory discriminant validity, the AVE from a construct should be greater than the variance shared between the construct and other constructs in the model. For each construct, the square root of the average variance extracted should exceed the construct's correlation with every other construct. The results indicates that the AVE for each construct is larger than the correlation of that construct with all the other constructs in the both models, thus ensuring discriminant validity of the constructs (see Table 4). To ensure that multicollinearity does not pose a problem, we checked values for the index of variance inflation factor (VIF). Our results ranged from 1.00 to 2.120, well below the threshold value of 10, recommended by Harter et al. [16]. The results indicate that it is unlikely that multicollinearity poses a serious concern for this study.

Table 4. Discriminant validity and correlation of constructs

	AVE	C.R.	ACC	CD	JP	SP	RES	SD	TD
ACC	0.612	0.825	**0.782**						
CD	1.000	1.000	0.233	**1.000**					
JP	0.556	0.862	0.424	0.140	**0.746**				
SP	0.609	0.821	−0.196	−0.364	−0.127	**0.781**			
RES	0.608	0.823	0.396	0.130	0.600	−0.086	**0.780**		
SD	1.000	1.000	0.242	0.267	0.211	−0.442	0.184	**1.000**	
TD	1.000	1.000	−0.083	0.230	−0.037	−0.078	0.023	0.311	**1.000**

Note:
(1) Square root of AVE for each latent construct is given in diagonals.
(2) C.R: Composite Reliability; AVE: Average Variance Extracted; ACC: Accessibility; CD: Cultural Distance; JP: Job Performance; SP: Subjective Proximity; RES: Responsiveness; SD: Spatial Distance; TD: Temporal Distance.

Given the structure of the model, the statistical analysis is expected to employ hierarchical linear regression [24] to take into account the different impacts of different sets of independent variables. In particular, we enter the interaction terms of different dimensions of objective distance into the model and regress it to psychological distance in order to verify their non-additive effects. Table 5 represents the results of the model test. Model 1 examines the effects of the control variables on psychological distance. The results indicate that organizational tenure has a negative influence on psychological distance. Three dimensions of objective distance were entered into Model 2. The results show that spatial distance significantly positively influences psychological distance, whereas temporal and cultural distances have no significant influence on psychological distance. Interaction terms between different dimensions of object distance were entered as independent variables into Model 3. The results show that significant interaction effects exist between spatial and cultural distance; spatial and temporal distance; and spatial, temporal, and cultural distance, which account for 12 % of the variance of psychological distance.

Table 5. The results of hierarchical regression analysis

	Model 1	Model 2	Model 3	Model 4	Model 5	Model 6
	Psychological distance			Job performance		
Gender	0.06	0.05	0.04	0.15	0.13	0.08
Age	0.09	0.058	0.04	0.16	0.12	0.08
Organizational tenure	−0.20*	−0.19*	−0.17*	0.18*	0.18*	0.05
SD		0.26**	0.23*		0.12	0.00
TD		0.05	0.43		−0.17	−0.04
CD		0.07	0.07		0.08	0.07
SD x TD			0.22**			
SD x CD			0.30*			
TD x CD			0.32			
SD x TD x CD			0.46*			
Psychological distance						−0.46***
R^2	0.05	0.13	0.25	0.08	0.13	0.44
ΔR^2		0.08	0.12		0.05	0.31

6 Discussion

The results showed that psychological distance was the main determinant of job performance and that the different dimensions of objective distance increased psychological distance in a nonlinear fashion. The results showed that interaction effects exist between each dimension of objective distance. That is, the different objective distances increased the psychological distance in a non-additive way. We found that neither cultural nor temporal distance by themselves increased psychological distance but cultural and temporal distance interacted with spatial distance to produce greater psychological distance than did the simple combination of the two dimensions of the objective distance.

Two questions arise. Why is the relationship non-linear, and why is the interaction of objective distance factors more salient than the factors themselves? With increased distance (of any kind) comes a loss of contextual detail, which may hinder collaboration unless it is compensated for. Increases in distance may not produce linear, but instead discrete losses in capability, such as cultural difference becoming too great to understand others' verbal language unambiguously. Bodenhausen [4] found that making judgments at non-optimal times of the day according to people's circadian cycle led to stereotypical and thus disproportionally poor judgments.

We assume that some such distance-based collaboration hindrances can be compensated for by other means. Just as individuals possess cognitive reserves by which they can overcome some brain pathologies [e.g., 29] and still function properly, we may think of people's *collaborative reserves*, which allow them to overcome collaboration hindrances. For example, a misunderstanding of verbal language may be compensated for by the interpretation of body language. Hence, VT workers may compensate for some levels of cultural distance, but if it interacts with temporal distance (e.g., time zone difference resulting in tiredness and thus poor judgment), then the interaction of both effects may become too much to compensate for, thus leading to a highly salient degradation of collaboration effectiveness.

6.1 Theoretical Implications

Technology-enabled and physically dispersed VTs have emerged as a critical organizational form for structuring work on a global scale [13]. Despite the great potential benefits of VTs, many virtual workers report negative experiences, such as communication depersonalization, conflict, feelings of isolation, and lack of shared knowledge, all of which may negatively influence the virtual worker's job performance [14]. To address these challenges, research has focused on the effects of objective distance on work outcomes. However, the conflict surrounding the paradox of the "far-but-close" experience for VTs is yet to be reconciled.

By providing a consistent and solid foundation for diagnosis and assessment of psychological distance, this study contributes to VT literature. The findings of this research significantly shift academic and practical attention from objective distance toward subjective distance. A more nuanced understanding of how psychological distance is formed by the different dimensions of objective distance and how psychological distance influences job performance is of academic value.

6.2 Practical Implications

The overarching practical implication of this study is that virtual workers' psychological distance should be carefully monitored and managed to improve their job performance. Our measurement for objective and psychological distance helps VT managers predict more precisely potential challenges a virtual worker may experience. Given that each VT member has varying degrees of objective distance, VT managers need to pay greater attention to those who have high degrees of distance in its two or more sub-dimensions. VT managers should also carefully monitor virtual workers' psychological distance at the team level when the team is highly dispersed. Furthermore, our findings imply that VT members' psychological distance can be mitigated by altering virtual workers' perceptions of responsiveness, subjective proximity, and accessibility. Technological affordances that can promote emotional and social interaction (e.g., interactivity support, self-presentation, identity expression) may help to mitigate psychological distance.

Acknowledgement. This research was supported in part by grants No. CityU 21500714 from the Research Grants Council of the Hong Kong SAR awarded to the first author. The research reported in this article was supported in part by the Hong Kong SAR Research Grants Council under Project No. CityU 194613 awarded to the second author.

References

1. Ambos, T.C., Ambos, B.: The impact of distance on knowledge transfer effectiveness in multinational corporations. J. Int. Manag. **15**, 1–14 (2009)
2. Ayoko, O., Konrad, A., Boyle, M.: Online work: managing conflict and emotions for performance in virtual teams. Eur. Manag. J. **30**, 156–174 (2012)
3. Berson, Y., Halevy, N., Shamir, B., Erez, M.: Leading from different psychological distances: a construal-level perspective on vision communication, goal setting, and follower motivation. Leadersh. Q. **26**, 143–155 (2015)
4. Bodenhausen, G.V.: Stereotypes as judgmental heuristics: evidence of circadian variations in discrimination. Psychol. Sci. **1**, 319–322 (1990)
5. Cha, M., Park, J.G., Lee, J.: Effects of team member psychological proximity on teamwork performance. Team Perform. Manag. **20**, 81–96 (2014)
6. Colazo, J., Fang, Y.: Following the sun: temporal dispersion and performance in open source software project teams. J. Assoc. Inf. Syst. **11**, 684–707 (2010)
7. Cramton, C.D.: The mutual knowledge problem and its consequences for dispersed collaboration. Manag. Sci. **12**, 346–371 (2011)
8. Cramton, C.D., Hinds, P.J.: Subgroup dynamics in internationally distributed teams: ethnocentrism or cross-national learning? In: Staw, B., Kramer, R. (eds.) Research in Organizational Behavior, vol. 26, pp. 233–265. Elsevier, New York (2005)
9. Cramton, C.D., Webber, S.: Relationship among geographic dispersion, team processes, and effectiveness in software development work teams. J. Bus. Res. **58**, 758–765 (2005)
10. Espinosa, J., Cummings, J., Wilson, J., Pearce, B.: Team boundary issues across multiple global firms. J. Manag. Inf. Sys. **19**, 157–190 (2003)
11. Espinosa, J., Salughter, S.A., Kraut, R., Herbsleb, J.: Team knowledge and coordination in physically distributed software development. J. Manag. Inf. Syst. **24**, 135–169 (2007)
12. Fujita, K., Trope, Y., Liberman, N., Levin-Sagi, M.: Construal levels and self-control. J. Pers. Soc. Psychol. **90**, 351–367 (2006)
13. Gibson, C., Gibbs, J., Stanko, T., Tesluk, P., Cohen, S.: Including the "I" in virtuality and modern job design: extending the job characteristics model to include the moderating effect of individual experience of electronic dependence and copresence. Organ. Sci. **22**, 1481–1499 (2011)
14. Guinea, A., Webster, J., Staples, D.: A meta-analysis of the consequences of virtualness on team functioning. Inf. Manag. **49**, 301–308 (2013)
15. Hansen, M., Lovas, B.: How do multinational companies leverage technological competencies? Moving from single to interdependent explanations. Strateg. Manag. J. **25**, 801–821 (2004)
16. Harter, J.K., Schmidt, F.L., Hayes, T.L.: Business-unit-level relationship between employee satisfaction, employee engagement, and business outcomes: a meta-analysis. J. Appl. Psychol. **87**, 268–279 (2002)
17. Ho, C., Ke, W., Liu, H.: E-learning system implementation: implications from the construal level theory. In: Pacific Asia Conference on Information Systems, Paper 243, Jeju Island, Korea (2013). http://aisel.aisnet.org/pacis2013/243
18. Hoegl, M., Weinkauf, K., Gemuenden, H.G.: Interteam coordination, project commitment, and teamwork in multiteam R&D projects: a longitudinal study. Organ. Sci. **15**, 38–55 (2004)
19. Hoegl, M., Ernst, H., Proserpio, L.: How teamwork matters more as team member dispersion increases. J. Prod. Innov. Manag. **24**, 156–165 (2007)

20. Kahn, W.: Psychological conditions of personal engagement and disengagement at work. Acad. Manag. J. **33**, 692–724 (1990)
21. Kanawattanachai, P., Yoo, Y.: The impact of knowledge coordination on virtual team performance over time. MIS Q. **31**, 783–808 (2007)
22. Klitmøllera, A., Lauring, J.: When distance is good: a construal level perspective on perceptions of inclusive international language use. Int. Bus. Rev. **25**, 276–285 (2016)
23. Lim, S., Cha, S.Y., Park, C., Lee, I., Kim, J.: Getting closer and experiencing together: antecedents and consequences of psychological distance in social media-enhanced real-time streaming video. Comput. Human Behav. **28**, 1365–1378 (2012)
24. Lindenberger, U., Poetter, U.: The complex nature of unique and shared effects in hierarchical linear regression: Implications for developmental psychology. Psychol. Methods **3**, 218–230 (1998)
25. O'Leary, M.B., Cummings, J.N.: The spatial, temporal, and configurational characteristics of geographic dispersion in teams. MIS Q. **31**, 433–452 (2007)
26. Mehra, A., Kilduff, M., Brass, D.: The social networks of high and low self-monitors: implications for workplace performance. Adm. Sci. Q. **46**, 121–146 (2001)
27. Raab, K., Ambos, B., Tallman, S.: Strong or invisible hands? - Managerial involvement in the knowledge sharing process of globally dispersed knowledge groups. J. World Bus. **49**, 32–41 (2013)
28. Siebdrat, F., Hoegl, M., Ernst, H.: Subjective distance and team collaboration in distributed teams. J. Prod. Innov. Manag. **31**, 765–770 (2013)
29. Stern, Y.: What is cognitive reserve? Theory and research application of the reserve concept. J. Int. Neuropsychological Soc. **8**, 448–460 (2002)
30. Suh, A., Shin, K., Ahuja, M., Kim, M.: The Influence of Virtuality on Social networks: a multi-level approach. J. Manag. Inf. Syst. **28**, 351–386 (2011)
31. Trope, Y., Liberman, N., Wakslack, C.: Construal levels and psychological distance. J. Consum. Psychol. **17**, 83–95 (2007)
32. Trope, Y., Liberman, N.: Construal-level theory of psychological distance. Psychol. Rev. **117**, 440–463 (2010)
33. Van Boven, L., Kane, J., McGraw, A.P., Dale, J.: Feeling close: emotional intensity reduces perceived psychological distance. J. Pers. Soc. Psychol. **98**, 872–885 (2010)
34. Walther, J., Bunz, U.: The rules of virtual groups: trust, liking, and performance in computer-mediated communication. J. Commun. **55**, 828–846 (2005)
35. Wilson, J., O'Leary, M., Metiu, A., Jett, Q.: Perception of proximity in virtual work: explaining the paradox of far-but-close. Organ. Study **29**, 979–1002 (2008)
36. Wilson, J., Crisp, C., Mortensen, M.: Extending construal-level theory to distributed groups: understanding the effects of virtuality. Organ. Sci. **24**, 629–644 (2013)

Training Tactical Combat Casualty Care with an Integrated Training Approach

Lisa Townsend[1](✉), Laura Milham[1], Dawn Riddle[1],
CDR Henry Phillips[1], Joan Johnston[2], and William Ross[3]

[1] Naval Air Warfare Center Training Systems Division (NAWC-TSD),
Orlando, FL, USA
{lisa.townsend, laura.milham, dawn.riddle,
henry.phillips}@navy.mil
[2] Army Research Lab (ARL) Human Research and Engineering Directorate
(HRED) Advanced Training and Simulation Division (ATSD),
Orlando, FL, USA
joan.h.johnston.civ@mail.mil
[3] Cognitive Performance Group (CPG), Orlando, FL, USA
bill@cognitiveperformancegroup.com

Abstract. Tactical medical situations require squads to coordinate achieving tactical mission objectives while providing competent medical treatment. A tactical situation may require foregoing all but the most essential point-of-wounding care until tactical dangers are suppressed (effective shooting stops) and security allows for more definitive treatment. Core knowledge and skills, within the content areas of *advanced situational awareness, resilience, tactical combat casualty care, and team performance* can help teams coordinate medical and tactical team decisions and tasks. The objective of the Squad Overmatch Tactical Combat Casualty Care (SOvM TC3) project was to improve individual and team performance within the context of tactical medical care. To do this, the team utilized the Team Dimensional Training (TDT) model to integrate and train the above skills through guided team self-correction [3]. The empirically derived expert model of teamwork (TDT) has been found to be effective in a variety of team settings. Smith-Jentsch, Cannon-Bowers, Tannenbaum, and Salas (2008) demonstrated that teams who participated in facilitator-led guided self-correction developed more accurate mental models of teamwork, demonstrated superior teamwork processes, and achieved more effective performance outcomes than did those briefed and debriefed using a traditional method. This effort extended the TDT model to the core skills within an integrated training curriculum for tactical medical skills. This paper discusses team members' reported efficacy of the TDT approach in fostering individual and team process skills.

Keywords: Team performance · Integrated Training Approach (ITA) · Tactical Combat Casualty Care (TC3) · Team Dimensional Training (TDT) · Live training · Simulation-Based Training (SBT)

Disclaimer: The views expressed herein are those of the authors and do not necessarily reflect the official position of the organizations with which they are affiliated.

D.D. Schmorrow and C.M. Fidopiastis (Eds.): AC 2016, Part II, LNAI 9744, pp. 253–262, 2016.
DOI: 10.1007/978-3-319-39952-2_25

1 Introduction

Tactical Combat Casualty Care (TC3) is team decision-making under stress. It requires interdependent squad members, performing their role-based critical tasks, to make decisions that achieve a set of common goals under extreme circumstances. Squads must be able to flexibly and simultaneously accomplish mission objectives while treating their wounded in a fluid tactical environment. This requires squad leader situational awareness of the tactical medical situation and squad leadership coordinated with TC3 first responders, or the casualty himself, providing life-saving treatment. Failure to manage the tactical situation can lead to more casualties or mission failure. Not treating life-threatening injuries can lead to preventable combat death. The challenge that squads face is in the implementation of tactics, techniques and procedures that enable mission completion and life-saving without becoming distracted by one or the other. Becoming distracted when there are combat casualties can have catastrophic consequences, as decision-making, information processing, attention, and situational awareness is impaired [5]. Having squads engage in realistic TC3 scenarios, during a high stress unit level event, could optimize squad leadership, teamwork, and tactical and medical skills required to succeed in these challenging situations and develops resiliency for future situations.

However, Medics/Corpsman and infantry units rarely train together at the company level or below prior to training for a specific deployment. Various medical training centers exist (e.g., Medical Simulation Training Center (MSTC), Defense Medical Readiness Training Institute (DMRTI), Medical Simulation Training Centers (MSTC), and the Brigade Combat Team Trauma Training (BCT3)) to sustain and certify skills. But, no formal curriculum exists to support the integration of these medical skills into tactical operational environments. Providing infantry and their Medics/Corpsman the opportunity to train at the team level has been the focus of a joint effort called Squad Overmatch TC3 Training for Readiness and Resilience (SOvM TC3). Building on the SOvM studies started in 2012 by the U.S. Army Study Board [1]. The current effort is managed by the Program Executive Office for Simulation, Training, and Instrumentation (PEO STRI), with collaboration between the Army Research Laboratory, Human Research and Engineering Directorate (ARL HRED) and the Naval Air Warfare Center Training Systems Division (NAWCTSD). The objective of the SOvM TC3 2015 demonstration at FT Benning, GA was to develop and test instruction, simulations, and training technology prototypes embedded in Live scenarios using an Integrated Training Approach (ITA) that could foster individual and team process skills within the context of tactical medical care, rather than to focus solely on tactical outcomes. As such, this effort emphasized process skills, those skills that enable squad members to achieve targeted tactical outcomes and ultimately, improve mission performance.

The goal of this paper is to describe self-report results obtained during the demonstration with participants that included four U.S. Army and three U.S. Marine Corps Squads, each augmented with an Army Medic or U.S. Navy Hospital Corpsman, respectively. We describe how the Team Dimensional Training (TDT) model was used to enable squads to practice and apply knowledge and skills within the training content areas developed for SOvM TC3: TC3, Advanced Situational Awareness (ASA), and

Resilience/Performance Enhancement (R/PE). We describe the ITA approach utilized and discuss the self-report measures from squad members on the degree to which they felt the TDT approach fostered individual and team process skills during virtual and live training.

TDT was developed as part of a program sponsored by the Office of Naval Research (ONR) called Tactical Decision-making Under Stress (TADMUS) as a training methodology for enhancing performance through improved team processes [3]. The methodology helps teams diagnose and correct their own performance problems during an Integrated After Action Review (IAAR). This trains teams to adapt quickly to unfolding events and to learn from and build on their previous experiences together. The foundation of TDT was determining "What makes a team of experts an expert team?" The TADMUS effort identified four critical dimensions of teamwork (and their associated subcategories) that help teams monitor and regulate their own performance:

- Information Exchange – *knowing what information to pass to whom and when*
  - Using available sources
  - Passing information before being asked
  - Providing situation updates
- Communication Delivery – *how information is delivered*
  - Using correct terms
  - Providing complete reports
  - Using brief communications
  - Using clear communications
- Supporting Behavior – *compensating for one another in order to achieve team objectives*
  - Correcting errors
  - Providing and requesting backup
- Initiative/Leadership – *behaviors that provide direction for the team*
  - Providing guidance
  - Stating priorities

Research has shown that by focusing on and evaluating these areas of team performance each time a training exercise or combat situation has been concluded, the performance of the team can be significantly improved to meet future training and real life situations [4]. Furthermore, Smith-Jentsch, Cannon-Bowers, Tannenbaum, and Salas (2008) demonstrated that teams who participated in facilitator-led guided self-correction developed more accurate mental models of teamwork, demonstrated superior teamwork processes, and achieved more effective performance outcomes than did those briefed and debriefed using a traditional method. The TDT model is particularly suited for application in the TC3 domain and has been utilized within numerous operational and training environments where individuals and teams are required to make critical decisions during changing and intense situations [2]. To perform successfully in tactical and medical environments, team members must be able to assess situations quickly, perform TC3 skills when necessary, and engage in R/PE methods to quickly recover from stressful situations.

2   SOvM TC3 Integrated Training Approach (ITA)

The SOvM TC3 ITA is a three day curriculum beginning with classroom instruction, moving on to skills practice in Simulation-Based Training (SBT), and then Live training exercises. Subject Matter Experts (SMEs) developed curricula to emphasize building communication and decision-making skills in managing combat casualties during Care Under Fire and Tactical Field Care situations. SMEs identified the key TDT teamwork behaviors within each of the foundational topics of TC3, ASA, and R/PE. They analyzed the content areas to determine instances of TDT behaviors that contribute to mission success (see Table 1 below for a subset of examples) and these points were instructed and demonstrated during the ITA.

Table 1. TDT related behaviors in ASA, TC3, and R/PE content areas

	ASA	TC3	R/PE
Information Exchange	Utilizing available sources - Proxemics, kinesics, autonomics/ biometrics, geographics, atmospherics are all sources that provide critical information. Providing situation updates - Tactical patience is necessary to develop a clear picture of the situation before providing a situation update.	Utilizing available sources - The TC3 card is a source of information, informing squad members of a casualty's severity of injuries and progress in treatment Passing information – Especially during Care Under Fire, information must be passed before having to be asked for it.	
Communication Delivery	Using correct terms – Battlefield Geometries require accurate Fields of Fire/Observation/Intelligence being communicated using a common frame of reference and standard phraseology.	Providing complete report - During tactical medical communications required reports must include the right pieces of information, in the right order (e.g., MEDEVAC Request). Using brief/clear communications - Stressful TC3 events require brief and clear communications.	
Supporting Behavior	Providing/requesting backup - Guardian Angels provide backup, acting as the eyes and ears of someone else who is otherwise engaged.	Providing backup -Providing support directly to a casualty and providing back up while self-care or first responder care is provided under fire by another squad member is vital. Asking for support if you cannot provide self-care is as important.	Providing/requesting backup and correcting errors - Back up and error correction are necessary when squad members are observed not performing or have frozen. Personal awareness is key as well - seek back up if/when needed. Self and buddy-talk, deliberate breathing, and grounding are R/PE tools to help during these times.

(Continued)

Table 1. (*Continued*)

	ASA	TC3	R/PE
Team Initiative/ Leadership	Providing guidance - Guardian Angels may need to direct a squad member's attention to something they may not see.	Stating priorities – During stressful TC3 events priorities may shift often and will need to be shared with the squad. Providing guidance – TC3 events require guidance both to and from squad members, especially as the Medic/Corpsman's demands are dispersed.	Stating priorities - When focusing on W.I.N. (What's Important Now), accept that priorities may change based on circumstances Providing guidance – Guidance and leadership are required if squad members are emotionally and physically impacted by stressful events.

2.1   Classroom Instruction

On day 1, instruction provided squad members with opportunities to acquire specific knowledge and included PowerPoint, interactive discussion, scenario diagnostic exercises, and hands on part-task medical simulators.

TC3. TC3 SMEs developed the classroom instruction to focus on the efficient communication and coordination behaviors needed between the squad leader, Fire team leaders, and the Medic or first responder. Communications to determine mission success provide the squad leader with information about his capability, allowing decisions to be made about continuing the mission. Communications about severity of wounds allows the Medic to make decisions about priority and resource needs.

ASA. ASA SMEs developed curriculum focused on providing knowledge and developing skills in pattern/threat recognition and decision-making to include behavioral profiling skills (i.e. proximity between people as an indicator of relationship), kinesics (i.e., nonverbal body language), autonomics (i.e., observable physiological signals), geographics (e.g., patterns of how individuals move through an environment) atmospherics (e.g., new rubble, bullet holes), and heuristics (e.g., using tactical cunning, tactical patience, keeping an overwatch/"guardian angel," and building relationships/"good shepherd"). In addition to the development of individual situational awareness, it is critical that the team members share this information across the squad to ensure that they have a more complete picture of the situation, and to pass that information to the squad leader for situational awareness, and for decision-making. Given this, the coordination of the team was defined in terms of the teamwork behaviors that facilitated a shared understanding of the situation.

R/PE. R/PE SMEs developed curriculum focused on providing knowledge and developing skills in maintaining tactical effectiveness under combat stress (acceptance, what's important now, deliberate breathing, self-talk and buddy talk, grounding, and Personal After Action Review (AAR). This involves both individual skills, as well as team supporting behaviors. With respect to teamwork, team members were encouraged to provide positive communication to other team members who were struggling with a stressful event, to try to refocus them on the mission task.

TDT/IAAR. TDT SMEs developed curriculum that focused on introducing the four dimensions of teamwork and how the TDT model (Prebrief, Perform, Debrief) can be used to facilitate discussions involving the teamwork behaviors identified in the TC3, ASA, and R/PE instruction. Emphasis was on mastery of team-level processes rather than maximization of scenario-specific outcomes. Then curriculum focused on how the IAAR enables the squad to discuss team TC3, ASA, and R/PE behaviors in the context of the four teamwork dimensions. The IAAR uses guided team self-correction, which refers to the use of a facilitator who (a) keeps the squad's discussion focused, (b) establishes a positive climate, (c) encourages and reinforces active participation, (d) models effective feedback skills, and (e) coaches team members in stating their feedback in a constructive manner [3] to diagnose team strengths and weaknesses, identify solutions, and establish goals for improvement.

2.2 Simulation-Based Training (SBT)

On day 2, the Virtual Battlespace 3 (VBS3) training simulation was used to provide SBT. VBS3 is an Army Training Program of Record platform for practicing within a semi-immersive environment with dynamic terrain. For this effort, VBS3 was integrated with a medical simulation program, TC3Sim, which supports the assessment and treatment of casualties. SMEs developed six tactical/medical event-based scenarios to enable squads to practice what they had learned in the classroom and to conduct IAARs. The Combined Arms Collective Training Facility (CACTF) - McKenna Military Operations on Urban Terrain 2 (MOUT) site used for the live exercises (described below) was modeled in the VBS3 urban terrain to increase the transfer of skills from simulation to the live environment. TDT behaviors were identified in the event-based scenarios so that the TDT/IAAR model could be applied, allowing squads to collectively (and even individually) engage in a cycle of practice, application, and feedback to create self-monitoring and correcting teams. During the pre-brief, mission clarification was emphasized, the teamwork development focus of the exercise was stressed (process skills), and any previously set goals for improvement were stated.

2.3 Live Training Exercise

On day 3, two Live training exercises were conducted at the CACTF MOUT site with scenario events designed to be very similar to the ones developed in VBS3. The site was outfitted with a suite of TC3 simulators and a wide variety of other Virtually Enhanced Live Technologies in order to significantly increase the number of realistic TC3 tasks that could be trained. This included:

- Simulated battlefield effects provided audio of combat sounds (e.g. gunshots), artillery, and Improvised Explosive Device (IED) blasts;
- Live role-players acting as key leaders, townspeople, and casualties made up with moulage (e.g. wearable wound models) and simulated injuries to increase realism and incorporation into triage and TC3 scenario management;

- A variety of interactive virtual enemy combatants projected on walls of MOUT buildings playing characters that could be shot and illustrate wounds;
- Interactive modeled components: tourniquets, nasal pharyngeal airway, chest decompression needle, chest seal, TC3 card, bandage, and compression bandage.

Squad members and role-players were equipped with the Multiple Integrated Laser Engagement System (MILES) gear, which was augmented with a prototype Electronic Casualty Display Device (ECDD). This device displayed information about the medical condition of a patient such as changing health status (e.g., pulse, respiration, and pain level), and ability to communicate and move. This enabled TC3 responders to identify, prioritize and succeed or fail to provide appropriate treatment according to realistic timelines and prognoses. Trainees could render medical aid with their sensored first aid kit, the Improved First Aid Kit (IFAK II) Simulators for Medical Devices. IAARs were conducted after each scenario. As with the VBS3 scenarios, TDT behaviors were identified in the event-based live scenarios so that the TDT/IAAR model could be implemented.

3 Findings

After each day of SBT and Live training, squad members were administered questionnaires asking the degree to which the VBS3 and Virtually Enhanced Live Technologies allowed them to practice teamwork behaviors. Seventy-one Army and Marine squad members participated in the demonstration, each going through the same ITA.

3.1 VBS3 Technology Survey

Trainees scored items on a 5-point Likert scale, rating whether they agreed that the VBS3 training technology supported the learning objectives: 1 (completely disagree), 2 (disagree), 3 (not sure), 4 (agree), and 5 (completely agree). Selected questionnaire items that focus on the degree that VBS3 supported team dimensions and team performance are presented in Table 2.

3.2 Virtually Enhanced Live Technologies and Overall Impact of Live Training Surveys

Trainees were instructed to provide ratings for those Virtually Enhanced Live Technologies encountered. For Table 3, trainees rated the effectiveness on a 5-point Likert scale from: 1 (not at all), 2 (a limited amount), 3 (adequately) and 4 (extremely well). Trainees were also instructed to provide ratings regarding the overall impact of Live Training. Table 4 reports on a 5-point Likert scale: from 1 (completely disagree), 2 (disagree), 3 (not sure), 4 (agree), and 5 (completely agree).

For VBS3 and the Virtually Enhanced Live Technologies, trainees agreed that training provided opportunities to practice team performance skills. In VBS3, squad members agreed with statements that they could practice communications in support of

Table 2. VBS3 and Teamwork

What was the degree that VBS3 supported team dimensions?	Mean	Std. Dev.
1. *I communicated information with my team members to determine if cues were normal or anomalies.*	4.3	0.7
2. *I practiced reporting key casualty information to my Team Leader or Squad Leader.*	4.1	0.9
3. *The squad engaged in a TDT Pre-brief and clarified the mission, introduced tactical objectives, focused attention on the four teamwork dimensions, and restated tactical and teamwork goals.*	4.4	0.6
4. *VBS provides an environment to practice and develop my TDT skills.*	4.2	0.7
5. *My squad effectively used the VBS scenarios to practice and develop TDT skills.*	4.3	0.8
6. *My squad engaged in a focused hotwash after each vignette.*	4.4	0.6
7. *My squad set goals at the end of the IAAR that were reviewed as part of the mission Pre-Brief.*	4.6	0.6
8. *VBS3 is an effective tool for me to practice TDT skills.*	4.2	0.9
9. *The virtual environment provided you with opportunities to engage in a successful team self-correction debrief.*	4.3	0.7
10. *The virtual environment provided you with opportunities to exchange information about the situation within the squad.*	3.6	1.2
11. *The virtual environment provided you with opportunities to support the actions of squad members when they are struggling.*	3.7	1.1
12. *The virtual environment provided you with opportunities to report information about the situation accurately.*	3.9	1.0
13. *The virtual environment provided you with opportunities to keep the Platoon informed of the situation without being asked.*	3.9	1.0
14. *The virtual environment provided you with opportunities to engage in effective error detection and team self-correction.*	3.9	1.1

determining anomalies (M = 4.3, SD = .7), a component of developing team ASA. Also, squad member agreed with the statement that they could practice sending key casualty information to other team members (M = 4.1, SD = .9). In the Live scenarios, all representations of combatants adequately supported communicating information on targets, key to team ASA (pop-up targets, M = 3.1, SD = 1.5, live role players M = 3.9, SD = .4, interactive virtual characters M = 3.6, SD = .7, and non-interactive virtual characters M = 3.6, SD = .9). For the team dimensions, squad members agreed that the live training overall provided the ability to practice. Specifically, live training supported Information Exchange (M = 4.3, SD = .7), Communication Delivery (M = 4.3, SD = .7), and Supporting Behaviors (M = 4.3, SD = .6). As VBS3 and Live Technologies are part of the overall training approach for team performance, these results suggest that the technologies support squads' ability to effectively practice team dimensions. This practice supports team members in developing an understanding of how the roles (and individuals in the roles) exchange information, communicate, and support each other. In future work, it may be helpful to provide squads with feedback about the impact of

Table 3. Virtually enhanced live technologies and teamwork

What was the degree that the Virtually Enhanced Live Technologies supported team dimensions?	Mean	Std. Dev.
1. *Pop up targets provide opportunities for me to practice effectively communicating information about suspected targets to others in my squad.*	3.1	1.5
2. *Live Role Players provide opportunities for me to practice effectively communicating information about suspected targets to others in my squad.*	3.9	0.4
3. *Dynamic Interactive Virtual Characters provide opportunities for me to practice effectively communicating information about suspected targets to others in my squad.*	3.6	0.7
4. *Virtual characters provide opportunities for me to practice effectively communicating information about suspected targets to others in my squad.*	3.6	0.9
5. *Simulated explosive effects provide opportunities for me to practice effectively communicating information to others in my squad.*	3.9	0.5
6. *Simulated wound effects provide opportunities for me to practice effectively communicating information to others in my squad.*	3.8	0.4
7. *The electronic casualty card (ECC) provides opportunities for me to practice effectively communicating information to others in my squad.*	3.6	0.6

Table 4. Overall impact of live training on teamwork

1. *The live training allowed my squad to exchange information about the situation within the squad.*	4.3	0.7
2. *The live training allowed my squad to support the actions of squad members when they are struggling.*	4.3	0.7
3. *The live training allowed my squad to report information about the situation accurately.*	4.3	0.7
4. *The live training allowed my squad to keep the Platoon informed of the situation without being asked.*	4.4	0.6
5. *The hot washes after VBS3 scenarios provided suggestions for improvement that I was able to use in later scenarios.*	4.4	0.7
6. *The IAARs after the first Live scenario helped me improve my performance during the second scenario.*	4.4	0.7
7. *The live training allowed my squad to engage in effective error detection and team self-correction.*	4.3	0.6
8. *The improved IFAK provides opportunities for me to practice effectively communicating information to others in my squad.*	3.7	0.7

coordination on medical and mission outcomes, such as number of casualties and time and accuracy in managing combatants. Feedback data could be fed forward into IAAR, to provide squads with the natural consequences of good or poor team performance.

4   Conclusion and Future Research

Future analyses will include reviewing the individual and team related TDT survey questions asked after classroom instruction, as the focus of the current paper was on SBT and Live training days. This will also include reviewing survey questions that focus on the other three content areas (TC3, ASA, and R/PE) and whether team members felt the ITA in these content areas fostered individual and team process skills. Currently, a SOvM TC3 experiment is planned for June 2016 in Fort Benning, GA. While SOvM TC3 2015 (the focus of this paper) was considered a demonstration, SOvM 2016 will be a training effectiveness evaluation conducted using a quasi-experimental design comparing the perceptions and performance of warfighters completing the ITA with warfighters completing similar exercises in a control condition. Lessons learned from SOvM TC3 2015 will be applied, including an additional half day of training to offer a Live test scenario, to evaluate the impact of the ITA curriculum on performance.

Acknowledgments. The authors would like to thank the Defense Medical Research and Development Program through Joint Program Committee 1 (JPC-1: Medical Training and Health Information Services) for sponsorship and funding of this critical effort. The authors would also like to thank the four U.S. Army and three U.S. Marine Corps Squads, as well as the Medics and U.S. Navy Hospital Corpsmen who contributed their time to this effort.

References

1. Brimstin, J., Higgs, A., Wolf, R.: Stress exposure training for the dismounted squad: the human dimension. In: The Proceedings of the Interservice/Industry Training, Simulation, and Education Conference [CD-ROM]. Orlando, FL (2015)
2. Smith-Jentsch, K.A., Cannon-Bowers, J.A., Tannenbaum, S.I., Salas, E.: Guided Team Self-Correction
3. Impacts on team mental models, processes, and effectiveness. In Small Group Research, vol. 39, no. 3, pp. 303–327 (2008)
4. Smith-Jentsch, K.A., Payne, S.C., Johnston, J.H.: Guided team self-corrections: a methodology for enhancing experiential team training. In: Smith-Jentch (Chair), K.A. (ed.) When, How, and Why Does Practice Make Perfect? Symposium Conducted at the 11th Annual Conference of the Society of Industrial and Organizational Psychology, San Diego, CA (1996)
5. Smith-Jentsch, K.A., Zeisig, R.L., McPherson, J., Acton, B.: Team dimensional training: a strategy for guided team self-correction. In: Cannon-Bowers, J.A., Salas, E. (eds.) Decision Making Under Stress: Implications for Individual And Team Training, pp. 271–297. American Psychological Association, Washington, DC (1998)
6. Stokes, A.F., Kite, K.: Flight Stress: Stress, Fatigue, and Performance in Aviation. Ashgate, Burlington (1994)

Exploratory Trajectory Clustering
with Distance Geometry

Andrew T. Wilson$^{(\boxtimes)}$, Mark D. Rintoul, and Christopher G. Valicka

Sandia National Laboratories, Albuquerque, NM 87185, USA
atwilso@sandia.gov

Abstract. We present here an example of how a large, multi-dimensional unstructured data set, namely aircraft trajectories over the United States, can be analyzed using relatively straightforward unsupervised learning techniques. We begin by adding a rough structure to the trajectory data using the notion of distance geometry. This provides a very generic structure to the data that allows it to be indexed as an n-dimensional vector. We then do a clustering based on the HDBSCAN algorithm to both group flights with similar shapes and find outliers that have a relatively unique shape. Next, we expand the notion of geometric features to more specialized features and demonstrate the power of these features to solve specific problems. Finally, we highlight not just the power of the technique but also the speed and simplicity of the implementation by demonstrating them on very large data sets.

1 Introduction

Recent advances in sensing technologies have resulted in ever-higher numbers of scientific and technical data sets being created at ever-higher fidelity. As with many other data types, this trend holds true for *trajectory data*, broadly defined as timestamped sequences of positions for uniquely identified objects. Trajectory data can be obtained from many different sources. Remote sensing systems track the movement of many objects through areas of sensor coverage. Individual objects such as taxi cabs, aircraft, seacraft, mobile phones, humans carrying GPS receivers, and even the occasional bear, turtle or penguin also record and broadcast their own position and movement. Video sensors (traffic or security cameras) combined with machine vision algorithms can track the appearance, motion and disappearance of objects in a scene. As with so many other real-world data sources, the ongoing explosion of trajectory data shows no signs of abating.

Trajectories are consumed and analyzed by a broad variety of research communities. Biologists use them to study wildlife movement [14]. Sociologists study human behavior [17]. Transit agencies and travel websites mine taxi trajectories to search for better driving directions [16]. Molecular dynamicists track molecules and individual atoms to study proteins, polymers, and transitions between different molecular conformations.

© Springer International Publishing Switzerland 2016
D.D. Schmorrow and C.M. Fidopiastis (Eds.): AC 2016, Part II, LNAI 9744, pp. 263–274, 2016.
DOI: 10.1007/978-3-319-39952-2_26

As a specific example, consider the Automatic Identification System (AIS) currently used for maritime ship tracking and cooperative collision avoidance. Given the amount of world commerce that depends on container ships and tankers, marine traffic safety and security is of incalculable importance – a perfect domain for trajectory analysis. Pallotta et al. [13] present an algorithm for automatically determining shipping routes given AIS ship trajectories for the purposes of anomaly detection and route prediction.

Both prediction and anomaly detection can be used to aid collision avoidance. However, such algorithms can also be extended to address the broader question of classifying ship behavior. Establishing patterns of normal and anomalous behavior is as useful to the large-scale problems of efficiency, security and resource allocation as tracking nearby objects for collision avoidance is at small scale.

Commercial airlines use similar pattern-finding analyses [1] to optimize the use of airspace resources such as flight paths, fuel and takeoff/landing permits. They are aided by the Aircraft Situation Display to Industry (ASDI) data set, a metadata-rich feed that provides frequent updates on nearly all non-sensitive civilian traffic in US airspace.

All of these analyses incorporate an assumption that we can identify and isolate patterns within the data. This brings us back to classic machine learning problems: finding instances of specifically described behavior, clustering items into groups (with or without ground truth), finding items similar to a provided exemplar, and labeling new data based on the information in a training set. Metadata (any information in the data feed beyond position, time, and object ID) and derived data (speed, heading, distance from origin, other quantities computed from the original data) help with this, but to date most of the job of labeling trajectories as normal or anomalous still relies on human knowledge and manual effort. Since humans still do not scale well we turn to algorithmic approaches.

Many approaches to trajectory analysis describe and compute the distance between each position of a trajectory. Amongst others, these approaches include hidden Markov models [3], Hausdorff-like distances [8], Bayesian models [10], the earth-mover's distance [4], and Fourier descriptors [2]. Alternatively, the approach mentioned in [15] makes use of trajectory features in order to provide trajectory comparisons that appeal to human intuition and significantly reduce the computational intensity required for those comparisons to allow for timely analysis of large sets of trajectory data.

In this paper we report on an experimental analysis of a large set of aircraft trajectories using feature vectors. For clarity, we formalize our definition of a trajectory as follows:

A *trajectory* Z is a sequence of n points $z_1 \ldots z_n$. Each point z_i exists in a normed vector space and is annotated with a timestamp t_i. We assume that the moving object described by Z moves directly from each point z_i to its successor z_{i+1} with uniform velocity, leaving z_i at t_i and arriving at z_{i+1} at t_{i+1}.

We now present a brief survey of previous work on trajectory analysis and clustering before describing our own experiments and their results.

2   Previous Work

The problem of classifying trajectories in an unsupervised manner has been tackled in a number of different ways, mostly focused around classic machine learning techniques. Hidden Markov Models (HMMs) have been applied to groups of trajectories [12] in order to divide them into different patterns. This has been reasonably effective, although the model building process can be time-consuming and it can sometimes be difficult to understand the underlying reasons for the assignment of the trajectories into different patterns. Similar approaches using Bayesian models have also been employed [10]. One can also develop distance metrics that can be defined between two individual trajectories and apply clustering techniques that use only the distance between two individual trajectories [4]. There are clustering techniques that can be applied with only a distance matrix between all of the points, but this can be large and potentially computationally expensive and can also limit the types of clustering techniques that can be used.

One of the primary problems of applying many types of unsupervised learning approaches is that many of the techniques, especially clustering, most naturally apply to n-dimensional vectors of data. The problem then becomes one of translating the trajectory representation in to that of a vector of real numbers that can have a simple and meaningful distance metric applied to it for clustering purposes. Annoni and Forster [2] have demonstrated this using Fourier descriptors to build the representations of the data. This approach has also been used [11] where the trajectories are represented not by a vector or points, but instead a vector of line segments that have been extracted from the straighter parts of the trajectory. However, their approach is inherently focused around trajectories that are naturally geographically aligned.

The unsupervised learning method we propose here uses has much in common with many of the previous works, but is tailored to have these key properties:

1. It must be fast enough to work at scales greater than 10^6 trajectories.
2. It must be generic enough to use with diverse types of trajectories.
3. It must not require a large number of user tunable parameters in order to work effectively.
4. The separation into different clusters should have a physically meaningful and intuitive interpretation.
5. It must not require geometric alignment of input trajectories in order to perform similarity calculations.

3   Overview

3.1   Intended Workflow

Our intent was to model a workflow that would let an investigator make sense of a large body of trajectories through a process of generating cluster labels, inspecting the results, extracting a subset and computing new cluster labels.

In order to create such a workflow we need a useful characterization of a trajectory's features and an unsupervised clustering algorithm that can operate on those features. For the purposes of this paper we will focus on the clustering step rather than the query and subset steps of the proposed workflow.

3.2 Feature Vectors

We describe trajectories using feature vectors in order to focus the clustering on characteristics of our own choice instead of point-by-point alignment. We tried two different kinds of feature vectors: one using the idea of distance geometry and one using several different geometric features. The main advantage of feature vectors over a divergence score computed directly between trajectories is that it allows us to use popular clustering algorithms that require (and benefit from) normed vector spaces.

Distance Geometry. We found feature vectors based on *distance geometry* [6] to be most expressive of the available options. We compute a *distance geometry signature* as follows:

1. Select an integer $k \geq 1$.
2. For each $1 \leq j \leq k$, select $j+1$ uniform sample points along a trajectory Z to yield sample points $s_0, s_1 \ldots, s_{j+1}$, where s_0 and s_{j+1} represent the beginning and end points of the trajectory, respectively. Interpolate between trajectory points z_i as necessary to construct these points.
3. For each j where $1 \leq j \leq k$, calculate the distance $d_{j,01}, d_{j,12}, \ldots, d_{j,j-1j}$ of each of the j sub-trajectories.
4. Normalize the distances by dividing each $d_{j,m-1m}$ by the length of the portion of the trajectory between s_{m-1} and s_m. For example, $d_{1,01}$ will be divided by the length of the entire trajectory, while $d_{j,m-1m}$ will be divided by one jth of the overall length.
5. Arrange these normalized distances into a vector. The actual order does not matter as long as it is consistent from one trajectory to the next. For convenience, we usually place $d_{1,01}$ first, followed by $d_{2,01}$ and $d_{2,12}$ and so forth. The distances $d_{k,k-1k}$ go at the end of the vector.

Observe that at a conceptual level, these signatures quantify how straight the trajectory is at different scales and different positions. The resulting signatures allow shape-based comparison independent of translation, rotation, reflection and uniform scale. This proves to be a major advantage. At the same time, it is also the major disadvantage of distance geometry since it is unaware of any property more complex than point-to-point distance. Finally, we note that a distance geometry signature based on k sample points yields a feature vector with $\frac{k(k+1)}{2}$ components. This raises the specter of the curse of dimensionality as we experiment with larger values of k.

Geometric Features. Besides distance geometry signatures, it is often useful to define other functions that measure specific geometric features within a trajectory. These provide traction when an analyst has a specific property in mind that helps differentiate among trajectory behaviors. We have used the following features in the past:

- End-to-end distance of the trajectory
- Total length of trajectory
- Total curvature (sum of signed turn angles)
- Properties of the convex hull of the trajectory including:
  • Area
  • Aspect ratio
  • Centroid
  • Perimeter

In general, there are not many requirements for a geometric feature. The two primary ones are that they should be simple to calculate in one pass through the data, and that they should be relatively insensitive to point sampling frequency and spatial noise on the trajectory. This second condition is usually the one that is more difficult to fulfill. For example, the total curvature is relatively insensitive to fluctuations in the heading due to the fact that the errors tend to cancel each other out. However, if one was interested in the total amount of absolute heading change between points (to attempt to distinguish straight flights from meandering flights), any sort of fluctuation in the heading will strongly affect the outcome. This measure is also very sensitive to the sampling rate along the curve.

3.3 Clustering

Two principles guide our selection of a clustering algorithm. First, in analysis and sensemaking tasks, the category of "things not similar to any we have seen before" is especially important since it may indicate the presence of new or overlooked classes of behavior. Since this is the very definition of an outlier, we prefer clustering algorithms that can explicitly identify outliers. Second, since we have no idea how many interesting classes exist in the data, we prefer nonparametric clustering algorithms that can choose a number of clusters on the fly.

Both of these criteria point strongly toward density-based clustering algorithms such as DBSCAN [7]. We choose HDBSCAN [5] for both of these properties as well as its ability to identify clusters with varying densities.

4   Implementation and Results

4.1   Data Set

We tested our approach on a database of aircraft trajectories. These were originally collected from the Aircraft Situation Display to Industry (ASDI) feed that originates at the US Federal Aviation Administration.

We perform minimal preprocessing of the data. First, we discard obviously invalid points (those missing coordinates, an ID or a timestamp). Second, we assemble points into trajectories by grouping them by flight IDs and sorting by timestamp. We begin a new trajectory for a given flight ID when we find a delay of more than 20 min or a distance of more than 100 km between successive points. These numbers were arbitrarily chosen but correspond well with observed practice at busy airports. Third, we discard trajectories that last less than one hour as uninteresting.

We tried two separate databases of trajectories. The smaller one contains 83,431 trajectories that fall on July 10 and 11, 2013. These dates are notable for a large system of thunderstorms that swept through the central and eastern United States and caused widespread disruption at several major airports. The larger set contains 359,940 trajectories from July 1–15, 2014. All trajectories were at least one hour long.

4.2 Feature Vectors

First, we tried clustering trajectories using distance geometry signatures with a maximum of 5 ($k = 4$), 10 ($k = 9$) and 15 ($k = 14$) sample points. Since the length of each feature vector is proportional to the square of the number of sample points we expected runtimes to increase accordingly. The resulting feature vectors had dimension 10, 45 and 105.

We also tried feature vectors made from various combinations of a trajectory's length, end-to-end distance and convex hull aspect ratio.

4.3 Runtime

For the purposes of this paper, runtime is not our primary concern. However, most current implementations of HDBSCAN have worst-case algorithmic complexity $O(n^2)$ with respect to the number of items being labeled. We emphasize *worst case* because in our experience the runtime depended more on the dimension of the feature space than on the number of items. See Table 1 for our observations.

5   Discussion

Our first observation was that distance geometry was far better at discriminating different behavior than any of the combinations of individual features that we tried. We attribute this strength to its multiscale representation of trajectory shape, an attribute not yet captured with our approach to custom features. The geometric features were able to distinguish the approximate straightness or roundness of a trajectory but little beyond that.

Second, we note that the runtime of the clustering algorithm depends only indirectly upon the number of items being labeled. We conjecture instead that runtime is dominated by the HDBSCAN step where a minimum spanning tree

Table 1. Typical runtimes and cluster size results for selected data sets. N refers the total number of trajectories and DG refers to the maximum number of distance geometry points used. We believe that the large difference in runtime between 10 and 15 distance geometry samples is a symptom of choosing too many sample points for distance geometry.

N	DG	Runtime	Largest cluster	Outliers	Other cluster sizes
83K	5	00:00:08	68,195 (82 %)	14,460 (17 %)	477, 137, 42, 14 (x2), 13, 12 (x3), 11 (x3), 10
83K	10	00:00:50	80,574 (97 %)	2,153 (2.6 %)	557, 124, 12, 11
83K	15	00:11:10	76,448 (92 %)	6,285 (7.5 %)	524, 112, 17, 13, 11 (x2), 10
359K	5	00:00:48	328,056 (91 %)	29,853 (8.3 %)	1044, 305, 78, 27, 26 (x2), 22 (x2), 21 (x3), 20 (x2), < 20 (x25)
359K	10	00:12:20	334,969 (93 %)	22,084 (6.1 %)	1863, 683, 34, 30 (x2), 24, 22, 20, < 20 (x12)
359K	15	03:23:56	339,796 (94 %)	18,208 (5.1 %)	1089, 490, 39, 29, 27, 25, 24, < 20 (x15)

is computed over a (notionally complete) distance matrix. Although McInnes's HDBSCAN implementation is heavily optimized and makes use of spatial data structures and parallelization wherever possible, the minimum spanning tree algorithm is still $O(E) = O(n^2)$ for a complete graph. We further conjecture that this distance graph grows denser as distances between feature vectors become more uniform – a known symptom of the curse of dimensionality. We do not yet understand fully how to choose the number of distance geometry samples for an entire corpus. If we choose too few samples then we can identify only coarse classes of behavior. If we choose too many, too much behavior winds up lumped into the large central cluster.

Now we turn to the actual clustering results. In each case, the cluster labels were dominated by one very large class comprising about 90 % of the input trajectories. Upon inspecting the distance geometry signatures we found that the members of this class were flights that took off, flew directly to their destination, maneuvered very briefly and then landed. This makes sense: it is the most efficient way to operate a commercial airline where time and fuel are both major expenses.

The outlier class also contained a wealth of diverse, interesting behavior. It typically contained about 5 % of the trajectories in the data set. Since the outliers are (by definition) data points that did not fit into any cluster, further exploration must incorporate other approaches. Here we appeal to our notional workflow where an analyst has information foraging and query tools available.

Further classes identified using distance geometry tend to be quite succinct. As we had hoped, distance geometry was able to identify trajectories that not only shared common behavior but shared it at similar distances along the trajectory. Figures 1, 2, 3, 4 and 5 show some examples. In each figure, the red end of a trajectory is its origin and the blue end is its destination.

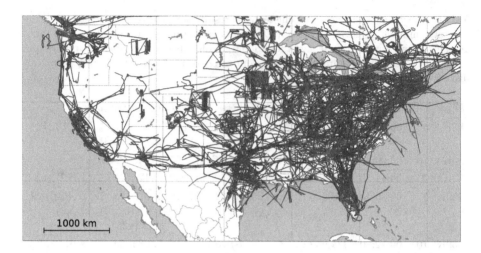

Fig. 1. The "noise" cluster from HDBSCAN contains plenty of interesting behavior. Since the members of this cluster are (by definition) unlike other items in the database we will need additional foraging and sensemaking tools for the user. These additional tools may be as simple as clustering using different feature measures. This particular cluster contains 2,153 trajectories and was identified with 10-point distance geometry over 83,000 trajectories.

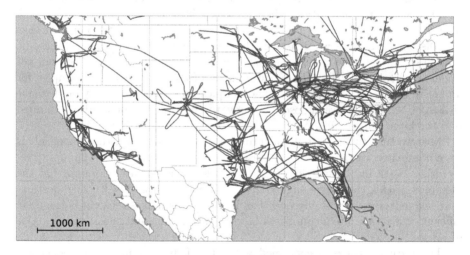

Fig. 2. Out-and-back flights (those that leave one place, fly to another, then return to their origin) are particularly easy for distance geometry to pick out. This set contains 557 trajectories identified with 10-point distance geometry over 83,000 trajectories.

The invariance of distance geometry signatures to rigid transformations was not as great a strength as we had hoped. While an out-and-back trajectory 100 km long has the same shape as one 2000 km long, an observer might reasonably conclude that their behavior was quite different. The former is a quick hop lasting less than an hour. The latter is a multi-hour odyssey. This suggests that

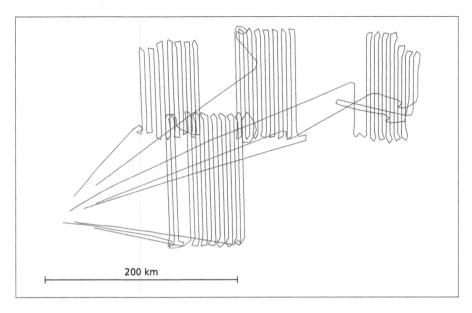

Fig. 3. A portion of a cluster of 683 flights exhibiting strong back-and-forth behavior typical of mapping and survey flights. This particular set of trajectories leaves from and returns to a small airfield near Bend, Oregon.

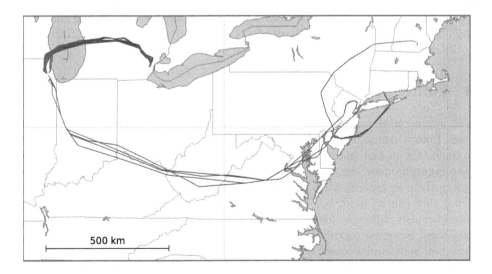

Fig. 4. Many instances of a single flight with a distinct shape that travels from Chicago to Detroit. Note that distance geometry pulls in additional flights with very similar shapes (Chicago to New York; New Haven, Connecticut to Philadelphia; and a single flight from Manchester, New Hampshire to Philadelphia). The differing sizes and orientations of these flights illustrate the invariance of distance geometry signatures under rigid transformation.

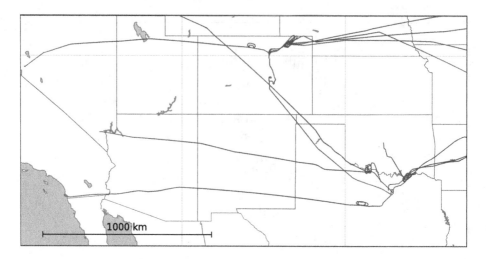

Fig. 5. Part of a cluster of 17 flights that all include a holding pattern (oval loop) at approximately the same point in their travel. This cluster was extracted using 15 distance geometry samples (a 105-dimensional feature space), offering very high sensitivity to localized features at the cost of runtime and the influence of the curse of dimensionality. This cluster came from the larger set of 360,000 trajectories.

we remove some of the invariance by adding a term to the feature vector that represents trajectory length. If done right, this would discourage the clustering algorithm from grouping trajectories with similar shape but vastly different scales. As usual, "if done right" is likely to be the hard part.

6   Future Work

The approach we have described in the previous sections forms a fundamental base, from which many potential improvements and extensions could derive. It is important to first note that trajectory clustering, like many applied machine learning techniques, can be difficult to judge on an objective basis. In some cases where there is ground truth associated with the trajectories (such as aircraft type) that can be used, but this doesn't necessarily divide the trajectories up into obviously different shapes. In other cases the results of the clustering could be judged based on very different metrics depending on the interest of the user. Any notion of improvement must be tempered by the application.

One of the primary difficulties in using many unsupervised machine learning algorithms is that there is ultimately a number of choices that must be made with respect to how data is structured and what choices are made with respect to algorithm parameters. This work primarily focuses on the distance geometry features because of their generality in describing trajectory shapes, but of course any numerical features could also be used. However, with too many features the algorithms run much more slowly; worse, the effects of important features are lost in the "curse of dimensionality" [9]. Techniques based on variable correlation studies could be used to reduce the dimensionality of the feature space. Additionally, there are linear algebra techniques such as PCA (Principal Component Analysis) that can be used to create more economical feature sets. Another potential source of improving the algorithm would be to have a weighted metric on the distances within the feature space that would scale the distances in the different dimensionalities based on a set of weights that would not necessarily be equal for each dimension.

Acknowledgements. We are grateful to AirNav Systems LLC for providing access to the ASDI data feed. We also applaud Leland McInnes for his highly optimized Python implementation of HDBSCAN.

References

1. Amidan, B., Ferryman, T.: Atypical event and typical pattern detection within complex systems. In: 2005 IEEE Aerospace Conference, pp. 3620–3631, March 2005
2. Annoni, R., Forster, C.: Analysis of aircraft trajectories using fourier descriptors and kernel density estimation. In: 2012 15th International IEEE Conference on Intelligent Transportation Systems (ITSC), pp. 1441–1446, September 2012
3. Bashir, F.I., Khokhar, A.A., Schonfeld, D.: Object trajectory-based activity classification and recognition using Hidden Markov Models. IEEE Trans. Image Process **16**, 1912–1919 (2007)
4. Boem, F., Pellegrino, F.A., Fenu, G., Parisini, T.: Multi-feature trajectory clustering using earth mover's distance. In: CASE, pp. 310–315. IEEE (2011). http://dblp.uni-trier.de/db/conf/case/case2011.html#BoemPFP11
5. Campello, R.J.G.B., Moulavi, D., Zimek, A., Sander, J.: Hierarchical density estimates for data clustering, visualization, and outlier detection. ACM Trans. Knowl. Discov. Data **10**(1), 5:1–5:51 (2015). http://doi.acm.org/10.1145/2733381
6. Crippen, G., Havel, T.: Distance geometry and molecular conformation. Chemometrics series. Research Studies Press (1988). http://books.google.com/books?id=5CPwAAAAMAAJ
7. Ester, M., Peter Kriegel, H., Sander, J., Xu, X.: A density-based algorithm for discovering clusters in large spatial databases with noise, pp. 226–231. AAAI Press (1996)
8. Guan, B., Liu, L., Chen, J.: Using relative distance and Hausdorff distance to mine trajectory clusters. TELKOMNIKA Indonesian J. Electr. Eng. **11**(1), 115–122 (2013). http://iaesjournal.com/online/index.php/TELKOMNIKA/article/view/1877
9. Guyon, I., Elisseeff, A.: An introduction to variable and feature selection. J. Mach. Learn. Res. **3**, 1157–1182 (2003). http://dl.acm.org/citation.cfm?id=944919.944968
10. Kooij, J.F.P., Englebienne, G., Gavrila, D.M.: A non-parametric hierarchical model to discover behavior dynamics from tracks. In: Fitzgibbon, A., Lazebnik, S., Perona, P., Sato, Y., Schmid, C. (eds.) ECCV 2012, Part VI. LNCS, vol. 7577, pp. 270–283. Springer, Heidelberg (2012). http://dx.doi.org/10.1007/978-3-642-33783-3-20

11. Lee, J.G., Han, J., Li, X., Gonzalez, H.: Traclass: trajectory classification using hierarchical region-based and trajectory-based clustering. Proc. VLDB Endow. **1**(1), 1081–1094 (2008). http://dx.doi.org/10.14778/1453856.1453972
12. Nascimento, J., Figueiredo, M., Marques, J.: Trajectory classification using switched dynamical Hidden Markov Models. IEEE Trans. Image Process. **19**(5), 1338–1348 (2010)
13. Pallotta, G., Vespe, M., Bryan, K.: Vessel pattern knowledge discovery from ais data: a framework for anomaly detection and route prediction. Entropy **15**(6), 2218 (2013). http://www.mdpi.com/1099-4300/15/6/2218
14. Patterson, T.A., Thomas, L., Wilcox, C., Ovaskainen, O., Matthiopoulos, J.: State space models of individual animal movement. Trends Ecol. Evol. **23**(2), 87–94 (2008). http://www.sciencedirect.com/science/article/pii/S0169534707003588
15. Rintoul, M.D., Wilson, A.T.: Trajectory analysis via a geometric feature space approach. Stat. Anal. Data Min. **8**(5–6), 287–301 (2015). http://dx.doi.org/10.1002/sam.11287
16. Yuan, J., Zheng, Y., Xie, X., Sun, G.: Driving with knowledge from the physical world. In: Proceedings of the 17th ACM SIGKDD International Conference on Knowledge Discovery and Data Mining, KDD 2011, pp. 316–324. ACM, New York (2011). http://doi.acm.org/10.1145/2020408.2020462
17. Zheng, Y., Zhang, L., Xie, X., Ma, W.Y.: Mining interesting locations and travel sequences from gps trajectories. In: Proceedings of the 18th International Conference on World Wide Web, WWW 2009, pp. 791–800. ACM, New York (2009). http://doi.acm.org/10.1145/1526709.1526816

Interaction in Augmented Cognition

Serial Sequence Learning on Digital Games

Eduardo Adams², Anderson Schuh[1(✉)], Marcia de Borba Campos¹, Débora Barbosa²,
and João Batista Mossmann²

[1] Faculty of Informatics (FACIN), Pontifical Catholic University of Rio Grande Do Sul (PUCRS),
Porto Alegre, Brazil
{anderson.schuh,marcia.campos}@pucrs.br
[2] Feevale University, Novo Hamburgo, Brazil
eba.adams@gmail.com, deboranice@feevale.br, mossmann@gmail.com

Abstract. The execution of sequential tasks tightly bound to the daily lives of people. Being possible to identify it during the keyboard typing, creating sequences of actions on the steering wheel or even playing a musical instrument. Researches shows is possible use the sequence learning as an executive function training. Which is considered essential skills for fiscal and mental health, life and scholar success, in addiction of the cognitive, social and psychological development. Other possible way to train executive functions is the use of digital games. In this context, in this work was developed a prototype of a digital game that permits a player to train the executive function working memory. The game permits the player to interact with a serial sequence, while his reaction time are collected for the progress evaluate during a match.

Keywords: Sequence learning · Executive function · Cognition · Neuroscience · Digital games

1 Introduction

The Sequence Learning (SL) can be considered one of the most essential cognitive abilities. This is because people's daily lives is filled with sequential activities, like walking, cooking, writing or even speaking. Consequently, AS has been the subject of several studies, ranging from implicit learning to the acquisition of speech and writing skills [1]. The nervous system has the ability to represent environmental events, associating them with other events and establishing causal relationships between them. This ability provides adaptation gains because it allows the anticipation of environmental events, generating behavioral actions that do not need to occur in response to the environmental events, but rather as representing environmental contingencies, enabling behaviors generated from previous experiments [2].

One approach for the SL can be given by serial reaction time task. This approach has been widely used in various researches and involves the response assessment time of an individual given a featured serial stimulus [2]. [1] Perform a version of this test using a computer application that required the user to click on squares arranged in the four screen edges. Assessing the trajectory of the mouse and the reaction times to the

D.D. Schmorrow and C.M. Fidopiastis (Eds.): AC 2016, Part II, LNAI 9744, pp. 277–284, 2016.
DOI: 10.1007/978-3-319-39952-2_27

course of the test batteries, the researchers could evaluate the SL from the forecast skill over the applied serial sequence [1].

The Serial Learning sequences can be used as a way to perform the training of the Working Memory. Using the AX-12 task-based in serial sequences [3], it was possible to verify that there is an improvement in the capacity of the Working Memory after some training in this [3] task.

Working Memory (WM) is a mental process that involves keeping the information in mind while working mentally. It is critical to understand something that unfolds over time, and requires that the information is kept in memory about what happened at the beginning of this deployment, in order to report something that will occur at the end. WM is one of the main Executive Functions (EF), which is a set of mental processes required for tasks that need concentration, attention or the control of instinctual drives that cannot be good for the individual. EFs are still composed of Inhibition Control (IC) and Cognitive Flexibility (CF) [4].

Given the context, this study has as its main contribution the development of two game modes for mobile devices that demonstrate the learning in serial sequences and therefore, the stimulation of the executive functions related to the Working Memory. The article is organized in this way: the second section presents related studies, the third section presents the two game modes, the fourth section presents the experiment carried out with the results and, finally, it is performed the conclusion.

2   Related Works

Papers with the of [5], verified if the use of the digital game in real-time strategy (RTS) could be used as a form of training of EF prelated to CF. From an experiment using the Blizzard Star Craft game, the scientists could verify that after the training with the digital game, the volunteers had a CF significant improvement [5].

Using the serial reaction task, researchers [6] conducted an experiment with two groups of volunteers, wherein one of the groups responded to stimuli that appear randomly and other that responded stimuli that appeared in a sequential manner. From the volunteers' reaction times, the researchers could verify a decrease in the group's reaction time that auditioned with the sequential version compared to the group that did the test with the random version [6]. [7] It was applied a serial reaction test based on the experiment [6]. In the test, two groups, one composed of pianists and other by non-pianists, carried out a serial sequence while undergoing functional magnetic resonance imaging. After the test, the researchers could verify that all participants were able to detect the serial sequence to which they were exposed. But when checking the areas of the brain that were activate during the tests, they found that the pianists had more active areas in the brain during the experiment that the non-pianists, thus demonstrating implicit learning brought from the piano playing task [7].

3   EF IMPROVER Digital Game

Under this context it was developed a prototype of digital game, called EF IMPROVER in order to allow the serial sequences learning and the EF stimulus related to WM. The EF IMPROVER has two game modes, each of the game modes will be explained next.

The first of the game mode is the EF IMPROVER ER. This game mode is a reproduction of the experiment [6] focused on the serial reaction time. Thus, this game mode aims to capture the user's reaction time over a sequence displayed to it. The game also has a division in two modes, the first is called ER 1, which uses a static serial sequence of 10 elements (D-B-C-A-C-B-D-C-B-A), the same is used in the experiment [6]. While the second modality, called ER 2, shows a completely random sequence.

When starting the EF IMPROVER ER game, it is presented to the player a screen with 4 white squares. After 500 ms from the white squares appearance, one of the squares is painted in blue, thus representing a stimulus. Each match consists of 8 attempts blocks with 100 stimuli each. Each stimulus is represented by an element of the fixed or random sequence. Whenever the blue is presented square, the player must press it as quickly as possible, because, after pressing the blue square, the squares become all white again and the next stimulus is presented after 500 ms, as may be seen in Fig. 1. At the end of a block, the player can rest for 1 min before the beginning of the next block. Throughout the match it is captured the player's reaction times, which is given by the interval of time between the appearance of the stimulus to the response given by the player.

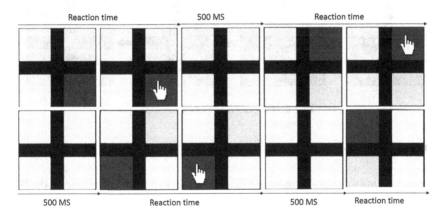

Fig. 1. Execution of ER game mode

The second game mode is called EF IMPROVER EG. This game mode is a version of the game Genius (Simon). Thus, this game mode has the objective of capture the player's reaction time and progress over a sequence presented to him. The game also has a division in two modes, the first is called EG 1, which uses a static serial sequence of 10 elements (D-B-C-A-C-B-D-C-B-A), the same used in the experiment of [6], while the second mode, called EG 2, presents a totally random sequence.

When starting FE IMPROVER EG, a screen of 4 squares is presented to the player, each one with a color. After 500 ms, the attempt is started, being that each one is represented by the reproduction of a 10 elements sequence, either sequential or random. The execution of the game is as follows: at the beginning of the game, the first sequence element is presented to the player after this presentation, where the player must reproduce the sequence presented to him/her as soon as possible. Whenever the player reproduces the sequence in the correct way, the sequence is reintroduced, increased by an additional element, and each time the sequence is reintroduced, the player must perform a complete reproduction of it, until it reaches a maximum of 10 elements, thus completing a challenge. If the player cannot reproduce the sequence presented to him/her, the challenge is given as an error, and the partial progress of the player is computed, as may be seen in Fig. 2. Each game consists of 8 attempts blocks with 10 challenges each. Each challenge is represented by 10 elements, at the end of each block the player may rest for 1 min before the beginning of the next block.

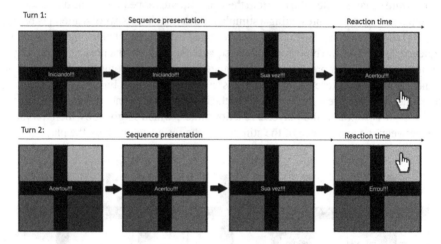

Fig. 2. Execution of EG game mode

4   Experiment

Two experiments were conducted using EF IMPROVER, one for each game mode. Both tests were applied from the same methodology, which consisted of the presentation of the theoretical background and the game mode functioning assigned to him/her for the test. After the presentation, the volunteers signed a free and informed consent form, and with it signed, the volunteers answered the participant's profile questionnaire and performed the test with the game assigned to them. At the end of the execution, the volunteers answered a questionnaire about the experiment.

4.1   EF IMPROVER ER Experiment

Four volunteers participated in the experiment with the game mode EF IMPROVER ER, all male, aged between 23 and 34 years, of which 2 are studying Bachelor of

Information Systems, one studying BA in Computer Science and 1 studying Master in Creative Industries. All the participants had experience with mobile devices like tablets and smartphones. One of the participants reported that he had contact with digital games, while others claimed to practice at least 10 h per week. Two of the volunteers said that they already have participated in a test like this, while the other two volunteers reported to be the first time in an experiment of this kind.

Based on the reaction times collected during the experiment, it was observed that the two participants who performed the test with the sequential version of EF IMPROVER ER test achieved a decrease in reaction time over the tests blocks. Since the two volunteers who used the random version showed a smaller decrease in the reaction time from the start to the end of the experiment. Figure 3 shows the graphical comparison of the average reaction times (represented by Axis Y) within each block (represented by Axis X). In the color blue we can see the results of the group that used the random version, while in orange we have the results of the group that used the version with the fixed sequence.

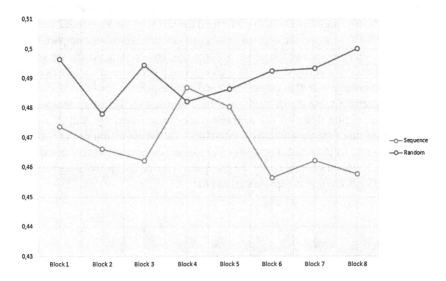

Fig. 3. Average reaction time of ER game mode test

Analyzing the graph, it is possible to verify irregularities in the reaction times, where we find increases at this time. These changes occurred because the freedom that the volunteers had to handle the tablet used to perform the experiment. Whenever there was a change in the tablet placement, or in the number of fingers used to run the experiment, it was noticed an increase in the reaction time.

At the end of the experiments, it was asked to the participants if they have identified a serial sequence. The participants who used the sequential version responded positively, and one of the participants who used the random version also responded positively to the question. When asked to the participants to reproduce the sequence, the two participants in the sequential mode succeeded to reproduce part of the sequence, while the participant who performed the sequential version claimed to have seen geometric shapes. This participant's observation of the random release was due to the disposal of the squares that provided the imagination of shapes like squares and triangles in accordance to the appearance of random stimuli.

4.2   EF IMPROVER EG Experiment

Four volunteers participated in the experiment with the game mode EF IMPROVER ER, of these, three are males and one is female, aged between 21 and 24 years, of whom, three are studying Technician in Digital Games at Feevale University, and one is formed in Technician in Digital Games at Feevale University. All the participants had experience with mobile devices like tablets and smartphones. One of the participants stated that he practices digital games 40 h per week while the others stated that they practice up to 10 h per week. Only one of the participants said that he had participated in experiments like this before.

Based on the reaction times and collected successes during the experiment, it was observed that the two participants who performed the test with the sequential version of EF IMPROVER EG test had the highest number of correct responses compared to the two volunteers who carried out the game with the random version. As for the reaction times, it was possible to verify that the two groups had a decrease in the reaction times during the experiment, but the group that used the sequential version of the game received a greater decrease in the reaction time compared to the group that used the random version. Figure 4 shows the average score (represented by Axis Y) and the average reaction times (represented by the bubbles diameters) within each experiment blocks (represented by Axis X). The group that carried out the test with the sequential version is represented in orange, while the group that carried out the random version of the FE IMPROVER EG test is represented in blue.

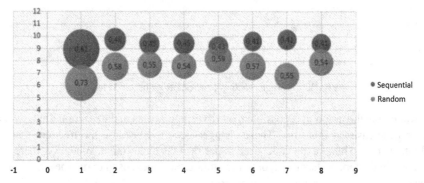

- Heights of the balls representes hit average.
- Diameter of the balls representes reaction time averege

Fig. 4. Average reaction time and hit of EG game mode test

At the end of the experiments, it was asked to the participants if they have identified a serial sequence. All the participants answered positively. The participants' positive answer about the random version is justified by the game mode, which presents a gradual way sequence, however, there were no repetitions of sequences between the attempts in this game mode. When it was asked to the participants to reproduce the sequence, the two participants in the sequential mode succeeded to reproduce the entire sequence, while one of the participants who performed the sequential version claimed to have seen geometric shapes. This participant's observation of the random release was due to the disposal of the squares, that provided the imagination of shapes like squares and triangles in accordance to the appearance of the random stimuli.

5 Conclusion

At the end of this study, it was possible to verify that for both tests, EF IMPROVER ER and EF IMPROVER EG, the groups that used the versions with static serial sequences obtained the this knowledge. This can be evidenced from the decrease of the reaction times during the experiments and in the answers collected at the end of the experiment, in which for both modes of the game, the participants who used the static sequential version were able to demonstrate the existence of the same, even without the prior knowledge.

Evaluating the results obtained in each one of the EF IMPROVER EG game modes, it is possible to verify the same pattern found [6] in their experiment, where the participants that used the sequential versions obtained a noticeable decrease in the reaction times collected from the beginning to the end of the experiment, while the participants who used the random versions had very small decrease in the reaction time.

However, there are some limitations to be improved, as it was perceived during the ER experiment, in which the reaction time is affected by the change in the positioning or number of fingers used to carry out the experiment. In this case, it is intended to create a protocol to standardize the form and run the tests. Other external factors such as noise in the environment where the test was carried out also affected the reaction and successes times. In this case, the next tests will be carried out in a more controlled environment.

We also intended to make changes to the EF IMPROVER digital game in order to improve existing features or even add new features, such as adding scores, sounds and animations that give feedback to the player, and the creation of new modes game that allow the training of other EF related to IC and CF. For the next experiments, it will be used a larger number of volunteers in order for the collected data be more consistent.

References

1. Berends, F., Hommel, B., Kachergis, G., de Kleinjn, R.: Trajectory Effects in a Novel Serial Reaction Time Task (2014)
2. Pavão, R.: Entropia informacional e aprendizagem de sequências (2011)
3. Krueger, K.A.: Sequential learning in the form of shaping as a source of cognitive flexibility (2011)

4. Diamond, A.: Intervations shown to a id executive function development in children 4 to 12 years old (2011)
5. Love, B.C., Glass, B.D., Moggox, W.T.: Real-time strategy game training: emergence of a cognitive flexibility trait. PLoS ONE **8**(8), e70350 (2013)
6. Nissen, M.J., Bullemer, P.: Attentional requirements of learning: evidence from performance mensures. Cogn. Psychol. **19**(1), 1–32 (1987)
7. D'esposito, M., LandaU, S.M.: Sequence learning in pianists and nonpianists: an fMRI study of motor expertise. Cogn. Affect. Behav. Neurosci. **6**(3), 246–259 (2006)

Text Simplification and User Experience

Soussan Djamasbi[1(✉)], John Rochford[2], Abigail DaBoll-Lavoie[1],
Tyler Greff[1], Jennifer Lally[1], and Kayla McAvoy[1]

[1] User Experience and Decision Making Research Laboratory,
Worcester Polytechnic Institute, Worcester, USA
{djamasbi,amdabolllavoie,tgreff,jmlally2,
kmmcavoy}@wpi.edu
[2] Eunice Kennedy Shriver Center, University of Massachusetts Medical School,
Worcester, USA
john.rochford@umassmed.edu

Abstract. Research provides ample evidence of the impact web page design has on comprehension; and that Generation Y users are impatient and dislike reading text. Yet there has been little research that focuses on content, in particular to examine the impact of text simplification on younger users' processing of textual information. To address this need, we report the initial steps of a larger research effort that focuses on developing a set of guidelines for designing simple and effective text passages. Specifically, we compiled a set of existing plain language rules and tested its effectiveness of conveying information to Generation Y users. The results suggest the compiled set of rules can serve as an appropriate tool for designing textual passages to reduce cognitive effort and improve readability of textual content for Generation Y users. Also, the results show that eye tracking serves as an excellent objective measurement for examining the effectiveness of text simplification.

Keywords: Plain language standards (PLS) · Text simplification · Text comprehension · Eye-Tracking · Cognitive effort · Performance · Generation Y

1 Introduction

According to a recent PEW report, 87 % of adults (18 +) and 95 % of teens (12 to 17) in the United States (U.S.) are Internet users [9, 10]. An overwhelming majority of U.S. users (90 %) report that Internet technologies have served as useful tools in their personal lives. Another notable majority (76 %) think the Internet is beneficial for society [6]. Because the Internet has become an essential source of information for the majority of people in the U.S., effective communication of that information is of great importance.

Many organizations pay close attention to how effectively they communicate information to their users through their websites [3, 4]. A significant recommendation is that web pages communicate information to users easily and quickly [7]. To address this issue, a great number of investigators have examined the impact of visual arrangements on the successful communication of information on webpages [5]. Despite that important information is often conveyed in textual format, eye-tracking

© Springer International Publishing Switzerland 2016
D.D. Schmorrow and C.M. Fidopiastis (Eds.): AC 2016, Part II, LNAI 9744, pp. 285–295, 2016.
DOI: 10.1007/978-3-319-39952-2_28

studies show viewers often pay little attention to text [4, 5]. For example, users read only about 20 % of text that is provided on a webpage [8]. These findings may suggest that simplifying text on websites is likely to improve the effectiveness of communication. However, little work has been done to provide a set of guidelines that (1) can significantly increase comprehension; and (2) can be tested for effectiveness with user subjective and objective reactions. We address this gap by testing the effectiveness of a comprehensive set of rules we compiled from various sources of plain language standards. We used eye tracking to capture user fixation during reading. Because fixation serves as a reliable measure of cognitive effort [4], eye tracking is a particularly useful tool to capture effort objectively and unobtrusively. We focus on Generation Y users only because research suggests this group of users particularly dislike reading text [4]. Hence, this generation is likely to benefit from this research.

1.1   Plain Language Guidelines

Plain language refers to clear writing that can be understood the first time it is read. In an effort to improve the public's understanding of the work U.S. federal agencies perform on the public's behalf, all were mandated to use plain language as of 2010 [11]. Such simplification is intended to improve access for the public, and is likely to improve engagement. For example, comprehensibility tends to be a universal characteristic of popular blogs, books, and novels [12]. Thus, a complete set of rules to compose simplified text could serve as an important tool for designing successful websites. To address this, we conducted a systematic search for plain language guidelines from various published sources. We consolidated the guidelines, including removing duplicates, to develop a comprehensive set for designing simple text (Table 1).

1.2   Research Motivation

While text simplification can improve accessibility of information for people with limitations in cognition and/or literacy, we argue that in today's digital world, text simplification will benefit all, not just those with such limitations. Simple text enables users to easily and quickly gather information. This is likely to be particularly important for Generation Y users, who tend to avoid reading textual information, find it boring to read long blocks of text, and prefer image based communication [4, 5]. In order to test the effects of simplified text on Generation Y users, we targeted college students and conducted two studies, which are described in the following section.

2   Method

We used plain language rules, listed in Table 1 below, to simplify text passages for two studies. In each study, we used two text passages (passage A and passage B) from two actual websites. Each text passage had two versions, original and simplified; hence each study had 4 different text passages (Original-A, Simplified-A, Original-B,

Table 1. Plain Language Guidelines

Rules	
• Identify and write for your audience	• Write short sentences (20-25 words), be succinct
• Avoid slang, jargon, colloquialisms, non-literal text	• Short paragraphs (no more than 150 words in 3-8 sentences)
• Use short, simple words (no more than ~ 3 syllables)	• Use transition words in paragraphs (pointing words, echo links, explicit connectives)
• Use concrete, familiar words/combinations of words	• Check/use correct grammar and spelling
• Use "must" instead of "shall" ("must not" vs. "shall not")	• Use "you" and other pronouns to speak to the reader
• Use an active voice, simple present tense	• Organize document chronologically
• Avoid weak verbs (def: a verb that is	• Use lists
made past tense by adding -ed, -d, -t)	• Use tables to make complex material easier to understand
• Use parallel sentence structure	• Do not use ALL CAPS for emphasis
• Use positive terms (avoid "don't" or "didn't")	• Do not use underlining for emphasis
• Avoid multiple negatives ("don't forget to not…")	• Use bold and italics for emphasis
• Explain all acronyms/abbreviations and avoid if possible	
Sources	
• WebAIM, http://webaim.org/techniques/writing/	
• WebAIM – WAVE, http://wave.webaim.org/cognitive	
• Plain Language Association International, http://plainlanguagenetwork.org/plain-language/what-is-plain-language/	
• Plain Language Action and Information Network, http://www.plainlanguage.gov/site/about.cfm	
• U.S. Federal Plain Language Guidelines, http://www.plainlanguage.gov/howto/guidelines/FederalPLGuidelines/index.cfm	

Simplified-B). Two research team members first independently constructed the simplified passages. They then compared the two passages, and selected the best version, or constructed a best one from the two versions, for use as the final simplified text passage in the study.

2.1 Study 1

The objective of this initial study was to gather information about subjective user reactions to an initial set of simplified text. User reactions were captured via a short survey and interview questions. We used the plain language rules to simplify two text passages (A or B) from two websites in the entertainment, movies, and games industries. These passages are displayed in Fig. 1. We asked 58 students from various disciplines in a university in the Northeast to read the two versions of each text passage, which were presented to them in random order displayed on web pages. We asked participants, after reading each passage, to evaluate (5-point rating scale: 1 = very hard, 5 = very easy) the readability of the text passage they just read. As displayed in Fig. 2 below, the simplified versions of the two text passages were perceived as very easy or "sort of" (somewhat) easy to read by the majority of the participants (91 % and 82 % for the movie and the game text passages respectively). The percentages of perceived

---

Original (A)

Lux Level is a luxurious, in-theatre dining experience at select theatres. Movie-goers can indulge themselves with premium reserved-seating, in-seat dining throughout the show, as well as other special amenities. Each seat is equipped with a server call button so your server is always there when you need them. This truly is the finest movie-going experience available today.

Original (B)

Welcome to Miniclip.com, the leading online games site, where you can play a huge range of free online games including action games, sports games, puzzle games, games for girls, mobile games, iPhone games, Android games, Windows Phone, games for kids, flash games and many more.

Simplified (A)

Lux Level is a rare movie theatre that acts as a place where you can eat while you are watching your desired movie. If you hit the button that is on the seat, a waiter or waitress will come and serve you.

Simplified (B)

Miniclip.com offers a wide range of games for all users, including:
- Action
- Sports
- Puzzles
- Mobile games
    a. iPhone
    b. Android
- and more!

Fig. 1. Text passages used in Study 1

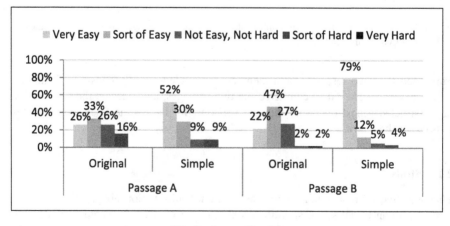

Fig. 2. Survey Results

very easy or somewhat easy ratings were much lower for the original versions of the two text passages (69 % and 59 % respectively).

The results of a t-tests, as displayed in Table 2, showed that text, simplified with plain language rules for both versions, were reported significantly (p = 0.004 and p = 0.000) easier to read than the original text.

Table 2. t-tests Comparing Text Passages

	Original text	Simplified text
Passage A	3.69 (1.03)	4.24 (0.97)
Passage B	3.84 (0.86)	4.67 (0.74)
	df = 110, t Stat = 2.91, p = 0.004	*df = 106, t Stat = 5.36, p = 0.000*

Participants' comments, collected in a brief interview after the participants completed rating the text passages, supported the above survey analysis. They indicated participants preferred reading simplified text. The comments describing reactions to the simplified text included statements such as "details are there and understandable," "extremely basic description," "quick and to the point," "shorter sentences," "not wordy," "no fluff," and "can easily skim and still understand the information". The comments describing reactions to the original text included statements such as "takes more time to read and understand," "easy to lose track," "zoned out while reading it," "very dense, many will glance over it," "not quick or to the point," and "used unnecessary words".

These results suggest the rules in Table 1 may serve as an appropriate tool for developing easy to read text passages for Generation Y users.

2.2   Study 2

To examine the impact of plain language rules (Table 1) on effective communication, we conducted a laboratory eye tracking study to objectively measure effort, comprehension, and performance. Effort plays an important role in how people use information systems [1]. Thus, the degree to which people are willing to expend effort when reading text is likely to affect comprehension of the available information.

We recruited 18 participants from the same pool as that of the first study. We focused on websites that provided information about health and wellness. We selected two health-related text passages from two blog posts (Fig. 3). These two text passages were longer than the text passages used in Study 1. One provides information about the importance of a healthy breakfast in maintaining healthy weight. The other provides tips for taking action against indoor and outdoor allergies. We created simplified versions of each using the same procedure described for Study 1. To prevent a possible comprehension-bias effect that could have occurred had participants read original text passages followed by simplified versions of them, we presented only one version (Original or Simplified) of each passage to each participant.

We showed four pages to each participant. Page 1 displayed a text passage. We asked participants to read it, then to navigate to a second page, by invoking a "next" button, once they were finished reading.

Page 2 displayed a set of questions related to the passage just read, and the passage itself. The display of both the questions and the related text passage enabled participants to refer easily to the passage while answering the questions. We asked participants to answer the questions, and then to navigate to a third page via a "next" button.

Pages 3 and 4 operated as pages 1 and 2, but with a different text passage (Fig. 3.)

Original (A)

Don't want eggs for breakfast? No problem! According to researchers, another popular breakfast food –oats – can also help you fill you up. A study from the University of California, Berkeley analyzed six years of nutrition data and found that people who ate breakfast had a lower body mass index (BMI) than people who skipped breakfast, and that those who ate cooked cereal, like oats, had a lower BMI than any other breakfast-eating group.

Simplified (A)

Want a food other than eggs for breakfast? No problem! Oats can help you fill you up. The University of California, Berkeley analyzed six years of data. They found that people who ate breakfast had a lower body mass index (BMI). Those who ate oats had the lowest index.

Original (B)

1. Track your triggers.

As the weather gets warmer, pollens and molds float into the air. If you have seasonal allergies, check your local pollen forecast in case you need to limit your outdoor time on high-count days.

2. Protect your bed.

You spend a third to half your life in your bedroom, so make sure allergens like dust mites don't, too. If you've had your pillow and mattress for several years, replace them. Encase new ones in allergen-proof covers that zip closed. Keep pets and clothes you wear outside out of the bedroom.

Simplified (B)

1. Track your triggers.

As the weather warms, pollens and molds float around. If you have allergies, check your local pollen count. You must limit your outdoor time on high-count days.

2. Protect your bed.

You spend almost half your life in your bedroom. Make sure allergens are removed. Replace your pillow and mattress after several years. Encase new ones in allergen-proof covers that zip closed. Keep pets and worn clothes outside out of the bedroom.

Fig. 3. Text passages used in Study 2

2.3   Measures

Fixations, or relatively steady gazes that are at least 60 ms long, are reliable indicators of cognitive processing when reading text passages [3]. We thus used gaze analysis to measure cognitive effort. We used the Tobii $\times$ 300 eye tracker to capture participants' eye movements unobtrusively. Before starting the task, each participant went through a brief calibration procedure, which enabled us to collect the participant's eye movements. We used the accuracy of the answers to gauge performance.

3   Results

An overall look at the data showed more correct answers to questions related to simplified text passages. As shown in Fig. 4, the means of correct answers for both simplified text passages were larger than those for the original text passages (1.78 vs. 1.61). Additionally, 83 % of participants were able to answer all questions correctly for the simplified text, while a lower number (67 %) were able to do the same for the original text passages (Fig. 4b). We observed an upward trend in performance for both simplified text passages. However, this trend was more nuanced for passage A (Fig. 4).

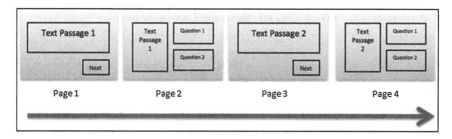

Fig. 4. The flow of pages presented to each user. Latin square design was used to avoid order effect.

Eye tracking data revealed that participants read the simplified text passages in a shorter time regardless of whether they were reading passage A or B (Fig. 5). This trend suggests participants processed simplified text passages more efficiently, with less effort. Unsurprisingly, the results show participants took longer to read passage B, which was longer than passage A.

Looking at the distribution (Fig. 6) on fixations of text passages and questions on the pages (2 & 4) that contained both of these components, we can see participants attended more to answering questions than to reading the text passages. This is not surprising because participants were able to read the text passages on the previous pages (1 & 2), and therefore were using the text passages more as a reference for answering questions.

The data show that the difference between the distribution for simplified and original versions was more pronounced on the set of passage As. Fixation duration was largest when participants responded to the questions for the simplified version of passage A, and shortest when they referred to its related text passage on the same screen. These results, along with performance data (100 % accuracy for simplified passage A), suggest that the simplified version of passage A was processed more efficiently and effectively than the other passages. While the reported differences in this section were not significant, together, the results indicated an upward trend in efficiency and performance for the simplified text (Fig. 7).

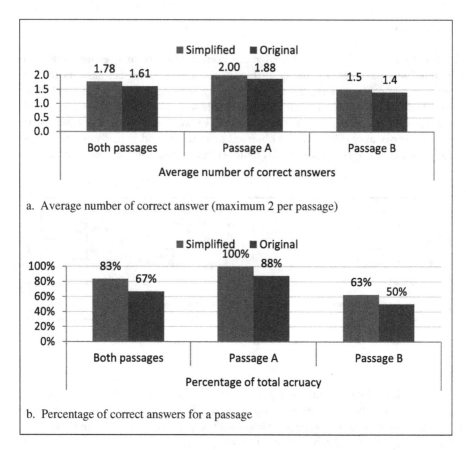

a. Average number of correct answer (maximum 2 per passage)

b. Percentage of correct answers for a passage

Fig. 5. Performance

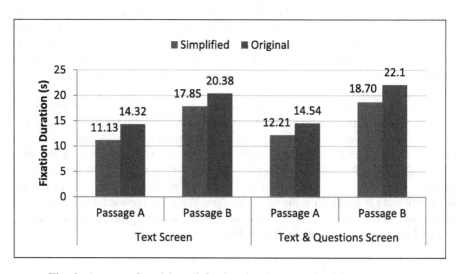

Fig. 6. Average of participants' fixation duration on each of the two screens

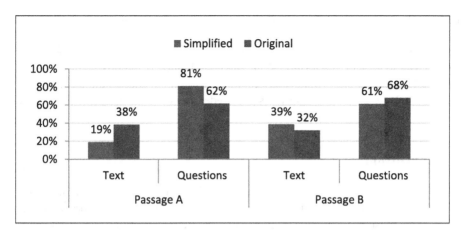

Fig. 7. Distribution of fixation duration on text & questions screen

4 Discussion

The objective of this study was to examine the impact of text simplification on effective communication. To do so, we compiled a comprehensive set of rules obtained from existing sources that define plain language standards. We used the compiled data set to simplify a set of text passages from actual websites.

We then conducted a preliminary study to see whether users responded well to simplified text. The results of this initial study showed that people provided significantly better comprehension ratings for the simplified text. Their comments indicated that they preferred reading simplified text on web pages.

In the second study, we tested objective reactions to another set of passages that were slightly longer in length. The eye movement data suggested that participants processed simple text passages more efficiently. The performance data showed that, on average, people answered more questions correctly when reading simplified text. Hence, the performance data suggested that simplified passages were easier to understand. Together, these results suggested that text simplification improves the effectiveness of information communicated to Generation Y users.

The results of this study also suggest that our compiled set of standards provided an appropriate initial set of guidelines for constructing simplified text that can improve reading comprehension and performance.

The results of this study have important theoretical and practical implications. Given the importance of cognitive effort in effective usage of computerized information tools [1], the results provide a theoretical direction for further development of text simplification guidelines. Because the results show that Generation Y users prefer simplified text, they also provide insight for HCI research that focuses on younger users. Generation Y's eye movement data generally reveal an "impatient" pattern of viewing [2, 4, 5]. This may be because younger users dislike reading text [4, 5]. Thus having guidelines for simplifying text is of great importance in designing effective communication for Generation Y users. From a practical point of view, the results provide guidelines that can be used to design websites with effective communication in mind. Given today's crowded web environment, providing effective communication could serve as invaluable strategy to drive behavior and improve market share.

As with any study, the results of our study are limited to the task and to the study setting. The sample size is yet another limiting factor in our study. Future studies with larger sample sizes and different tasks are needed to verify our results and to extend their generalizability.

5 Conclusion

The objective of this study was to compile a set of standards for simplifying textual information, and to test its effectiveness on communicating textual information with Generation Y users. Testing the original passages and the simplified passages together allowed for a direct comparison regarding the effectiveness of the compiled set of standards. The results show that the compiled set of rules in our study has the potential to effectively reduce users' cognitive effort and thus improve their performance when reading text. The results also show that eye tracking serves as an excellent tool for this line of research because it can capture effort objectively, continuously, and unobtrusively. The results have important theoretical implications for HCI researchers who study the impact of cognitive effort on comprehension and performance. The results have also important implication for designers who focus on Generation Y users.

References

1. Djamasbi, S.: Does positive affect influence the effective usage of a decision support system? Decis. Support Syst. **43**(4), 1707–1717 (2007)
2. Djamasbi, S., Hall-Phillips, A.: Eye tracking in user experience design, pp. 27–43. Morgen Kaufmann (2014). http://digitalcommons.wpi.edu/uxdmrl-pubs/42
3. Djamasbi, S., McAuliffe, D., Gomez, W., Kardzhaliyski, G., Liu, W., Oglesby, F.: Designing for success: creating business value with mobile user experience (UX). In: Nah, F.F.-H. (ed.) HCIB 2014. LNCS, vol. 8527, pp. 299–306. Springer, Heidelberg (2014)
4. Djamasbi, S., Siegel, M., Skorinko, J., Tullis, T.: Online viewing and aesthetic preferences of generation Y and the baby boom generation: testing user web site experience through eye tracking. Int. J. Electron. Commer. **15**(4), 121–158 (2011)
5. Djamasbi, S., Siegel, M., Tullis, T.: Generation Y, web design, and eye tracking. Int. J. Hum Comput Stud. **68**(5), 307–323 (2010)
6. Fox, S., Rainie, L.: The Web at 25 in the US, Pew Research Center (2014). http://www.pewinternet.org/2014/02/27/the-web-at-25-in-the-u-s/
7. Krug, S.: Don't Make Me Think: A Common Sense Approach to Web Usability. Pearson Education, India (2005)
8. Nielsen, J.: How little do users read? Nielsen Norman Group (2008). http://www.nngroup.com/articles/how-little-do-users-read/
9. PEW: Teens Fact Sheet. Pew Research Center (2012). http://www.pewinternet.org/fact-sheets/teens-fact-sheet/

10. PEW: Internet Overtime. Pew Research Center (2014). http://www.pewinternet.org/datatrend/Internet-use/Internet-use-over-time/
11. The Plain Language Action and Information Network (PLAIN), Plain Language: Improving Communications from the Federal Government to the Public (2011). http://www.plainlanguage.gov/
12. Snow, S.: This Surprising Reading Level Analysis Will Change the Way You Write, The Content Strategist (2015). https://contently.com/strategist/2015/01/28/this-surprising-reading-level-analysis-will-change-the-way-you-write/

A Proposed Approach for Determining the Influence of Multimodal Robot-of-Human Transparency Information on Human-Agent Teams

Shan Lakhmani[1(✉)], Julian Abich IV[1], Daniel Barber[1], and Jessie Chen[2]

[1] University of Central Florida (UCF), Institute for Simulation and Training (IST), Orlando, FL, USA
{slakhman,jabich,dbarber}@ist.ucf.edu
[2] U.S. Army Research Laboratory, Orlando, FL, USA
jessie.chen@us.army.mil

Abstract. Autonomous agents, both software and robotic, are becoming increasingly common. They are being used to supplement human operators in accomplishing complex tasks, often acting as collaborators or teammates. Agents can be designed to keep their human operators 'in the loop' by reporting information concerning their internal decision making process. This transparency can be expressed in a number of ways, including the communication of the human and agent's respective responsibilities. Agents can communicate information supporting transparency to human operators using visual, auditory, or a combination of both modalities. Based on this information, we suggest an approach to exploring the utility of the teamwork model of transparency. We propose some considerations for future research into feedback supporting teamwork transparency, including multimodal communication methods, human-like feedback, and the use of multiple forms of automation transparency.

Keywords: Multimodal communication · Human-robot interaction · Transparency · Human-agent teaming

1 Introduction

There is an increasing reliance on autonomous agents to perform functions previously done by human actors. Agents are being used in business to maintain interactivity between businesses and their customers [1]; in the U.S. military to conduct dangerous activities such as explosive disposal and firefighting [2]; and in Homeland Security to help analysts process vast quantities of intelligence information [3]. As technology improves, so too does the need to understand how agents can be implemented in a way that yields the most effective partnership between humans and technology [4].

1.1 Agents and Their Roles in Human-Agent Teams

The progression of technology has led to circumstances where complex tasks can be delegated to a machine, automated, and thus be done with fewer errors and by fewer

© Springer International Publishing Switzerland 2016
D.D. Schmorrow and C.M. Fidopiastis (Eds.): AC 2016, Part II, LNAI 9744, pp. 296–307, 2016.
DOI: 10.1007/978-3-319-39952-2_29

people [5, 6]. One means of implementing automation is through an agent. Agents are hardware or software-based computer system that are characterized by four properties: autonomy, (the ability to operate without direct human intervention for a significant length of time); social ability, (the capacity to interact with humans or other agents using language); reactivity, (the ability to perceive the environment and react to it); and proactiveness, (ability to exhibit goal directed behavior in anticipation of future events) [6–9]. In this manuscript, references to 'agents' will use this definition. Robots, by definition, are a kind of agent that are physically embodied [2, 10]. In systems where humans work with agents as team members rather than operators, agents usually play one of three roles: individual support, team support, or team member [9, 10]. When agents support individual team members, they can either be person-specific or task-specific [9]. When agents support a team as a whole, they act to facilitate the group's teamwork [10]. When agents assume the role of an equal team member, they are expected to act similarly to their human teammates [9, 10]. Thus, similar to a human team member, an agent in a human-agent team must also communicate relevant information to their teammate to maintain shared knowledge and shared intent [9].

In many circumstances, the introduction of automation has changed the human operator's task to that of monitor and backup [5, 11]. Autonomous agents and their ability to choose goals and act independently also require coordination and cooperation [12]. In systems with flexible automation, agents act in tandem with humans to make decisions, mirroring the relationship between a human and a subordinate [2]. The flexibility gained by this joint decision-making requires continuous collaboration and communication [2]. Human teams have the advantage of flexible communication strategies. Team members elicit relevant information from other team members, which in turn supports development of effective shared mental models [13]. However, in human-agent teams, the agent team members often cannot effectively share information without some means of translating their 'understanding' [3, 14]. By establishing a common understanding of the situation, the task, the team members and their respective duties, human teams are able to coordinate effectively [13, 15]. Similarly, effective human-agent teams also maintain a shared understanding of the situation and of their teammates [9]. When both parties maintain a shared understanding of the team environment, they can give, seek, and receive clarifying feedback, which are critical actions for teamwork.

To support the shared awareness and intent needed to perform as an effective human-agent team member, the agent must share information pertaining to its historical and current operation, how the underlying algorithms of the agent govern its behavior (the agent's "reasoning"), and the extent to which it acts in accordance with the designer's intent and the operator's goals [2, 16, 17]. Agents that communicate their performance abilities, intent, reasoning process, and future plans in a way that facilitates operators' comprehension of such provide transparency [18, 19].

2 Transparency

2.1 Transparency Overview

In the context of human-agent interaction, transparency has been described as a method by which a human and a machine can gain shared intent and awareness [19]. A transparent system facilitates this understanding by explaining its choices and behaviors, allowing its human operators to understand the way it works [20]. One approach, the Belief, Desire, and Intention (BDI) view describes the agent as having mental attitudes [11, 21]. The BDI approach to transparency, communicating the information, motivational, and deliberative states of the agent, helped inspire the Situation awareness-based Agent Transparency (SAT) model [18, 21]. The SAT model informs the design of transparent systems by supporting the human operator's situation awareness [18]. In the SAT model, a transparent system communicates three levels of information [18]:

- Level 1 describes the agent's current actions and plans and its knowledge of the environment,
- Level 2 describes the agent's underlying reasoning behind its actions and plans, and
- Level 3 describes the agent's predictions about its future state or outcomes of its planned actions

Given the complexities of the transparency construct and the information needed to support it, Lyons divides transparency into two categories, Robot-to-Human transparency and Robot-of-Human transparency, a useful demarcation when describing humans and autonomous agents as teammates [19].

2.2 Models of Transparency

Robot-to-Human Transparency describes models of transparency which focus on the agent's information about the world [19]. The following models are in this category: the intentional model, the task model, the analytical model, and the environment model [19]. The *intentional* model focuses on communicating the purpose of the system through the use of social intent cues; the *task* model focuses on communicating information pertaining to the agent's task, expressing its goals and its progress towards meeting those goals, its capabilities, and its performance while pursuing those goals; the *analytical* model focuses on the underlying principles the agent uses to make decisions; and the *environment* model focuses on communicating variance in terrain, weather, and temporal constraints to humans [17, 19].

Robot-of-Human Transparency describes two models of transparency focusing on the communication of the agent's awareness of the state of human teammates [19]. The *teamwork* model focuses on the division of labor between the agent and the human and the *human state* model focuses on the agent's communicating their understanding of the human's cognitive, emotional, and physical state [19]. This delineation of models is particularly important to keep in mind, given the parallels between human teams and human-agent teams. Robot-to-Human agent transparency models describe information relevant to task performance, while Robot-of-Human transparency models focus on the members of the human-agent team.

2.3 Effects of Transparency

The implementation of features that support agent transparency can have a positive influence on the relationship between the human and the agent working together. Depending on the kind of transparency explored and the amount of information presented to the user, information supporting transparency can influence operator trust, situation awareness, and workload.

Trust. In the context of a human-agent team, trust can be defined as "the attitude that an agent will help achieve an individual's goals in a situation characterized by uncertainty and vulnerability" [16]. In a transparent system, human observation of the agent's actions—such as its history of action, capability, and reliability—should be supplemented by information concerning the goals, reasoning, and situational information that led to these actions [5, 16, 22]. By providing this information, which supports transparency, the human's trust in the agent can be reasonably informed and more solidly held [7, 16]. However, trust is continuously updated [7]. If the agent communicates uncertainty or reports incorrect information, the human operator can use that information to calibrate their trust, matching their trust with the system's capabilities, leading to appropriate use [7, 16].

With the incorporation of agents into teams as equal team members, however, humans and agent system designers must account for both trust in the agent as an automated system as well as trust in a teammate to act in the best interests of the team [9, 16]. In pursuit of transparency, system designers attempt to make sure that the agent communicates knowledge about itself, its goals, its underlying reasoning, and its awareness of environmental factors, but this communication of information is most frequently one-way [2, 17, 18].

Situation Awareness. When humans work with robots, the human needs to maintain situation awareness (SA) in order to make appropriate decisions [23]. Situation awareness refers to the process by which a human attempts to understand their environment and use that understanding to perform competently in a situation as it occurs [24]. When working with agents, SA may include awareness of the environment in which agents may be located or what the agent is doing [23, 25]. Agent transparency can be used to keep the human operator from being pulled 'out of the loop' by allowing human operators to focus only on information relevant to the mission [2, 25]. Contextual awareness of an agent is a key factor in the success of human operators, and the communication of the agent's intent can facilitate overall SA [25–27]. Global SA requires awareness of not only the immediate working environment, but the relationship between the agent and the human within that environment, so transparency specific to the human-agent relationship can support that awareness.

Workload. A perennial concern is the impact of adding more information to an interface. Supporting transparency could require additional information, which may affect the human's workload [18]. Although a unitary definition of workload does not exist, it can be conceptualized as the perceived impact of task demand imposed on the human operator and the associated physiological responses [28, 29]. Additional information supporting transparency may cognitively overload the operator, leading to performance decrements [30]. However, if additional information mitigates workload that would have been caused by having to recall or estimate information, the added information may lead to similar, if not lower, levels of workload overall [18, 30]. If overload is a concern, then features that reduce workload to a more manageable level are preferred. In two studies on joint human-agent decision-making, increased amounts of information supporting transparency were added to an interface without a significant increase to workload [31, 32]. Thus, transparency can possibly lead to benefits without a noticeable increase to the human teammates' workload.

2.4   Communication and the Teamwork Model of Transparency

In the pursuit of transparency, agent interfaces have been designed to communicate the agent's behaviors, goals, reasoning, and environmental constraints to the human operator in order to facilitate shared intent and shared awareness [17, 18]. While information encompassed by the Robot-to-Human transparency models has been explored as a means of supporting humans' understanding of their agent teammates, less work has been done exploring the influence of Robot-of-Human transparency. While research concerning automated systems responding to human physiological states and the dynamic division of labor between humans and agents exist, fewer studies focus on the transparency of these systems [2, 19].

A particular area of interest is how agents can express the human's and agent's fulfillment of their responsibilities, and how the communication of this information could influence the human's relationship with their agent team member. In human teams, team members can engage in mutual performance monitoring, a behavior where team members keep track of all team members' performance, which can be coupled with feedback [33, 34]. This kind of feedback reflects the agent's model of the human operator back to that selfsame operator, allowing the human and agent to establish a greater shared awareness of both the human's and agent's roles in the team and how they fulfill those roles [16, 34].

One study found that humans who worked with a highly autonomous robot attributed more blame to the robot than those who worked with a low autonomy robot [35]. While increased transparency led to a marginally significant reduction in the attribution of credit to other group members working with the highly autonomous robot, the robot's feedback did not influence credit or blame to the robot or the self [35]. While an explanation of the robot's reasoning did not influence the aforementioned factors, feedback concerning the robot's and human's performance of their roles may do so. While human and robot role responsibility feedback may lead to different credit and blame attribution, feedback concerning human operators' shortfalls may influence the human's perception of their own trustworthiness. Similarly to how humans can determine the trustworthiness of an agent through its history of action, capability, and reliability, they may also determine their own trustworthiness by seeing this same information about themselves [5, 16]. However, if the human feels that their own trustworthiness is low, they may feel the need to delegate tasks to the agent [16]. The impact of this kind of information, especially with robots and other embodied agents, is underexplored, despite the implications it may have towards the relationship between humans and agents. The means by which this information is communicated, however, may emphasize benefits or mitigate the possible negative repercussions of this communication. Hence, an exploration of different modes of communication is of interest.

2.5 Multimodal Feedback

Research in the field of agent transparency focuses on the communication of different kinds of information in order to maintain shared intent and awareness [19]. While the content of this communication is important, the means by which it is communicated is notable as well. Content is most frequently communicated through auditory or visual methods [36]. Humans can only process a limited amount of visual or auditory information, and the available mental effort used for each is distinct, so communicating information across multiple modes can extend mental limitations by splitting the burden across multiple channels [37]. Multimodal communication, communication across more than one sensory channel, allows for an increased complexity in communication through the use of redundant or non-redundant signals. The transmission of redundant signals can ensure that the message is received; the transmission of non-redundant signals can communicate two separate messages simultaneously, the modulation of a message, or the communication of an entirely new message [38]. Multimodal communication, can influence workload, which in turn can affect error rate and operator effectiveness [36, 38]. There are several methods in which agents can effectively integrate visual and auditory feedback.

Visual feedback. The most common form of feedback is visual, with multimodal research investigating the effects of supplementing the visual modality [36]. In learning environments, information is usually presented to learners visually, either through text or graphics [39]. Text feedback has the advantage of facilitating understanding of complex, semantically-rich content [40]. In addition to the content of the message, the social presentation can influence humans' responses to what was written. Increased etiquette, expressed by automated systems warning operators before giving them support and avoiding interruptions during requested actions, has been shown to lead to better performance and improved trust, though it has hampered situation awareness [7, 41]. The ubiquity of text means that it is frequently supplemented by other methods of communication [42]. Text-based feedback has been paired with graphics and speech, yielding more comprehensible output and more creative solutions [43, 44]. While agents can use disembodied text to communicate information, an agent with a human-like avatar can potentially provide an emotional connection that can create a more positive relationship between the agent and their human operator [42].

Software agents that are depicted using virtual characters are capable of communicating using human-like verbal and nonverbal signals [45]. A virtual character can provide feedback through the use of facial expressions or gaze [7, 45]. Positive facial expressions on pedagogical agents' characters have been used to facilitate learning, motivate learners, and aid in attitudinal learning [45]. Gestures as social cues can be used to draw attention to an important feature in an interface or can be coupled with speech to improve the recall of verbal information and captivate the human operator [42, 46]. When robot gestures were combined with synthetic speech, it was more positively evaluated than when it communicated using speech alone [47].

The desired type of agent feedback—gestures, facial expressions, and so on—informs the design of a robot. A robot's shape can potentially influence how it is seen; in one study, spider-legged robots were seen as more aggressive than wheeled robots, while robots with arms were seen as more intelligent than those without [48]. An agent with a human face or avatar may be more likely to engender human-like treatment from their human teammates, but human-like treatment may not be the desired response [49]. These different shapes are conducive to different gestures. A robot with arms and legs can make different gestures than a robot with no arms and wheels. The addition of expressive lights can add an entirely new dimension in communication, with speed, regularity, and color providing an avenue through which messages can be communicated [50]. The major limit in visual communication seems to lie in physical feasibility and human understanding.

Auditory feedback. Sound has often been used as a social cue to focus people's attention and provide feedback [36]. One study found that when earcons (i.e., abstract musical tones) were used to indicate movement of an interface element, it led to slower completion of a highlighting task than visual highlighting alone [36]. When abstract tones were used as robot feedback, participants did not extend assistance to it as much as when it had a voice, either synthetic or human [51]. When working with a mix of synthetic and human speech, users' perception of their own performance was higher than users who only received a synthetic voice, but their actual performance in a series of office tasks was worse than their counterparts who only received synthetic speech [52]. Synthetic speech, unfortunately, is judged based on its intelligibility, naturalness, and acceptability to the human [53]. Participants exhibited faster response latencies when listening to natural voice compared to those who were listening to a synthetic voice [54]. Overall, speech is suited for presenting short, semantically simple content which carries only essential information [40, 42].

3   Experimental Approach

The exploration of human-agent teams, agent transparency, and multimodal communication has set the stage for a proposed approach to the investigation of transparency in human-agent teams. Specifically, this investigation seeks to make the case that the influence of an agent's multimodal feedback in response to human operators' meeting and not meeting their responsibilities within the division of labor is an area of research that has not yet been plumbed.

3.1 Experimental Considerations

A central question in the exploration of information concerning division of labor is how that information is expressed to the human operator. In tasks where humans and agents must work together to complete a task, the teamwork model of transparency suggests that the agent inform the human about their respective responsibilities and if they are being fulfilled. If an agent communicates to its human counterpart that they are fulfilling or failing to fulfill their responsibilities, how will that communication influence the human's performance and their relationship with that agent? Establishing how feedback concerning division of labor can influence the relationship between human and agent may be useful. Additionally, a human-appearing agent leads to human-like expectations from it, which may or may not be desired [17, 49]. Will human-like social cues and non-human-like social cues yield equal benefits of transparency? Would teamwork transparency alone provide the same benefits that robot-to-human transparency does, or would they work better together? Scales pertaining to Workload, Trust, and Situation Awareness are useful indicators to determine the extent to which the information supporting teamwork transparency facilitates a beneficial relationship between the agent and the human.

3.2 Research Questions

Information pertaining to division of labor can be communicated multimodally, with human-like interfaces, using a human-like avatar and natural voice feedback, or non-human interfaces, using flashing lights and beeps. One aim of this approach is to determine the extent to which a human-like presentation of information supporting transparency influences operator behaviors. Human-like robots have resulted in a specific behavioral pattern from human operators [49].

Additionally, information supporting the teammate transparency model may require precise communication, so the use of non-redundant multimodal messaging should be explored as well. Non-redundant multimodal signals can be used to communicate modulated messages, which allows for a finer-tuned message concerning division of labor [38].

Furthermore, another area that bears exploring is the coordination of different models of transparency. Would a model of transparency, such as the SAT model, benefit from the addition of information supporting teamwork transparency? Would the operator attend to features of the interface supporting their situation awareness if periodically reminded of their responsibilities? Given the parallels between human teamwork and human-agent teamwork, determining the utility of information supporting teamwork transparency on its own and combined with a task-oriented transparency is a key area of exploration.

4 Evaluation

Dependent variables pertaining to the utility of human-agent transparency include performance, how well the agent supports the operator, and the human operator's relationship with the agent. Performance, a key dependent variable, can include the successful completion of decision-making tasks, comprehension of presented information, and search tasks. The human's performance and perceptions of their performance should be measured. An agent can support the operator by assisting in the maintenance of situation awareness and workload in a way that serves performance, so these two factors should be evaluated. The human operator's relationship with the agent includes trust, which influences automation use, disuse, and overreliance [16]. Given the large impact that trust can have, it should be evaluated as well. Additionally, it is also important to evaluate the human's perception of the agent, including technology acceptance and perceived usability.

5   Conclusion

To maintain the benefits of keeping the human operator 'in the loop,' autonomous agents must maintain transparency. As agents are increasingly tasked to act as teammates, however, they need to also communicate information to support teamwork, rather than just information to support operators' tasks. Like mutual performance monitoring can aid human teams, the presentation of information supporting the teamwork model of transparency should benefit human-agent teams. The communication of role responsibility informs operators of the agent's understanding of the humans' and agents' responsibilities in the system and how those responsibilities are being fulfilled. Providing feedback about the human's actions as a team member may allow for greater teamwork between humans and agents. Presentation of this information by an agent may have unintended consequences, though, so research should look at presenting information using both visual and auditory communication methods, both human-like and non, and with other forms of automation transparency. This research will inform the design of agents for human-agent teams where an authentic artificial teammate is desired. As agents become more complex and are able to do more, our understanding of how humans treat their teammates, human or not, becomes even more necessary to facilitate effective performance from human-agent teams.

References

1. Saade, R., Vahidov, R., Yu, B.: Agents and E-commerce: beyond automation. In: Americas Conference on Information Systems. Puerto Rico (2015)
2. Chen, J.Y., Barnes, M.J.: Human–agent teaming for multirobot control: a review of human factors issues. IEEE Trans. Hum.-Mach. Syst. **44**(1), 13–29 (2014)
3. Yen, J., et al.: Agents with shared mental models for enhancing team decision makings. Decis. Support Syst. **41**(3), 634–653 (2006)
4. Sheridan, T.B., Parasuraman, R.: Human-automation interaction. Rev. Hum. Factors Ergon. **1**(1), 89–129 (2005)
5. Parasuraman, R., Sheridan, T.B., Wickens, C.D.: A model for types and levels of human interaction with automation. IEEE Trans. Syst. Man Cybern. Part A Syst. Hum. **30**(3), 286–297 (2000)

6. Zhu, H., Hou, M.: A Literature Review on Operator Interface Technologies for Network Enabled Operational Environments Using Complex System Analysis. W7711-083931/001/ TOR: Defence R & D Canada, Toronto (2009)
7. de Visser, E.J., Cohen, M., Freedy, A., Parasuraman, R.: A design methodology for trust cue calibration in cognitive agents. In: Shumaker, R., Lackey, S. (eds.) VAMR 2014, Part I. LNCS, vol. 8525, pp. 251–262. Springer, Heidelberg (2014)
8. Wooldridge, M., Jennings, N.R.: Intelligent agents: theory and practice. Knowl. Eng. Rev. **10**(2), 115–152 (1995)
9. Sycara, K., Sukthankar, G.: Literature review of teamwork models, Carnegie Mellon University CMU-RI-TR-06-50 (2006)
10. Sukthankar, G., Shumaker, R., Lewis, M.: Intelligent agents as teammates. In: Theories of Team Cognition: Cross-Disciplinary Perspectives, pp. 313–343 (2012)
11. Urlings, P., et al.: A future framework for interfacing BDI agents in a real-time teaming environment. J. Netw. Comput. Appl. **29**(2), 105–123 (2006)
12. Atkinson, D.J., Clancey, W.J., Clark, M.H.: Shared awareness, autonomy and trust in human-robot teamwork. In: Papers from the 2014 AAAI Spring Symposium on Artificial Intelligence and Human-Computer Interaction (2014)
13. Shah, J., Breazeal, C.: An empirical analysis of team coordination behaviors and action planning with application to human–robot teaming. Hum. Factors J. Hum. Factors Ergon. Soc. **52**(2), 234–245 (2010)
14. Cannon-Bowers, J.A., Bowers, C.A., Sanchez, A.: Using synthetic learning environments to train teams. Work group learning: Understanding, improving and assessing how groups learn in organizations, pp. 315–346 (2008)
15. Cannon-Bowers, J.A., Salas, E.: Reflections on shared cognition. J. Organ. Behav. **22**(2), 195–202 (2001)
16. Lee, J.D., See, K.A.: Trust in automation: designing for appropriate reliance. Hum. Factors J. Hum. Factors Ergon. Soc. **46**(1), 50–80 (2004)
17. Lyons, J.B., Havig, P.R.: Transparency in a human-machine context: approaches for fostering shared awareness/intent. In: Shumaker, R., Lackey, S. (eds.) VAMR 2014, Part I. LNCS, vol. 8525, pp. 181–190. Springer, Heidelberg (2014)
18. Chen, J.Y., et al.: Situation Awareness-Based Agent Transparency. Army Research Laboratory (ARL): ARL-TR-6905, Aberdeen Proving Grounds, MD (2014)
19. Lyons, J.B.: Being transparent about transparency: a model for human-robot interaction. In: 2013 AAAI Spring Symposium Series (2013)
20. Cramer, H., et al.: The effects of transparency on trust in and acceptance of a content-based art recommender. User Model. User-Adap. Inter. **18**(5), 455–496 (2008)
21. Rao, A.S., Georgeff, M.P.: BDI agents: from theory to practice. In: ICMAS (1995)
22. Hoffman, R.: An integrated model of macrocognitive work and trust in automation. In: AAAI Spring Symposium: Trust and Autonomous Systems (2013)
23. Adams, J.A.: Human-robot interaction design: understanding user needs and requirements. In: Proceedings of the Human Factors and Ergonomics Society Annual Meeting. SAGE Publications (2005)
24. Smith, K., Hancock, P.: Situation awareness is adaptive, externally directed consciousness. Hum. Factors J. Hum. Factors Ergon. Soc. **37**(1), 137–148 (1995)
25. Miller, C.A.: Delegation and transparency: coordinating interactions so information exchange is no surprise. In: Shumaker, R., Lackey, S. (eds.) VAMR 2014, Part I. LNCS, vol. 8525, pp. 191–202. Springer, Heidelberg (2014)
26. Mercado, J.E., et al.: Effects of agent transparency on multi-robot management effectiveness. Army Research Laboratory (ARL): ARL-TR-7466, Aberdeen Proving Grounds, MD (2015)

27. Stubbs, K., Wettergreen, D., Hinds, P.H.: Autonomy and common ground in human-robot interaction: a field study. IEEE Intell. Syst. **22**(2), 42–50 (2007)
28. Abich, J.: Investigating the universality and comprehensive ability of measures to assess the state of workload. Doctoral Dissertation, University of Central Florida (2013)
29. Hart, S.G.: NASA-task load index (NASA-TLX); 20 years later. In: Proceedings of the Human Factors and Ergonomics Society Annual Meeting. Sage Publications (2006)
30. Hancock, P., Warm, J.: A dynamic model of stress and sustained attention. Hum. Factors **31**(5), 519–537 (1989)
31. Mercado, J.E., et al.: Intelligent agent transparency in human-agent teaming for multi-UxV management. Human Factors. In Press
32. Wright, J., et al.: Agent Reasoning Transparency's Effect on Operator Workload. Manuscript Submitted for Publication (2016)
33. Mathieu, J., et al.: Team effectiveness 1997-2007: a review of recent advancements and a glimpse into the future. J. Manage. **34**(3), 410–476 (2008)
34. Salas, E., et al.: Does team training work? principles for health care. Acad. Emerg. Med. **15**(11), 1002–1009 (2008)
35. Kim, T., Hinds, P.: Who should I blame? effects of autonomy and transparency on attributions in human-robot interaction. In: The 15th IEEE International Symposium on Robot and Human Interactive Communication, 2006. IEEE (2006)
36. Vitense, H.S., Jacko, J.A., Emery, V.K.: Multimodal feedback: an assessment of performance and mental workload. Ergonomics **46**(1–3), 68–87 (2003)
37. Wickens, C.D.: Multiple resources and mental workload. Hum. Factors J. Hum. Factors Ergon. Soc. **50**(3), 449–455 (2008)
38. Partan, S.R., Marler, P.: Issues in the classification of multimodal communication signals. Am. Nat. **166**(2), 231–245 (2005)
39. Moreno, R., Mayer, R.: Interactive multimodal learning environments. Educ. Psychol. Rev. **19**(3), 309–326 (2007)
40. Merkt, M., et al.: Learning with videos vs. learning with print: The role of interactive features. Learn. Instruction **21**(6), 687–704 (2011)
41. Parasuraman, R., Miller, C.A.: Trust and etiquette in high-criticality automated systems. Commun. ACM **47**(4), 51–55 (2004)
42. Woo, H.L.: Designing multimedia learning environments using animated pedagogical agents: factors and issues. J. Comput. Assist. Learn. **25**(3), 203–218 (2009)
43. Beskow, J.: Animation of talking agents. In: Audio-Visual Speech Processing: Computational & Cognitive Science Approaches (1997)
44. Mayer, R.E.: The promise of multimedia learning: using the same instructional design methods across different media. Learn. Instruction **13**(2), 125–139 (2003)
45. Krämer, N.C.: Psychological research on embodied conversational agents: the case of pedagogical agents. J. Media Psychol. **22**, 47–51 (2010)
46. Moreno, R., Reislein, M., Ozogul, G.: Using virtual peers to guide visual attention during learning. J. Media Psychol. **22**(2), 52–60 (2010)
47. Salem, M., et al.: Generation and evaluation of communicative robot gesture. Int. J. Soc. Rob. **4**(2), 201–217 (2012)
48. Ososky, S., et al.: Building appropriate trust in human-robot teams. In: 2013 AAAI Spring Symposium Series (2013)
49. Perzanowski, D., et al.: Building a multimodal human-robot interface. IEEE Intell. Syst. **16**(1), 16–21 (2001)

50. Baraka, K., Paiva, A., Veloso, M.: Expressive lights for revealing mobile service robot state. In: Reis, L.P., Moreira, A.P., Lima, P.U., Montano, L., Muñoz-Martinez, V. (eds.) Robot 2015: Second Iberian Robotics Conference. Advances in Intelligent Systems and Computing, vol. 417, pp. 107–119. Springer, Heidelberg (2016)
51. Sims, V.K., et al.: Robots' auditory cues are subject to anthropomorphism. In: Proceedings of the Human Factors and Ergonomics Society Annual Meeting. SAGE Publications (2009)
52. Gong, L., Lai, J.: Shall we mix synthetic speech and human speech?: impact on users' performance, perception, and attitude. In: Proceedings of the SIGCHI Conference on Human Factors in Computing Systems. ACM (2001)
53. Delogu, C., Paoloni, A., Pocci, P.: New directions in the evaluation of voice input/output systems. IEEE J. Sel. Areas Commun. 9(4), 566–573 (1991)
54. Reynolds, M.E., Isaacs-Duvall, C., Haddox, M.L.: A comparison of learning curves in natural and synthesized speech comprehension. J. Speech Lang. Hear. Res. 45(4), 802–810 (2002)

Assessment of Visualization Interfaces for Assisting the Development of Multi-level Cognitive Maps

Hengshan Li, Richard R. Corey, Uro Giudice, and Nicholas A. Giudice[✉]

Spatial Informatics Program: School of Computing and Information Science, University of Maine,
348 Boardman Hall, Orono, ME 04469, USA
Hengshan.li@umit.maine.edu,
{richard.corey,nicholas.giudice}@maine.edu, uro@vemilab.org

Abstract. People often become disoriented and frustrated when navigating complex, multi-level buildings. We argue that the principle reason underlying these challenges is insufficient access to the requisite information needed for developing an accurate mental representation, called a multi-level cognitive map. We postulate that increasing access to global landmarks (i.e., those visible from multiple locations/floors of a building) will aid spatial integration between floors and the development of these representations. This prediction was investigated in three experiments, using either direct perception or Augmented Reality (AR) visualizations. Results of Experiment 1 demonstrated that increasing visual access to a global landmark promoted multi-level cognitive map development, supporting our hypothesis. Experiment 2 revealed no reliable performance benefits of using two minimalist (icon-based and wire-frame) visualization techniques. Experiment 3, using a third X-ray visualization, showed reliably better performance for not only a no-visualization control but also the gold standard of direct window access. These results demonstrate that improving information access through principled visualizations benefit multi-level cognitive map development.

Keywords: Multi-level indoor wayfinding · Multi-level cognitive maps · Human factors · Visualization interface design · X-ray visualization

1   Introduction

Most travelers can recall an unpleasant memory of becoming disoriented when navigating inside a large building. These buildings usually have a complex multi-story structure with many levels and confusing staircases. Getting lost wastes our time and energy, not to mention being stressful and frustrating. It is widely accepted that to efficiently find our destination in complex environments without becoming lost, navigators rely on the support of cognitive maps—an enduring, observer-free spatial representation of the environment [1, 2]. Similarly, to accurately and efficiently find targets located on different floors, people must form a globally coherent mental representation of the multi-level built environment, which has been termed a multi-level cognitive map [3, 4]. Multi-level cognitive maps are postulated as consisting of: (1) a set of superimposed single-level cognitive maps; (2) between-floor connectivity information (e.g.,

© Springer International Publishing Switzerland 2016
D.D. Schmorrow and C.M. Fidopiastis (Eds.): AC 2016, Part II, LNAI 9744, pp. 308–321, 2016.
DOI: 10.1007/978-3-319-39952-2_30

elevators, staircases, escalators, etc.); (3) between-floor alignment information (e.g., indicating what is directly above/below one's current location); and (4) encoding of the z-axis (e.g., rough estimates of floor heights) [3]. The notion of multi-level cognitive maps of complex built environments is different from the concept of a true 3D spatial representation (see reviews in [5–7]), as the vertical axis of a multi-level cognitive map is not encoded with the same representational structure and fidelity as the x, y axis [3]. Although previous literature has found evidence that the hippocampus can represent 3D volumetric space using a uniform and nearly isotropic rate code along three axes, as with Egyptian fruit bats [6, 8], no evidence for such 3D representations has been observed in humans. By contrast, Jeffery and colleagues [7] suggested a bicoded representational structure—where space in the plane of locomotion is represented differently from space in the orthogonal axis. On this basis, they argued that "the mammalian spatial representation in surface–traveling animals comprises a mosaic of these locally planar bicoded map fragments rather than a fully integrated volumetric map" [7]. Indeed, there has been a lively debate concerning the efficacy of this bicoded representation. However, little hard evidence is available to support whether humans were born with the capacity to construct true 3D spatial representations in the brain [7, 9–11]. The consensus is that humans have the capability to encode elevation and z-axis offset in both outdoor and indoor spaces, even if not in a precise 3D manner [12, 13]. For instance, previous studies have found clear evidence that differences in terrain elevation are encoded in cognitive maps of outdoor environments [12]. With regard to indoor environments, a growing body of evidence also suggests that the integration of multi-level spatial knowledge (learned from different floors) can be consolidated into a multi-level cognitive map, but this process is challenging and error-prone for humans to perform [4, 13–16]. Addressing this challenge, the primary goal of the current work is to investigate whether increasing visual access to a global landmark from within a multi-level building could facilitate users' development of a multi-level cognitive map.

Global landmarks are salient environmental features visible at a large spatial scale from within the environment, e.g., a prominent building. Previous literature on outdoor wayfinding has found clear evidence that these global landmarks provide a fixed spatial reference frame for navigators to integrate local spatial knowledge into a global cognitive map (see [17] for review). However, there is no empirical evidence on the effect of global landmarks observed from within a building in supporting the development of multi-level cognitive maps. This issue is evaluated in Experiment 1. In the three experiments discussed here, users' development of multi-level cognitive maps are measured by three cross-level spatial tasks including pointing and wayfinding between floors and a cross-floor drilling task. The present research also aims to investigate whether visual access to global landmarks can facilitate users' integration of outdoor and indoor spaces, called OI-spaces, which has attracted increasing attention in recent years (see [18] for review). In the current studies, OI-space integration was measured by pointing latency and error performance when pointing from indoor locations (e.g., the building's rooms) to an outdoor location, e.g., a parking lot.

Global landmarks are often not available in multi-level indoor environments due to: (1) interior objects such as walls, ceilings, and other obstacles limiting visual access, and (2) the external windows or large atriums that might be used to facilitate access are frequently only visible from specific locations in the building. As a result, the advantage of global landmarks—serving as a fixed spatial reference frame—is often greatly reduced when learning and navigating through indoor environments [18]. If visual access to global landmarks is found to facilitate the development of a multi-level cognitive map, as we predict, the question remains as how to best leverage this benefit for the majority of complex buildings without direct visual access to these landmarks. It is obviously impractical to modify the physical building to increase access but an alternative and economical solution is to use visualization techniques such as Augmented Reality (AR). AR technology can be used to superimpose virtual information on the physical environment from a perception-friendly first-person perspective and thus enhance users' spatial awareness of the environment by showing occluded information that they otherwise cannot directly perceive [19]. If we can use AR technology to increase visual access to global landmarks, as is investigated in Experiments 2 and 3, the benefit of these cues for providing a fixed frame of reference can be extended to all matter of complex multi-level buildings and thereby facilitate users' development of multi-level cognitive maps. All experiments discussed in this article were conducted using virtual environments (VEs), as VEs best facilitate manipulation of building layout and information content, as well as tracking of movement behavior.

2   Experiment 1

We propose that a global landmark, serving as a fixed global spatial reference, helps users to consolidate single-level spatial knowledge into a consistent/global multi-level cognitive map. Thus, our hypothesis in Experiment 1 is that users would develop a more accurate multi-level cognitive map when they could see the global landmark from both floors of the experimental building rather than from only a single floor. As shown in Fig. 1, we designed an outdoor global landmark (a church) and an indoor global landmark (a statue in an atrium), both of which were visible from within the building over multiple locations.

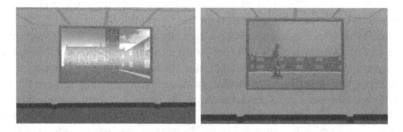

Fig. 1. Outdoor and indoor global landmarks

In a previous study, we investigated whether two vertically-aligned chandeliers co-located on separate floors, called contiguous landmarks, could serve as a global landmark and facilitate users' development of a multi-level cognitive map [4]. However, we observed no reliable effects of contiguous indoor landmarks and very few users even noticed that the chandeliers were vertically aligned. We interpreted this absence of an effect as owing to the fact that users had to perceive each chandelier discretely on separate floors, making it hard for them to mentally link the two inter-floor locations without having direct access to each other. These results suggest that indoor global landmarks for multi-level built environments need to be more than co-located at the same x-y coordinates between floors, they must also be directly perceivable from multiple locations/levels of the building. Therefore, we predict that both a statue in an atrium and an external landmark, as shown in Fig. 1, can serve as a global landmark, as they are directly perceivable from multiple locations/levels in the building. This assertion was evaluated in the current study.

2.1   Method

Participants: Sixteen participants (eight females and eight males, mean age = 20.1, SD = 2.0) were recruited from the University of Maine student body. All participants self-reported as having normal (or corrected to normal) vision. All gave informed consent and received monetary compensation for their time.

Materials and Apparatus: The experimental environments were displayed on a Samsung 43" Class Plasma HDTV monitor running at 60 Hz and at a resolution of 1024 × 768. The desktop VEs were run with a MacBook Pro (2.2 GHz Intel Core i7). The Unity 5.1 VR engine (Unity Technologies, http://unity3d.com) was used as the VE platform supporting users' real-time navigation and recording their trajectory and test performance. Our environments comprised four two-level buildings, as shown in Fig. 2. Participants used an elevator to move between floors. All buildings were matched for layout complexity and topology.

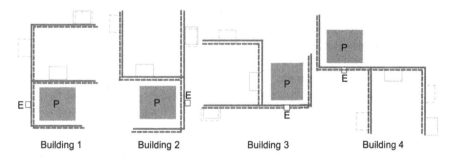

Building 1   Building 2   Building 3   Building 4

Fig. 2. Floor layouts. The (*solid line*) represents the first-floor layout. The (*dashed line*) represents the second-floor layout. "E" represents the elevator. "P" represents the parking lot.

Each virtual building contained four target rooms: a bathroom, a dining room, a conference room, and an office. In addition, each environment had a number of empty rooms located throughout the building, as shown in Fig. 3. A set of fire extinguishers or water fountains were located directly above/below target rooms, and served as the targets for the drilling task, as described in the experimental procedure. Each environment included a global landmark—either a church or a statue in an atrium—visible from a single floor or from both floors. As shown in Fig. 3, each floor consisted of a number of windows, through which users had visual access to the global landmark. Each environment also contained a parking lot. Participants were positioned at the parking lot at the beginning of the experiment. However, when inside the building, the parking lot was only visible from the window opposite the elevator, as shown in Fig. 3. Thus, the parking lot was not a global landmark in the current studies, but it served as a fixed geo-reference for the outdoor environment. We tested users' integration between indoor and outdoor spaces by asking them to point from rooms inside the building to this parking lot.

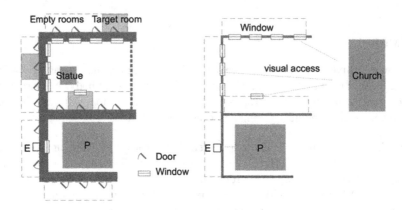

Fig. 3. Visual access to the indoor and outdoor global landmark

2.2 Procedure

A within-subject design was adopted, with the sixteen participants running in all four conditions: (1) single-floor visual access to an outdoor global landmark, (2) single-floor visual access to an indoor global landmark, (3) two-floor visual access to an outdoor global landmark, and (4) two-floor visual access to an indoor global landmark). There were five phases in the experiment.

Phase 1: Practice. Subjects were familiarized with the apparatus and navigation behavior in the VE. All experimental tasks were explained and demonstrated before starting the experimental trials.

Phase 2: Learning. At the beginning of the experiment, participants were positioned at the parking lot. A red arrow on the ground indicated north. Participants were asked to turn in-place and to note the presence/location of the global landmark (e.g., church or statue) from this position. Participants were then guided by blue arrows on the ground to learn the whole building. When they passed by a target room, an audio signal was played that indicated its name, e.g. conference room.

Phase 3: Pointing criterion task. This task was designed to test whether participants had successfully learned the four target rooms. They were first randomly positioned at the doorway of one room and a red arrow appeared to indicate north. The experimenter then asked them to look around and use what they could see of the building's layout, along with the provided north arrow, to get oriented. When participants were ready, they walked to the center of the room and turned to face north, indicated by the red arrow. The experimenter then asked them to turn to face a straight line to the elevator on the current floor as quickly as possible without compromising accuracy. To perform this task, participants rotated in the VEs by twisting the joystick and when they felt they were facing toward the elevator, pulled the trigger to log their response. A red crosshair on the screen indicated participants' facing direction. To meet the criterion, they needed to point to the elevator within a tolerance of 20 degrees. If they failed the first iteration, the Phase 2 learning and Phase 3 pointing criterion tests proceeded until they either successfully met criterion or until they made five incorrect attempts. All participants passed the criterion test within five iterations ($M = 1.5$).

Phase 4: Pointing task. Participants were first randomly positioned at the doorway of a room and were told its name, e.g., "you are facing the conference room". They were encouraged to orient themselves as they did in Phase 3. The experimenter then gave a target room name and asked them to turn to face a straight line to that target. If the target room was on a different floor, they were instructed to ignore the height offset and to point as if the target was on the same plane as their current floor. They pulled the joystick's trigger when they felt they were oriented so as to indicate a straight line to the requested target. The experimenter then asked them to point to the global landmark and the parking lot in the same manner. Two dependent variables for the pointing task were analyzed: pointing latency and absolute pointing error.

Phase 5: Wayfinding task. Participants were first randomly positioned at the doorway of a room and received self-orientation as they did in Phase 3. They were then given one target room name and asked to navigate to it using the shortest possible route. Upon reaching the door where they believed the target was located, they turned to face it and pulled the joystick's trigger. The door opened if they were correct. If incorrect, they were guided to the correct location before proceeding to the next trial. Two dependent variables were analyzed for this task: navigation accuracy (whether participants indicated the correct location and orientation of the target room) and navigation efficiency (shortest route length over traveled route length).

Phase 6: Drilling task. After participants had entered a room in the wayfinding task (above), the experimenter asked them which room or object was directly above/below their current location. There were four options: (1) a target room, (2) an empty room, (3) fire extinguishers or water fountains, and (4) nothing. The dependent variable for the drilling task was drilling accuracy (whether participants successfully indicated which room or object was immediately above/below their current location). The drilling task tested whether participants successfully learned between-floor alignment information, which is an important component of the multi-level cognitive map.

2.3   Results and Discussion

The five dependent measures (pointing latency, absolute pointing error, navigation accuracy, navigation efficiency, and drilling accuracy) were analyzed for each participant. A 2 (visual access: single-floor vs. two-floor) × 2 (global landmark type: indoor vs. outdoor) × 3 (pointing target type: global landmark, parking lot, and building rooms) repeated-measures ANOVA was conducted for each of the two dependent measures of pointing latency and absolute pointing error. Significant main effects of visual access were observed for both measures, with pointing in the two-floor visual access condition being faster and more accurate than pointing in the single-floor visual access condition: pointing latency, $F(1, 63) = 11.151$, $p = .001$, $\eta^2 = .150$; and absolute pointing error, $F(1, 63) = 10.057$, $p = .002$, $\eta^2 = .138$. Significant main effects of target type were also observed for both pointing latency and absolute pointing error: latency, $F(2, 126) = 58.361$, $p < .0001$, $\eta^2 = .481$; and error, $F(2, 126) = 15.631$, $p < .0001$, $\eta^2 = .199$. Subsequent pairwise comparisons showed that pointing to the global landmark was faster and more accurate than pointing to the parking lot and the internal rooms (all $ps < .001$). A significant global landmark type by pointing type interaction was observed for pointing error, $F(2, 126) = 7.198$, $p = .001$, $\eta^2 = .103$. Subsequent pairwise comparisons demonstrated that this significant interaction was driven by the trials requiring pointing to the parking lot, which was reliably more accurate in the outdoor global landmark conditions than with the indoor global landmark conditions (all $ps < .05$).

A 2 (visual access) × 2 (global landmark type) repeated-measures ANOVA was conducted for each of the three dependent measures of navigation accuracy, navigation efficiency, and drilling accuracy. A significant main effect of global landmark type was observed for drilling accuracy, with drilling performance in the outdoor global landmark condition found to be more accurate than performance in the indoor global landmark condition, $F(1, 63) = 4.817$, $p = .032$, $\eta^2 = .071$. There were no significant main effects of visual access (all $ps > .172$) or global landmark type (all $ps > .242$) on navigation accuracy or navigation efficiency.

In Experiment 1, we investigated whether increasing visual access to an indoor or outdoor global landmark observed through the building's windows would assist users' development of a multi-level cognitive map. As we predicted, the results demonstrated that users' pointing was reliably faster and more accurate in the two-floor visual access condition than in the single-floor visual access condition, providing clear evidence that a global landmark (both indoor and outdoor) can serve as a fixed spatial reference frame for navigators to integrate multi-level spatial knowledge into a globally coherent multi-level cognitive map. These findings provide important empirical foundations for the design of Augmented Reality (AR) models used in Experiments 2 and 3, which aim to use AR technology to extend the benefit of global landmarks providing a fixed spatial reference frame to buildings that otherwise do not have visual access to this cue.

With respect to the variable of global landmark type (indoor vs. outdoor), the results showed that the indoor global landmark was as efficient as the outdoor global landmark for promoting users' pointing between building rooms and pointing to the global landmark. However, results also demonstrated that the outdoor global landmark yielded better pointing performance than the indoor global landmark when pointing to the parking lot, suggesting that an outdoor reference is better in facilitating users' integration between indoor and outdoor spaces. This finding is likely due to the nature of indoor global landmarks, which are often not visible from the outdoor space (e.g., the statue in the atrium was not readily visible from the parking lot in the current study). By contrast, an outdoor global landmark is often visible from both indoor and outdoor spaces. We believe that the difference found in integrating these environments is due to this disparity in information access and would be eliminated if the indoor and outdoor global landmarks had the same visual access from both within and outside the building. This prediction will be evaluated in a future project. There was a small effect of global landmark type on drilling accuracy, suggesting that the outdoor global landmark was more efficient for promoting users' learning of vertical alignment information than the indoor global landmark. However, the effect of visual access on drilling accuracy was not observed, meaning that two-floor visual access to a global landmark was not more efficient than single-floor access for promoting drilling accuracy. Indeed, we believe that drilling accuracy may have been elevated for all conditions in Experiment 1 because the fire extinguishers and water fountains were always located directly above/below a target room and some participants indicated that they used this as a cue. This issue is addressed in Experiment 2.

3   Experiment 2

The results of Experiment 1 showed that increasing visual access to a global landmark observed through the building's windows promoted users' development of multi-level cognitive maps. However, as discussed earlier, direct access to global landmarks is often not available from within buildings, and increasing visual access through structural modifications is impractical. Thus, Experiment 2 aimed to use AR technology to extend the benefits found in Experiment 1 to many buildings without physical visual access to global landmarks. We proposed and evaluated two AR models to improve visualization (an icon-model vs. a wireframe-model), as shown in Fig. 4.

Fig. 4. Icon-model and wireframe-model of the global landmark

An icon-model uses a visual symbol to indicate the global landmark's direction. By contrast, a wireframe-model indicates not only the direction of the global landmark, as the icon-model does, but also the perspective from which users can see the landmark, and its edges, as shown in Fig. 4. Users' performance with the two AR visualization techniques were compared to two control conditions: (1) no visual access to outdoor spaces, which is the baseline control condition, and (2) a window-access condition. The two AR models require fewer computational resources to render and take less time to create when compared to other visualization techniques, as reviewed in [19]. Thus, if one (or both) were found to be as efficient as the window-access condition in facilitating multi-level cognitive map development and subsequent cross-floor spatial behaviors, we would have an economical and broad-based solution for improving indoor visualization.

Sixteen new students participated in Experiment 2. The design was similar to that of Experiment 1, except for the following changes: (1) only the church was used as the global landmark, and (2) the locations of the fire extinguishers and water fountains were adjusted to ensure that only a subset of them were vertically aligned with the target rooms.

3.1 Results and Discussion

A 4 (visual access: no visual access, icon-model, wireframe-model, and window-access) × 3 (pointing target type: global landmark, parking lot, and building rooms) repeated-measures ANOVA was conducted for each of the two dependent measures of pointing latency and absolute pointing error. A significant main effect of visual access was observed for absolute pointing error, $F(3, 189) = 14.925$, $p < .0001$, $\eta^2 = .192$, with pointing in the window-access condition being more accurate than the no visual access condition and the two AR interface conditions (all ps < .0001). This finding suggests that the visualization of the global landmark provided by the two AR conditions was not as effective as the "gold standard" of direct window access in assisting users' development of a multi-level cognitive map. Significant main effects of target type on pointing performance were observed for both pointing latency and absolute pointing error: latency, $F(2, 126) = 25.420$, $p < .0001$, $\eta^2 = .287$; and error, $F(2, 126) = 7.175$, $p = .001$, $\eta^2 = .102$. Subsequent pairwise comparisons showed that pointing performance to the global landmark was more accurate than pointing to the parking lot ($p < .005$) but not more accurate than pointing to the building's rooms ($p = .080$). Even though users were assisted with the AR visualizations of the global landmark (i.e., the church), no reliable differences were found between pointing to the church and to the building's rooms, suggesting that the two AR models were not as effective as direct window access in enhancing users' spatial awareness of the church and thus, it failed to serve as a "global landmark" in this study. One explanation for this result is the lack of depth information about the global landmark conveyed by the two AR models. Without access to this depth information, users may have perceived the global landmark to be "floating" in space, leading to an erroneous perception of its true location. In addition, no outside boundary information of the building was visible from the AR visualizations, as could be seen through the building's windows.

A repeated-measures ANOVA was conducted for each of the three dependent measures of navigation accuracy, navigation efficiency, and drilling accuracy, with the four conditions of visual access as a within-subject factor. There was no significant main effect of visual access for any measure (all ps > .05). The average drilling accuracy ($M = 57.4 \%$, $SE = 1.9 \%$) was significantly lower than that found in Experiment 1 ($M = 89.8 \%$, $SE = 1.9 \%$), $t(510) = 8.935$, $p < .0001$, supporting our assertion that the design of the buildings in Experiment 1 artificially elevated users' drilling accuracy performance. Even with these modifications, drilling accuracy was still not promoted by the window-access condition, suggesting that direct visual access to a global landmark alone does not facilitate users' learning of between-floor alignment. It appears that accurate between-floor alignment information, needed in the drilling task, was not sufficiently provided by global landmarks in the current study. We believe that to promote drilling accuracy, the AR interface must also assist users to visualize the objects above/below their current location. This assertion is evaluated in Experiment 3.

4   Experiment 3

The AR visualization models used in Experiment 2 had three shortcomings: (1) they provided no depth information about the global landmark, (2) they could not help users perceive what was directly above or below their current location, and (3) users were constantly exposed to the AR information through an always-on interface. On the basis of the Experiment 2 findings and acknowledging these limitations, we redesigned an X-ray visualization technique in Experiment 3 by allowing navigators to see transparent walls, the global landmark, and the horizon of the outdoor space, as shown in Fig. 5. The X-ray visualization provides access to depth information about the global landmark, similar to the access afforded through the building's windows. Thus, it is anticipated to be as efficient as direct window access in assisting users' development of multi-level cognitive maps. Importantly, the X-ray visualization also facilitates users to perceive what is directly above or below their current location. Thus, it is also predicted that users' drilling accuracy will be promoted by access to this AR interface in Experiment 3. In addition, users could turn on/off the AR information on-demand.

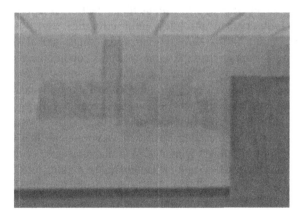

Fig. 5. An X-ray visualization with depth information

A second goal of Experiment 3 was to investigate whether visual access to multiple global landmarks is more efficient than visual access to a single global landmark for users' development of multi-level cognitive maps. Previous literature has discussed several methods for how humans use landmarks for self-localization, such as computing position using bearing and distance to a single landmark, computing position using distances to multiple landmarks (trilateration), and computing position using bearings or bearing differences to multiple landmarks (triangulation), as reviewed in [20]. Visual access to multiple global landmarks has been used to help self-localization in outdoor spaces (see [17] for review). However, little is known about the effect of having visual access to multiple global landmarks in multi-level built environments, and there is no empirical evidence on the effect of access to global landmarks perceived through AR interfaces on users' development of a multi-level cognitive map. This issue is evaluated in the current study.

In Experiment 3, we evaluated the X-ray visualization with two global landmark conditions (single global landmark access vs. multiple global landmarks access), compared to two control conditions (no visual access to outdoor spaces vs. direct window-access), as were used in Experiment 2. In addition to the church, four distinctive town houses were located on one side of the building, serving as landmarks. In the single global landmark access condition, only the church was visible through the X-ray visualization, whereas in the multiple global landmarks condition, both the houses and the church were visible throughout the building via the X-ray visualization. Sixteen new students participated in Experiment 3. The design was the same as Experiment 2, except that only one visualization interface was evaluated but with two global landmark conditions.

4.1 Results and Discussion

A repeated-measures ANOVA was conducted for each of the two dependent measures of pointing latency and absolute pointing error, with the four conditions of visual access and three pointing target types as two within-subject factors. A significant main effect of visual access was observed for absolute pointing error, $F(3, 189) = 10.746$, $p < .0001$, $\eta^2 = .146$, with pointing in the X-ray visualization (single global landmark access) condition being more accurate than the window-access condition and no visual access condition (all $ps < .0005$). Interestingly, the results demonstrated that the X-ray visualization (single global landmark access) outperformed the gold standard of window-access in promoting users' development of multi-level cognitive maps. We interpret this superior pointing performance as providing evidence that the X-ray visualization affords even better visual access in the multi-level built environment than is possible from observation through the building's windows. With the assistance of the X-ray visualization, users had visual access to the global landmark, the parking lot, and the building's rooms from anywhere in the building. Thus, they could learn the spatial relations between places within the multi-level built environment from any location, and this increased spatial visualization aided the development of a multi-level cognitive map.

No significant effect between the two global landmark conditions of the X-ray visualization was observed (single global landmark access vs. multiple global landmark access) ($p = .284$). This result suggests that increasing visual access to multiple global landmarks did not improve multi-level cognitive mapping performance. The larger numeric absolute pointing error observed in the multiple global landmark access condition is not surprising for two reasons: first, users only required one global landmark (the church) for self-localization in the current studies. Second, users had difficulty in extracting each of the global landmarks from the AR interface, as it was cluttered with too much information, which made it less effective.

A repeated-measures ANOVA was conducted for each of the three dependent measures of navigation accuracy, navigation efficiency, and drilling accuracy, with the four conditions of visual access as the within-subject factor. There was no significant main effect of visual access on navigation accuracy, $F(3, 189) = .539$, $p = .656$, $\eta^2 = .014$; or navigation efficiency, $F(3, 189) = .550$, $p = .649$, $\eta^2 = .009$. These results are consistent with the earlier two experiments. This lack of effect is likely due to the environments tested; e.g. all buildings in the current studies had congruent floor layouts without any loops and each building consisted of only one elevator. As a result, navigators could find the target room using the shortest path based on accessing two accurate single-floor cognitive maps, or even from route knowledge formed during the learning phase. In a previous study, we investigated how the realism of a virtual environment model impacts human wayfinding in a multi-level building [14]. The virtual multi-level building in that study had two elevators and the results showed that a sparsely rendered model significantly promoted users' navigation accuracy and efficiency. Thus, we predict that the X-ray visualization used in Experiment 3 could also promote users' wayfinding performance in a complex building with multiple elevators, which will be the topic of a future experiment.

Of note, a significant main effect of visual access was observed for the drilling task, $F(3, 189) = 5.548$, $p = .001$, $\eta^2 = .081$. Subsequent pairwise comparisons showed that the drilling accuracy in the X-ray visualization (single global landmark access condition) was significantly higher than the no visual access condition ($p = .001$) and the window-access condition ($p = .039$). This was not surprising for the no visual access condition but very meaningful for the window-access condition. The finding that the X-ray visualization outperformed the window-access condition in promoting users' drilling accuracy suggests that this interface is a more than adequate substitute for the gold standard of windows. As predicted, it provided clearer inter-floor visualization than was possible from the windows. Taken together, the results of Experiment 3 provide compelling evidence that the X-ray visualization is an effective approach for promoting users' development of a multi-level cognitive map.

5   General Discussion

The primary goal of this work was to investigate whether visual access to a global landmark from within a multi-level building, either through direct window access or AR technology, could help multi-level cognitive map development. A multi-level cognitive map represents the globally coherent mental representation of a multi-story built environment. It was evaluated in the current studies using three cross-level spatial tasks including pointing and wayfinding between floors and a cross-floor drilling task.

The most important finding from Experiment 1 is that increasing visual access to a global landmark (both indoor and outdoor) through direct window access significantly promotes users' development of a multi-level cognitive map. This finding supports our hypothesis that both an outdoor and indoor global landmark can serve as a fixed spatial reference frame for navigators to integrate multi-level spatial knowledge. The results also demonstrated that the outdoor global landmark not only aided with the development of multi-level cognitive maps, but also assisted with the integration of indoor and outdoor spatial reference frames. Previous literature has discussed how increasing visual access to important level-related building features such as elevators could support users' spatial learning and wayfinding of multi-level buildings [14, 15]. Our current research extends these earlier studies and demonstrates that increasing visual access to a global indoor or outdoor landmark can also facilitate the development of a multi-level cognitive map. This research also provides new insights into our understanding of the underlying mental processes involved in the integration of multi-level spatial knowledge into a multi-level cognitive map; for instance, users could learn between-floor alignment by computing the bearing difference to a global landmark, rather than constantly updating their heading directions during vertical travel. In this case, the difficulty of learning a multi-level building with confusing elevators/staircases could be greatly reduced (or alleviated) if navigators have direct or indirect (via AR visualization) access to a global landmark.

On the basis of the Experiment 1 findings, we proposed and evaluated three AR interfaces in Experiments 2 and 3 (an icon-model, a wireframe-model and an X-ray visualization), compared to two control conditions. The results of Experiment 2 showed that the two simply rendered AR models, although resource efficient, did not provide sufficient visualization fidelity, and thus, were not effective for facilitating multi-level cognitive map development. The most important finding from Experiment 3 is that the X-ray visualization was not only effective but actually outperformed the "gold standard" of window-access in promoting users' development of multi-level cognitive maps. This finding suggests that increasing visual access with AR techniques is not merely an alternative and economical approach, but a more effective way for overcoming the disadvantage of limited visual access in built environments and improving the development of multi-level cognitive maps. This finding has important practical significance in that the AR technology could make a local landmark that is not physically visible in multiple locations/levels in a building to be a "global" landmark and thereby provide a generalizable, broad-based solution for improving spatial behaviors in complex buildings.

Taken together, the findings of these experiments provide three Human-computer interaction principles for cognitively motivated visualization techniques for development of indoor navigation systems: first, designers should provide the depth information of global landmarks on the AR interface by showing transparent walls, occluded hallways, and the horizon. Second, designers should keep the AR visualization uncluttered, i.e. showing multiple global landmarks is not necessarily helpful. Third, designers should allow users to turn on/off the AR visualization on demand rather than having them constantly expose to this information.

Acknowledgements. This research was supported by NSF grant CHS-1425337 and NIH grant R01-EY019924-07.

References

1. Tolman, E.C.: Cognitive maps in rats and men. Psychol. Rev. **55**, 189–208 (1948)
2. O'Keefe, J., Nadel, L.: The hippocampus as a cognitive map. Oxford University Press, Oxford (1978)

3. Li, H., Giudice, N.A.: Using mobile 3D visualization techniques to facilitate multi-level cognitive map development of complex indoor spaces. In: Graf, C., Giudice, N.A., Schmid, F. (eds.) Proceedings of the International Workshop on Spatial Knowledge Acquisition with Limited Information Displays, SKALID 2012, Monastery Seeon, Germany, pp. 31–36, August 2012

4. Li, H., Giudice, N.A.: The effects of 2D and 3D maps on learning virtual multi-level indoor environments. In: Proceedings of the 1st ACM SIGSPATIAL International Workshop on Map Interaction, pp. 7–12. ACM, Orlando (2013)

5. Vidal, M., Berthoz, A.: Navigating in a virtual 3D maze: body and gravity, two possible reference frames for perceiving and memorizing. Spat. Cogn. Comput. **5**, 139–161 (2005)

6. Yartsev, M.M., Ulanovsky, N.: Representation of three-dimensional space in the hippocampus of flying bats. Science **340**, 367–372 (2013)

7. Jeffery, K.J., Jovalekic, A., Verriotis, M., Hayman, R.: Navigating in a three-dimensional world. Behav. Brain Sci. **36**, 523–587 (2013)

8. Finkelstein, A., Derdikman, D., Rubin, A., Foerster, J.N., Las, L., Ulanovsky, N.: Three-dimensional head-direction coding in the bat brain. Nature **517**, 159–164 (2014)

9. Hölscher, C., Büchner, S., Strube, G.: Multi-floor buildings and human wayfinding cognition. Behav. Brain Sci. **36**, 551–552 (2013)

10. Klatzky, R.L., Giudice, N.A.: The planar mosaic fails to account for spatially directed action. Behav. Brain Sci. **36**, 554–555 (2013)

11. Wang, R.F., Street, W.N.: What counts as the evidence for three-dimensional and four-dimensional spatial representations? Behav. Brain Sci. **36**, 567–568 (2013)

12. Garling, T., Böök, A., Lindberg, E., Arce, C.: Is elevation encoded in cognitive maps? J. Environ. Psychol. **10**, 341–351 (1990)

13. Tlauka, M., Wilson, P.N., Adams, M., Souter, C., Young, A.H.: An investigation into vertical bias effects. Spat. Cogn. Comput. **7**, 365–391 (2007)

14. Giudice, N.A., Li, H.: The effects of visual granularity on indoor spatial learning assisted by mobile 3D information displays. In: Stachniss, C., Schill, K., Uttal, D. (eds.) Spatial Cognition 2012. LNCS, vol. 7463, pp. 163–172. Springer, Heidelberg (2012)

15. Hölscher, C., Meilinger, T., Vrachliotis, G., Brösamle, M., Knauff, M.: Up the down staircase: wayfinding strategies in multi-level buildings. J. Environ. Psychol. **26**, 284–299 (2006)

16. Carlson, L.A., Hölscher, C., Shipley, T., Conroy, D.R.: Getting lost in buildings. Curr. Dir. Psychol. Sci. **19**, 284–289 (2010)

17. Steck, S.D., Mallot, H.A.: The role of global and local landmarks in virtual environment navigation. Presence Teleoperators Virtual Environ. **9**, 69–83 (2000)

18. Giudice, N.A., Walton, L.A., Worboys, M.: The informatics of indoor and outdoor space: a research agenda. In: 2nd ACM SIGSPATIAL International Workshop on Indoor Spatial Awareness, pp. 47–53 (2010)

19. Dey, A., Sandor, C.: Lessons learned: evaluating visualizations for occluded objects in handheld augmented reality. Int. J. Hum Comput Stud. **72**, 704–716 (2014)

20. Loomis, J.M., Klatzky, R.L., Golledge, R.G., Philbeck, J.W.: Human navigation by path integration. Wayfinding Behav. Cogn. Mapp. other Spat. Process 125–151 (1999)

Interactive Visualization of Multivariate Time Series Data

Shawn Martin[(✉)] and Tu-Toan Quach

Sandia National Laboratories, Albuquerque, NM 87185, USA
{smartin,ttquach}@sandia.gov

Abstract. Organizing multivariate time series data for presentation to an analyst is a challenging task. Typically, a dataset contains hundreds or thousands of datapoints, and each datapoint consists of dozens of time series measurements. Analysts are interested in how the datapoints are related, which measurements drive trends and/or produce clusters, and how the clusters are related to available metadata. In addition, interest in particular time series measurements will change depending on what the analyst is trying to understand about the dataset.

Rather than providing a monolithic single use machine learning solution, we have developed a system that encourages analyst interaction. This system, *Dial-A-Cluster* (DAC), uses multidimensional scaling to provide a visualization of the datapoints depending on distance measures provided for each time series. The analyst can interactively adjust (dial) the relative influence of each time series to change the visualization (and resulting clusters). Additional computations are provided which optimize the visualization according to metadata of interest and rank time series measurements according to their influence on analyst selected clusters.

The DAC system is a plug-in for Slycat (slycat.readthedocs.org), a framework which provides a web server, database, and Python infrastructure. The DAC web application allows an analyst to keep track of multiple datasets and interact with each as described above. It requires no installation, runs on any platform, and enables analyst collaboration. We anticipate an open source release in the near future.

Keywords: Multivariate time series · Multidimensional scaling · Interactive visualization · Slycat

1 Introduction

There are numerous problems from different fields that produce time series data, including chemical engineering [27], intrusion detection [31], economic forecasting [28], gene expression analysis [21], hydrology [23], social network analysis [32], and fault detection [11]. Fortunately, there are just as many algorithms available for analyzing time series data [9]. These algorithms involve tasks including queries [9,10], anomoly detection [2], clustering [4,20], classification [3,9], motif discovery [9,24], and segmentation [16]. From a practical point of view, these

© Springer International Publishing Switzerland 2016
D.D. Schmorrow and C.M. Fidopiastis (Eds.): AC 2016, Part II, LNAI 9744, pp. 322–332, 2016.
DOI: 10.1007/978-3-319-39952-2_31

algorithms share basic data processing goals starting with pre-processing and normalization [9], representation [17], and similarity computation [9,15].

In addition to the large body of algorithms available for mining time series data, there is an additional set of techniques available for visualization of time series [1,22,26]. These techniques belong to the field of Visual Analytics, or sometimes Interactive Visual Analytics [14,30], and include methods such as Parallel Coordinates [12], multiple views, brushing, selection, and iteration. Researchers in Visual Analytics have called out the need for greater integration with underlying algorithms [5].

In between these two fields of research there is a smaller body of work which investigates the interactive visualization of multivariate time series data [18,25,29]. Most of this work focuses on visualization and interaction with multivariate time series plots. Our work fits within this area, but with an emphasis on the algorithms used in the visualization. We provide a layer of abstraction by providing an interactive visual summary of the data, rather than just looking at the time series themselves.

In this paper, we describe a lightweight system for analyzing multivariate time series data called *Dial-A-Cluster* (DAC). DAC is designed to provide a straightforward set of algorithms focused on allowing an analyst to visualize and interactively explore a multivariate time series dataset. DAC requires precomputed distance matrices so it can exploit a large number of available algorithms related to time series representation and similarity comparison [9]. The DAC interface uses a multidimensional scaling [6] to provide a visualization of the dataset. The analyst can adjust the visualization by interactively weighting the distance measures for each time series. A modification of Fisher's discriminant [8] can be used to rank the importance of each time series. Finally, an optimized weighting scheme for the visualization can be used to maximally correlate the data with analyst specified metadata.

DAC is implemented as a plugin for Slycat (slycat.readthedocs.org) [7], a system which provides a web server, a database, a Python infrastructure for remote computation (on the web server). The Slycat DAC plugin is a web application which provides the previously described time series analysis algorithms. It requires no installation and is platform independent. In addition, DAC supports (via Slycat) management of multiple users, multiple datasets, and access control, therefore encouraging collaboration while maintaining data privacy. Slycat and DAC are implemented using JavaScript and Python. Slycat is open source (github.com/sandialabs/slycat).

2 Algorithms

The primary goal of DAC is to provide a no-install, interactive user interface which can be used to organize and query multivariate time series data according to the interests of the analyst. There are three algorithms which support this goal: visualization using multidimensional scaling, identifying time series most responsible for differences in analyst selected clusters, and optimizing the visualization according to analyst specified metadata.

2.1   Multidimensional Scaling

DAC uses classical multidimensional scaling (MDS) to compute coordinates for a dataset, where each datapoint is a set of time series measurements. To be precise, suppose we have a dataset $\{x_i\}$, where x_i is a datapoint, for example an experiment or a test. Each datapoint consists of a number of time series measurements, which we write as a vector $x_i = [\mathbf{t}_{ik}]$, where $\mathbf{t}_{ik}$ is the kth time series vector for datapoint x_i. Note that we are abusing notation here, because each vector $\mathbf{t}_{ik}$ may be a different length, but that we require that the $\mathbf{t}_{ik}$ have the same length for the same k. We also assume that we are given distance matrices

$$D_k = \begin{bmatrix} d_k(x_1, x_1) & d_k(x_1, x_2) & \cdots \\ d_k(x_2, x_1) & d_k(x_2, x_2) & \cdots \\ \vdots & \vdots & \ddots \end{bmatrix}$$

for each time series measurement, where $d_k(x_i, x_j)$ gives a distance between datapoint x_i and x_j for time series k. For example using Euclidean distance we would have

$$d_k(x_i, x_j) = d(\mathbf{t}_{ik}, \mathbf{t}_{jk}) = \sqrt{\sum_l (t_{ikl} - t_{jkl})^2},$$

where $\mathbf{t}_{ik} = [t_{ikl}]$ is the kth time series vector $\mathbf{t}_{ik}$ for datapoint x_i indexed by l. Other distances can be used, so that each time series distance metric can be tailored to the type of measurement taken.

Now let $\boldsymbol{\alpha} = [\alpha_k]$ be a vector of scalars, with $\alpha_k \in [0, 1]$. The vector $\boldsymbol{\alpha}$ contains weights so that we may compute weighted versions of our datapoints, defined as $\boldsymbol{\Phi}(x_i) = [\alpha_k \mathbf{t}_{ik}]$, where we are again abusing notation since the vectors $\mathbf{t}_{ik}$ are allowed to have different lengths. Now we define a distance matrix D of pairwise weighted distances between every datapoint, where the entries of D are given by

$$d^2(x_i, x_j) = \boldsymbol{\Phi}(x_i)^T \boldsymbol{\Phi}(x_j) = \sum_k \alpha_k^2 d_k^2(x_i, x_j).$$

The matrix D is the matrix of pairwise distances between datapoints used as input to MDS within DAC. The weights α_k are adjustable by the analyst. Note that using these definitions

$$D = \sqrt{\sum_k \alpha_k^2 D_k^2}.$$

For completeness, we describe the MDS algorithm operating on the matrix D. First, we double center the distance matrix, obtaining

$$B = -\frac{1}{2} H D^2 H,$$

where D^2 is the componentwise square of D, and $H = I - II^T/n$, n being the size of D. Next, we perform an eigenvalue decomposition of B, keeping only the two largest positive eigenvalues λ_1, λ_2 and corresponding eigenvectors $\mathbf{e}_1, \mathbf{e}_2$. The MDS coordinates are given by the columns of $E\Lambda^{1/2}$, where E is the matrix containing the two eignvectors $\mathbf{e}_1, \mathbf{e}_2$ and Λ is the diagonal matrix containing the two eigvenvalues λ_1, λ_2.

Finally, we note that the eigenvectors computed by MDS are unique only up to sign. This fact can manifest itself as disconcerting coordinate flips in the DAC interface given even small changes in $\boldsymbol{\alpha}$ by the analyst. To minimize these flips, we use the Kabsch algorithm [13] to compute an optimal rotation so that the newly computed coordinates are as closely aligned to the existing coordinates as possible. The Kabsch algorithm uses the Singular Value Decomposition (SVD) to compute the optimal rotation matrix. If we assume that matrices P and Q have columns containing the previous and new MDS coordinates, then we form $A = P^T Q$ and use the SVD to obtain $A = U\Sigma V^T$. If we denote $r = \text{sign}(\det(VU^T))$ then the rotation matrix is given by

$$R = V \begin{bmatrix} 1 & 0 \\ 0 & r \end{bmatrix} U^T.$$

2.2 Time Series Differences

In addition to using MDS to visualize the relationships between the datapoints, DAC allows the user to select subsets of the dataset and upon request ranks the time series according to how well each time series separates those subsets. DAC allows two different selections and ranks the time series according to Fisher's Discriminant [8].

To be precise, for each distance matrix D_k, we compute the values of Fisher's Discriminant $J_k(u, v)$, where $u, v \subset \{x_i\}$ are two groups that we wish to contrast. By definition,

$$J_k(u, v) = \frac{\|\bar{u} - \bar{v}\|^2}{S_u^2 + S_v^2},$$

where $S_u^2 = \sum_i \|u_i - \bar{u}\|^2$, $S_v^2 = \sum_j \|v_j - \bar{v}\|^2$, and $\bar{u}, \bar{v}$ are averages over the sets $\{u_1, \ldots, u_n\}, \{v_1, \ldots, v_m\}$. Although we do not provide the algebraic derivation, we claim that

$$\|\bar{u} - \bar{v}\|^2 = \frac{1}{n}\frac{1}{m} \sum_{ij} d^2(u_i, v_j) - \frac{1}{2n^2} \sum_{ik} d^2(u_i, u_k) - \frac{1}{2m^2} \sum_{jk} d^2(v_j, v_k),$$

where k varies over i for $\sum_{ik}$ and k varies over j for $\sum_{jk}$. We similarly claim that $S_u^2 = \frac{1}{2n} \sum_{ik} d^2(u_i, u_k)$ and $S_v^2 = \frac{1}{2m} \sum_{jk} d^2(v_j, v_k)$. Now we can compute $J_k(u, v)$ using only submatrices of the distance matrices D_k.

DAC ranks the time series in descending order of the values of $J_k(u, v)$. Since a higher value of Fisher's Discriminant $J_k(u, v)$ indicates a greater separation between the selections, this ranking reveals the time series which exhibit the greatest differences between the subsets.

2.3   Clustering by Metadata

Often an analyst will be interested in metadata describing the datapoints. Questions might include: does the dataset cluster relative to a particular metadata variable?; can we make the dataset cluster relative to the metadata variable by adjusting the α weights of the time series?; and which time series are most affected by a metadata variable? To address these questions, we incorporate a supervised optimization of the visualization which correlates the distances between time series with the distances between metadata values.

Specifically, we compute α such that the distances in $D^2 = \sum_k \alpha_k^2 D_k^2$ are as close as possible to the distances in the matrix D_p^2, where D_p is a pairwise distance matrix for a given metadata property p. In other words, we want to solve

$$\min_\alpha \ \sum_{ij}(\sum_k \alpha_k^2 d_k^2(x_i, x_j) - d_p^2(x_i, x_j))^2$$
$$\text{s.t. } \alpha_k \in [0, 1],$$

where $d_p(x_i, x_j)$ is the property distance between x_i and x_j, i.e. $d_p(x_i, x_j) = |p_i - p_j|$, where p_i is the metadata property of x_i and p_j is the metadata property of x_j. Note that for MDS, we can scale α by a positive scalar with no effect, so that the constraint $\alpha \in [0, 1]$ is unnecessary. If we let $\beta_k = \alpha_k^2$ we have

$$\min_\beta \ \sum_{ij}(\sum_k \beta d_k^2(x_i, x_j) - d_p^2(x_i, x_j))^2$$
$$\text{s.t. } \beta_k \geq 0.$$

In the Frobenius matrix norm, we have

$$\min_\beta \ \| \sum_k \beta_k D_k^2 - D_p^2 \|_F^2$$
$$\text{s.t. } \beta_k \geq 0.$$

Now if we let $U = [D_1^2, D_2^2, \cdots]$, where each D_k^2 is written as a column vector, and $V = [D_p^2]$, where D_p^2 is written as a column vector, then we have

$$\min_\beta \ \|U\beta - V\|^2$$
$$\text{s.t. } \beta \geq 0.$$

This is known as a non-negative least squares problem [19]. Once we compute β we can obtain time series weights α corresponding to an MDS visualization optimized to a particular metadata property value.

3   User Interface

The DAC user interface allows access to the algorithms discussed in Sect. 2. DAC assumes that the time series data has been pre-processed, metadata has been collected, and distance matrices have been computed. These assumptions allow flexibility in terms of representing the time series data and computing similarities, two steps in time series analysis served by a wide variety of different algorithms [9]. In addition, pre-computing the distance matrices ensures that DAC will operate in real-time for reasonable dataset sizes (up to ∼5000 datapoints).

The DAC user interface consists of sliders to adjust α_k values (labelled using variable names meaningful to analysts), a canvas to display the MDS visualization, traditional time series plots, and a table displaying metadata. The interface is shown in Fig. 1.

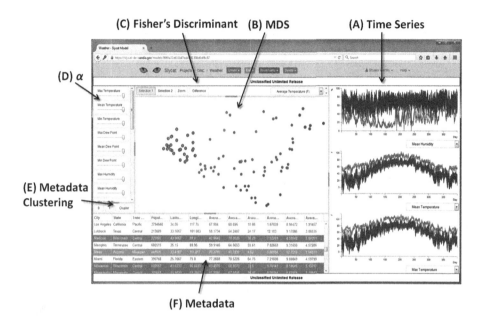

Fig. 1. DAC user interface. Here we show DAC running in Firefox on a Windows PC. Reading the labels counter-clockwise from the upper right: (A) time series data is displayed in the traditional manner; (B) MDS is used to provide a visual representation of the datapoints in the dataset, shown as circles; (C) Fisher's Discriminant can be used to order the time series to maximize the difference between analyst selected red and blue groups; (D) time series measurements can be weighted to adjust the visualization according to analyst preference; (E) the weights can be computed optimally to correlate with an analyst chosen metadata field; and (F) metadata can be examined. (Color figure online)

The DAC interface is a Slycat plugin (slycat.readthedocs.org) [7]. Slycat supports the management of multiple users, multiple datasets, and access controls. Both Slycat and DAC are implemented using JavaScript and Python. DAC is written in JavaScript using jQuery for the controls. The time series and MDS plots are rendered and animated using D3, and the metadata table uses Slick-Grid. Calculations are performed on the Slycat webserver using Python and NumPy. Slycat is open source (github.com/sandialabs/slycat) and DAC will be released as open source in the near future.

4   Example

To demonstrate how DAC might be used by an analyst, we provide an example using publicly available weather data. The data consists of weather time

Fig. 2. DAC weather data. On the left (A), we show the DAC MDS visualization of the cities in the weather dataset. In the middle (B), the visualization is colored by average temperature, where yellow is low and brown is high. On the right (C), the visualization is colored by annual precipitation, where yellow is again low and brown is high. (Color figure online)

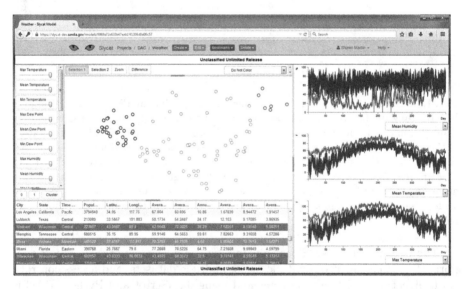

Fig. 3. DAC analyst selections. Here we show two selections made by the analyst, cities on the left hand side of the visualization are selected in blue, and cities in the upper right are selected in red. The same coloring scheme is automatically reflected in the metadata table and colored time series plots are shown on the right. The blue cities include Madison, WI and Milwaukee, WI, and the red cities include Mesa, AZ. By pushing the difference button, DAC ranks and orders the time series plots in the right hand panel of the interface. In this case, humidity gives the greatest difference between the red and blue cities, followed by temperature. (Color figure online)

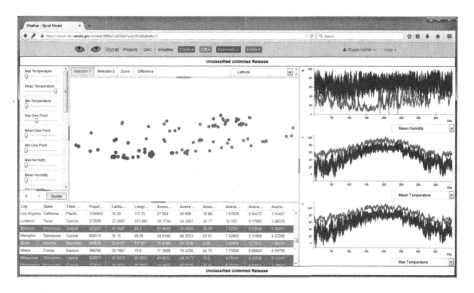

Fig. 4. DAC optimal MDS. Here we show the optimal MDS coordinates correlated with latitude, computed according to the algorithm in Sect. 2.3. The α values are automatically adjusted to show that temperature, dew point, and sea level pressure are best suited to represent latitude, and the previous city selections show that the cold wet cities tend to be in the north and the hot dry cities tend to be in the south. (Color figure online)

series data from Weather Underground (www.wunderground.com) during the year 2014 for the 100 most populated cities in the the United States. The time series measurements include temperature, dew point, humidity, sea level pressure, visibility, wind speed, precipitation, cloud cover, and wind direction. Metadata for the cities includes city name, state, time zone, population, latitude, longitude, average temperature, average humidity, annual precipitation, average windspeed, average visibility and average cloud cover.

Upon starting, DAC produces an MDS visualization of the dataset assuming $\alpha = 1$. For the weather data, this visualization is shown in Fig. 2(A). Among the simplest functions provided by DAC is the ability to color the datapoints according to analyst selected metadata. A coloring of the weather data by average temperature is shown in Fig. 2(B) and by annual precipitation in Fig. 2(C).

From the coloring, it appears that cities on the left hand side of the visualization are cold and wet, while cities on the upper right are hot and dry. This can be confirmed by selecting cities in these areas of the visualization and examining their metadata and time series, as shown in Fig. 3. The selections show that cities on the left (blue selections) are indeed cold and wet and are located in the northern and eastern parts of the country, while the cities in the upper right (red selections) are hot and dry and are located in Arizona and Nevada. By pushing the difference button, Fisher's Discriminant is computed against the red and blue selections to rank the time series plots in the right hand panel of the DAC interface, showing that humidity and temperature give the greatest differences between the two selections.

Finally, the analyst might speculate that the latitude has a significant correlation with the MDS coordinate visualization. Coloring by latitude and pushing the cluster button produces the visualization shown in Fig. 4. This visualization is computed according to the optimization in Sect. 2.3 to obtain the MDS coordinates that best correlate with latitude. The analyst's speculation is confirmed in that the red cities are positioned on the upper right and the blue cities are positioned on the lower left. In addition, the α values computed show that temperature, dew point, and sea level pressure are the most significant weights in the optimized MDS coordinates. Unsurprisingly, temperature is the main influence.

5   Conclusion

Interactive visualization of multivariate time series data is a challenging problem. In addition to organizing what can be large quantities of data for display, there are many potential algorithms available for analyzing the data. We have designed a lightweight web application to bridge the gap between these two problems.

Our system, *Dial-A-Cluster* (DAC), allows an expert data mining practitioner to pick and choose among the available algorithms for time series representation and similarity comparison to pre-compute distance matrices for use with DAC. (Alternatively, a novice practitioner can use very simple pre-processing and Euclidean distance to compute the matrices for DAC.)

DAC in turn provides a subject matter expert a lightweight, no-installation, platform independent interface for examining the data. DAC implements a real-time MDS coordinate based abstraction for the dataset, as well as an interactive interface for examining the actual time series data and metadata. DAC uses Fisher's Discriminant to rank and order the time series according to analyst selections. Finally, DAC provides an optimized computation for determining which time series measurements are correlated with metadata of interest to the analyst.

Instead of making the analyst an evaluator of the data mining results, DAC provides an easy to use interface which encourages the analyst to explore the data independently. Further, since DAC is implemented as a Slycat plugin, management of multiple datasets, multiple users, and access controls are also provided, encouraging collaboration between multiple anlaysts while maintaining data privacy.

Acknowledgements. Sandia National Laboratories is a multi-program laboratory managed and operated by Sandia Corporation, a wholly owned subsidiary of Lockheed Martin Corporation, for the U.S. Department of Energy's National Nuclear Security Administration under contract DE-AC04-94AL85000. This work was funded by Sandia Laboratory Directed Research and Development (LDRD).

References

1. Aigner, W., Miksch, S., Schumann, H., Tominski, C.: Visualization of Time-Oriented Data. Springer, London (2011)
2. Aggarwal, C.C.: Outlier Analysis. Springer, New York (2013)
3. Bakshi, B., Stephanopoulos, G.: Representation of process Trends-IV. Induction of real-time patterns from operating data for diagnosis and supervisory control. Comput. Chem. Eng. **18**(4), 303–332 (1994)
4. Berkhin, P.: A survey of clustering data mining techniques. In: Kogan, J., Nicholas, C., Teboulle, M. (eds.) Grouping Multidimensional Data, pp. 25–71. Springer, Heidelberg (2006)
5. Bertini, E., Lalanne, D.: Surveying the complementary role of automatic data analysis and visualization in knowledge discovery. In: Proceedings of the ACM SIGKDD Workshop on Visual Analytics and Knowledge Discovery (VAKD 2009), pp. 12–20 (2009)
6. Borg, I., Goenen, P.J.F.: Modern Multidimensional Scaling. Springer, New York (2005)
7. Crossno, P.J., Shead, T.M., Sielicki, M.A., Hunt, W.L., Martin, S., Hsieh, M.-Y.: Slycat ensemble analysis of electrical circuit simulations. In: Bennett, J., Vivodtzev, F., Pascucci, V. (eds.) Topological and Statistical Methods for Complex Data. Mathematics and Visualization, pp. 279–294. Springer, Heidelberg (2015)
8. Duda, R.O., Hart, P.E., Stork, D.G.: Pattern Classification. John Wiley and Sons, Hoboken (2000)
9. Esling, P., Agon, C.: Time-Series data mining. ACM Comp. Surv. **45**(1), 12 (2012)
10. Faloutsos, C., Ranganathan, M., Manolopulos, Y.: Fast subsequence matching in time-series databases. SIGMOD Rec. **23**, 419–429 (1994)
11. Fontes, C.H., Pereira, O.: Pattern recognition in multivariate time series - a case study applied to fault detection in a gas turbine. Eng. Appl. Artif. Intell. **49**, 10–18 (2016)
12. Inselberg, A.: A survey of parallel coordinates. In: Hege, H.-C., Polthier, K. (eds.) Mathematical Visualization, pp. 167–179. Springer, Heidelberg (1998)
13. Kabsch, W.: A solution for the best rotation to relate two sets of vectors. Acta Crystallogr. Sect. A **32**(5), 922–923 (1976)
14. Keim, D.A., Kohlhammer, J., Ellis, G., Mansmann, F.: Mastering the information age - solving problems with visual analytics. Eurographics (2010)
15. Keogh, E., Kasetty, S.: On the need for time series data mining benchmarks: a survey and empirical demonstration. Data Min. Knowl. Discov. **7**(4), 349–371 (2003)
16. Keogh, E., Chu, S., Hart, D., Pazzani, M.: Segmenting time series: a survey and novel approach. Data Min. Time Ser. Databases **57**, 1–22 (2004)
17. Keogh, E., Lonardi, S., Ratanamahatana, C.: Towards parameter-free data mining. In: Proceedings of the 10th ACM International Conference on Knowledge Discovery and Data Mining, pp. 206–215 (2004)
18. Konyha, Z., Lez, A., Matkovic, K., Jelovic, M., Hauser, H.: Interactive visualization analysis of families of curves using data aggregation and derivation. In: Proceedings of the 12th International Conference on Knowledge Management and Knowledge Technologies, pp. 1–24 (2012)
19. Lawson, C.L., Hanson, R.J.: Solving Least Squares Problems, vol. 161. Prentice-Hall, Upper Saddle River (1974)
20. Lin, J., Keogh, E.: Clustering of time-series subsequences is meaningless: implications for previous and future research. Knowl. Inf. Syst. **8**(2), 154–177 (2005)

21. Lin, T., Kaminski, N., Bar-Joseph, Z.: Alignment and classification of time series gene expression in clinical studies. Bioinf. **24**(13), 147–155 (2008)
22. Muller, W., Schumann, H.: Visualization methods for time-dependent data - an overview. In: Proceedings of the Winter Simulation Conference, pp. 737–745 (2003)
23. Ouyang, R., Ren, L., Cheng, W., Zhou, C.: Similarity search and pattern discovery in hydrological time series data mining. Hydrol. Process. **24**(9), 1198–1210 (2010)
24. Patel, P., Keogh, E., Lin, J., Lonardi, S.: Mining motifs in massive time series databases. In: Proceedings of the IEEE International Conference on Data Mining (ICDM 2002), pp. 370–377 (2002)
25. Peng, R.: A method for visualizing multivariate time series data. J. Stat. Soft. **25**(1), 1–17 (2008)
26. Silva, S.F., Catarci, T.: Visualization of linear time-oriented data: a survey. In: Proceedings of the International Conference on Web Information Systems Engineering, p. 310 (2000)
27. Singhal, A., Seborg, D.E.: Clustering multivariate time-series data. J. Chemometr. **19**(8), 427–438 (2005)
28. Song, H., Li, G.: Tourism demand modelling and forecasting - a review of recent research. Tour. Manag. **29**(2), 203–220 (2008)
29. Thakur, S., Rhyne, T.-M.: Data vases: 2D and 3D plots for visualizing multiple time series. In: Bebis, G., Boyle, R., Parvin, B., Koracin, D., Kuno, Y., Wang, J., Pajarola, R., Lindstrom, P., Hinkenjann, A., Encarnação, M.L., Silva, C.T., Coming, D. (eds.) ISVC 2009, Part II. LNCS, vol. 5876, pp. 929–938. Springer, Heidelberg (2009)
30. Thomas, J. J., Cook, K. A.: Illuminating the path: the research and development-agenda for visual analytics. Nat. Vis. & Anal. Ctr. (2005)
31. Zhong, S., Khoshgoftaar, T., Seliya, N.: Clustering-Based network intrusion detection. Int. J. Reliab. Qual. Saf. Eng. **14**(2), 169–187 (2007)
32. Zhu, J., Wang, B., Wu, B.: Social network users clustering based on multivariate time series of emotional behavior. J. China Univ. Posts Telecom. **21**(2), 21–31 (2014)

Investigation of Multimodal Mobile Applications for Improving Mental Health

Sushunova G. Martinez[1]([✉]), Karla A. Badillo-Urquiola[1],
Rebecca A. Leis[1], Jamie Chavez[2], Tiffany Green[2],
and Travis Clements[3]

[1] Institute for Simulation and Training, Orlando, FL, USA
{smartine, kbadillo, rleis}@ist.ucf.edu
[2] University of Central Florida, Orlando, FL, USA
{jamchavez, tiffany.green}@knights.ucf.edu
[3] Valencia College, Orlando, FL, USA
t.clements2461@gmail.com

Abstract. The National Alliance on Mental Illness reports that one in four adults experience mental health issues in a given year. Stigmas surrounding mental health issues often leave those afflicted reluctance to seek treatment. Those individuals that do decide to pursue treatment are often denied because of cost and lack of health care coverage or simply do not know where to find it. Assisted technologies can bridge these gaps, providing not only information on how to manage symptoms, but viable treatment options (e.g., adaptive management plans and training, physiological sensing, and alerts for physical symptom onset). The pairing of wearable technology, smart applications, and blended learning techniques can teach patients and caregivers the skills needed for lifetime management. The present theoretical paper provides a literature review of current technology platforms that can be utilized by the mental health domain and explores viable mental health technology options for the next five years.

Keywords: Wearable devices · Anxiety disorders · Mental health · Blended therapy

1 Introduction

On the morning of the October 2, 2006, 32 year old Charles C. Roberts marched into a one-room Amish school house ready to avenge a 20-year old grudge. Roberts instructed the boys to exit the classroom, leaving the remaining girls to cower in fear. During the course of the incident Roberts proceeded to kill five and wound seven female victims before committing suicide [1]. Though Roberts had no prior history of psychiatric illness, it was clear that he was suffering from some kind of mental health crisis. Had Roberts received proper psychiatric care, would this incident have occurred? This type of question, raised by the media after a mass shooting, often leads the public to stigmatize and criminalize all mental health issues. Metzl and MacLeish [2] detail four assumptions that often surface after mass shootings: "(1) that mental illness causes gun violence, (2) the psychiatric diagnosis can predict gun crime, (3) that shootings

© Springer International Publishing Switzerland 2016
D.D. Schmorrow and C.M. Fidopiastis (Eds.): AC 2016, Part II, LNAI 9744, pp. 333–343, 2016.
DOI: 10.1007/978-3-319-39952-2_32

represent the deranged acts of mentally ill loners, and (4) that gun control 'won't prevent' another [mass school shooting]." This overgeneralization, however, is often unfounded, as most mental health patients do not exhibit violent behavior and 95–97 % of violent acts involving guns are not committed by individuals exhibiting acute mental illnesses [3]. The flawed perceived association between gun violence and mental illness is perpetuated by the media, often feeding cultural, political, socio-economical, stereotypes, creating obscured views, and stigmatizing individuals diagnosed with mental health conditions [2]. In order to better understand the challenges facing both therapists and patients an evaluation of current method of treatments and the possibilities of expanding resources is required.

The National Alliance on Mental Illness [4] reports that one in four adults experience mental health issues (e.g., schizophrenia, major depression, and bipolar disorder) in a given year. However, because of social stigma, monetary limitations (e.g., costs of treatment, lack of healthcare), or inconvenience, individuals often resist seeking treatment or discontinue treatment prior to completion upon pursuing such treatment; this is particularly true amongst military populations [5–7]. The effects of these barriers and setbacks are evident as approximately one third of 40 million affected Americans receive treatment [8]. Additionally, those afflicted may fail to self-identify as having a disorder, may mistrust treatment as an effective option, may not wish to seek outside assistance, and/or may believe that the symptoms will dissipate overtime [9].

The present paper provides a brief literature survey of the current treatment options available for a subgroup of mental health conditions – Anxiety Disorders (due to the prevalence), as well as details recommendations for integrating these established treatment options with blended learning (multimodal) techniques, utilizing online, mobile, and wearable technologies. The purpose of this paper is to initiate discussion points for current technological capabilities within the mental health system that addresses accessibility and adoptability gaps, as well as list potential variables for longitudinal data collection.

2 Anxiety Disorders

Anxiety disorders are the most common type of mental health condition afflicting over 40 million Americans [10], with a *specific (simple) phobia* as the most common [11]. Diagnosis is typically determined through interviews and questionnaires to rule out whether other medical conditions/disabilities are present [12]. However, it is often difficult to diagnose anxiety disorders due to comorbidity (an individual with co-occurring of two or more disorders [13]). Meaning, several symptoms overlap between multiple disorders, such as general anxiety and major depression, as both types of patients typically exhibit symptoms of fatigue and insomnia [14, 15]. Although these conditions are similar in nature, the following paragraphs summarize and distinguish specific details between common anxiety disorders.

Generalized anxiety disorder has a prevalence rate within the U.S. of 3.1 % for the general population [14]. Those individuals afflicted with generalized anxiety disorder exhibit defining features and at least one coexisting condition – excessive worry and major depression [14]. Clinicians often observe generalized anxiety disorder patients citing somatic symptoms such as headaches or gastrointestinal distress, but these individuals rarely report worry [14]. Other symptoms include fatigue, insomnia, restlessness, difficulty concentrating, irritability, muscle tension, and sleep disturbances [14, 16].

Social anxiety disorder (social phobia), prevalent in 12 % of the population, involves fear and avoidance of social circumstances such as public speaking [17]. It encompasses the feeling of humiliation or embarrassment, as well as rejection [18]. Social anxiety disorder (social phobia) symptoms include blushing, profuse sweating, trembling, nausea, abdominal distress, rapid heartbeat, shortness of breath, dizziness, lightheadedness, headaches, and feelings of detachment [16]. Another common symptom of this disorder is elevated levels of anger, particularly while receiving criticism or negative evaluations [19].

Another prevalent disorder (12.5 % of the population) is *specific phobia*. Specific phobias are classified into four subtypes: *animal, natural environment, situational, blood-injection injury,* and *other* (provided for phobias that do not conform to the four subtypes) [20]. Those afflicted with a specific phobia show strong fear reactions and avoid common places, situations, or objects that have no danger [16].

Post-traumatic Stress Disorder (PTSD) is measured by three levels: *acute* (persisting for less than three months), *chronic*, and *delayed* (occurs six months after event) [21]. Several risk factors (i.e., intensity of trauma, pre-trauma demographics, and temperament traits) can help identify individuals that may potentially develop this condition. PTSD symptoms are classified into three groups: re-experience, avoidance, and increased arousal. To be diagnosed with PTSD, patients must exhibit these symptoms following the traumatic event; meaning, they should not have occurred prior to the event. In the present paper, specific consideration is given to the treatment of anxiety disorders, particularly utilizing multimodal and blended learning techniques combined with traditional therapy.

3 Current Treatments for Anxiety Disorders

Multiple treatment options are available for individuals diagnosed with anxiety disorders, including psychotherapy, medication, complementary or alternative treatment, support groups, and in severe cases, hospitalization [22]. The following sections provide a brief overview of common treatments.

3.1 Psychotherapy

Psychotherapy (also known as counseling) is the application of psychological principles indented to improve an individual's behaviors, emotions, or cognitions. Much of the research on psychotherapy highlights cognitive behavior therapy, specifically prolonged exposure therapy and eye movement desensitization and reprocessing (EMDR) [23].

A common psychotherapy procedure for treating anxiety disorders is *cognitive behavior therapy* (CBT) [24]. It involves utilizing basic cognitive and behavioral principles to identify, understand, and change specific feelings, thoughts, and behaviors.

Previous research suggests that CBT is more effective for alleviating physiological arousal, fear, and re-experiencing symptoms, than behavioral avoidance, impaired social functioning, anger management, and social skill deficits [25]. CBT (especially exposure therapy) is considered the most effective treatment for anxiety disorders, such as PTSD [25]. Prolonged Exposure Therapy (PE), is "the main components of prolonged exposure are in vivo and imaginal exposure to stimuli related to the traumatic experience, in addition to psycho-education and controlled breathing [26]."

3.2   Complementary and Alternative Treatment

In today's society, increased open-access to healthcare information elicits an interest in homeopathic and alternative therapies. Complementary and alternative medicines (CAM) are considered to be methods used jointly with conventional medical U.S. practices. Typical types of CAM for anxiety disorders are relaxation techniques, yoga, and acupuncture. Although there is not sufficient evidence to support the substitution of clinical practices with CAM (nor would it be a favorable outcome), research has suggested several of these practices to be effective when paired with traditional therapeutic techniques.

3.3   Pharmacotherapy/Medications

The changes that occur in the hypothalamus-pituitary-adrenal axis, the serotonergic system, and the noradrenergic neurotransmitter systems as a result of PTSD are often treated with medications [27]. However, there is conflicting evidence as to the relative efficacy of most of the medications involved with this disorder. The majority of studies related to pharmacotherapy for PTSD support the conclusion that selective serotonin reuptake inhibitors (SSRIs) can improve symptoms and prevent relapse. There is also evidence to suggest that treatment with SSRIs may be beneficial in the long-term; as a result, this specific class of drugs is considered the first line agents in treating PTSD [27]. More specifically, patients who were placed under 24 weeks of treatment in a double-blind, placebo-controlled trial of fluoxetine improved significantly on the clinical and PTSD severity scores as well as in anxiety and depression symptoms [27].

4   Anxiety Disorders and Assistive Technologies

Assistive technologies are quickly evolving to include more capable devices for tracking a person's day-to-day experiences. Specifically for mental health symptom management, assistive technologies can be implemented by professional therapists as a supplemental means of therapy. Typically assistive technologies refer to equipment that aid individuals with physical or cognitive impairments, such as hearing aids, brail keyboard, or braille embossers; however, in this paper, assistive technologies refers generally to technologies used to assist disabled individuals, including those with mental health conditions. The following paragraphs detail modalities of treatments including online platforms, mobile technology, simulation, and wearable technology.

4.1   Online Platforms

Online platforms allow individuals with mental health conditions the ability to asynchronously access useful and individualized symptom management information. These types of platforms also allow the individual distributed access to his/her clinician. Utilizing an online platform can replace *some* (not all) face-to-face sessions. These online sessions tend to be more cost efficient and convenient for the patient [28, 29]. Additionally, clinicians can organize online platforms to connect patient to additional resources, meaning the online platform can double as a distributed repository of symptom management techniques, group discussion boards (online support groups), and self-paced learning modules. This type of platform can also reduce the fear associated with others' perceptions of clinical help (stigmas) [28, 29]. In particular, CBT has been shown to easily adapt to online platforms and some argue that online CBT sessions can be as effect as face-to-face treatment [29]. Psychiatrists can also benefit from the CBT online platform. Typically in face-to-face therapy, the clinician makes quick decisions throughout the session. Online CBT allows a psychiatrist the ability to take time and consider the best possible decision for a patient [29].

These benefits prove advantageous to both patient and clinician, but online CBT also has a few disadvantages. One disadvantage of online CBT is the impracticality of integrating particular components of CBT, such as exposure therapy into an online platform. Exposure therapy is best implemented under the guidance of a psychiatrist. Having a clinician present ensures that the patient will be properly cared for if an episode is triggered during exposure therapy. Alternatively, journaling thoughts, feelings, or emotions can work as effectively as exposure therapy [28]. Journaling is easily adoptable within an online platform. Further, another disadvantage of online therapy platforms is that alone these systems cannot fully replace the entire therapeutic process. Specifically, an online platform does not allow clinicians to formally diagnosis in accordance with the DSM and HIPAA laws [29]. In order to mitigate risks and reduce disadvantages, a blended approach integrating online CBT with traditional techniques should be utilized.

4.2   Mobile Technology

In an effort to continue treatment outside the therapy session, multimodal techniques should be implemented, integrating various aspects of the overall treatment plan into a patient's life. CBT is readily adaptable to a mobile platform [25]. The rate of technology advancement (increased phone processor speed and open-source software development capabilities) has evolved quickly, making smart-phone mobile technologies "a very attractive tool for use in mental health interventions," [5]. Mobile capabilities such as live connections to remote server and interface hardware to interact with user provide useful as treatment options as this allows for real-time and longitudinal data collection, as well as the option of pairing mobile technology with wearable devices further enhancing options for treatment. Application developers have already proceeded to create assistive mental health applications (refer to Table 1 for specific details on current and developing application for PTSD). For example, PTSD Coach is an online and mobile application assistive service. PTSD Coach categorizes specific mental health issues into separate modules, allowing psychiatrists the ability to provide an individualized treatment plan, designed to best meet the needs of the patient. The online application takes the user to a list prompting, "I want to work on my…" The user then chooses from a list of ten options (e.g., worry, anxiety, and disconnection). Choosing a topic takes you to an introductory video and various exercises enabling the user to manage symptoms appropriately.

Table 1. Current mobile application for PTSD symptom management

application name	Available platforms	Features	Compatible devices
MyBivy	IOS, Android, and PC	Monitors heartrate and sleep; Has smart alarm	Pebble smartwatch. Potential for more devices as development progresses
PTSD Coach	IOS and Android	Provides Self-assessment tools, symptom management, local treatment facilities, and suicide prevention hotline in case of emergency	No current compatibility with off-the-shelf wearables
Optimism	Mac, Windows, IOS, Web	Helps detect patterns in mood, wellness plan, and coping mechanisms	No current compatibility with off-the-shelf wearables
MCalm	Under Development	Detects blood volume pulse, electrodermal activity to track triggers for therapist evaluation	Wristband sensor specific to application

4.3 Virtual Reality

In addition to both online and mobile platforms, virtual reality can also benefit mental health patients. Difficulty in using imagery and in vivo therapy has led to the use of virtual reality based exposure therapy (VRET). VERT exposes a patient to a specific fear or object that triggers anxiety in a safe and controlled (by the psychiatrist) environment [30]. By using auditory, tactile, and proprioceptive stimuli, VRET provides a versatile environment that can be modified for several types of anxieties [26, 31]. Meyerbroker & Emmelkamp [32] studied the efficacy of VRET for anxiety disorders. This analysis resulted in a review of 20 studies, of which two disorders, aviophobia (fear of flying) and acrophobia (fear of heights), had significant evidence for efficacy. Several recent studies have found VRET, for treatment of PTSD, to be as effective as traditional exposure therapy, and potentially offers additional advantages (e.g., reducing dropouts and aversion to prolong exposure) [26].

4.4   Wearables

While online, mobile, and virtual reality technologies can assist in the delivery of information, wearables are more commonly utilized for patient data collection or to mitigate episodes. An individual's physiological response (heart rate, respiration, sleep pattern, etc.) to a particular event can be measured utilizing current wearable technologies (see Tables 2, 3 and 4 for specific measurement capabilities per wearable). Professional Clinicians can utilize wearables as a means of tracking different physiological symptoms that are associated with anxiety disorders. Wearable technologies are referred to as behavioral intervention technologies (BITs) and defined as the application of behavioral and psychological intervention strategies through the use of technology features to address behavioral, cognitive and affective targets that support physical, behavioral and mental health [33]. Throughout the treatment process, clinical psychiatrists sometimes request logs or journals of from each patient detailing behaviors, thoughts, and feelings. BITs can passively record daily activities and can detect instances in which intervention is needed [33]. The tables presented below includes a list of known wearables, specific features for each device, and recommendations as to whether or not the wearable could be easily integrated into a blended/multimodal therapeutic approach.

Table 2. Potential fitness devices for symptom management

Device Name	Features	Paired Applications	Rec.	Disorders and Conditions Utilized	Common and Potential Issues
Nike Fuel	Tracks movement and heartrate	Nike + Fuel app	N	N/A	Unreliable sleep monitoring; only compatible with IOS platform
Fitbit	Tracks activity, sleep patterns, and heartrate; alarm system	Fitbit app and custom apps available	Y	PTSD & Schizophrenia	Sync delay, no direct access to vibrate feature
Jawbone UP	Tracks activity, sleep patterns, and heartrate; alarm system	Jawbone app and custom apps available	Y	PTSD, stress, and sleeplessness	None cited
Microsoft Band 2	Tracks activity, sleep patterns, and heartrate; alarm system	Microsoft health and custom apps available	Y	PTSD, stress, and sleeplessness	Uncomfortable design
Garmin Vivosmart HR	Tracks activity, sleep patterns, and heartrate; alarm system	Garmin Connect and custom apps available	Y	PTSD, stress, and sleeplessness	Not currently compatible on PC

Table 3. Potential smart watch for symptom management

Device name	Mobile platform	Features	Paired applications	Rec.	Disorders and conditions utilized
Pebble	IOS, Android and PC	Monitor sleep patterns, alarm system, displays text on screen	Custom apps available.	Y	PTSD and other anxiety disorders if paired with external HRM
Samsung Gear	Android only and PC	Monitor sleep patterns and heartrate, alarm system, displays text on screen	S Health Google Fit, custom apps available	Y	PTSD and other anxiety disorders

Table 4. Potential heart rate monitors for symptom management

Device name	Mobile platform	Features	Fitness tracking apps	Rec.	Mental health related use
Wahoo Fitness	IOS and Android	Heartrate and movement (not sleep activity)	Wahoo app and custom apps available	Y if paired, not alone	PTSD and other anxiety disorders if paired with sleep/activity tracker
Polar H7	IOS, Android and PC	Heartrate only	Polar apps and customs apps available	Y if paired, not alone	PTSD and other anxiety disorders if paired with sleep/activity tracker
Zephyr HxM Smart	IOS, Android and PC	Heartrate and movement (not sleep activity)	Zephyr apps and custom apps available	Y if paired, not alone	PTSD and other anxiety disorders if paired with sleep/activity tracker

5   The Future of Online/Wearable Devices in Therapy

Traditional therapy involves: traveling to a specific office and individualized treatment based on patient needs; however, active treatment typically ceases after the sessions ends. What if treatment progressed beyond the session? How can technology assist therapeutic implementation beyond these sessions? How can we adapt these methods for mental health issues? As we have already seen, these capabilities allow for the Therapists to transcend present therapy sessions, allowing greater access to current, and potential mental health patients. This strategy is similar to the "Blended Learning" technique found in pedagogical research, in which knowledge is presented online or via mobile technologies and allows for greater time in the therapy session to be dedicated to specific exercises for understanding ways in which a patient can mitigate triggers using cognitive behavioral therapy.

Currently, only a few mobile applications online assist users in managing mental health including PTSD, depression, and bipolar disorder. The majority of the health related applications are designed for the patient as a user, however just one application, MCalm, allows the therapist to track specific metrics and triggers. By providing this type of information the Therapist can tailor the sessions based on known triggers and may result in more effective treatment [34].

Another resource is the online-group therapy which is equivalent to student discussion boards where users can relate to each other and provide different perspectives on coping with their issues. It is a method that is easily accessible and users can log on anytime of day. Online methods are available as the first steps for individuals that may not be able to leave their house.

A blend of online and individual face-to-face therapy is an alternative method that meets individual patient needs while also reducing time, cost, and therapist workload. Allowing access to distributed information or long-distance therapists, provides higher quality interactions between therapists in the individualized sessions. This "Blended Therapy" approach utilizes multiple electronic modes for informing patients and caregivers about information on a particular mental health issue using a mix of online methods of treatment, mobile methods of treatment, simulation based treatment, wearables, and in-therapy sessions. Future treatment should aide both the therapist and the patient by providing multiple means of symptom management and detection.

6 Conclusion

Challenges to treating mental health issues arise from stigmas, healthcare cost, and patient unresponsiveness. Mental health disorders, specifically those related to anxiety, are prevalent issues that can be treated using several techniques, the most effective being cognitive behavioral therapy. Current technologies may provide alternative methods for continuing patient treatment outside of the clinic. By providing blended therapy and implementing multimodal applications the patient can benefit more from the individualized sessions. Several online tools and assistive technologies can supplement recovery and may prevent relapse. Future recommendations include providing specified blended therapy techniques for anxiety disorders.

References

1. Kocieniewski, D.: Man shoots 11, killing 5 girls, in Amish school. The New York Times, 3 October 2006. http://www.nytimes.com/2006/10/03/us/03amish.html?pagewanted=2&_r=1
2. Metzl, J.M., MacLeish, K.T.: Mental illness, mass shootings, and the politics of American firearms. Am. J. Public Heath 105(2), 240–248 (2015)
3. Mental Health America. Position Statement 72: Violence: Community Mental Health Response (2014). http://www.mentalhealthamerica.net/positions/violence. Accessed
4. National Alliance on Mental Illness. Mental Illness Facts and Numbers, March 2013. www.nami.org: http://www2.nami.org/factsheets/mentalillness_factsheet.pdf. Accessed
5. Fletcher, R.R., Tam, S., Omojola, O., Redemske, R., Kwan, J.: Wearable sensor platform and mobile application for use in cognitive behavioral therapy for drug addiction and PTSD. In: Proceedings in 33rd Annual International Conference of the IEEE EMBS, Boston, Massachusetts, USA, August 30th–September 3 2011
6. Gulliver, A., Griffiths, K.M., Christensen, H.: Percieved barriers and facilitators to mental health help-seeking in young people: a systematic review. BCM Psychiatry 10(113), 113–120 (2010)
7. Ritterfeld, U., Jin, S.: Addressing media stigma for people experiencing mental illness using an entertainment-education strategy. J. Health Psychol. 11(2), 247–267 (2006)
8. Anxiety and Depression Association of America, Facts & Statistics, September 2014. www.adaa.org: http://www.adaa.org/understanding-anxiety. Accessed
9. Kohn, R., Saxena, S., Levav, I., Benedetto, S.: The treatment gap in mental health care. Bull. World Health Organ. 82, 858–866 (2004)
10. Anxiety and Depression Association of America. Facts & Statistics, September 2014. www.adaa.org: http://www.adaa.org/about-adaa/press-room/facts-statistics. Accessed
11. Rowney, J., Hermida, T., Malone, D.: Anxiety Disorders. Center for Continuing Education, Cleveland Clinic (2010)
12. Lang, R.J., McTeague, L.M.: The anxiety disorder spectrum: fear imagery, physiological reactivity, and differential diagnosis. Anxiety, Stress Coping. 22(1), 5–25 (2009)
13. Brown, T.A., Campbell, L.A., Lehman, C.L., Grisham, J.R., Mancill, R.B.: Current and lifetime comorbidity of the DSM-IV anxiety and mood disorders in a large clinical sample. J. Abnorm. Psychol. 110(4), 585–599 (2001)
14. Stein, M.B., Sareen, J.: Generalized anxiety disorder. New England J. Med. 373(21), 2059–2068 (2015)
15. Kessler, R.C., Gruber, M., Hettema, J.M., Hwang, I., Sampson, N., Yonkers, K.A.: Co-morbid major depression and generalized anxiety disorders in the national comorbidity survey follow-up. Psychol. Med. 38, 365–374 (2008)
16. Anxiety and Depression Association of America. Symptoms (Generalized Anxiety Disorder), October 2015. www.adaa.org: http://www.adaa.org/understanding-anxiety/generalized-anxiety-disorder-gad/symptoms. Accessed
17. Schneier, F.R.: Social anxiety disorder. New England J. Med. 355(10), 1029–1036 (2006)
18. Heimberg, R.G., Hofmann, S.G., Liebowitz, M.R., Schneier, F.R., Smits, J.A., Stein, M., Craske, M.G.: Social anxiety disorder in the DSM-5. Depress. Anxiety 31, 472–479 (2014)
19. Versella, M.V., Piccirillo, M.L., Potter, C.M., Olino, T.M., R., G.H.: Anger profiles in social anxiety disorder. J. Anxiety Disord. 37, 21–29 (2016)
20. Choy, Y., Fyer, A.J., Lipsitz, J.D.: Treatment of specific phobia in adults. Clin. Psychol. Rev. 27, 266–286 (2007)
21. Javidi, H., Yadollahie, M.: Post-traumatic stress disorder. Int. J. Occupational Environ. Med. 3, 2–9 (2012)

22. Mental Health America. Mental Health Treatment (2016). www.mentalhealthamerica.net: http://www.mentalhealthamerica.net/types-mental-health-treatments. Accessed
23. Bradley, R., Breene, J., Russ, E., Dutra, L., Westen, D.: A multidimensional meta-analysis of psychotherapy for PTSD. Am. J. Psychiatry **162**(2), 214–227 (2005)
24. Krijn, M., Emmelkamp, P.M.G., Olafsson, R.P., Beimond, R.: Virtual reality exposure therapy of anxiety disorders: A review. Clin. Psychol. Rev. **24**, 259–281 (2004)
25. Beidel, D.C., Frueh, B.C., Uhde, T.W., Wong, N., Mentrikoski, J.: Multicomponent behavioral treatment for chronic combat-related posttraumatic stress disorder: a randomized controlled trial. J. Anxiety Disord. **25**, 224–231 (2011)
26. Botella, C., Serrano, B.C., Banos, R.M., Garcia-Palacios, A.: Virtual reality exposure-based therapy for the treatment of post-traumatic stress disorder: a review of its efficacy, the adequacy of the treatment protocol, and its acceptability. Neuropsychiatric Disease Treatment. **11**, 2533–2545 (2015)
27. Ipser, J.C., Stein, D.J.: Evidence-based pharmacotherapy of post-traumatic stress disorder (PTSD). Int. J. Neuropsychopharmacol. **15**(6), 825–840 (2012)
28. Klein, B., Austin, D., Pier, C., Kiropoulos, L., Shandley, K., Mitchell, J., Gilson, K., Ciechomski, L.: Internet-based treatment for panic disorder: does frequency of therapist contact make a difference? Cogn. Behav. Ther. **38**(2), 100–113 (2009)
29. Ruwaard, J., Lange, A., Schrieken, B., Dolan, C.V., Emmelkamp, P.: The effectiveness of online cognitive behavioral treatment in routine clinical practice. PLoS ONE, **7**(7), 1–9 (2012)
30. Repetto, C., Gaggioli, A., Pallavicini, F., Cipresso, P., Raspelli, S., Riva, G.: Virtual reality and mobile phones in treatment of general anxiety disorders: a phase-2 clinical trial. Pers. Ubiquit. Comput. **17**, 253–260 (2013)
31. Motraghi, T.E., Seim, R.W., Meyer, E.C., Morissette, S.B.: Virtual reality exposure therapy for the treatment of post-traumatic stress disorder: a methodological review using CONSORT guidelines. J. Clin. Psychol. **70**(3), 197–208 (2014)
32. Meyerbroker, K., Emmelkamp, P.M.G.: Virtual reality exposure therapy in anxiety disorders: a systematic review of process-and-outcomes studies. Depress. Anxiety **27**, 933–944 (2010)
33. Mohr, D.C., Burns, M.N., Schueller, S.M., Clarke, G., Klinkman, M.: Behavioral intervention technologies: evidence review and recommendations for future research in mental health. Gen. Hosp. Psychiatry **35**(4), 332–338 (2013)
34. Puiatti, A., Mudda, S., Giordano, S., Mayora, O.: Smartphone-centered wearable sensors network for monitoring patients with bipolar disorder. In: 33rd Annual International Conference of the IEEE EMBS, Boston

Integrating Methodology for Experimentation Using Commercial Off-the-Shelf Products for Haptic Cueing

LT Joseph E. Mercado[✉], Nelson Lerma, Courtney McNamara,
and LT David Rozovski

Naval Air Warfare Center Training Systems Division (NAWCTSD), Orlando, USA
{joseph.mercado,nelson.lerma,courtney.mcnamara,
david.rozovski}@navy.mil

Abstract. Although haptic cueing is well researched, its effects on performance accuracy and workload are mixed (Hancock et al. 2013). As such, there is still a need to further develop our understanding of the effects of haptic cueing on performance and workload. The objective of this effort is to develop a cost-effective and non-invasive experimental methodology to investigate the effects of haptic cueing on unmanned aerial vehicle operator performance and workload utilizing commercial off-the-shelf products, specifically, Unity 3D™ - Game Engine and an Xbox 360™ controller.

Keywords: Haptic cueing · Performance · Workload · Usability

1   Introduction

For unmanned aerial vehicle (UAV) operators, searching displays for critical cues is an essential responsibility. As a result, research on a human's ability to visually search is well documented (Wolfe et al. 2005).

Research has shown that visual search can become progressively demanding when a large number of targets are present or in multitasking environments (Prewett et al. 2012). In addition, in environments where the number of targets is low but numerous distractors exist, humans are susceptible to a vigilance decrement (Hancock 2013; Warm 1984). As a result, research has shifted to investigate the effects of cueing to aid visual search, specifically haptic cueing, which are haptic signals that aid the attentional system in detecting signals.

Although haptic cueing is well researched, its effects on performance accuracy and workload are mixed (Hancock et al. 2013). Haptic cueing often results in improved response time but at a cost to accuracy. In addition, perceived workload ratings do not positively correlate with objective measures of workload (Mercado et al. 2014). As such, there is still a need to further develop our understanding of the effects of haptic cueing on performance and workload.

However, the cost of conducting research using haptic cueing aids is expensive. Haptic cueing devices such as a haptic belt or haptic car seat can cost thousands of dollars. In addition, many of the haptic cueing methods utilized in previous research are invasive. For example, Merlo et al. (2006) and Hancock et al. (2013) utilized a belt like

© Springer International Publishing Switzerland 2016
D.D. Schmorrow and C.M. Fidopiastis (Eds.): AC 2016, Part II, LNAI 9744, pp. 344–350, 2016.
DOI: 10.1007/978-3-319-39952-2_33

device with eight vibrotactile actuators to provide participants with messages and haptic cueing, respectively. This belt like device was wrapped tightly around the participant's torso directly on their skin.

Van Erp and Van Veen (2004) utilized a vibrotactile display, consisting of eight vibrating factors that were mounted in a driver's seat to provide haptic cueing as part of a GPS system. Four factors were placed under each participant's thigh in a straight line from the front to the rear of the seat. In addition, Van Erp et al. (2007) utilized a 60-element tactile torso display to capture a pilot's attention in a hyper-gravity state. Similar to the belt-like device utilized by Hancock and colleagues, participants had the 60-element tactile torso display wrapped around their torso directly on their skin. Thus, there is a need to integrate a cost-effective and non-invasive experimental methodology to investigate the effects of haptic cueing on operator performance and workload.

This paper addresses the need for a cost-effective and non-invasive integration methodology for experimentation by utilizing commercial off-the-shelf (COTS) products, specifically, Unity 3D™ - Game Engine and an Xbox 360™ controller. It is important that this integration methodology be non-invasive because it may provide richer data. Specifically, a large portion of the potential participant pool (college students) is already familiar with using an Xbox 360 controller. Thus, they have experienced the Xbox 360 controller's haptic vibration. In addition, the participants will not have the factors connected to them. Thus, the factors will not distract the participants from their task. Familiarity and comfort are important for experimental methodology because an invasive apparatus can affect performance, workload, usability, and trust data (Hall 2001; Kendall 1983).

COTS systems are ubiquitous; however, utilizing COTS systems for research can be a difficult undertaking. The lack of source code availability can be a barrier when leveraging COTS systems for research. If researchers can overcome this barrier, COTS systems make for great research apparatus because of their large feature sets, ease of use, and cost-effectiveness (Hopkinson et al. 2003). Unity 3D is a low-cost, adaptable, cross-platform game engine aimed to create multiplatform 2D and 3D interactive experiences and games. This platform allows designers to build complete environments on personal computers, mobile devices, and websites (Creighton 2010). The Xbox 360 controller is a flexible device that users can connect to a computer via wire or wireless technology. This capability, along with its built-in vibrating motor, makes a great low-cost controller to pair with Unity 3D. Although this integration methodology for experimentation is generalizable to operators across many domains, we utilizing UAV operators as our framework. This allows us to be as detailed as possible in our integration methodology.

2   Integration Methodology for Experimentation

Research has been conducted to understand the benefits of haptic cueing in many settings, but investigating and measuring UAV operator performance and workload when they are provided with haptic cueing has been limited. Integrating a proper experimental methodology is essential to assess questions concerning how cost-effective and non-invasive haptic cueing influences an operator's performance and workload.

2.1 Equipment

The apparatus used to assemble the simulator include one laptop, one LCD monitor, and one Xbox 360 controller. These apparatus will be controlled by a purpose-created Unity 3D Game Engine that will synchronize the respective program and record response times and accuracy rates for each participant. The LCD monitor will be centered directly in front of the participant. All participants will be unaware of the cueing reliability, which will be set at 100 %, which is the optimal level for the mission. The middle of the LCD monitor will display an UAV traveling along a predetermined route. The top of the screen will display the UAV's speed. The left hand side of the screen will display the UAV's altitude, messages (similar to a chat room), and alerts (see Fig. 1).

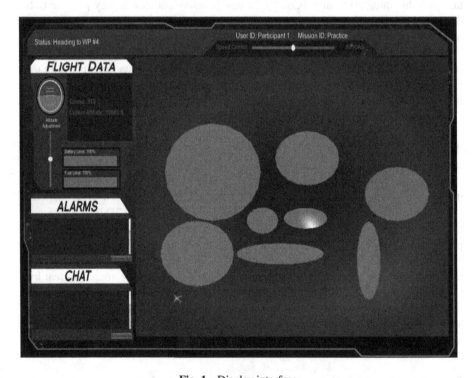

Fig. 1. Display interface

Selection of the Xbox 360 Controller. The Xbox 360 controller was chosen as a cost-effective haptic cueing device because it provides great integration flexibility with existing cost-effective gaming engines, such as Unity 3D. The Xbox 360 contains two variable vibration motors at each end of the game controller that can be dually or individually activated for a given duration. The vibration in the motors can be adjusted for both frequency and intensity, which allows for multiple alert types during a task. The low cost, availability, and integration ease of these controls make the Xbox 360 controller an ideal haptic cueing device that can be easily deployable and tailored to various simulation platforms.

Integration of Xbox and Unity 3D. The simulator consisted of a windows laptop, an Xbox 360 controller, and gaming software called Unity 3D. The Xbox 360 controller is a legacy controller, which has been predominantly used by the gaming community along with the Xbox 360 game console. The online community support for both Unity 3D and the Xbox 360 controller is large, which allows developers a wide range of custom applications.

For this experiment, the Xbox 360 controller was integrated into the Unity 3D Game Engine using the XInputDotNet.dll, an open source C# wrapper around XInput. XInput served as a DirectX API that allowed the Xbox 360 controller to be used on the Windows computer. In order to execute the Xinput API, XInputDotNet.dll was included in the Unity 3D C# project so calls could be made to adjust each of the rumble packs in the controller. Cross communication between the Xbox 360 controller and Unity 3D was accomplished by mapping the controller inputs into Unity 3D to allow the user response through the Xbox 360 controller's joystick and buttons to be transferred to appropriate commands on the game scenario. Unity 3D Game Engine will collect the data and generate a CSV file for each participant, time stamping all of the Xbox controller inputs, along with when the participant received haptic cueing (for the haptic cueing scenario only).

2.2 Procedures

The experiment will be conducted in a controlled laboratory environment, free of competing noise or vibration. Before beginning any of the scenarios, the participant will be given a short briefing to explain their role in monitoring the UAV and sign the informed consent materials. The participant will be shown how to precisely increase/decrease altitude and airspeed and acknowledge messages from their commander and alerts. The participant will be informed to respond as quickly and accurately as possible. In addition, the participant will be informed as to the nature of each area of the display they have to monitor and how it relates to the overall mission. Lastly, the participant will be provided with a training scenario to become familiar with the mission and the haptic cueing of the Xbox 360 controller. The participant will not be made aware of any potential failures of the haptic cueing. However, in the present experiment, for the purpose of ecological validity, there will be no incorrect cueing information.

After completing the training, the participant will begin the experimental scenarios. The participant's primary job in each scenario is to make sure that the UAV does not fly into predefined no-fly zones. Their secondary task, which will be aided by haptic cueing during the cueing condition, will be to monitor the four sections of the LCD monitor mentioned earlier. The participants will have to monitor airspeed and altitude to make sure they are both within predetermined limits. If either moves out of those limits, the participant will have to adjust the UAV accordingly using the Xbox 360 controller. In the haptic cueing condition, the Xbox 360 controller will increasingly vibrate once the UAV is outside of its predefined speed or altitude. In regards to messaging, the participant will monitor the chat room for messages from their commander (the commander's chat name will be predefined). Once the participant notices a message from their commander, they will click an "acknowledge" button using the Xbox 360 controller. The alerts will work similarly to the messages. Once the participant notices an alert, they will click a separate "acknowledge" button using the Xbox 360 controller. For both the messages and alerts, during the haptic cueing condition, the Xbox 360 controller will vibrate simultaneously with the arrival of a message or alert. Each individual scenario will last approximately 10 min. Once the participant has completed each scenario, they will complete the NASA-Task Load Index (TLX; Hart and Staveland 1988), System Usability Scale (SUS: Brooke 1996), and the Experience-based Questionnaire for Usability Assessments Targeting Elaborations (EQUATE; Atkinson et al. in progress) for that specific scenario and then continue to the last scenario. After the participants complete the two scenarios they will be debriefed and allowed to depart the experiment.

3   Selecting Measures

The last step in integrating a methodology for experimentation is selection measures, as a proof of concept, which allow us to understand how cost-effective non-invasive haptic cueing influences an operator's performance and workload.

3.1   Independent Variables

The independent variables in this experiment will be the type of cueing (i.e., no cueing or haptic cueing) to support visual identification of stimuli changes (i.e., airspeed, altitude, messages from commander, aircraft system alerts) in the display and the type of haptic cueing (increasing vibration or steady vibration).

There will be 40 changes presented in each scenario, and they will be divided such that 10 changes per task type (monitor airspeed, attitude, messages, and aircraft system alerts) will occur. Changes will be presented at irregular intervals throughout each individual participant's series of trials so that for any single participant there will be no identifiable temporal pattern. In the haptic cueing condition the cueing will be presented simultaneously with the change in stimuli (i.e., decrease/increase in airspeed, decrease/increase in altitude, messages from commander, aircraft system alerts). However, the type of haptic cueing will vary. When the UAV is outside of the predefined airspeed and altitude limits, the haptic cueing vibration will increase steadily the further the UAV goes outside of the limits. In regards to messages and alerts, the haptic cueing will be a steady vibration. The issue of task difficulty and the potential for asymmetric transfer effects will be addressed in the following manner: First, the number of changes in stimuli will match previous studies (Hancock et al. 2013; Merlo and Hancock 2011), in which participants perceived that task as low/medium workload. In addition, the two scenarios will be counterbalanced across individual participant presentation. The participants will be divided into two groups that will undertake the sequence of different scenarios in differing testing orders (group 1 – scenario 1 then 2, group 2 –scenario 2 then 1).

3.2 Dependent Variables

The dependent variables will be objective measures of performance, experienced cognitive workload as assessed by the NASA-TLX, and perceived usability as assessed by the SUS and EQUATE. Objective measures of performance include response time and accuracy rate. Response time is defined as the latency between the onset of the change in stimuli (alert, airspeed outside of limits, etc.) and the subsequent corrective action. Accuracy rate will include: correct response (hit), response omissions (misses), and false alarms (incorrect action when there was no change in stimuli). The NASA-TLX measures a total weighted workload score based on six subscales: mental physical, and temporal demands, as well as effort, performance, and frustration. The SUS is a 10-question scale designed to measure users' overall feelings of usability (efficiency, efficacy, and satisfaction) with the interface and is scored on a 5-point Likert scale. The EQUATE measures usability based on 16 categories using a 5-point Likert scale.

4   Conclusion

The integration methodology for experimentation presented in this paper is intended to extend to any human-computer system involving human operators that provides haptic cueing. This novel approach, utilizing COTS products and focusing on a non-invasive experimental methodology, will afford more researchers the opportunity to contribute to haptic research and expand their knowledge base.

Acknowledgment. This work was supported by the Office of Naval Research In-house Laboratory Independent Research (ILIR) program. The views expressed herein are those of the authors and do not necessarily reflect the official position of the Department of Defense, its components, or the organizations with which the individuals are affiliated.

References

Atkinson, B.F.W., Kaste, K., Tindall, M.: The psychometric development and validation of the EQUATE. Theoretical Issues in Ergonomics Science. Manuscript ready for submission (In progress)

Brooke, J.: SUS - a quick and dirty usability scale. In: Jordan, P.W., Thomas, B., Weerdmeester, B.A., McClelland, I.L. (eds.) Usability Evaluation in Industry, pp. 189–194. Taylor & Francis, London (1996)

Creighton, R.H.: Unity 3D Game Development by Example: A Seat-of-Your-Pants Manual for Building Fun, Groovy Little Games Quickly. Packt Publishing Ltd., Olton (2010)

Hall, M.A.: Arrow on trust. J. Health Polit. Policy Law **26**(5), 1131–1144 (2001)

Hancock, P.A.: In search of vigilance: the problem of iatrogenically created psychological phenomena. Am. Psychol. **68**(2), 97 (2013)

Hancock, P.A., Mercado, J.E., Merlo, J., Van Erp, J.B.: Improving target detection in visual search through the augmenting of multi-sensory cues. Ergonomics **56**(5), 729–738 (2013)

Hart, S., Staveland, L.: Development of NASA TLX (task load index): results of empirical and theoretical research. In: Hancock, P., Meshkati, N. (eds.) Human Mental Workload, pp. 139–183. Elsevier, Amsterdam (1988)

Hopkinson, K.M., Birman, K.P., Giovanini, R., Coury, D.V., Wang, X., Thorp, J.S. EPOCHS: integrated commercial off-the-shelf software for agent-based electric power and communication simulation. In: Proceedings of the 2003 Winter Simulation Conference, 2003, vol. 2, pp. 1158–1166. IEEE, December 2003

"How Unity3D Became a Game-Development Beast". Slashdot.org. Dice, 3 June 2013. Accessed 23 November 2015

Kendall, P.C.: Methodology and cognitive—behavioral assessment. Behav. Psychother. **11**(4), 285–301 (1983)

Mercado, J.E., Reinerman-Jones, L., Barber, D., Leis, R.: Investigating workload measures in the nuclear domain. In: Proceedings of the Human Factors and Ergonomics Society Annual Meeting, vol. 58, no. 1, pp. 205–209. SAGE Publications, September 2014

Merlo, J., Hancock, P.: Quantification of tactile cueing for enhanced target search capacity. Mil. Psychol. **23**(2), 137 (2011)

Merlo, J.L., Stafford, S., Gilson, R., Hancock, P.A.: The effects of physiological stress on tactile communication. In: Proceedings of the Human Factors and Ergonomics Society Annual Meeting, vol. 50, no. 16, pp. 1562–1566 (2006)

Prewett, M.S., Elliott, L.R., Walvoord, A.G., Coovert, M.D.: A meta-analysis of vibrotactile and visual information displays for improving task performance. IEEE Trans. Syst. Man Cybern. Part C: Appl. Rev. **42**(1), 123–132 (2012)

Van Erp, J.B., Van Veen, H.A.: Vibrotactile in-vehicle navigation system. Transp. Res. Part F: Traffic Psychol. Behav. **7**(4), 247–256 (2004)

Van Erp, J.B., Eriksson, L., Levin, B., Carlander, O., Veltman, J.A., Vos, W.K.: Tactile cueing effects on performance in simulated aerial combat with high acceleration. Aviat. Space Environ. Med. **78**(12), 1128–1134 (2007)

Warm, J.S. (ed.): Sustained Attention in Human Performance, pp. 1–14. Wiley, New York (1984)

Wolfe, J.M., Horowitz, T.S., Kenner, N.: Rare items often missed in visual searches. Nature **435**, 439–440 (2005)

Understanding Older Adults' Perceptions of In-Home Sensors Using an Obtrusiveness Framework

Blaine Reeder[1(✉)], Jane Chung[2], Jonathan Joe[3], Amanda Lazar[3], Hilaire J. Thompson[3], and George Demiris[3]

[1] University of Colorado Anschutz Medical Campus, Aurora, CO, USA
blaine.reeder@ucdenver.edu
[2] University of New Mexico, Albuquerque, NM, USA
jchung@salud.unm.edu
[3] University of Washington, Seattle, WA, USA
{jjoe,alaz,hilairet,gdemiris}@uw.edu

Abstract. The aim of this study was to determine if dimensions and sub-categories of a previously-tested obtrusiveness framework were represented in interviews conducted with community-dwelling older adults at three- and six-month study visits during an in-home sensor study. Secondary analysis of interviews was performed using a codebook based on an obtrusiveness framework. Eight community-dwelling older adults aged 79–86 participated in 15 interviews. One participant died between the three- and six-month interviews. Some elements of the obtrusiveness framework were present at three months but not at six months, indicating that perceptions of obtrusiveness of in-home sensors may decline over time. Findings highlight the importance of privacy issues and perceived usefulness for sensor technology use and adoption. There is a need to develop an obtrusiveness assessment instrument that enables nuanced measurements based on specific contexts and types of technologies.

Keywords: Sensors · Obtrusiveness · Technology acceptance · Older adults · Aging

1 Introduction

1.1 Aging and Technology

An increase in the worldwide population of older adults is driving the need for innovative solutions to help older adults maintain independence at home and foster health. Smart home technologies, defined as sensing technologies embedded in the residential infrastructure to facilitate passive monitoring, have the potential to enable lasting independence. One potential application of smart home technologies to foster maximal health of older adults is through collection of information about activity levels in the home to support augmented cognition. This could enable older adults to monitor their own activity levels, leading to behavior change and more efficient self-management of health, or alert care providers and family members about changes in patterns that could indicate functional decline.

© Springer International Publishing Switzerland 2016
D.D. Schmorrow and C.M. Fidopiastis (Eds.): AC 2016, Part II, LNAI 9744, pp. 351–360, 2016.
DOI: 10.1007/978-3-319-39952-2_34

Technology is increasingly used to help older adults stay independent and connected to their health care providers [1]. Technology acceptance is an important factor in technology adoption and use [2]. Therefore, there is a need for research to identify what features and types of home monitoring technologies that are acceptable to older adults [3]. Over 93 % of older adults in the United States live independently in community settings [4] but not all people age the same way [5], or have the same views about the acceptability of technology [6] and health information sources [7]. Thus, determining the views of community-dwelling older adults regarding in-home sensors is important if these technologies are to be designed appropriately for different types of people and play a role in everyday health maintenance.

1.2 Obtrusiveness

Obtrusiveness, defined as "a summary evaluation by the user based on characteristics or effects associated with the technology that are perceived as undesirable and physically and/or psychologically prominent" [8] (p. 430), is a factor in technology acceptance. While there is a recognized need to understand older adults' views about obtrusiveness of smart home technologies and how these views change over time, validated instruments that measure obtrusiveness of technology do not yet exist [9]. Hensel et al. developed a conceptual framework that describes eight broad dimensions of obtrusiveness for smart home technologies [8] (see Fig. 1).

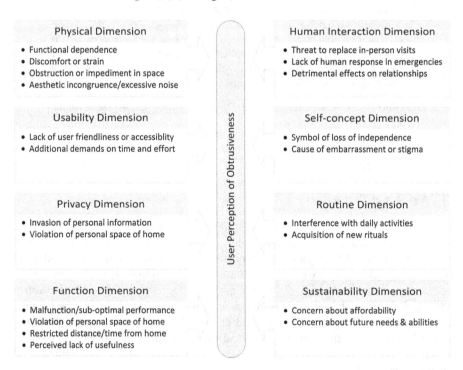

Fig. 1. Obtrusiveness framework with dimensions and subcategories based on Hensel et al. [8]

Courtney et al. validated this framework [10] with older adults at a continuing care retirement community (CCRC) [11] and two residential care communities [12]. The framework has subsequently been used to engage older adults regarding their perceptions of technology obtrusiveness to aid the creation of design guidelines for smart home technologies [13] and to determine the effect of distinct sensing approaches on older adults' perceptions of technologies [14]. However, the views of community-dwelling older adults regarding the obtrusiveness of smart homes technologies installed in their homes remain largely unexplored, and individual studies do not evaluate changes in older adults' perceptions of obtrusiveness over long periods of time. Therefore, the aim of this study was to determine if the dimensions and sub-categories of an obtrusiveness framework were represented in technology acceptance interviews with community-dwelling older adults through secondary analysis of interview data collected at three- and six-month study visits during an in-home sensor study.

2   Methods

This study was a secondary analysis of interviews conducted as part of a six-month feasibility study of smart home technologies [15] installed in the homes of community-dwelling older adults in the Pacific Northwest region of the United States. The study setting was an independent retirement community in the Pacific Northwest region of the United States [15]. All residents are independent living. The community consists of a mix of 1-, 2- and 3-bedroom apartments with communal living spaces such as a gym, patio and library available to residents. All residences are provided with Internet access.

A convenience sample of participants was recruited through a presentation at the study setting and through the use of snowball sampling procedures. Inclusion criteria were to be a resident within the participating retirement community 65 years of age or older and able to speak and understand written English. Written informed consent was obtained from participants prior to study procedures. All study procedures were approved by the Institutional Review Board of the University of Washington.

All participants were administered a battery of standardized instruments that measured a variety of physical, psychosocial, and cognitive parameters at baseline and 6-month data collection visits. A full description of the study protocol, instruments administered and data collection schedule for each instrument is available in the primary study publication [15]. All participants were found to have normal cognition after screening for cognitive impairment using the Mini-Cog cognitive screening tool [16]. At the three- and six-month visits, semi-structured interviews to solicit participants' attitudes toward in-home sensor technologies were conducted and recorded with a digital audio recorder. Interview questions related to obtrusiveness, usefulness and acceptability of technology. The full interview guide is available in the primary study publication [15].

2.1   Sensor System

The smart home technologies used in this study consisted of in-home sensor systems that used commercially available passive infrared motion sensors, a gateway and a secure web-based interface for system administration and sensor data visualization. Sensor data were transmitted wirelessly to the gateway and then transferred over the Internet to a remote server. Sensors were installed in the living spaces of each participant including bedrooms, living rooms, kitchens, dining rooms and bathrooms. The number of sensors installed in each residence varied based on the size and layout of the residence. Additional details about the sensor system and installations are available in the primary study publication [15].

Sensor systems were installed in the home of each participant during enrollment. The function of the sensor system was described to participants during recruiting efforts and enrollment procedures. Specifically, participants were informed that the sensor system did not collect video data or personally identifiable information beyond activity levels. Specific information regarding the obtrusiveness framework was not provided to study participants.

2.2 Data Analysis

A secondary analysis of technology acceptance interviews from the main study was performed using a theory-driven coding approach [17]. The approach was theory-driven in that it relied on a codebook based on the obtrusiveness framework [8, 10]. A version of this codebook was previously used to analyze qualitative data obtained in studies of older adults at a continuing care retirement community and two residential care communities [10]. The codebook was obtained from one of the developers of the framework.

Interviews were transcribed verbatim. The coding team consisted of the study leader and three research team members. The study leader had five years of extensive qualitative data collection and analysis experience. One of the study PIs provided guidance and oversight regarding application of the codebook. This PI originally trained the study leader in qualitative data analysis and was one of the developers of the obtrusiveness framework and codebook. The three research team members were doctoral students with qualitative analysis experience obtained through graduate course work and from projects within the research group.

The three research team members independently coded transcripts from 3 month (n = 8) and 6 month interviews (n = 7). The study leader, acting as a fourth coder, independently analyzed sets of coded transcripts and noted disagreements between coders. Disagreements were reconciled through discussion during in-person meetings of all coders until consensus was reached about application of codes.

Our total data set consisted of 15 interviews. Within the focus and constraints of our study, we believe that data saturation was reached. O'Reilly and Parker note that data saturation is a contentious issue with complexities such that the concept may not plausibly transfer in the same way across qualitative approaches [18]. For data-driven qualitative analysis, Guest et al. showed that 94 % of all high-frequency codes were identified within the first six interviews and 97 % within the first 12 interviews [19]. For theory-based studies, Francis et al. recommend specifying an initial sample size and an additional number of interviews as a stopping criterion, demonstrating the approach with retrospective analysis of 10 and 3 interviews [20]. Given our sample size and approach, our study functionally satisfies the recommendations of both Guest et al. [19] and Francis et al. [20].

3   Results

Eight participants ranging in age from 79 to 86 years (mean age 83 ± 2.2) enrolled in the study. All participants were Caucasian and 75 % had completed graduate school. One participant died between the three- and six-month study visits. Table 1 shows the dimensions and subcategories of the obtrusiveness framework that were represented in three- and six- month interviews. Check marks represent instances where participant responses indicated the dimension or subcategory was a concern.

Table 1. Representation of obtrusiveness dimensions and subcategories at 3 and 6 months

Dimension	Subcategory	3 mos.	6 mos.
Physical	Functional dependence	–	–
	Discomfort or strain	–	–
	Obstruction or spatial impediment	–	–
	Aesthetic incongruence or excessive noise[a]	✓	–
Usability	Lack of user friendliness or accessibility	–	–
	Additional demands on time and effort	–	–
Privacy	Invasion of personal information	✓	✓
	Violation of personal space of the home	✓	✓
Function	Malfunction or unreliable performance	✓	✓
	Inaccurate measurement	✓	✓
	Restriction in distance or time from home	–	–
	Perceived lack of usefulness	✓	✓
Human Interaction	Threat to replace in-person visits	–	–
	Lack of human response in emergencies	–	–
	Detrimental effects on relationships	–	–
Self-Concept	Symbol of loss of independence	–	–
	Cause of embarrassment or stigma	–	–
Routine	Interference with daily activities	✓	–
	Acquisition of new rituals	✓	–
Sustainability	Concern about affordability	–	–
	Concern about future needs and abilities	–	–

[a]This row combines two subcategories per Courtney et al.'s recommendation [10].

3.1   Physical Dimension

Overall, participants found the smart home technologies installed in their homes to be non-obtrusive, as illustrated by the following quote. *"I don't even remember they're there. Most of the time, I don't even think about it. It wouldn't occupy a tenth of 1 % of my time. I just come in and live in here"* (participant at 3 months). The only subcategory represented in this dimension was "Aesthetic incongruence or excessive noise". Referring to the gateway hardware, one participant commented: *"I wanted to push this thing out of the way so it wouldn't look so obvious"* (at 3 months). In addition, she stated that visitors frequently asked about the sensor system: *"The only time I think about it is when someone says, and this happens fairly often, 'What the heck are those supposed to be doing?'"* (at 3 months) but later observed: *"I don't think anyone's said anything about them for a couple of months"* (at 6 months). Another participant did not find the system obtrusive but noted that others might: *"If you are someone who insists on décor then it might be bothersome"* (at 6 months).

3.2   Usability Dimension

The technology used in this study consisted solely of sensors and gateways that were installed by members of the research team and were at no point operated by the residents. As such usability issues resulting from a potential interaction with the system were not applicable to this study.

3.3   Privacy Dimension

There were few instances where perceptions pertaining to the subcategory "Invasion of personal information" emerged in participants' responses. Participants discussed their assumptions that personal activity data would be de-identified and secured: *"It's fine. Nobody knows who I am, what I do"* (participant at 3 months) and *"I just trust the people that would be gathering this information that they keep it"* (participant at 3 months). Regarding the "Violation of personal space" subcategory, one participant reported having to renegotiate his understanding of how the system worked when he noticed a sensor in the bathroom: *"Every once in a while I think that: 'No, that thing is not taking pictures'"* (at 3 months). Later, he stated: *"Early on I noticed them when I went in the bathroom, and then it would dawn on me: 'No, that's not a camera.' So it was just reminding myself what it really was and then I forgot all about it"* (at 6 months).

3.4   Function Dimension

Issues related to the "Malfunction or unreliable performance" and "Inaccurate measurement" subcategories were represented as doubts about unproven technology in both three- and six-month interviews. For example, one participant was concerned that measurements from the sensor in her laundry room might be inaccurately mistaken for bathroom sensor measurements. Her comment was: *"Do they remember that I said this is my laundry? This is where I do the washing and the ironing. So I may be in there ironing and listening to the radio for a couple of hours or maybe a ten minute session if I'm just pressing something. But you know, I think: 'So what difference does it make? But I want them to know I'm not ill.* (laughs) *I'm healthy and hearty at the moment"* (at 6 months).

For the "Perceived lack of usefulness" subcategory, coded responses about the usefulness of activity data from smart home technologies were mixed. One view was that health care providers should have as much information as possible: *"I think they should know as much as they can know about because otherwise it's hard for them to treat us*" (participant at 3 months). However, this same participant did not see the usefulness of smart home technologies for herself. Another participant commented: "*I would like to see the results of the finished project but I have no idea whether it would have any usefulness to me*" (at 3 months). Another participant felt that personal activity data could be useful in interactions with health care providers when discussing issues related to chronic pain: "*I tell him: 'I have sleep interruptions.' 'How do you know that?' 'Well, I say, I've got data*" (at 3 months).

3.5 Human Dimension

"Lack of human response in emergencies" was not seen as a concern. To the contrary, technology was seen as potentially supportive of human response in an emergency. The following quote exhibits a preventive mindset: "*If I get to the point where I am falling, I want a sensor. I don't want to lay here for two days without anybody knowing there is something wrong with me*" (participant at 6 months). This participant acknowledged the need for technology to alert people to respond in the event of an emergency. Likewise, the same held true for the "Detrimental to relationships" subcategory; several participants reported that they volunteered information about the study to visiting family members and friends.

3.6 Self-concept Dimension

Subcategories in this dimension were not represented.

3.7 Routine Dimension

Issues related to the "Interference with daily activities" and "Acquisition of new rituals" subcategories were raised by one participant. His concern related to having to sign in and out of the building so the system would not raise alarms due to lack of motion in his residence. In discussion of schedule coordination with activity data, he commented: "*That would require that I somehow notify the system that I'm gonna be gone, and you know, that would be the same as my signing out. I don't do it and I wouldn't be likely to do it*" (at 3 months).

3.8 Sustainability Dimension

The "Affordability" or "Concern about future needs and abilities" (as they relate to participant capacity to operate or use the technology) subcategories were not represented. This absence may be due to participant thinking about the need (or lack thereof) for smart home technologies. For instance, when asked about sharing personal activity data, one participant expressed a lack of concern about need for technology and an overall comfort with the stability of her physical abilities: "*I don't think so at the moment. Not unless my behavior, my physical condition, changes considerably. But I'm pretty much the way I've been for the past I don't know how many years"* (at 3 months). In addition, the affordability issue may not have been raised because the technology in the study was installed free of charge.

4 Conclusion

This study explored the dimensions of an obtrusiveness framework with community-dwelling older adults living in an independent retirement community whereas prior research did so with residents of a CCRC and two residential care communities [10]. A particular strength of this study is that our protocol was longitudinal in nature, giving us the opportunity to compare differences in presence of elements of the obtrusiveness framework from participant interviews at three and six months. As such, this study contributes to knowledge about aging and technology regarding obtrusiveness and its dimensions.

Participants expressed minor concerns in the Physical and Routine dimensions during 3 month interviews. Issues regarding aesthetic incongruence and changes in routine raised during 3 month interviews resolved themselves for study participants by the 6 month visit. These results suggest that some older adult concerns about technologies installed their homes diminish over time. This is consistent with other studies of home based technologies that indicate that home care patients had a more positive attitude towards the technology as time passed [21].

Noting potential limitations when comparing different interview protocols and study aims we contrast our results to prior research that tested the obtrusiveness framework with participants from different settings [10]. The Privacy (Invasion of personal information and Violation of personal space of the home) and Function (Perception of lack of usefulness) dimensions were represented in data collected from community-dwelling older adults in this study and in prior studies with residents of residential care facilities and CCRCs [10]. This finding confirms the acknowledged importance of privacy issues and perceived usefulness concerning health-related technology use and adoption. Conversely, whereas the dimensions of Human Interaction (Lack of human response in emergencies), Self-Concept (Symbol of loss of independence, Cause of embarrassment or stigma) and Sustainability (Concern about affordability) were present in interviews of residents of residential care facilities and CCRCs [10], these dimensions were absent in our interviews of community-dwelling older adults. This finding suggests that independent living community-dwelling older adults may not have concerns in these areas because of differences in circumstances related to health or living situation. An important area for future work would be to confirm this initial understanding by comparing older adults' perceptions across settings in a single study. This would also assist in the development of instruments to measure obtrusiveness.

Limitations of this study include a small sample size with a racially homogenous sample with a higher level of educational attainment than the general US population of adults 65 years of age and older. Thus, the findings may not generalize to larger populations of older adults within or external to the US. However in spite of these limitations, the study provides insight into older adults' perceptions of obtrusiveness in a longitudinal study of smart home technologies, providing new understanding in an underexplored area.

Deployments of smart home technologies will vary based on context and the target population who use them because people age differently and have different needs. The technologies deployed in this study included commercially available sensors that have been deployed in other smart home studies [22]. Since more than 93 % of older adults in the United States live independently in community settings [4], one of our study aims was to determine technology perceptions for healthy community-dwelling older adults to inform future preventive interventions.

While the obtrusiveness framework used in this study should be further validated, its dimensions appear to hold for older adults in a range of different settings. The implications are that the construct of the framework seems valid but the prevalence of dimensions varies by context. This idea suggests the need to develop an instrument that affords nuanced, context-based measurements of the obtrusiveness of smart home technologies. Thus, an instrument to measure obtrusiveness of smart home technologies may require modification based on specific contexts and technologies. Therefore, future research to develop a validated instrument should focus on the type and frequency of concerns as they relate to the dimension of the obtrusiveness framework when it is administered across settings and to individuals across a range of older adult's health status.

References

1. Reeder, B., Chung, J., Stevens-Lapsley, J.: Current telerehabilitation research with older adults at home: an integrative review. J. Gerontological Nurs. (In press)
2. Davis, F.D.: Perceived usefulness, perceived ease of use, and user acceptance of information technology. MIS Q. **13**, 319–340 (1989)
3. Kang, H.G., Mahoney, D.F., Hoenig, H., Hirth, V.A., Bonato, P., Hajjar, I., Lipsitz, L.A.: In situ monitoring of health in older adults: technologies and issues. J. Am. Geriatr. Soc. **58**, 1579–1586 (2010)
4. United States Federal Interagency Forum on Aging-Related Statistics: Older Americans 2010: Key Indicators of Well-Being. Government Printing Office, Washington, DC (2010)
5. Zaslavsky, O., Cochrane, B.B., Herting, J.R., Thompson, H.J., Woods, N.F., Lacroix, A.: Application of person-centered analytic methodology in longitudinal research: exemplars from the Women's Health Initiative Clinical Trial data. Res. Nurs. Health **37**, 53–64 (2014)
6. Caine, K.E., Fisk, A.D., Rogers, W.A.: Benefits and privacy concerns of a home equipped with a visual sensing system: A perspective from older adults. In: Proceedings of the Human Factors and Ergonomics Society Annual Meeting, vol. 50, pp. 180–184. Sage Publications (2006)
7. Le, T., Chaudhuri, S., White, C., Thompson, H., Demiris, G.: Trust in health information sources differs between young/middle and oldest old. Am. J. Health Promot. AJHP **28**, 239–241 (2014)
8. Hensel, B.K., Demiris, G., Courtney, K.L.: Defining obtrusiveness in home telehealth technologies a conceptual framework. J. Am. Med. Inf. Assoc. **13**, 428–431 (2006)
9. Daniel, K.M., Cason, C.L., Ferrell, S.: Emerging technologies to enhance the safety of older people in their homes. Geriatr. Nurs. **30**, 384–389 (2009)

10. Courtney, K.L., Demiris, G., Hensel, B.K.: Obtrusiveness of information-based assistive technologies as perceived by older adults in residential care facilities: A secondary analysis. Med. Inf. Internet Med. **32**, 241–249 (2007)

11. Demiris, G., Rantz, M.J., Aud, M.A., Marek, K.D., Tyrer, H.W., Skubic, M., Hussam, A.A.: Older adults' attitudes towards and perceptions of 'smart home' technologies: a pilot study. Inf. Health Soc. Care **29**, 87–94 (2004)

12. Courtney, K.L.: Privacy and senior willingness to adopt smart home information technology in residential care facilities. Methods Inf. Med. **47**, 76–81 (2008)

13. Meulendijk, M., Van De Wijngaert, L., Brinkkemper, S., Leenstra, H.: Am I in good care? Developing design principles for ambient intelligent domotics for elderly. Inf. Health Soc. Care **36**, 75–88 (2011)

14. Demiris, G.: Privacy and social implications of distinct sensing approaches to implementing smart homes for older adults. Engineering in Medicine and Biology Society, 2009, EMBC 2009, Annual International Conference of the IEEE, pp. 4311–4314. IEEE (2009)

15. Reeder, B., Chung, J., Lazar, A., Joe, J., Demiris, G., Thompson, H.J.: Testing a theory-based mobility monitoring protocol using in-home sensors: a feasibility study. Res. Gerontol Nurs. **6**, 253–263 (2013)

16. Borson, S., Scanlan, J., Brush, M., Vitaliano, P., Dokmak, A.: The mini-cog: a cognitive 'vital signs' measure for dementia screening in multi-lingual elderly. Int. J. Geriatr. Psychiatry **15**, 1021–1027 (2000)

17. Boyatzis, R.E.: Transforming qualitative information: thematic analysis and code development. Sage Publications, Thousand Oaks (1998)

18. O'Reilly, M., Parker, N.: 'Unsatisfactory Saturation': a critical exploration of the notion of saturated sample sizes in qualitative research. Qual. Res. **13**, 190–197 (2013)

19. Guest, G., Bunce, A., Johnson, L.: How many interviews are enough? Field Methods **18**, 59–82 (2006)

20. Francis, J.J., Johnston, M., Robertson, C., Glidewell, L., Entwistle, V., Eccles, M.P., Grimshaw, J.M.: What is an adequate sample size? Operationalising data saturation for theory-based interview studies. Psychol. Health **25**, 1229–1245 (2010)

21. Demiris, G., Speedie, S.M., Finkelstein, S.: Change of patients' perceptions of TeleHomeCare. Telemed. J. e-Health **7**, 241–248 (2001)

22. Reeder, B., Meyer, E., Lazar, A., Chaudhuri, S., Thompson, H.J., Demiris, G.: Framing the evidence for health smart homes and home-based consumer health technologies as a public health intervention for independent aging: A systematic review. Int. J. Med. Inf. **82**, 565–579 (2013)

The Role of Simulation in Designing Human-Automation Systems

Christina F. Rusnock[✉], Jayson G. Boubin, Joseph J. Giametta, Tyler J. Goodman,
Anthony J. Hillesheim, Sungbin Kim, David R. Meyer, and Michael E. Watson

Air Force Institute of Technology, Wright-Patterson AFB, Dayton, OH, USA
christina.rusnock@afit.edu

Abstract. Human-machine teaming is becoming an ever present aspect of executing modern military missions. In this paper, we discuss an extensive line of research currently being conducted at the Air Force Institute of Technology focused specifically on using simulation in the design of automated systems in order to improve human-automation interactions. This research includes efforts to predict operator performance, mental workload, situation awareness, trust, and fatigue. This research explores using simulation to design interfaces, perform trade studies, create adaptive systems, and make task allocation decisions.

Keywords: Human-machine teaming · Human-performance modeling · Simulation · System design

1 Introduction

Human-machine teaming is becoming an ever present aspect of executing modern military missions. Human-machine teaming can be seen across a large spectrum of automation capabilities, from traditional automation, to robots, to semi-autonomous systems, and even to autonomous teammates. Designing these systems requires not only great technical skill, but also requires a deep understanding of the interaction between the human operator and the automated system. Design decisions made early in the system development life cycle can have long-term repercussions for the effectiveness and utility of the system, and thus it is vital to have an effective mechanism for predicting and evaluated these interactions and for predicting how automation design decisions can influence the human's performance and the overall system/team performance. Simulation is one such mechanism. It is relatively cost and time efficient, allows designers to easily explore a large option space, and can be used early in the design process, before the system is built, and before key design decisions are made.

The purpose of this paper is to explore the role that simulation can play in the design of automated systems in order to improve human-automation interactions. This discussion includes current human-performance simulation research being performed at the Air Force Institute of Technology (AFIT) aimed at evaluating team performance and operator mental workload in order to make system design tradeoffs, perform task allocation, design adaptive systems, and design interfaces. In addition to predicting team

© Springer International Publishing Switzerland 2016
D.D. Schmorrow and C.M. Fidopiastis (Eds.): AC 2016, Part II, LNAI 9744, pp. 361–370, 2016.
DOI: 10.1007/978-3-319-39952-2_35

performance, this line of simulation research is also seeking novel methods to evaluate situation awareness, trust, and fatigue.

2   Performance and Performance Tradeoffs

Performance is an important consideration in system design, which often includes component-level and integrated testing in order to ensure actual system performance is commensurate with the planned/desired level of performance. When evaluating system designs, the human operator is often treated as a reliable, error-free, high-performing external actor. However, in order to truly evaluate the overall system performance, the performance of the user with respect to their interaction with the system must be taken into account. Of course, in achieving desired system and/or human performance, sometimes tradeoffs need to be made with other factors such as system cost or size [1–3], and user manning or workload [4, 5]. For example, in order to increase overall system performance, user manning may need to be increased. In turn, this might necessitate an increase in system size, resulting in higher system cost.

Automation can sometimes be used to offset human performance [6, 7]. For example, implementing system automation could be used to augment the user's performance of tasks, thus increasing the overall performance of the human-system team while also mitigating the need for other tradeoffs (e.g. increased manning or task allocation) to achieve the same level of performance.

Simulation can be used to conduct trade studies on performance in order to estimate the efficacy of potential design decisions or potential re-design options. Each design option can be modeled as a separate alternative system, and the results from the simulation runs will reveal the expected performance outcomes as well as unanticipated emergent behavior.

For example, research performed by Watson [8] used simulation to demonstrate the value of considering human performance when making system design tradeoff decisions. The study used a threat detection scenario in which automation was implemented as a way to augment user performance. The Improved Performance Research Integration Tool (IMPRINT) was used to simulate six automation alternatives with varying design parameters in order to predict which automation produced both the largest increase in team performance and decrease in user mental workload. The study showed that by performing these simulated tradeoff analyses, the effect of the human's performance on overall system performance can be seen, thus enabling more informed design decisions.

3   Task Allocation

In addition to system-level trades, when designing human-machine teams, another important design decision is which tasks should be allocated to the human and which ones should be allocated to the automated system. Automated systems and human operators bring unique qualities and abilities to the work environment. Automated systems do not lose vigilance and can perform certain tasks–such as computations–almost instantly. However, automated systems often lack flexibility since they operate within the bounds of their code. Humans may lose vigilance in monitoring tasks [9], but are flexible decision makers in response to unusual or unforeseen circumstances. Additionally, humans and automation can also have overlapping abilities in which a task could be performed suitably by either [10]. Task allocation decisions should consider: the abilities and limitations of both the human and the system; the other tasks that each is also managing; and the required handoffs that occur due to the division of tasks.

Modeling and simulation provides an opportunity to examine how variations in task allocation and handoff interactions affect human behavior and workload, as well as entire system performance. In dynamic environments, it is too costly to perform human test subject experiments to the extent that is necessary to discover preferred task allocation. Therefore, well-designed models are cost effective measures to adequately predict the effects of task allocation in response to environmental changes.

For example, research conducted by Goodman et al. [11] evaluated task allocation options using an automated route-generation aid in an Air Traffic Control-style task. The objective of the Air Traffic Control task is to direct incoming ships to their corresponding destinations, while avoiding negative outcomes, such as ship collisions. There are two high-level functions: identifying an incoming ship and creating a route. In this research, the automated aid was given responsibility to identify an incoming ship and the human with route creation. SysML activity diagrams [12], in conjunction with the IMPRINT simulation tool [13], were developed to assess task allocation. This research revealed that modeling task allocation requires careful consideration of human-automation communication actions. Explicit depictions of outputs and inputs are necessary to properly model interactions. Another consideration is human behavior adjustments in response to automation's actions. It should not be assumed the human will consistently perform the same behaviors when working with an automated teammate as he/she would if working solo. It is important to capture dynamic human decision making, such as acting upon the automation's suggestions, ignoring the automation, or additional human activities specifically aimed at maintaining situation awareness.

4 Design of Adaptive Systems

In addition to traditional allocation decisions, human-machine teaming systems have seen a rise in the interest in adaptive automation, in which the task allocation decisions are made dynamically according to factors such as the state of the human operator, environment, system, or other information [14]. In these systems, the automation provides assistance to the operator on an as-needed basis. Compared with static automation, adaptive automation based on operator need has the benefit of minimizing the risks of automation (e.g. increased boredom, decreased situation awareness) while maximizing the benefits (e.g. reduced workload, increased performance) [15]. Dynamic physiological assessment has been suggested as a potential method for measuring operator need in adaptive systems [16]. Recent studies at AFIT have used discrete event simulation (DES) and physiological recording (i.e. electrocardiogram (ECG), electroencephalogram (EEG), and electrooculogram (EOG)) to explore different methods that can be used to dynamically assess operator need and inform adaptive augmentation decisions.

Giametta and Borghetti [17] recently demonstrated the effectiveness of physiologically-based assessment in remotely piloted aircraft (RPA) surveillance tasks. The group used supervised machine learning techniques to link physiological features, collected from EEG recordings to periods of additional workload caused by multi-tasking. The EEG-based classifiers were able to correctly identify periods of increased workload 80.9 and 83.4 percent of the time in two different multiple-objective RPA scenarios.

In a similar study involving the same RPA scenarios, Smith et al. [18] used IMPRINT to provide detailed user activity data to supervised machine learning techniques. Rather than using coarse task classifications labels (e.g. high workload, low workload) that were found in the majority of EEG–based classification studies, the group created continuous analytic workload profiles (CAWPs) that provided unique workload values for each second of user activity. The CAWPs enabled "detailed application and research analysis not possible with subjective measures alone" [19].

Recently, Giametta [20] used stochastic simulation techniques to overcome the real-world challenges of creating second-by-second CAWPs for dynamic user tasks. His work showed that representative workload profiles could be crafted using CAWPs from a small set of previously observed subjects performing similar tasks. After identifying and observing user activities that governed task difficulty and timing in RPA simulations, stochastic variables were fit to distributions that matched each of the observed actions then resampled multiple times to create representative workload profiles. Supervised machine learning models were then calibrated for new subjects by collecting only EEG data during training tasks, then pairing them with the previously created representative profiles.

Studies at AFIT continue to focus on assessing operator need using physiological data. DES has given their researchers a unique view of operator workload during dynamic tasks. This has allowed them to link physiological features to workload in multiple military scenarios, which will ultimately enable the design of effective adaptive systems.

5   Interface Design

The effectiveness of the human-machine team is highly dependent upon the mechanism that the human and machine use to communicate with each other—the interface. Poorly designed interfaces could cause either teammate to misinterpret the goals, intentions, or information being conveyed by the other. Simulation enables designers to explore a range of interface design options, across a variety of design detail levels.

Work by Rusnock and Geiger [21] used human-performance simulation to model the cognitive workload of an operator performing intelligence, surveillance, and reconnaissance tasks using remotely-controlled unmanned ground and aerial systems. The study evaluated the relative performance and expected workload for three types of interface redesigns for the control system: keyboard, voice recognition, and touch screen. Through this evaluation the study was able to find the alternative that offered both workload and performance improvements.

Goodman, et al. [22] evaluated the timing of automation intervention route-generation aid in an Air Traffic Control-style task. A DES, validated by human-in-the-loop experimentation, revealed that agent intervention timing has a significant impact on human behavior, workload, and team performance. Further simulations suggested agent intervention timing should not be static, but rather a function of environmental event rates.

Kim [23] used simulation to evaluate the use of a 3D audio interface for multiple aircraft control. The aims of this research were to see if the workload and performance of an operator responsible for tracking radio traffic of multiple unmanned aircraft could be improved through the use of a 3D audio system over the current system. The 3D audio system uses a voice recognition system to automatically differentiate critical information (i.e., radio calls including the call sign of an aircraft under control) from distractive information (i.e., radio calls including other call signs) and present these information to different ears of the operator. The researchers used IMPRINT simulations to predict the effects of the 3D audio system, which showed promising effects of the 3D audio system in reducing UAV operators' workload and response time. The simulation predicted that the operator would shed the more complex cognitive and physical tasks associated with call sign recognition and relevance determination, instead performing the simpler perceptual task. This conversion of the tasks would permit the operators to quickly distinguish critical from distractive information, thus reducing workload, when using the 3D audio system. Furthermore, one interesting expectation from the results of the simulation was that the operators' workload and performance would not be influenced by the number of call signs the operator controls while using the 3D audio system. These simulation results were later confirmed through the use of human-subjects experimentation.

6   Assessing Situation Awareness

As automated teammates take over an increasingly larger number of tasks previously performed by humans, one major concern for human-machine teaming is the potential loss of operator situation awareness (SA). Situation awareness is the operator's perception (or mental model) of elements in the environment within a volume of space and time, the comprehension of their meaning, and the projection of their status into the future [24, 25]. For example, the ability of a pilot to conceive of an aircraft's whereabouts, status, weather, fuel state, terrain, and, in combat, enemy disposition is critical to effective aircraft operation. In critical phases of flight, poor weather, or in the face of systems malfunctions, appropriate SA can mean the difference between mission success and failure or even survivability [26].

Because of the critical effects situation awareness has on mission outcome and survivability, designers and operators both have a vested interest in maintaining a high level of SA. Operators develop procedures and train to maximize the use of all available tools and observations to increase SA [26]. Designers can incorporate technology specifically designed to enhance SA such as heads-up displays (HUD), multi-function displays, automation aids, expert systems, advanced avionics, and sensors that provide more information in a more useful manner [24]. Designing for enhanced SA must consider the number of required tasks, the workload of those tasks, and the information provided to the operator during their completion [27]. In order to design for SA, we must be able to predict/estimate SA during the design process.

Recently, Meyer [26] demonstrated the use of discrete-event simulation, to measure potential SA. While this simulation inherently reflects an optimistic estimation, it can model the complex relationship between operator workload and SA as the human interacts with the machine. This method is done with two separate algorithms: workload-dependent and task-dependent. The workload-dependent measure, Strategic SA, is computed from the cognitive workload experienced below the overload threshold. This corresponds with Endsley's theory that high SA can be maintained under increasing workload conditions until approaching overload, at which point, it deteriorates rapidly [28]. Strategic SA allows the operator to have independent and unpredictable priorities for information gathering. The task-dependent measure, Tactical SA, evaluates the information gathered from accomplishing a specific task. Some tasks, such as actuating a button or switch, provide no SA, while others, such as reading an instrument or display, provide noticeable SA. Summing Tactical and Strategic SA together yields Total SA [26].

This approach was first used in a study of airlift missions comparing two different C-130 aircraft conducting both a formation airdrop, and a single-aircraft approach and landing with maximum effort procedures. The older C-130H aircraft had a cockpit crew of four (pilot, copilot, navigator, and flight engineer) and predominantly analog instrumentation, while the newer C-130 J aircraft had a cockpit crew of two (pilot and copilot) with modern digital avionics and enhanced automation features. Each cockpit crew member was modeled with discrete-event simulation to measure workload and situation awareness both as individuals and as a team. Results showed that operators were able to maintain high SA during periods of high workload, if the workload was attributed towards tasks that gained SA. Also, while the modern avionics were able to substitute for human operators, it did not result in significantly improved SA for the C-130 J in either simulation [26].

By using simulation to estimate SA, designs of human-machine teaming systems can be effectively evaluated and potential degradations in human and mission performance can be identified.

7 Assessing Trust

Another key factor in the proper application of automation in human-machine teaming is characterizing operator trust in the automation. Trust is defined as the human's confidence that an automated system will help him/her achieve his/her goals in a situation characterized by uncertainty and vulnerability [29].

Characterizing and modeling trust in human-automation interactions is imperative for successful performance and reduced workload, because operators that distrust an automated system will not use it effectively, thus losing the expected benefits from the automation. Calibrating an operator's trust in a system is necessary to prevent overtrust or distrust in the automation. Calibration references the relationship between an operator's trust in the automation and the automation's true capabilities [30]. Overtrust refers to poor calibration in which trust exceeds the automation's capabilities and distrust refers to trust falling short of the automation's capabilities [30].

In order to model and simulate trust in automation, trust needs to be quantified. Recent work by Boubin et al. [31] has sought to quantify two aspects of trust: reliance and compliance. Reliance pertains to the human operator's state when an alert or alarm is silent [32]. Boubin et al. extend the definition of reliance to mean the acceptance of an automation's non-action. Inversely, compliance addresses the operator's response when the alarm sounds whether true or false. Boubin et al. extend the definition of compliance to mean the acceptance of an automation's action. Using data collected from a human-in-the-loop experiment, Boubin et al. were able to create mathematical functions which model compliance and reliance based on taskload and the automation type. These functions can be used by simulation models to capture impacts of trust on human-machine team performance. This work is being extended to examine how a user's reliance and compliance rates are affected by degraded automation reliability. The research hopes to provide further insight into how reliability can affect human operator's performance based on the level of trust the operator has in the system.

In another experiment Goodman et al. [22] incorporated similar reliance functions accounting for task load and agent response timing into discrete event simulation models. These reliance functions were developed from previous experiments and produced a probability that the human would permit the agent to create a route. This function assumed that higher taskload would result in greater reliance. Agent response time was used to shift the function vertically, where quicker agent responses created higher probabilities of agent route creation and slower agent responses led to lower probabilities. There models were later supported by human-in-the-loop experimentation, which suggested that humans will take advantage of the opportunity to shed tasks as long as it is not detrimental to performance.

8 Assessing Fatigue

One of the many advantages of modeling is the ability to rapidly simulate human-machine teaming interactions that last for extended periods of time. Especially for military human-machine teams, it is not uncommon to have tasks that extend beyond an 8-hour work day, including night-shifts or even multi-day shifts. Over these long periods of time, it is important to account for changes in the human operator's cognitive and physical abilities. Unlike the automated counterpart, the human operator is susceptible to declines in performance due to fatigue. Assumptions that an operator's performance is constant, especially during extended task durations, would likely result in unrealistic over-estimates of team performance. Human cognitive and physical abilities degrade as time without sleep increases. This degradation causes can result in an increase in task times, error rates, and dropped tasks.

In order to effectively capture human-performance under fatigue conditions, it is necessary to create models which account for increased task failure and task time due to these fatigue conditions. Recent work at AFIT has built upon previous fatigue models, developed by Gunzelmann and Gluck [33] using ACT-R, to incorporate fatigue mechanisms which account for performance declines due to microsleeps. A microsleep describes a very short period of time where no cognition occurs (i.e. temporary episode of sleep lasting a fraction of a second). To properly implement microsleeps into an IMPRINT simulation model, unique functions were created for each task where microsleeps may occur. These functions determine the probability of a microsleep event occurring and are based on the amount of sleeploss and the number of microsleeps that have already occurred.

Fatigue modeling research at AFIT has also examined vigilance decrement. In situations where operators have had appropriate sleep, operators can still experience fatigue during the performance of vigilance tasks. Vigilance tasks are characterized by long periods of sustained attention, commonly requiring operators to identify stimuli that are occurring at very low event rates. Work at AFIT has incorporated functions established by Giambra and Quilter [34]—which describe the relationship between vigilance task time and the increase in reaction time—into human-performance simulations in the cyber domain. This model used the vigilance decrement function to portray the workload and performance effects of fatigue on Air Force cyber-defense operators monitoring network traffic.

By accounting for sleeplessness and vigilance decrement, modelers can have a better understanding of the performance of human operators in high stress, high-attention situations over long periods of time. By creating models which account for human fatigue, system designers are able to understand the interaction between the design and a fatigued operator, and thus more accurately account for expected operator performance. This awareness can inform designs of human-machine teaming systems, hopefully increasing effectiveness and reducing the likelihood of errors due to fatigue.

9   Conclusions

Simulation has the potential to play a crucial role in the design and development of human-automation systems. By not requiring physical prototypes or human subjects, simulation provides a safe, affordable, and time-effective, mechanism for evaluating system designs. These advantages make it easier to perform what-if analyses and explore many more design options than would be possible through live-testing. Additionally, simulation can be performed throughout all phases of the system development lifecycle, enabling early design decisions and trade-offs to account for human performance and human-machine interactions. The body of work described herein demonstrates how simulation is being used to capture complex human-machine interactions and to identify system-level, emergent performance outcomes which account for human qualities such as mental workload, situation awareness, trust, and fatigue. Properly accounting for human performance during system design and development will ultimately result in more effective human-machine teams.

10 Disclaimer

The views expressed in this paper are those of the authors and do not reflect the official policy or position of the United States Air Force, the Department of Defense, or the U.S. Government.

References

1. Crane, J., Hamilton, B.A., Brownlow, L., Hamilton, B.A.: Optimization of multi-satellite systems using integrated model based system engineering (MBSE) techniques (2015)
2. Do, Q., Cook, S., Lay, M.: An investigation of MBSE practices across the contractual boundary. Procedia Comput. Sci. **28**(Cser), 692–701 (2014)
3. Russell, M.: Using MBSE to enhance system design decision making. Procedia Comput. Sci. **8**, 188–193 (2012)
4. Allender, L.: Modeling human performance: impacting system design, performance, and cost. In: Proceedings Military, Government and Aerospace Simulation Symposium, 2000 Advanced Simulation Technologies Conference, vol. 32, no. 3, pp. 139–144 (2000)
5. Mitchell, D.K., Samms, C., Wojcik, T.M.: System-of-systems Modeling: The Evolution of an Approach for True Human System Integration
6. Mitchell, D.K., Samms, C.L., Henthorn, T., Wojciechowski, J.Q.: Trade Study: A Two-Versus Three-Soldier Crew for the Mounted Combat System (MCS) and Other Future Combat System Platforms (2003)
7. Colombi, J.M., Miller, M.E., Schneider, M., McGrogan, J., Long, D.S., Plaga, J.: Predictive mental workload modeling for semiautonomous system design: implications for systems of systems. Syst. Eng. **14**(3), 305–326 (2011)
8. Watson, M.E.: Improving System Design through the Integration of Human Systems and Systems Engineering Models. Air Force Institute of Technology (2016)
9. Parasuraman, R., Manzey, D.H.: Complacency and bias in human use of automation: an attentional integration. Hum. Factors **52**, 381–410 (2010)
10. Rouse, W.: Human-computer interaction in multitask situations. IEEE Trans. Syst. Man Cybern. **7**(5), 384–392 (1977)
11. Goodman, T., Miller, M., Rusnock, C.: Incorporating automation: using modeling and simulation to enable task re-allocation. In: Winter Simulation Conference (2015)
12. Delligatti, L.: SysML Distilled: A Brief Guide to the Systems Modeling Language. Addison-Wesley, Boston (2013)
13. Improved Performance Research Integration (IMPRINT) Tool: Army Research Laboratory (2010)
14. Johnson, A.W., Oman, C.M., Sheridan, T.B., Duda, K.R.: Dynamic task allocation in operational systems: Issues, gaps, and recommendations. In: 2014 IEEE Aerospace Conference, pp. 1–15 (2014)
15. Rouse, W.B.: Adaptive aiding for human/computer control. Hum. Factors **30**, 431–438 (1988)
16. Parasuraman, R., Bahri, T., Deaton, J.E., Morrison, J.G., Barnes, M.: Theory and Design of Adaptive Automation in Aviation Systems. Naval Air Warfare Center, Aircraft Division, Warminster (1992)
17. Giametta, J., Borghetti, B.J.: EEG-based secondary task detection in a multiple objective operational environment. In: Proceedings of the 14th International Conference on Machine Learning and Applications (ICMLA) (2015)

18. Smith, A.M., Borghetti, B.J., Rusnock, C.F.: Improving model cross-applicability for operator workload estimation. Proc. Hum. Factors Ergon. Soc. Annu. Meet. **59**(1), 681–685 (2015)
19. Rusnock, C., Borghetti, B., McQuaid, I.: Objective-analytical measures of workload – the third pillar of workload triangulation? In: Schmorrow, D.D., Fidopiastis, C.M. (eds.) AC 2015. LNCS, vol. 9183, pp. 124–135. Springer, Heidelberg (2015)
20. Giametta, J.: Cross-subject continuous analytic workload profiling using stochastic discrete event simulation. Air Force Institute of Technology (2015)
21. Rusnock, C.F., Geiger, C.D.: Using discrete-event simulation for cognitive workload modeling and system evaluation. In: Proceedings of the 2013 Industrial and Systems Engineering Research Conference (2013)
22. Goodman, T., Miller, M.E., Christina, F., Bindewald, J.: Timing within human-agent interaction and its effects on team performance and human behavior. In: Cogsima 2016 (2016)
23. Kim, S.: Unmanned Aerial Vehicle (UAV) Operators' Workload Reduction: The Effect of 3D Audio on Operators' Workload and Performance during Multi-Aircraft Control. Air Force Institute of Technology (2016)
24. Endsley, M.R.: Situation awareness global assessment technique (SAGAT). In: Aerospace and Electronics Conference 1988, NAECON 1988, Proceedings of IEEE 1988 National, pp. 789–795 (1988)
25. Endsley, M.R.: Situation awareness in aviation systems. In: Garland, D.J., Wise, J.A., Hopkin, V.D. (eds.) Handbook of Aviation Human Factors, pp. 257–276. Lawrence Erlbaum Associates, Mahwah (1999)
26. Meyer, D.R.: Effects of automation on aircrew workload and situation awareness in tactical airlift missions. Air Force Institute of Technology (2015)
27. Endsley, M.R.: Toward a theory of situation awareness in dynamic systems. Hum. Factors J. Hum. Factors Ergon. Soc. **37**(1), 32–64 (1995)
28. Endsley, M.R.: Situation awareness and workload: flip sides of the same coin. In: Proceedings of the 7th International Symposium on Aviation Psychology, pp. 906–911 (1993)
29. Ross, J.M., Szalma, J.L., Hancock, P.A., Barnett, J.S., Taylor, G.: The effect of automation reliability on user automation trust and reliance in a search-and-rescue scenario. Proc. Hum. Factors Ergon. Soc. Annu. Meet. **52**(19), 1340–1344 (2008)
30. Lee, J.D., See, K.A.: Trust in automation: designing for appropriate reliance. Hum. Factors J. Hum. Factors Ergon. Soc. **46**(1), 50–80 (2004)
31. Boubin, J.G., Rusnock, C.F., Bindewald, J.M., Miller, M.E.: Measuring human compliance and reliance with automated systems. In: Proceedings of the 2016 Industrial and Systems Engineering Research Conference (2016)
32. Dixon, S.R., Wickens, C.D.: Automation reliability in unmanned aerial vehicle control: a reliance-compliance model of automation dependence in high workload. Hum. Factors **48**(3), 474–486 (2006)
33. Gunzelmann, G., Gluck, K.A.: An integrative approach to understanding and predicting the consequences of fatigue on cognitive performance. Cogn. Technol. **14**(1), 14–25 (2009)
34. Giambra, L.M., Quilter, R.E.: A two-term exponential functional description of the time course of sustained attention. Hum. Factors **29**(6), 635–643 (1987)

Navigating with a Visual Impairment: Problems, Tools and Possible Solutions

Michael Schwartz[1($\boxtimes$)] and Denise Benkert[2]

[1] Deptartment of Psychology, University of Central Florida, Orlando, USA
schwartz.michael@knights.ucf.edu
[2] Modeling and Simulation Program, University of Central Florida, Orlando, USA
denise.benkert@gmail.com

Abstract. In this paper we discuss various navigational aids for people who have a visual impairment. Navigational technologies are classified according to the mode of accommodation and the type of sensor utilized to collect environmental information. Notable examples of navigational aids are discussed, along with the advantages and disadvantages of each. Operational and design considerations for navigational aids are suggested. We conclude with a discussion of how multimodal interaction benefits people who use technology as an accommodation and can benefit everyone.

Keywords: Multimodal interaction · Vibrotactile feedback · Auditory feedback · Visual impairment · Blind · Navigation

1 Introduction

Technologies that utilize multimodal interaction have the ability to benefit everyone. For example, commercial GPS devices, such as the Garmin Drive 60LM, use both visual and auditory alerts to assist drivers in navigating safely [1]. Automobile manufacturers have recognized the complex nature of operating a vehicle and have begun to incorporate multimodal systems into other aspects of vehicles (e.g., safety features) [2]. While the benefits and disadvantages of these new technologies have yet to be thoroughly assessed, many people would recognize the visual system's important role in mobility and orientation, whether driving or walking. For example, if a person is engaged in wayfinding (i.e., both orienting and navigating) she must determine her current location, find a suitable route, utilize cues or landmarks to plan the next step and detect arrival at the intended location [3]. Each step in the wayfinding process can be cognitively demanding; however, for sighted people the process is performed automatically and is less effortful than navigating without sight. In order to successfully navigate, people with a visual impairment must learn to interpret nonvisual sensory signals to assist with each of the four steps in a wayfinding task. Navigating via the use of non-visual means is typically less accurate than utilizing visual cues because tactile, olfactory, and audible landmarks can be temporary, confusing, and take longer to interpret [4]. Thus, wayfinding taxes the cognitive and attentional demands of people with a visual impairment more than their sighted counterparts and results in less precise outcomes [5].

© Springer International Publishing Switzerland 2016
D.D. Schmorrow and C.M. Fidopiastis (Eds.): AC 2016, Part II, LNAI 9744, pp. 371–381, 2016.
DOI: 10.1007/978-3-319-39952-2_36

Multimodal technologies are a possible solution to the problem of navigating with a visual impairment. Indeed, multiple resource theory (MRT) continues to have an impact on technological design [6]. While MRT was intended as a theory of simultaneous, multitask performance, attention remains a unified mental construct that cannot be ignored when designing technological interfaces [7]. The application of multimodal interfaces to the design of navigational technologies for those with a visual impairment offers numerous advantages. First, the technology can substitute the use of a non-visual sensory modality in place of an impaired visual system. Navigational aids that allow for sensory substitution are not necessarily multimodal (see Sect. 3 for a discussion of specific navigational aids); however, multimodal interfaces offer a second benefit: the ability to translate visual cues into the sensory modality that can best represent the information needed to successfully orient and travel. For example, finding an optimal route to travel can be indicated by vibrotactile stimulation and discovering information about a location (e.g., a store's hours of operation) can be indicated audibly. While Morse code could be used to convey textual information through vibrotactile means, this would require someone to know another language in order to accurately interpret the stimuli. Similarly, determining a correct path of travel could be accomplished by listening to auditory information; however, this can result in imprecise navigation due to the inexactness of spatial language (e.g., "take a slight right in 300 feet") [8]. Sensory substitution devices are also less invasive and more affordable than sensory replacement devices (e.g., cochlear implants).

2   Classifying Multimodal Functionality in Navigational Technologies for People with a Visual Impairment

2.1   Obstacle Detection vs Route Guidance

Tools for navigating with a visual impairment can be classified according to the primary goal of the technology: obstacle detection or route guidance. Mobility aids, such as a white cane or a dog guide, are primarily used for obstacle detection. Route Guidance is accomplished by using navigational aids (sometimes called electronic travel aids or ETAs). Mobility aids typically have a limited effective range of a few meters whereas ETAs are intended to provide more detailed information about the environment and have longer range [9]. Differences in the effective range of use of navigational technologies should be taken into consideration when designing travel aids. For example, vibrotactile feedback is appropriate for obstacle detection whereas auditory instructions can provide different information about objects and locations farther away. The way information is received and understood by the human brain plays a part. Vision, audition, and taction can be perceived spatiotemporally [7]. However, there are differences in how sensory input is understood and acted upon [10]. Tactile feedback may take less time to understand but audition may provide more readily understandable information. Individual differences in sensory integration and processing are further defined in populations with one or more disabilities as a result of the level of impairment [11]. Designers of navigational technologies must take these differences into account when deciding on the appropriate modes of sensory substitution and information presentation.

2.2   Camera, GPS, and Sonar Technologies

Navigational aids can also be defined by the type of sensors used to receive environmental information. Commonly used sensors include cameras, GPS, infrared sensors (IR), lasers, radio frequency identification (RFID), and sonic sensors (sonar). Any navigational aid using these types of sensors provides auditory or tactile feedback to the user, and sometimes both. Some devices provide multimodal feedback to the user without being designed to do so (e.g., white canes). There are advantages and disadvantages to each type of technology. Navigational devices that employ cameras, lasers, or sonar allow people with a visual impairment to sense objects up to several meters away and do not require the environment to be retrofitted. However, such devices do not work well in crowds and have trouble with moving objects. Sonar devices providing a high degree of resolution about the environment tend to have a steeper learning curve, thus requiring more time and effort to learn. Sonar can interfere with a person's hearing, a sensory modality heavily relied upon by someone with impaired or no vision. Infrared and RFID are effective in both indoor and outdoor environments; however, expensive retrofitting of the environment is required. Additionally, IR and RFID do not require line of sight in order to work but are limited in range. A more commonly used navigational aid, GPS, is highly customizable and allows pedestrians with a visual impairment to preview their routes before traveling. However, GPS does not work indoors and the degree of accuracy provided by GPS systems is not detailed enough for people with a visual impairment. The accuracy of GPS systems is further degraded by dense foliage, tall buildings, and cloud cover. Each technology has advantages and disadvantages and people with a visual impairment often compensate for the weaknesses in their devices by carrying multiple tools on each journey [12].

3   Discussion of Selected Navigational Technologies

The following passage discusses notable examples of navigational technologies for people with a visual impairment. This review is not a comprehensive list; instead, it is meant to emphasize important aspects of user interaction with navigational aids. For a thorough discussion of navigating with a visual impairment and navigation aids for people with a visual impairment, see Blasch and Welsh's book on orientation and mobility [13]. Technologies that magnify objects (e.g., screen readers, monocular devices) are not included in this paper.

3.1   White Cane

The white cane is a symbol of having a visual impairment; indeed, all 50 of the United States have "White Cane" laws, which protect pedestrians who have a visual impairment [14]. While a cane may not be considered to be an advanced technological device, contemporary white canes can be found in many variants according to user preference. Different cane tips provide varying degrees of tactile information and produce distinct sounds when coming into contact with objects. Materials such as aluminum and graphite are used in construction to keep the cane strong while reducing weight. The white cane was intended to be used as an extension of touch; people receive tactile feedback when the cane encounters objects in the environment; however, the cane also produces sounds when interacting with objects. The maximum effective range of the white cane is thus extended when experienced users learn to detect large objects nearby (or the absence of those objects, such as a passage between buildings) using echolocation. The remaining technologies discussed here are not intended to replace the white cane; rather, they are complementary devices.

3.2   Ultra Cane

The Ultra Cane, developed by Sound Foresight Technology Ltd, utilizes ultrasonic technology to detect potential hazards at a range of two to four meters in front of the user [16]. The cane can sense objects on the ground or in front of the user's head and torso, thus detecting obstacles that would normally be missed by a traditional white cane. Feedback about obstacle location is delivered in the form of vibrotactile stimulation in the handle of the cane. Ground level obstacles are signaled with activation of the rear vibromotor; head level obstacles are indicated by activation of the forward vibromotor. Although the Ultra Cane can detect hazards not ordinarily detected by a traditional white cane, the Ultra Cane is bulkier, heavier, and more expensive. As with any ultrasonic technology, line of sight is required for reliable obstacle detection. The Ultra Cane's vibrotactile feedback may increase the user's cognitive workload as he spends time and effort discerning which signals are from the device's vibromotors and which are from contact with the environment.

3.3   Sonic Pathfinder

The Sonic Pathfinder, developed by Perceptual Alternatives, is a head-mounted device that warns the user via musical notes of obstacles in the path of travel [17]. As users approach an obstacle, notes produced by the Pathfinder descend the musical scale indicating proximity to an object. Orientation of the object to the user is indicated by location of the note (i.e., left and/or right ear detects the signal). A distinctive feature of the Pathfinder is that the effective range is determined by the user's walking speed, which allows for a greater degree of control. The distinctive appearance of the device is also a disadvantage. People who have a visual impairment do not want public perception to be focused on their disability [18]. The Pathfinder's use of musical notes to convey information to the user means that the person's hearing is at least partially blocked. For people who have little or no vision, the sense of hearing becomes even more important, especially when navigating.

3.4   Nurion Laser Cane

Similar to the Ultra Cane, the Nurion Laser Cane detects obstacles in front of the user; however, instead of ultrasonic transducers, the Laser Cane utilizes diode lasers

[19]. Information about the location of obstacles is delivered to the user via auditory and vibrotactile feedback. As with ultrasonic technology, line of sight is required to use the Laser Cane.

3.5 BrainPort V100

The BrainPort V100, developed by Wicab, employs a tactile display and camera to convey information about objects to users [20]. The camera is mounted on a pair of sunglasses and connects to the tactile display, which sits on the user's tongue. The tactile "picture" communicated to the user has a maximum resolution of 400 by 400 pixels, which allows the person to discern objects in the environment. The BrainPort has not yet seen widespread adoption, however, the tongue display draws on decades of research with tactile displays for the abdomen and back [21–23]. Users may not want to travel in public with a cord hanging out of the mouth; however, the potential benefits offered by the system may warrant using the device while traversing problematic routes (e.g., near construction sites).

3.6 Talking Signs

Talking Signs, developed by the San Francisco based Smith-Kettlewell Eye Research Institute, is an audible signage system composed of a handheld IR receiver and strategically placed IR transmitters. The user waves the device around until a signal is located and, once a signal is detected, the handheld receiver decodes the audio message conveyed by the transmitter. Audio messages can describe aspects of the environment (e.g., "ticket kiosk") and can guide users to a location by honing in on the IR signal, which is directional in nature. Talking Signs can work in both indoor and outdoor environments and the system is an orientation device since both wayfinding information and landmark identification are provided.

3.7 CINVESTAV

A navigational aid in the form of smart glasses was developed at the Center for Research and Advanced Studies (CINVESTAV). The system combines GPS, ultrasound, cameras, and artificial intelligence (AI) to assist with visually impaired navigation [25]. Obstacle detection is provided by cameras and ultrasound technology while the GPS offers navigational capabilities. The AI can interpret text, colors, and recognize locations and relay the information through synthetic speech. The CINVESTAV glasses are not yet commercially available and behavioral studies are needed to confirm the usability and durability of the system.

3.8 GPS Units

GPS technology has greatly improved the navigational abilities of many drivers and pedestrians; however, many of the commercially available units are not accessible to people who must navigate with a visual impairment [15]. This is reflected in the high cost of GPS units developed specifically for people with impaired or no vision (usually several hundred to several thousand dollars). The BrailleNote GPS, developed by Sendero, can provide detailed verbal information about street names, locations, and points of interest. The system can be customized according to user preference and the software is accessible. The hardware is expensive, however, and additional software updates are required to be purchased in the future in order to maintain accurate guidance. Most importantly, without additional hardware a blind pedestrian will not be able to obtain precise location information from GPS technology alone. For example, although someone who is legally blind may be able to tell that the sidewalk is four feet away, a pedestrian that has no light perception (i.e., completely blind) could find herself lost in the middle of an intersection. Additionally, GPS does not work in interior environments and accuracy is degraded when the pedestrian is between tall buildings.

3.9   Smartphone Apps

Many smartphone navigation apps for people with a visual impairment give auditory directions; however, there are several apps that convey information via haptic or multi-modal means. Blindsquare is similar to GPS apps intended for use by sighted individuals [27]. Using a smartphone's onboard GPS technology, the application determines a user's current location and incorporates information from other apps (e.g., Foursquare) about the surrounding environment. Blindsquare allows a user to mark and save locations for easy referencing. Most notably, the app allows the user to customize the filters so that only relevant information is presented. Although not a navigation app, TapTapSee can assist people with a visual impairment in identifying landmarks and signage [28]. Object recognition and identification can be used to help a traveler know his current location, the first step in a wayfinding task. Smartphone technology has allowed for multiple functions to be incorporated into a handheld device, such that innovative apps and services can be obtained. Using the app Be My Eyes, a person with a visual impairment can use her phone to call someone for help and establish a live video connection with someone who can assist her with anything from finding items in a grocery store to knowing the expiration date on a jar of mayonnaise [29]. ARIANNA, an app for independent indoor navigation, allows a user to use his cellphone to detect colored lines on the floor of a building, such as those found in hospitals [30]. The user inputs his desired destination in the app and scans the environment with his phone until the correct colored line is detected. While following the path, his phone vibrates as long as his phone camera can detect the appropriate colored line in the middle of the screen. A disadvantage of this app is that it will only work if the colored lines are already in place, not hidden by objects in the way, and not too worn to be useful. ARIANNA's developers have suggested using infrared lines which can be detected by the IR sensors already in contemporary smartphones. Future smartphones may include more hardware, which could allow for the development of apps that will further assist in navigation, particularly for those with a visual impairment.

4 Future Development of Navigational Technologies for Those with a Visual Impairment

The rapid development of navigational technologies (e.g., GPS units) and smartphones, coupled with advances in imaging technology and processing power heralds an optimistic future for travelers, sighted or not. Unfortunately, our understanding of the human perceptual and cognitive systems does not advance as quickly. There is a need for behavioral research in every aspect of wayfinding: sensory perception, integration, and translation, cognitive and attentional demands of orienting and navigating, and usability research with regard to technologies used. The need for research in these areas is highlighted by the issues faced by people with a visual impairment.

4.1 Vibrotactile Feedback for Navigation

Vibrotactile feedback has been demonstrated to be effective at helping people to navigate, even under stressful conditions [31, 32]. Prior research has demonstrated that feedback from vibrotactile stimuli can result in faster orienting than spatial language with no loss of accuracy, even when participants were placed in total darkness [33]. The optimal form of a vibrotactile navigational aid may be a wearable unit, which allows for directional information to be mapped onto the body. Route guidance can be arranged spatially on the user's body while information about proximity is coded in another tactile dimension (e.g., amplitude) [34]. There is a need for more research investigating optimal locations on the body for receiving vibrotactile feedback for navigational purposes, especially with regard to the needs of people with a visual impairment (see Sect. 4.4 for a discussion) [35]. There is evidence to indicate that a multimodal navigational system can result in less direction and distance errors compared to unimodal interfaces, even if mental workload (e.g., demand on attentional resources) is increased [36].

4.2 Types and Levels of Automation to Assist the User

The proliferation and continued use of navigational technologies suggests that such systems are beneficial. The ways in which automation can assist a person who is utilizing navigational systems are described in a seminal work by Parasuraman, Sheridan, and Wickens. [37]. Returning to our earlier example of a person using a GPS unit to navigate, we see how automating the technology can benefit (or harm) her. When activated, a GPS unit automatically keeps track of the user's position; the system is engaged in information acquisition (receiving positional information from satellites) and performing at a high level of automation (level 10). Information acquisition by technology is analogous to sensory perception in humans. Our user decides to input a destination (more information is acquired, but at a much lower level of automation: (1) and the system computes an optimal path of travel (information analysis, similar to working memory in humans, occurs at level 7 of automation). The traveler approves of a route suggested by the system and the GPS unit provides route guidance. The above example is open to interpretation. For example, some GPS units may offer one suggestion for path of travel, others may offer several. By automating component processes of wayfinding (e.g., keeping track of position and heading), the mental workload of the traveler is reduced. Combining auto-mation with assistive navigational aids can result in improved performance, reduced mental workload, and/or greater feelings of safety and satisfaction. More research is needed to determine how the different types and levels of automation can affect navi-gating with a visual impairment. Further, there is a need for research investigating the aspects of how to optimally substitute sensory modalities, translate sensory information, and represent information in a multimodal way [36]. There is also a need for research investigating how information can be input into navigational systems via multimodal interaction.

4.3 Further Design Considerations

Considerations for the design of assistive navigational aids must take into account the population for which the device is being developed. An audible GPS unit would not benefit someone who is deaf and a visual display would not be advantageous, or usable, for someone who is completely blind. Despite a wide range of disabilities and functioning sensory systems, there are several design characteristics that have been identified as being beneficial for everyone [3]. First, a navigation system should be able to identify changes in the environment and notify the user. Changes in the envi-ronment can be incorporated via software updates or camera-based hardware coupled with an AI. A second consideration for device design is the need to reduce the number of devices people with a visual impairment have to carry in order to accom-modate for having an impairment. One method for ameliorating the problem is to incorporate new technologies into existing devices that people with a visual impair-ment are already carrying (e.g., smartphones). Furthermore, navigational aids, or any assistive device, should not increase the social stigma of having a disability by drawing unwanted attention [38]. Devices should be customizable; as a user's needs change (e.g., deteriorating vision) the device can continue to be used as an aid without having to be replaced or a having to learn a new device. Finally, incorpo-rating multimodal interaction into assistive devices, particularly navigational aids, is a critical step toward ensuring that these devices remain useful, usable, and enjoyable.

4.4 Accommodating for Aging, Multiple Impairments, Concomitant Medical Conditions

Many of the studies involving sensory substitution and multimodal interfaces involve young adults with no reported physical or mental disabilities [31–34]. For the purposes of this discussion, we have focused on visual impairments and presumed that limited or no vision was the only difference between people with a visual impairment and people without a disability. However, a visual impairment is oftentimes the result of a concom-itant medical condition (e.g., diabetic retinopathy, stroke) that can further impair some-one's ability to navigate, be mobile, and/or use technological aids. The vast majority of people with a visual impairment are not born with a disability; indeed, the opposite is true. Vision loss is mostly seen in adults older than 50 years of age. Aging can result in decrements in cognitive and physical ability. As such, hearing loss often occurs with vision loss and it is not uncommon for a visual impairment to develop alongside a tactile impairment. In no other population is the necessity of having multimodal technologies more apparent.

4.5 Customization to Account for Individual Differences

As mentioned in Sect. 4.3, navigational technologies should be customizable. This is not just to account for individual differences in sensory modalities, but also user preferences. Assistive technologies are abandoned for numerous reasons, even if a benefit is still provided through use of the technology [39–41]. Technological devices that allow for a desirable degree of individual customization, including the ability to operate the device via multimodal means, are likely to be more useful and desirable to users [42].

4.6 Advances in Multimodal Technology Can Benefit Us All

We have focused on how sensory substation and multimodal interaction have been employed in navigational aids for people with a visual impairment; however, technologies and environments that are more accessible for those with a disability are accessible for everyone. Multimodal interaction allows for a greater degree of interaction, freedom of choice, and user preference when interacting with a system. More research is needed in every aspect of multimodal interfaces; however, there is a need for such research with regard to individuals with a physical or cognitive impairment.

Acknowledgements. We extend our gratitude to Brian Michaels of Florida Blind Services and the staff of Lighthouse Central Florida for their assistance with understanding the wayfinding issues faced by people who have a visual impairment. Our thanks go to Jerry Aubert (UCF College of Medicine), Michael Judith (Innovative Space Technologies, LLC), David Metcalf (UCF Institute for Simulation and Training), and the Mixed Emerging Technology Integration Lab at the Institute for Simulation and Training. We are grateful for their support.

References

1. Garmin. http://www.garmin.com/en-US
2. Consumer Reports. http://www.consumerreports.org/cro/magazine/2015/04/cars-that-can-save-your-life/index.htm
3. Quinones, P.A., Greene, T., Yang, R., Newman, M.: Supporting visually impaired navigation: a needs-finding study. In: CHI 2011 Extended Abstracts on Human Factors in Computing Systems, pp. 1645–1650. ACM (2011)
4. Thinus-Blanc, C., Gaunet, F.: Representation of space in blind persons: vision as a spatial sense? Psych bull **121**(1), 20 (1997)
5. Rieser, J.J., Guth, D.A., Hill, E.W.: Mental processes mediating independent travel: implications for orientation and mobility. Vis. Impair Blindness **76**, 213–218 (1982)
6. Sarter, N.: Multiple-resource theory as a basis for multimodal interface design: Success stories, qualifications, and research needs. In: Attention Theory Practice, pp. 187–195 (2006)

7. Hancock, P.A., Oron-Gilad, T., Szalma, J.L.: Elaborations of the multiple-resource theory of attention. In: Kramer, A.F., Wiegmann, D.A.K. (eds.) Attention: From Theory to Practice, pp. 45–56 (2006)
8. Frank, A.U., Mark, D.M: Language issues for geographical information systems (1991)
9. Brabyn, J.: A Review of Mobility Aids and Means of Assessment. Martinus Nijhoff, Boston (1985)
10. Kunimi, M., Kojima, H.: The effects of processing speed and memory span on working memory. GeroPsych J. Gerontopsychology Geriatr. Psychiatry 27(3), 109 (2014)
11. Mangione, C.M., Phillips, R.S., Seddon, J.M., Lawrence, M.G., Cook, E.F., Dailey, R., Goldman, L.: Development of the 'Activities of Daily Vision Scale': a measure of visual functional status. Med. Care, 1111–1126 (1992)
12. Kane, S.K., Jayant, C., Wobbrock, J.O., Ladner, R.E.: Freedom to roam: a study of mobile device adoption and accessibility for people with visual and motor disabilities. In: Proceedings of the 11th International ACM SIGACCESS Conference on Computers and Accessibility, pp. 115–122. ACM (2009)
13. Blasch, B.B., Welsh, R.L., Wiener, W.R.: Foundations of Orientation and Mobility, 2nd edn. AFB Press, New York (1997)
14. Blasch, B., Stuckey, K.: Accessibility and mobility of persons who are visually impaired: a historical analysis. J. Vis. Impairment Blindness (JVIB), 89(5) (1995)
15. Giudice, N.A., Legge, G.E.: Blind navigation and the role of technology. Eng. handb. smart technol. aging disabil. independence, 479–500 (2008)
16. Sound Foresight. http://www.soundforesight.co.uk/
17. Perceptual alternatives. http://www.sonicpathfinder.org/
18. Williams, M.A., Hurst, A., Kane, S.K.: Pray before you step out: describing personal and situational blind navigation behaviors. In: Proceedings of the 15th International ACM SIGACCESS Conference on Computers and Accessibility, p. 28. ACM, October 2013
19. Nurion-Raycal. http://www.nurion.net/LC.html
20. Wicab. http://www.wicab.com/
21. Bach-Y-Rita, P.: Brain Mechanisms in Sensory Substitutions. Academic Press, New York (1972)
22. Bach-y-Rita, P., Tyler, M.E., Kaczmarek, K.A.: Seeing with the brain. Int. J. Hum. Comput. INTERACT. 15(2), 285–295 (2003)
23. Novich, S.D., Eagleman, D.M.: A vibrotactile sensory substitution device for the deaf and profoundly hearing impaired. In: Haptics Symposium (HAPTICS), p. 1. IEEE, February 2014
24. Crandall, W., Brabyn, J., Bentzen, B.L., Myers, L.: Remote infrared signage evaluation for transit stations and intersections. J. Rehab. Res. Devel. 36(4), 341–355 (1999)
25. CINVESTAV. http://www.cinvestav.mx/
26. Sendero. http://www.senderogroup.com/
27. Blindsquare. http://blindsquare.com/
28. TapTapSee. http://www.taptapseeapp.com/
29. Be My Eyes. http://www.bemyeyes.org/
30. Gallo, P., Tinnirello, I., Giarré, L., Garlisi, D., Croce, D., Fagiolini, A.: ARIANNA: pAth recognition for indoor assisted navigation with augmented perception (2013). arXiv preprint arXiv:1312.3724
31. Merlo, J.L., Terrence, P.I., Stafford, S., Gilson, R., Hancock, P.A., Redden, E.S., White, T.L.: Communicating through the use of vibrotactile displays for dismounted and mounted soldiers (2006)

32. Merlo, J.L., Stafford, S., Gilson, R., Hancock, P.A.: The effects of physiological stress on tactile communication. In: Proceedings of the Human Factors and Ergonomics Society Annual Meeting, vol. 50, No. 16, pp. 1562–1566. Sage Publications, October 2006

33. Faugloire, E., Lejeune, L.: Evaluation of heading performance with vibrotactile guidance: The benefits of information–movement coupling compared with spatial language. J. Exp. Psychol. Appl. **20**(4), 397 (2014)

34. van Erp, J.B., van Veen, H.A., Jansen, C., Dobbins, T.: Waypoint navigation with a vibrotactile waist belt. ACM Trans. Appl. Percept. (TAP) **2**(2), 106–117 (2005)

35. Machida, T., Dim, N.K., Ren, X.: Suitable body parts for vibration feedback in walking navigation systems. In: Proceedings of the Third International Symposium of Chinese CHI on ZZZ, pp. 32–36. ACM, April 2015

36. Fujimoto, E., Turk, M.: Non-visual navigation using combined audio music and haptic cues. In: Proceedings of the 16th International Conference on Multimodal Interaction, pp. 411–418. ACM, November 2014

37. Parasuraman, R., Sheridan, T.B., Wickens, C.D.: A model for types and levels of human interaction with automation. IEEE Trans. Syst. Man Cybern. Part A Syst. Hum. **30**(3), 286–297 (2000)

38. Shinohara, K., Wobbrock, J.O.: In the shadow of misperception: assistive technology use and social interactions. In: CHI 2011 - SIGCHI Conference on Human Factors in Computing Systems, pp. 705–714 (2011)

39. Riemer-Reiss, M.L., Wacker, R.R.: Factors associated with assistive technology discontinuance among individuals with disabilities. J. Rehabil. **66**(3), 44 (2000)

40. Jutai, J., Day, H.: Psychosocial impact of assistive devices scale (PIADS). Technol. Disabil. **14**(3), 107–111 (2002)

41. Federici, S., Borsci, S.: The use and non-use of assistive technology in Italy: preliminary data. In: 11th AAATE Conference: Everyday Technology for Independence and Care. (2011)

42. Oviatt, S.: Multimodal interfaces. Hum. Comput. Interact. Handb. Fundam. Evolving Technol. Emerg. Appl. **14**, 286–304 (2003). Chicago

A Systems Approach for Augmented Reality Design

Andrea K. Webb(✉), Emily C. Vincent, Pooja Patnaik, and Jana L. Schwartz

Draper, Cambridge, MA, USA
{awebb,evincent,ppatnaik,jana}@draper.com

Abstract. Effective ways of presenting digital data are needed to augment a user's experience in the real world without distracting or overloading them. We propose a system of systems approach for the design, development, and evaluation of information presentation devices, particularly augmented reality devices. We developed an evaluation environment that enables the synchronized presentation of multimodal stimuli and collection of user responses in an immersive environment. We leveraged visual, audio, thermal, and tactile information presentation modalities during a navigation and threat identification task. Twelve participants completed the task while response time and accuracy data were collected. Results indicated variability among devices and pairs of devices, and suggested that information presented by some pairs of devices was more effective and easily acted upon than that presented by others. The results of this work provided important guidance regarding future design decisions and suggest the utility of our system of systems approach. Implications and future directions are discussed.

Keywords: Augmented reality · Situation awareness · System of systems · Immersive environment

1 Introduction

We are surrounded by digital data and are faced with challenges in how to best acknowledge and use that data. Too much data or conflicting/confusing data has far-reaching implications and may lead to events such as friendly fire incidents, clinical errors (e.g., operating on the wrong body part or side), or civilian accidents (e.g., car accidents because of cell phone distractions). What is needed is a way to effectively present digital information that augments what the user experiences in the real world without distracting or overloading the user or making their task more difficult.

In order to address these types of challenges, a multidisciplinary and multifaceted approach is needed. The domain of Human Systems Technology requires a spectrum of user modeling, observation, and measurement techniques. We select techniques spanning from expert assessment through rigorous human subjects testing in order to meet the needs of a particular design challenge. Both ends of this spectrum have strengths and weaknesses: expert judgment is an interpolation based on experience and is thus limited in scope; human subjects testing – particularly in the applied research space – has come under scrutiny due to difficulties in reproducing results [1]. Taken together, these challenges point to the need for a different approach to leverage expert or user response to guide design decisions.

© Springer International Publishing Switzerland 2016
D.D. Schmorrow and C.M. Fidopiastis (Eds.): AC 2016, Part II, LNAI 9744, pp. 382–389, 2016.
DOI: 10.1007/978-3-319-39952-2_37

There are a number of systems engineering approaches that can help guide design decisions. There are several systems analysis tools and techniques that can be applied across the spectrum of design maturity [2]. However, both modeling and measurement are less mature for human-in-the-loop systems. Current laboratory measures and methods largely remove technology from its intended environment. This is problematic because out of context performance data tends to provide minimal design insight. Approaches we have leveraged to include and assess context include testing a single design across a number of user cases [3]; this approach provides robust findings but can be expensive and time consuming. Another approach is to measure multiple channels of data continuously during completion of a task, rather than relying solely on pre/post assessments [4]. An additional challenge is that we wish to provide feedback at the speed of design (e.g., over days), as opposed to the speed of academic publication (e.g., months or years).

How then do we develop an evaluation environment to support the design and development of a system of novel wearables, with the purpose of providing the user with a sense of immersive situation awareness (SA)? Our initial operational requirements were to measure situation awareness as a function of presentation and context. We define SA to be measured by accuracy moderated by response time, and our goal is to develop designs to maximize SA.

In order to ground our research in a specific use case with real-world implications, we selected a ground infiltration mission as our primary concept of operations. These users have several tasks they are trying to do concurrently while navigating their mission (e.g., watching for hazards, communicating with other team members). They have a number of tools available to them, such as handheld devices for navigation and monitoring, but they are often challenged to maintain a balance of heads down and heads up time to successfully execute their mission.

Our broader interest is to provide an evaluation solution that is useful and cost effective for the crowded small business and start-up space in augmented reality, university researchers, and the simulation and test community. This paper details the first implementation of our approach and provides important guidance for future revisions.

2   Method

2.1   Participants

Participants were 12 Draper employees. Of these, 8 (67 %) were male and 4 (33 %) were female. Participant age ranged between 23 and 52 ($M = 34.33$, $SD = 9.38$). Due to data collection issues, not all participants experienced all stimulus conditions. As such, statistical analysis was not performed; summary measures are reported below.

2.2   Testing Environment

We have developed a lab for the rapid design and evaluation of directed attention and performance augmentation devices that can be tested against metrics relevant in the operational space (accuracy, response time, psychophysiological response). The physical environment is comprised of eight identical ambient presentation panels, each of which can present local audio and visual stimuli. The baseline configuration for the panels is a uniform closed shape (an octagon), but the layout is dynamically configurable to provide a variety of orientations. This modular design provides flexibility for testing numerous devices and configurations with tasks of various degrees of flexibility and noise. Its scalability (from 1:8 or more panels) allows for enhancement with minimal added investment, using the same presentation and data collection infrastructure.

The physical octagon environment is grounded in a lab-centered, lab-fixed coordinate system. All lab infrastructure and all hardware units under test are referenced to this 3D coordinate space. Communication among lab and test devices, including timing synchronization, high level commands, and interdevice messaging, is enabled by the Draper Network Architecture for Java software framework (DNA4J). DNA4J is a pure Java solution enabling development on any platform with support for Java 1.6 or later. It has been tested on Windows, Linux, OSX, and also supports the Raspberry PI Raspian OS.

In addition to uniform presentation of lab and digital stimuli, the octagon further enables concurrent recording of user response. Each panel is equipped with a motion capture camera that can capture the 3D position of multiple points in a scene. To date we have collected rigid body data on the user's head, torso, and handheld devices. The DNA4J framework further enables time synchronized collection of task and user responses.

2.3   Test Devices

We performed an integrated data collection that leveraged four different input devices: augmented reality glasses that included a heads-up display for presentation of visual information, a wrist-worn thermal device for presentation of warm and cool temperatures, standard earbuds for presentation of audio information, and a chest-worn torque tactile device (TTD) that used torque for presentation of information. We also leveraged a handheld Android phone for presentation of visual information. Participants wore each device singly (Android handheld, AR glasses, thermal, audio, TTD) and in pairs (e.g., AR + TTD, thermal + audio, AR + Android handheld) for the trials discussed below.

2.4   Test Protocol

Participants were asked to complete a navigation and threat identification task in the octagon environment (see Fig. 1). Participants were presented with black and yellow circles on the handheld Android device. Participants were instructed to act upon the yellow circles by pressing the target button on the handheld device (see Fig. 2). After some trials, a threat was signaled on one of the octagon panels (northwest, southwest, southeast, northeast). There was no visual threat actually presented on the octagon panel. Participants were presented with a cue on each device or pair of devices signaling them to which panel to turn to then acknowledge the threat. For example, if the threat was on the southeast panel, the AR glasses would display an arrow pointing in the southeast direction, and the handheld Android device would present a symbol on the southeast panel on the display. Similarly, if thermal and TTD were paired, the thermal device would present a warm temperature, and the TTD would send signals to nudge the participant to the southeast panel. Participants completed 4 trials per device and device pairing (44 trials total) in the context condition in which a threat always appeared after a yellow circle, and 44 trials in the no context condition in which a threat could appear after a yellow or black circle. Response time and accuracy was assessed for each trial.

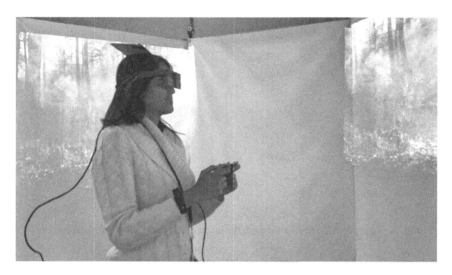

Fig. 1. The octagon environment

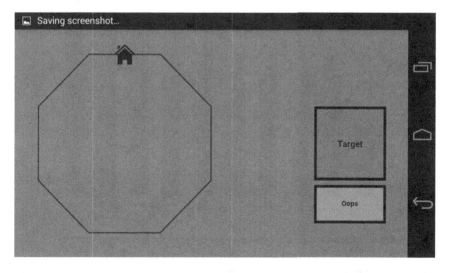

Fig. 2. Android handheld device interface for the navigation and threat identification task

3 Results

Response time and accuracy were assessed for each of the devices and pairs of devices. Response time data for trials where the threat was correctly localized are presented in Fig. 3, and accuracy data are presented in Fig. 4.

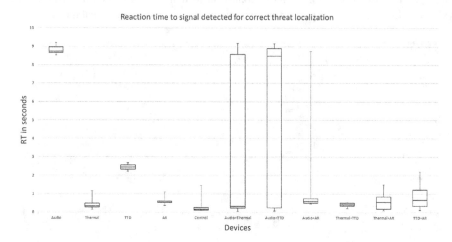

Fig. 3. Reaction time results for each device and pairs of devices for correct trials

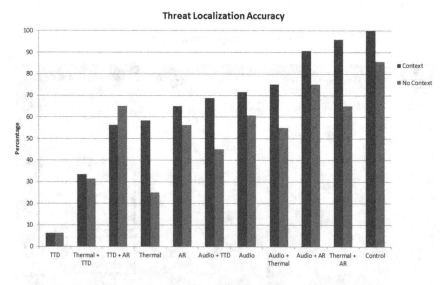

Fig. 4. Threat localization accuracy for each device and pairs of devices

It can be seen in these plots that there was a large amount of variability across devices – it was much easier to correctly detect a threat with cues from some of the devices (i.e., Android handheld and AR glasses) and pairs of devices (i.e., AR glasses + thermal, audio + AR) than it was for other devices (i.e., TTD). It also can be seen that response times were much longer for some devices (i.e., audio) than for others (i.e., AR). An examination of participant self-report responses and a close examination of the cues indicated that the audio cues took longer to complete than did the cues from other devices, and participants would wait until completion of the presentation before indicating the threat location. Participant self-report data also revealed that threat localization cues were easiest to detect with the AR glasses and Android handheld, whereas cues were most difficult to detect with the thermal, TTD, and audio devices. These self-report results are not unexpected and confirm the need to identify intuitive cues or provide learning trials (i.e., if using thermal cues, participants would need time to learn that cold = left, and hot = right). Despite the differences in response time and accuracy across devices and pairs of devices, the results were important for guiding future design decisions, as discussed below.

4 Discussion

Through our current work, we have come to believe that a true augmented reality system will encompass more than a set of AR goggles. In order to augment a human in a way that will be intuitive and actionable, we must move beyond focus on the visual and include multiple sensory modalities. This implies a focus on design of systems of systems that must work in synchronization across a user's senses. In order to achieve this tight synchronization we have found that applying a systems engineering lens enables us to better examine the interactions and dependencies between different display systems.

Our systems engineering approach led us to start building our test environment at the beginning of the project, co-incident with designing our system of displays. Building a test environment from scratch had a number of benefits for our team. We had full control of the system, which enabled us to make it ideal for the scenarios we were testing. It was large enough to block out the rest of the room and allow the participant to move around in which, when combined with 360 degrees of projection surface, provided enough of an immersive environment for the participant to accept it as "reality." Creating an acceptable "reality" against which to overlay augmentation is crucial for any augmented reality testing endeavor.

We did find it was a significant effort to build a 360 degree immersive environment from scratch. While the octagon that we built meets our needs and was on the whole less expensive than buying a CAVE system, there are some downsides to its design. It is less clean/professional looking and it took more time and labor on our end. However, the Octagon has the added bonus of flexible configuration. As noted previously, it does not need to remain in an octagon formation, and our future plans involve using those panels in different configurations.

We also found that while our systems approach recognized extensibility and a "system of systems" concept, our software implementation of the messaging between systems had to undergo multiple iterations to meet this goal. Our initial implementation had each device implementing its own messaging scheme. This introduced a significant burden to introducing new devices, which was one of the primary goals of this work. As such, we iterated on this software infrastructure in order to reduce the barrier to entry to an acceptably small level of effort that did not require expert support.

Through our desire to truly compare each device on a level playing field, we designed a single information scenario that all devices needed to display. This caused our results to show that some devices had better performance than others. However, we believe that this was due to not designing for each devices' specific strengths. We have begun to explore the differences in information type and style – such as how suddenly the information is available and how quickly the user needs to be aware of and react to that data. The goal for a future experiment phase is to create a holistic system design where each device plays to its strengths, which we recommend as an approach to AR systems.

5   Path Forward

There are a number of goals for our future work in this area. Our high level goal is to identify good combinations of systems that enable augmented reality in multiple fielded scenarios, ranging from the battlefield to the operating room to the analyst workstation. Our test environment approach needs to enable us to quickly integrate new display systems as they become available and to quickly configure and run tests on multiple combinations of new and existing systems. To this end, we plan to continue to build flexibility and extensibility into our software framework. This includes well documented APIs, generalizable messaging, and a general focus on adding extensibility to the software architecture. One specific action we are undertaking is to ensure that our messaging infrastructure sends information or data rather than commands on how to display that information. This will enable each device to make decisions on how best to display information and will de-centralize the intelligence of the system, making it easier to integrate new components without requiring changes in the core software.

We also have considered increasing the immersiveness of the testing environment, in order to increase the user acceptance of the "reality" with which our devices are augmented. Additional study is needed to determine how the immersion of our environment impacts the experimental results and generalizability of findings to the real world. Some augments to the immersiveness that we've considered are: full 360 degree motion environment though a gaming engine such as Unity, adding a 360 degree treadmill to enable participant movement, ambient sound, and ambient thermal. Future work will explore how close to a fully enclosed CAVE the environment needs to be or if a minimalist approach produces the same results.

Another approach to increasing the immersiveness of the test environment is to open up the octagon. The modularity of the octagon enables multiple configurations – our next planned experiment involves using a subset of the 8 panels to create a 180 degree environment that will simulate a driving scenario. We also have planned to break individual panels out and place them in an actual physical environment – such as a house or obstacle course – so that we can combine physical features and rooms with virtualized panels, similar to a haunted house experience.

Perhaps most importantly, we plan to bring new devices into our system of augmented reality devices and test environment. We are exploring multiple haptic feedback systems, such as vibrotactile boots, belts, and a headband. We also have started acquiring multiple brands of AR goggles and smart glasses. We continue to explore other sensory modalities that could be applicable, such as smell and taste. Lastly, we want to expand our testing to include immersive user input devices – devices that enable the user to communicate back to the system of systems in a manner that does not distract them from or interrupt their physical world task. These may initially include gesture, through use of hardware such as data gloves or vision, physical controls such as buttons, knobs, and touchscreens, implicit interactions such as gaze or head movement, and voice control, both audible and sub-vocal. We believe that immersing the user in physical and digital information is not enough to keep them from being heads down in their technology. We must also free them from the burden of inputting data into their augmentation systems. Taken together, these future research plans will provide a rich set of data and design guidelines that can be used by future developers of augmented reality devices and systems.

References

1. Collins, F.S., Tabak, L.A.: NIH Plans to enhance reproducibility. Nature **505**, 612–613 (2014)
2. Borer, N.K., Odegard, R.G., Schwartz, J.L., Arruda, J.R.: A unified framework for capturing concept development methods. In: Proceedings of the IEEE Aerospace Conference, Big Sky, Montana (2009)
3. Martin, D.J., Martin, J.Z., Webb, A.K., Horgan, A.J., Marchak, F.M.: Malintent Detection in Primary Screening Utilizing Noncontact Sensor Technology (2016, Manuscript in preparation)
4. Poore, J.C., Webb, A.K., Cunha, M.G., Mariano, L.J., Chappell, D.T., Coskren, M.R., Schwartz, J.L.: Operationalizing engagement as coherence to context: a cohesive physiological measurement approach for human computer interaction. IEEE T. Affect. Comput. (in press)

Social Cognition

Modeling of Social Media Behaviors
Using Only Account Metadata

Fernanda Carapinha[1], John Khoury[2], Shai Neumann[2],
Monte Hancock[1(✉)], Federico Calderon[1], Mendi Drayton[1],
Arvil Easter[1], Edward Stapleton[1], Alexander Vazquez[1],
and David Woolfolk[1]

[1] 4Digital, Los Angeles, USA
practicaldatamining@gmail.com
[2] Eastern Florida State College, Cocoa, USA

Abstract. Applications in Augmented Cognition can be hampered by obstacles to the effective instrumentation of the data space, making the collection of informative feature data difficult. These obstacles usually arise from technical limitations, but can also be present due to methodological and legal considerations. We address a specific instance of the difficulty of characterizing a complex behavior space under legally constrained data collection: the instrumentation of social media platforms, where privacy, policy, and marketing considerations can severely hamper 3rd-party data collection activities. This paper documents our constrained empirical analysis and characterization of the behaviors of Twitter account-holders from their account metadata alone. The characterization is performed by coding user account data as feature vectors in a low-dimensional Euclidean space, then applying parametric and non-parametric methods to the resulting empirical distribution. Suggestions for future work are offered.

Keywords: Twitter · Social media · Behavior modeling · Metadata

1 Background

Social Media is entrenched in the human psyche across the globe. Individuals feel its impact in relationships, knowledge, while businesses cite its effectiveness in brand management, public relations, and product promotion. Even government sees the value in utilizing social media to reach its citizens and promote policy as well as provide alerts and notifications in case of emergencies. As a result, social media has become a lucrative marketing and sales channel for businesses. It offers sellers immediate access to a demographically diverse, socially active, and relatively affluent international market. They interconnect users in social cliques, where buying and product experiences are shared, occasionally resulting in geometric growth of product awareness ("going viral") [1].

As technology progresses, how can users of this medium ensure their ROI? Twitter has been transformed from a personal microblogging site to a robust information portal. It has become a defacto media channel, and as such is concerned that its audience is engaged and authentic. These concerns are, however, not as easily determined as in

© Springer International Publishing Switzerland 2016
D.D. Schmorrow and C.M. Fidopiastis (Eds.): AC 2016, Part II, LNAI 9744, pp. 393–401, 2016.
DOI: 10.1007/978-3-319-39952-2_38

years past. Analyzing social media accounts' metadata can unlock clues to an its user authenticity. Does the account belong to active, passive, or anomalous users? These statuses are important to entities wishing to fully leverage the capabilities promised by Twitter's technology. After all, the Twittersphere is populated by countless users and the accuracy of their information, and identification provide real incentives for personal, economic and even political ends. Conversely, inaccurate identification and targeting can place the user at risk or at the very least exposed to unintended consequences.

The design of a reliable method of identification will ensure conditions are optimal to offer interested parties greater opportunity for the monetization of social media data, having overcome the present technical decision-theoretic challenges:

1. There are billions of individual social media accounts
2. Privacy controls limit access to the most informative data elements
3. Technology has reached a level where automated account-holders can impersonate human users, and these constitute a growing proportion of account-holders

2   Data

A large number of fields are available for collection via the Twitter API (Application Program Interface) and they are divided into five object classes. Those object classes are; Users, Tweets, Entities, Entities in Objects, and Places [2]. Due to the focus of this research on user metadata the APIs reviewed were almost exclusively from the "User" object class. Information from the Twitter Developer API guide was used to identify a number of metadata categories for the research team to collect and use in the Twitter-space behavioral data analysis. A bot program was written to collect the data for later inspection and calculations. The sample size for this research was 100,001 users and spanned 13 direct and 3 calculated data fields.

Each Twitter user has a unique 64 bit integer allocated to them for a user identifier, the field in the API is designated "id" and would be analogous to a Primary or Unique Key from a relational database. The id field is essential in separating information about one user from that of another. All the other user object data fields are related back to this unique identifier. In order to better understand these relationships and the possibilities therein, the following definitions provide the field identifiers.

Twitter API Fields Utilized.

1. id – The unique/primary identifier for the user (64 bit integer).
2. created_at – UTC date and time of the initial user creation.
3. default_profile – true/false identifier for whether the user has altered the default theme or background.
4. default_profile_image – true/false identifier for whether the user has replaced the default user avatar.
5. favorites_count – total lifetime number of tweets the user has favorited.
6. followers_count – total number of other users following that unique user.
7. friends_count – total number of users the user is following.

8. location – user provided location, not always accurate (e.g. Mars, etc.).
9. protected – indicates if the user's tweets are protected (only viewable by their followers).
10. statuses_count – total number of tweets sent by the user.
11. time_zone – user defined time zone, not always accurate (e.g. "Eastern Time (US & Canada)").
12. utc_offset – the offset from GMT/UTC described in seconds.
13. verified – user identity has been verified by Twitter (e.g. Joe Actor might be verified as being the real celebrity and not an impersonator).

3 Methodology

The purpose of this paper is to characterize categories of user behavior in communication via tweeting as these are reflected in the metadata only: no tweet content. Data mining technology is used with the aid of statistical methods: exploratory data analysis, cluster analysis, factor analysis, multiple regression, and multinomial logistic regression.

Given 19 variables and 100001 cases, various approaches were used to study the data. The data included both categorical and quantitative variables.

Data cleaning was performed prior to analysis. Evidence of corrupt data was found in the case of one of the features that involved ratio calculations. It appeared that the formula was not executed appropriately to all cases. After corrections were applied, the data set was reexamined and judged to be ready for analysis. There were no missing values in the data set. In addition, issues of division by zero or undefined non-linear transformations of some features were addressed prior to analysis.

In order to visualize the data, a number of graphs were investigated, such as histograms, scatter plots, box plots, and stem and leaf displays.

Descriptive statistics were obtained for each feature, including 5 number summary, outliers were identified.

The correlation among variables were calculated and analyzed.

Using SPSS, variable reduction techniques were applied to the original data, showing variable importance, leading to a smaller number of variables to be used in the two-step clustering on SPSS.

In total, two clustering techniques were applied to the data. A two-step clustering run on SPSS revealed primary clusters, including an order of importance of the variables. Consistent with this clustering technique, a multinomial logistic regression was run on SPSS to check accuracy of cluster assignment. Subsequent to the identification of primary clusters, two additional iterations for each cluster were performed using the same two-step clustering method. A second clustering technique created 200 clusters using a dedicated clustering program. Those 200 clusters were examined for distinctive characteristics with particular attention paid to small clusters involving high z scores in a number of features.

4 Analysis

The data set was examined at different levels. One dimensional review included a time series of account creation. It appears to reveal the period when Twitter actually took off and grew exponentially as a platform. That date and time corresponds to the South by South West Interactive conference in March 2007, some 234 days after the first account of the data set was created in July 2006. The distribution suggests that once the product reached a certain level of traction, rates of account creation may have been associated with world events [3].

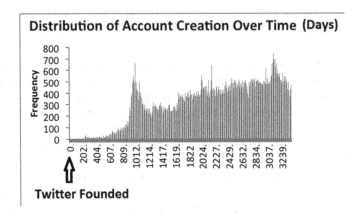

Two dimensional review of the data included creation of the correlation matrix (immediately below) and examination of scatter plots. Features that exhibited high correlation were later examined in the context of variable reduction.

	1-UP IDX	TwitterUserId	Day_Num	DefaultProfile	DefaultProfileImage	FavoritesCount	FollowersCount	FriendsCount	ProtectedUser	StatusesCount	TimeZone	UtcOffset	VerifiedUser
1-UP IDX	1.00												
TwitterUserId	0.99	1.00											
Day_Num	0.97	0.94	1.00										
DefaultProfile	0.15	0.14	0.15	1.00									
DefaultProfileImage	0.04	0.03	0.04	0.25	1.00								
FavoritesCount	-0.01	-0.01	-0.01	-0.03	-0.03	1.00							
FollowersCount	-0.01	-0.01	-0.01	-0.01	-0.01	0.02	1.00						
FriendsCount	0.00	0.00	0.00	-0.05	-0.03	0.07	0.16	1.00					
ProtectedUser	0.03	0.03	0.04	0.00	0.01	-0.02	-0.01	-0.04	1.00				
StatusesCount	-0.03	-0.03	-0.03	-0.08	-0.05	0.18	0.03	0.17	-0.04	1.00			
TimeZone	0.10	0.09	0.09	-0.04	-0.06	-0.02	0.01	0.08	0.00	0.02	1.00		
UtcOffset	0.16	0.15	0.15	0.13	0.05	-0.03	0.00	0.04	-0.01	-0.02	0.84	1.00	
VerifiedUser	-0.04	-0.04	-0.04	-0.03	-0.01	0.03	0.08	0.08	-0.02	0.02	-0.01	-0.03	1.00

The scatter plot for StatusesCount vs followers indicates that in a small number of cases accounts produce a lot of tweets and yet have few followers, while a small number of twitter accounts have many followers but they produce a small number of tweets.

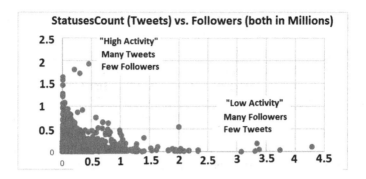

Similarly, the scatter plot for StatusesCount vs friends indicates the same phenomenon.

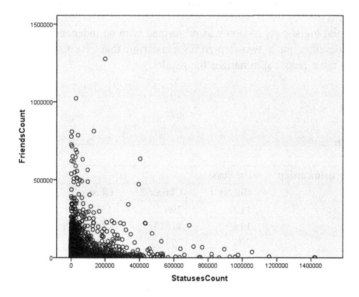

Another scatter plot that exhibited a noticeable characteristic was the "Followers-Favorites" ratio vs "Friends-Favorites" ratio. Multidimensional analysis was performed using SPSS and a dedicated clustering program. The Two Step Cluster Analysis procedure was used as an exploratory tool in order to reveal grouping (or clusters) within a large data set containing 23 variables and 100001 cases. The clusters were based on both categorical and continuous variables.

The following Five variables were selected as *Categorical:*

Default Profile; Default Profile image; Protected User; Verified User; Duplicates

The following seven variables were selected as *Continuous:*

Favorites Count; Epoch Time; Followers Friends Ratio KGH; Status Count; Friends Favorites Ratio KHF; Location_ Symbol; Friends Count

Factor Analysis and Principal Cluster Analysis, PCA, were used in order to reduce the Dimension of the space from 23 to 12. The number of clusters was selected automatically by the procedure, based on Schwartz's Bayesian Criterion. Then, each of the clusters were sub-clustered by repeating the two step clustering procedure.

The Likelihood Distance measure, which assumes that variables in the cluster are independent, was used. Continuous variables are assumed to have a Gaussian distribution and each categorical variable was assumed to have a multinomial distribution. However, the procedure is fairly robust to departures from both assumptions of independence and normality.

A model summary was created along with a fair cluster quality. The model showed 12 variables and 100001 cases were valid and no missing data. A Pie Chart revealed the percentages of cases in each cluster, along with a table showing the size of the smallest and largest cluster. Clusters profiles, centroids of each cluster, show clusters are well separated.

Multinomial logistic regression was performed with an independent variable being the cluster identified in a two-step SPSS clustering that resulted in three primary clusters. The table below summarizes the results

5   Results

Classification

Actual cluster membership	Predicted			
	Cluster 1	Cluster 2	Cluster 3	Percent correct
Cluster 1	1127	796	1333	34.6 %
Cluster 2	174	42873	47	99.5 %
Cluster 3	206	228	53217	99.2 %
Overall percentage	1.5 %	43.9 %	54.6 %	97.2 %

The results indicate that if a data point belongs to clusters 2 or 3, there is better than 99 % probability that the multinomial logistic regression procedure would correctly identify the data point as belonging to the correct cluster. If the data point belonged to cluster 1, which was the smallest cluster, there was only slightly more than one in three chance the multinomial logistic regression would identify the data point correctly. The overall percent accuracy from this perspective is 97.2 %. From another perspective, numbers in this table may be used to derive estimates of conditional probabilities of belonging to a cluster given a multinomial logistic regression prediction of belonging to a specific cluster. The results are as follows: P (belonging to cluster 1 given multinomial logistic regression predicts data point belongs to cluster 1) = 74.8 %, P (belonging to cluster 2 given multinomial logistic regression predicts data point belongs to cluster 2) = 97.7 %, P (belonging to cluster 3 given multinomial logistic regression predicts data point belongs to cluster 3) = 97.5 %. This seems to indicate that the multinomial logistic regression performs well in this context and can be used to validate cluster assignments. Numbers appear to confirm that clusters might be meaningful in this feature space.

Below is an oblique ortho-projection of the clustered account metadata. Notice the presence of a variety of coherent subpopulations. These correspond to the levels of activity described in the semantic:

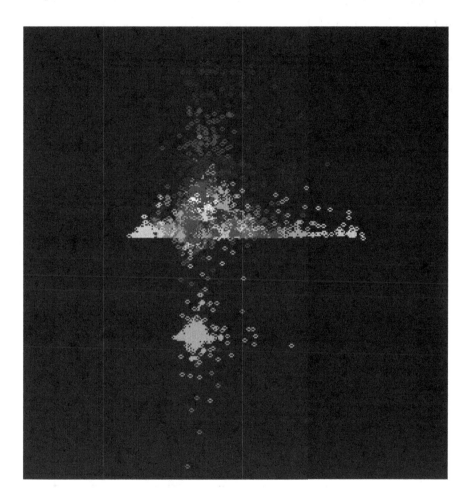

The charts below illustrate the sub-clustering of the primary cluster that contained 55566 cases leading to two sub-clusters, one that contains 45413 cases, the other 10153 cases.

Cluster Quality

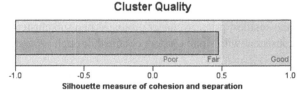

The Figure below shows Cluster profiles: the cells show different distributions of features within a single cluster for each varia

Additional Comments: In the future, we should collect more refined information on other properties of the variables with additional attributes, if available.

Other approaches could be used such as Simulation, Monte Carlo method, in order to construct some predictive regression model and use it on another more refined data.

200 Clusters: A dedicated clustering program was used to create 200 clusters for the original data set. Clusters varied in terms of number of cases, but of particular interest were small clusters that were characterized by high z-scores in one or more of the features. A number of clusters contained as few as 4 cases out of the 100001 and showed high z scores in a number of specific features. These small clusters represent cases that are far out in multidimensional feature space.

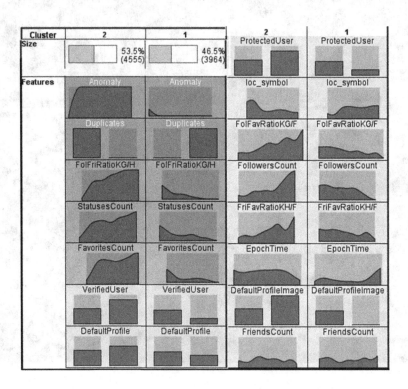

6   Future Work

Similarly, sub clustering of the smallest primary cluster produced two sub clusters, one that contains only 5 cases, consistent with small clusters obtained through separate 200 cluster procedure.

In this paper we presented an initial quantitative analysis based on the behavior of participating social media account users. During the analysis, a bot detection model was incorporated to collect and analyze data in an effort to investigate human and non-human behavior based on a structured framework. In the future, we aim to develop and incorporate prediction algorithms to assess the accuracy, scalability and resiliency of data based on selected features which would measure user's behavior.

References

1. Java, A., Song, X., Finin, T., Tseng, B.: Why we twitter: understanding microblogging usage and communities. In: Proceedings of the 9th WebKDD and 1st SNA-KDD 2007 Workshop on Web Mining and Social Network Analysis, pp. 56–65. ACM, August 2007
2. Twitter. API Overview, Object: Users. Twitter Developers Field Guide, 20 February 2016. https://dev.twitter.com/overview/api/users
3. Mischaud, E.: Twitter: expressions of the whole self. In: An Investigation into User Appropriation of a Web-Based Communications Platform. Media@lse, London (2007). Accessed 20 Oct 2011
4. Aladwani, A.M.: Facilitators, characteristics, and impacts of Twitter use: theoretical analysis and empirical illustration. Int. J. Inf. Manag. 15–25 (2015)
5. Chu, Z., Gianvecchio, S., Wang, H., Jajodia, S.: Detecting automation of Twitter accounts. IEEE Trans. Dependable Secure Comput. 1–14 (2012)
6. Cresci, S., Di Pietro, R., Petrocchi, M., Spognardi, A., Tesconi, M.: Fame for sale: efficient detection of fake Twitter followers. Decis. Support Syst. 56–71 (2015)
7. Ferrarra, E., Varol, O., Davis, C., Menczer, F., Flammini, A.: The Rise of Social Bots. Cornell University, New York (2015)
8. Kang, H., Wang, K., Soukal, D., Behr, F., Zheng, Z.: Large scale bot detection for search engine. In: WWW 2010 Proceedings of the 19th International Conference on World Wide Web, pp. 501–510. ACM, New York (2010)
9. Twitter. API Overview, Object: Users. Twitter Developers Field Guide, 20 February 2016. https://dev.twitter.com/overview/api/users
10. Xiao, C., Freeman, D.M., Hwa, T.: Detecting clusters of fake accounts in online social. In: AISec 2015 Proceedings of the 8th ACM Workshop on Artificial Intelligence and Security, pp. 91–101. ACM, New York (2015)

The Willful Marionette: Modeling Social Cognition Using Gesture-Gesture Interaction Dialogue

Mohammad Mahzoon, Mary Lou Maher[(✉)], Kazjon Grace, Lilla LoCurto,
and Bill Outcault

University of North Carolina at Charlotte, Charlotte, USA
{mmahzoon,m.maher,k.grace,llocurto}@uncc.edu,
loc.out@verizon.net

Abstract. In this paper we describe a cognitive model for provoking gestural dialogue with humans, embodied in an interactive marionette. The cognitive model is a framework for the design and implementation of a gesture to gesture interaction. The marionette *perceives* gestures of humans using a Microsoft Kinect, *reasons* about perceived gestures to determine a response, and then *performs* the selected response gesture. This simple cognitive model: perceive-reason-perform, operates in a social context where humans interact with the marionette. The marionette was built as a 3D replica of a human body. The marionette's responses were designed using interaction design techniques such as body storming, gesture elicitation, and the "Wizard of Oz" method to provoke an emotional response from humans. Several user studies were conducted during and after the design process to guide the design goal of achieving an engaging and provocative interaction. These studies showed that participants were encouraged to engage in a gesture-based dialogue with the marionette, and that they perceived the system to possess a kind of intelligence.

Keywords: Marionette · Gesture · Human-computer interaction

1 Introduction

As studies in cognition shift towards embodiment, researchers are considering the role that interaction with the environment plays in models of cognitive processes (Anderson 2003). According to research in embodied cognition, many cognitive processes are tightly coupled with the way the body interacts with the environment. The development of intelligence in humans depends as much on their interaction with the world in which they are embodied as it does on their individual brains (Anderson 2003). This trend has been reflected in recent research in implementing cognitive models in artificially intelligent systems. Sandini et al. (2007) implemented a kid-sized humanoid robot with 53 degrees of freedom, which could improve its skills through interacting with its environment.

In this paper we describe a cognitive model for a marionette interacting with humans. Our marionette interacts not with the physical world as in Sandini et al. (2007), but with humans in a social context. The marionette's interaction with humans takes the form of

© Springer International Publishing Switzerland 2016
D.D. Schmorrow and C.M. Fidopiastis (Eds.): AC 2016, Part II, LNAI 9744, pp. 402–413, 2016.
DOI: 10.1007/978-3-319-39952-2_39

gesture. The marionette detects human gestures, reasons about them, and responds by performing a sequence from its pre-designed set of gestures. The underlying cognitive model is based on this perception-reasoning-action cycle. The design process included abstracting a participant's behavior into meaningful gestures as well as designing and implementing marionette actions. To recognize complex and sophisticated human actions as discrete gestures, a gesture elicitation study was performed for both human gesture and marionette gesture classifications.

This paper first introduces the *willful marionette* as an art project, followed by an overview of related work on gesture design and interaction. The paper then presents the user experience and cognitive system design of the marionette. The cognitive model is comprised of three modules: gesture recognition, marionette gesture selection, and marionette gesture performance. The last section concludes with a summarization and reflection of the effectiveness of the cognitive model in provoking a human response through continued interaction, as well as a discussion of how participants ascribed human-like intelligence to the marionette.

2   The Willful Marionette

The synthesis of a traditional art form, the marionette, with a modality of human-machine gesture interaction, leads to a new kind of creative computation. The marionette evokes creative dialogue of gestures between humans and machines. A marionette is a string-operated puppet, a traditional art form that exists in many cultures (Chen et al. 2005). Modern marionette and puppetry artists often work with engineers and researchers to explore the possibility of integrating robotics into marionette performance (Yamane et al. 2004). In previous work on developing a robotic marionette, researchers explored the possibility of infusing robotic systems into the traditional art form of marionette theater (Chen et al. 2005), and to evoke and stimulate public interest (Robert et al. 2011; Sidner et al. 2005; Speed et al. 2014).

The design and construction of the *willful marionette* was a collaboration between artists Lilla LoCurto and Bill Outcault, and the Interaction Design Lab at UNC Charlotte. The artists' previous work focused on the human body as a three-dimensional form, re-representing it in ways that draw attention to the frailty of human physicality.

The *willful marionette* began as a 3D scan of Bill Outcault's body, which was then 3D printed in segments and constructed as a marionette. Little Bill is shown in Fig. 1, and stands about 3 feet tall. To create the marionette, the whole body was segmented into 17 parts. Segments are connected with hinge and socket joints based on the corresponding joints of the human body. Thirteen of the joints are connected to strings to enable movement. The movement of the strings is controlled by motors connected to a frame above Little Bill, which extend and retract the strings and cause joints to move up and down. Two Microsoft Kinects are attached to the frame, and capture the movement of people in the area around Little Bill, allowing the marionette to respond to them. Inside Little Bill's head a fourteenth motor controls his eye lids.

Fig. 1. The *Willful Marionette*, aka "Little Bill", a 3-foot tall naked, blue cognitive agent (Color figure online)

Little Bill provokes an interactive relationship between art object and audience member. Historically, the audience member is a passive viewer, watching a puppeteer perform with a marionette in a theatrical setting. With an interactive marionette, the audience becomes *active participants* in the performance, and the theatrical performance is replaced with an interactive dialogue. Without the context of a theatrical performance to capture viewers' attention, the puppet must act as a provocateur to engage the viewer. Once engaged, participants continue to interact with the *willful marionette* and to evoke the movements and reactions of the puppet. Interaction design in this context is about the interaction between participants and the 3D marionette. Participants differ from traditional conceptions of the "user" in HCI as they are not acting to further some goal but instead participating in a dialogue with an embodied cognitive agent. The marionette also differs from traditional conceptions of an "interface" as it is both socially and physically embodied within the same space as the humans with which it is interacting.

Interaction with the *willful marionette* is entirely based on the human body: both that of the participant and the machine. The marionette creates a dialogue of gestures that provoke movement and evoke emotional response. This form of dialogue both engages the audience and, as we determined through our user studies, can provoke a strong perception that the marionette possesses a form of intelligence.

3   Background

The goal of the marionette project was to design an interactive system that engaged people in a gestural dialogue. Doing so requires an understanding of the role of gestures in cognition (Baber 2014; Maher et al. 2014; Tversky et al. 2014). Past HCI research has striven to develop common sets of gestures for interaction (Card 2014; Jetter 2014; Karam 2005), and to evaluate the ease and effectiveness of those gestures for performing tasks (Ackad et al. 2014; Vanacken et al. 2014). In order to elicit a set of popular gestures (Seyed et al. 2012), several researchers have explored the design of gestures that people can easily learn or discover (Cartmill et al. 2012; Karam 2005).

Research in computational models of emotion (Marsella and Gratch 2009) and affective computing (Picard and Picard 1997) are also relevant to the marionette project, given the primacy of emotion in the body language that makes up a great deal of gestural interaction between people.

The *Viewpoints AI* system (Jacob et al. 2013), while virtual rather than physical, comes closest to the marionette project among past work of which the authors are aware. *Viewpoints* is a Kinect-based projection of a humanoid form that communicates with human dancers through the medium of dance: it will dance a duet with them, similar to the *willful marionette*'s gestural dialogue. One point of contrast in the dialogues the two systems construct is that *Viewpoints* begins by mimicking the human dancer to establish synchronicity, while the *willful marionette* strictly avoids mimicry to establish its autonomy and otherness.

Research into robotic marionettes has primarily focused on their application in the performing arts. Hoffmann (1996) developed a human-scale marionette that could, controlled by a human, enact a dance performance using motions based on human dancers. Hemami and Dinneen (1993) proposed a strategy for stabilizing a marionette through a system of unidirectional muscle-like actuators. The strategy provides positive force to the actuators analogous to the firing rate of natural muscles. Yamane et al. (2004), controlled the upper body of a marionette to perform dances using human motion. These projects show how a marionette performance can be automated, but not autonomous: they do not consider a marionette as an embodied actor interacting with and responding to human participants.

4   Gesture Design and Implementation

The first step in designing gestures for an interactive system is to understand the design space of possible gestures. Various design methods, such as bodystorming, role-playing, personas and image boards, were used in the early stages of the project to explore possible avenues for gestural interaction with the marionette. These methods provided the design team with the opportunity to explore the possibilities of both the hardware and software technologies that could be used in the development phase. In bodystorming and role playing, members of the design team played either a human participant or a marionette role, and acted out gestural dialogues. This enabled the design team to better understand how an embodied gestural interaction with a marionette could proceed.

Based on the initial prototypes and the results of bodystorming, a set of preliminary gestures were selected and implemented for the marionette. Each gesture was defined by specifying each motor's movement in time. This definition allowed us to write and store gestures for selection by the cognitive system, i.e. when a marionette gesture is selected in response to a perceived human gesture.

After the implementation of the selected gestures for the marionette, a preliminary evaluation study was performed to assess and refine them. The evaluation of this study was done using the Wizard of Oz technique, since the perceptual system that would sense human gestures and map them to marionette gesture responses had not been developed at that time. A human operator decided which marionette gesture to execute based on participants' gestures. The think aloud method was used to gather further data on how human participants perceived the interaction was progressing, and the reasons behind their gestural selections.

For this preliminary study we recruited twelve students as our participants. Each participant was asked to interact with the marionette spontaneously without specifying a specific task. Participants were asked to think aloud while interacting with the marionette in this study. After each session, an interview was conducted to collect additional insights about participant behavior through gestures. Video recording was used to capture each performed gesture along with notes taken by the design team.

One of the biggest challenges that distinguish Little Bill from other gesture-based interaction systems is that participants in this context are not given instructions or tasks. The most difficult moment is the "cold start": participants initially have no conception of the scope of the marionette's ability to perceive or respond to them. Seeing the marionette respond to their presence typically gives participants the confidence to initiate gesturing towards the marionette. Participants were more willing to continue the dialogue after they noticed that they got Little Bill's "attention" (i.e. eye contact). Based on this feedback we designed the interaction such that Little Bill "makes the first move" and directs its attention to the new participant. To achieve this, we added an "approach" gesture that the marionette perceives when a participant is approaching it. A corresponding "retreat" gesture was added, ensuring that walking away signifies to the system the participant has lost interest in Little Bill.

The full list of participant gestures elicited by the preliminary study was: waving, bending over, approaching, walking away, getting too close, and going behind the marionette. The last two gestures are detected by the angle and distance of the participant. Results of the gesture elicitation study and the interviews revealed that lifting the marionette's head to make eye contact, turning the marionette's body to follow the participant, and the marionette raising its hands were the three gestures that inspired the greatest emotions among the testers.

4.1 Gesture Implementation

The marionette gestures were designed to convey emotions of different kinds and were divided into the following five categories:

- Complex gestures: A subset of the marionette gestures involve large body movements that are intended to convey that the marionette is experiencing a strong emotional response. These gestures are implemented as a quickly executed series of movements across many degrees of freedom. Examples of the marionette's complex gestures include surprise and scared.
- Subtle gestures: Other, smaller gestures are intended to encourage continued interaction with the marionette. For instance, simply lifting the head of the marionette gives an impression of eye contact and, in our experiments, engaged participants and made them more likely to continue interacting. Similarly, a series of movements that convey a "quizzical look" from the marionette while participants wave for him can be intriguing and encourages continued interaction.
- Attentive gestures: These gestures are a direct response to participants' movement. For example, the marionette turns so that it tracks a participant, or turns its head such that it faces them. As another example, when participants walk away from the marionette, the marionette might shake its head as an attentive gesture to get their attention back.
- Living gestures: These gestures are designed to convey the impression that the marionette is alive, and involve movement that is not a direct response to perceived participant action. For example, the marionette possesses a motor behind its eyes that can execute a blinking gesture, which is performed at random times. Another example of this type of gesture is a "breathing" gesture, which moves the back of the marionette up and down very slowly such that it looks like it is breathing. These gestures prevent the marionette from being completely still.
- Restorative gestures: After performing some gestures the marionette might not be in a natural pose, or may have lost track of its exact pose due to technical limitations. To accommodate this lack of information, a restorative gesture was designed to adjust the marionette's position back to its initial position. One such gesture slightly lifts marionette up off the ground and returns it to its default position.

The cognitive model for the marionette has three components: participant gesture detection, marionette gesture selection and marionette gesture execution. Participant gesture detection uses the Microsoft Kinect and its SDK to detect and send human gestures to the marionette gesture selection program. The selection component selects the most relevant marionette gesture to execute, and sends the related action to the gesture execution component.

The next challenge was how to model the selection of a marionette gesture as a response to a human gesture. We developed a set of guidelines based on observations of human movement, particularly during dialogue:

- people are always moving;
- different people respond differently, particularly to a repeated event;
- people may respond by starting a conversation with another person;
- people shift their attention to a different object even when there is no obvious event.

In order to have the marionette's responses not become predictable, each participant gesture is mapped to a set of possible marionette responses from which a single response is stochastically chosen. This one-to-many relationship is used because the goal of the interaction is not to generate an expected response, but to encourage and provoke continued interaction. This is in contrast to the typical interaction design goal of learnable and predictable interaction between user and interface. The perceived autonomy of this simple random behavior is also intended to provoke the human to perceive intelligence in the marionette: human social interaction is not predictable, and systems intending to provoke dialogic interaction should be similarly opaque.

To define a set of appropriate marionette response gestures to participant gestures, the design team envisioned the set of probable emotional states that could cause the participant to perform each gesture. Since the gesture selection process cannot interpret participants' emotional states, the set of possible response actions was designed to cover all emotional states (such as surprised, shy or shocked) that were deemed probable causes. The cognitive model constructs a probability that participants would be in each emotional state, and selects a random gesture weighted by this probability distribution. This allowed the marionette to respond in a manner that responds to the most likely emotional state of the participant. As an example, a person who is bent over near the marionette is probably displaying curiosity or interest in it, which puts the marionette in the surprised, shocked or shirk state. Table 1 shows the mappings from each human gesture that the marionette can recognize to a list of possible marionette response gestures. Each gesture in Table 1 represents an emotional state and refers to one or more implementation on the marionette.

Table 1. The mapping from human to marionette gestures.

Human gestures	Marionette gestures
Approach	Scared, shirk, surprised
Wave	Stand straight, quizzical look
Bend over	Surprised, shocked, shirk
Walk away	Surprised, shy, shake head
Too close	Shy, shake head, stand straight, look up fast, walk backward

The marionette gesture selection component is also responsible for deciding which participant is the current focus of the marionette's attention. Participant interestingness is based on continued engagement (measured by amount of body movement) and the order that people approached the marionette. The marionette attends to the participant it perceives to be the most interesting, and rotates to follow their position. From the gesture elicitation study and participant interviews, it was determined that eye contact was the most important feature to participants, and resulted in the highest level of engagement. If a person was behind the marionette and no one was present in front, the marionette rotates to face them, allowing gestural interaction to continue.

The gestures of the marionette were divided into two categories based on its responsiveness. The first category is a set of "regular" gestures that are selected in response to participants' gestures, and the second one is a set of "idle" movements that are selected when no one interacts with the marionette for a defined amount of time. If no participants are detected the gesture selection component triggers an idle state, during which the marionette performs subtle gestures in an attempt to engage anyone present but not detectable by its perceptual system (due to the limited range or field of view of the Kinect sensors). Idle movements are actions that are short in terms of execution time, and are subtle movements designed to engage people to interact. This ensures the marionette is not still for lengthy periods.

5   Evaluation of Human Response to Gesture Dialogue

Once the gestures for the marionette were selected, refined through the preliminary study, and implemented, we conducted a user study to evaluate the effectiveness of the cognitive model for gesture dialogue. This study included 13 participants (a different set of users than the preliminary user study). Since the marionette is originally an art piece and it is expected to be placed in an art museum, we performed the study in a gallery setting. Participants visited the marionette individually, with nobody but the experiment facilitator present. Figure 2 shows some participants interacting with the marionette.

Fig. 2. Participants interacting with the *willful marionette*

Participants received a short verbal introduction to the project. This introduction provided an explanation of about the objective of the evaluation. The *willful marionette* was presented to the participants as shown in Fig. 1. Participants could see that the marionette was controlled electronically, but they were not given any information on how the processes for perception, reasoning and response. Similar to the initial user study, the participants were asked to interact with the marionette while thinking aloud. Participants were explicitly not given a task to perform, as the purpose of our system is exploratory gestural dialogue. Participants were made aware that they were being video recorded. An interview was conducted after each session to collect additional insights from the participants about their experience, expectations, the degree to which they felt that the marionette responded to their gestures, and any feedback or suggestions.

5.1   Evaluation Results

This section presents highlights and notable themes of the responses given during interviews performed in both the preliminary and the final user studies. By far the most common topic in the interviews was the participants' interest in the marionette. All of the participants found the marionette highly provocative and interesting. The human-like features of the marionette such as blinking and breathing, its responsiveness, and the complexity of its gestures were all given as reasons for participants' surprise, curiosity and interest. One of the participants said he hesitated in approaching the marionette due to the blinking of its eyes and the human-like nature of its movement. Our data, while small-scale, suggests that participants overwhelmingly associated the embodied form and clear responsiveness of the marionette with human behavior and assumed that it was intelligent far beyond its simple reasoning.

One of the common themes of participant responses concerned the first moments of their dialogue with the marionette. At first, most participants did not approach the marionette directly, keeping their distance and observing the marionette's idle actions. Several participants noted that at that time they did not believe that the marionette would respond to them, and that its movements were predetermined. However, when they saw the marionette's response to their approach, they became aware of its interactive nature and began to make various gestures actively. This initial surprise was mentioned as a cause of significant emotion in several users, both positive and negative. Participants discussed that the "back and forth" resulting from this initial exploration of the marionette's interactivity – their first gesture-based dialogue with an embodied cognitive agent – were unexpectedly engaging.

Another feature of the interaction with the marionette which led participants to comment on the intelligence of the marionette was its lack of mimicry behaviors. Three participants expected that the marionette would mirror their own movements, i.e. if they raised an arm, the marionette would also raise an arm. These participants said the interaction was more interesting than they expected because this behavior was absent – a conscious decision on the behalf of the design team. The fact that the interaction was based on an exploratory gestural dialogue, rather than simple mimicry, helped engage these participants.

Four of the participants tried to talk to the marionette, assuming that if it was capable of human gestural interaction then it would also be capable of hearing and understanding speech. Two of these participants referred to Siri, the digital personal assistant in Apple's iOS, and said they expected that the marionette could interact in a similar fashion.

Participants were asked to indicate which gestures they found most provocative. Three participants mentioned the blinking of the eyes during eye contact as highly provocative. Rotation of the marionette to track participants (especially when participants moved behind the marionette) was rated as most highly provocative by two other participants. One participant said that arm-related gestures, such as the marionette raising its arm as if to shield its face in response to a participant approaching, was highly provocative and caused a strong emotional response.

6   Discussion

The *willful marionette* is a contemporary interpretation of the marionette as a form of interactive installation based on an embodied cognitive agent. The system includes a cognitive model that perceives, reasons, and acts in order to engage humans in a gestural dialogue. By replacing the puppeteer and puppet with cognitive agent and an animatronic marionette, the performance becomes more physically and socially engaging: users are participants in an interactive dialogue rather than an audience. The *willful marionette's* control systems are deliberately exposed and clearly visible, serving to more greatly unnerve and fascinate users about its nature. The true unknown about the marionette is not how it is physically controlled, but the processes by which it decides to act in response to its environment. Even though its cognitive system is extremely simple, its physical embodiment in a human-like form, and the deceptively human-like behaviors it executes using that form, cause users to project onto it significant capacity for higher-level thought. Much like with the ELIZA program of mid last century (Weizenbaum 1966), it is very easy to attribute intelligence to a system that interacts with you in the way you interact with other humans. As an art piece the *willful marionette* exposes the fundamental frailty of human social interaction: we can be so captivated by simple randomness, so long as it is embodied to look and move like us! As an HCI research project the *willful* marionette demonstrates the possibilities of affective gestural inter-action that seeks to sustain engaging dialogue, rather than complete a task by the most effective route.

In summary, *the willful marionette* is an example of a simple interactive embodied cognitive system that draws participants into a gesture-based dialogue. Our evaluation of the cognitive model shows that people easily ascribe intelligence to the marionette because of the combination of its human-like form and its unexpected and provocative behavior. The core reasoning process for the marionette is a mapping algorithm that maps a detected gesture to a selection from a list of predefined gestures. This mapping was designed to produce unpredictable social interaction, and to leave ambiguous the question of the marionette's capacity for higher thought. Based on the results of our interviews with the human participants, we believe that the key factors that caused the participants to perceive machine intelligence are (1) the unpredictability of the perceive-reason-perform cognitive model (2) use of gesture dialogue as the mode of interaction (3) the human-like features and gestures of the marionette and (4) the proactive move-ments of the marionette: the idle gestures.

We developed a system that enables a novel gesture-gesture based dialogue in order to explore how embodied cognitive agents with human-like features could affect a phys-ical social context. Even though the resulting system's behavior is based on a simple cognitive model, users were more than willing to ascribe higher intellect to its actions due to its embodied nature. This result has implications for both art and the design of future interactive systems.

Acknowledgments. We would like to thank the following for their financial support for this project: Yi Deng, Dean of the College of Computing and Informatics at the University of North Carolina at Charlotte (UNCC); William Ribarsky, former Chair of the Department of Computer Science at UNCC; and Ken Lambla, Dean of the College of Art and Architecture at UNCC. We thank the many people that participated in the design and implementation of Little Bill: Alexander Adams, Trevor Hess, Yueqi Hu, Lina Lee, Steph Grace, and Katy Gero. We truly appreciate their help throughout the project.

References

Ackad, C., Kay, J., Tomitsch, M.: Towards learnable gestures for exploring hierarchical information spaces at a large public display. In: Gesture-Based Interaction Design: Communication and Cognition, CHI 2014 Workshop (2014)

Anderson, M.L.: Embodied cognition: a field guide. Artif. Intell. **149**(1), 91–130 (2003)

Baber, C.: Objects as agents: how ergotic and epistemic gestures could benefit gesture-based interaction. In: Gesture-Based Interaction Design: Communication and Cognition, CHI 2014 Workshop (2014)

Card, S.K.: A simple universal gesture scheme for user interfaces. In: Gesture-Based Interaction Design: Communication and Cognition, CHI 2014 Workshop (2014)

Cartmill, E.A., Beilock, S., Goldin-Meadow, S.: A word in the hand: action, gesture and mental representation in humans and non-human primates. Philos. Trans. Roy. Soc. B: Biol. Sci. 129–143 (2012)

Chen, I.M., Xing, S., Tay, R., Yeo, S.H.: Many strings attached: from conventional to robotic marionette manipulation. IEEE Robot. Autom. Mag. 59–74 (2005)

Hemami, H., Dinneen, J.A.: A marionette-based strategy for stable movement. IEEE Syst. Man Cybern. 502–511 (1993)

Hirai, K., Hirose, M., Haikawa, Y., Takenaka, T.: The development of Honda humanoid robot. In: Proceedings of IEEE International Conference on Robotics and Automation (ICRA 1998), pp. 1321–1326 (1998)

Hoffmann, G.: Teach-in of a robot by showing the motion. In: IEEE Proceedings of Image Processing, pp. 529–532. IEEE (1996)

Jacob, M., Coisne, G., Gupta, A., Sysoev, I., Verma, G.G., Magerko, B.: Viewpoints AI. In: AIIDE (2013)

Jetter, H.C.: A cognitive perspective on gestures, manipulations, and space in future multi-device interaction. In: Gesture-Based Interaction Design: Communication and Cognition, CHI 2014 Workshop (2014)

Kaneko, K., Kanehiro, F., Morisawa, M., Miura, K., Nakaoka, S., Kajita, S.: Cybernetic human HRP-4C. In: 9th IEEE-RAS International Conference on Humanoid Robots, Humanoids 2009, pp. 7–14 (2009)

Karam, M.: A taxonomy of gestures in human computer interactions (2005)

Maher, M.L., Clausner, T.C., Gonzalez, B., Grace, K.: Gesture in the crossroads of HCI and creative cognition. In: Gesture-Based Interaction Design: Communication and Cognition, CHI 2014 Workshop (2014)

Marsella, S.C., Gratch, J.: EMA: a process model of appraisal dynamics. Cogn. Syst. Res. **10**(1), 70–90 (2009)

Picard, R.W., Picard, R.: Affective Computing, vol. 252. MIT Press, Cambridge (1997)

Robert, D., Wistorrt, R., Gray, J., Breazeal, C.: Exploring mixed reality robot gaming. In: Proceedings of the Fifth International Conference on Tangible, Embedded, and Embodied Interaction, pp. 125–128. ACM (2011)

Sandini, G., Metta, G., Vernon, D.: The *iCub* cognitive humanoid robot: an open-system research platform for enactive cognition. In: Lungarella, M., Iida, F., Bongard, J., Pfeifer, R. (eds.) 50 Years of Artificial Intelligence. Lecture Notes in Computer Science, vol. 4850, pp. 358–369. Springer, Berlin (2007)

Seyed, T., Burns, C., Costa Sousa, M., Maurer, F., Tang, A.: Eliciting usable gestures for multi-display environments. In: Proceedings of the 2012 ACM International Conference on Interactive Tabletops and Surfaces, pp. 41–50. ACM (2012)

Sidner, C.L., Lee, C., Kidd, C.D., Lesh, N., Rich, C.: Explorations in engagement for humans and robots. Artif. Intell. 140–164 (2005)

Speed, C., Pschetz, L., Oberlander, J., Papadopoulos-Korfiatis, A.: Dancing robots. In: Proceedings of the 8th International Conference on Tangible, Embedded and Embodied Interaction, pp. 353–356. ACM (2014)

Tversky, B., Jamalian, A., Segal, A., Giardino, V., Kang, S.M.: Congruent gestures can promote thought. In: Gesture-Based Interaction Design: Communication and Cognition, CHI 2014 Workshop (2014)

Vanacken, D., Beznosyk, A., Coninx, K.: Help systems for gestural interfaces and their effect on collaboration and communication. In: Gesture-Based Interaction Design: Communication and Cognition, CHI 2014 Workshop (2014)

Weizenbaum, J.: ELIZA—a computer program for the study of natural language communication between man and machine. Commun. ACM 9(1), 36–45 (1966)

Yamane, K., Hodgins, J.K., Brown, H.B.: Controlling a motorized marionette with human motion capture data. Int. J. Humanoid Robot. pp. 651–669 (2004)

Improving Analysis and Decision-Making Through Intelligent Web Crawling

Jonathan T. McClain[✉], Glory Emmanuel Aviña, Derek Trumbo,
and Robert Kittinger

Sandia National Laboratories, Albuquerque, NM, USA
jtmccl@sandia.gov

Abstract. Analysts across national security domains are required to sift through large amounts of data to find and compile relevant information in a form that enables decision makers to take action in high-consequence scenarios. However, even the most experienced analysts are unable to be 100 % consistent and accurate based on the entire dataset, unbiased towards familiar documentation, and are unable to synthesize and process large amounts of information in a small amount of time. Sandia National Laboratories has attempted to solve this problem by developing an intelligent web crawler called Huntsman. Huntsman acts as a personal research assistant by browsing the internet or offline datasets in a way similar to the human search process, only much faster (millions of documents per day), by submitting queries to search engines and assessing the usefulness of page results through analysis of full-page content with a suite of text analytics. This paper will discuss Huntsman's capability to both mirror and enhance human analysts using intelligent web crawling with analysts-in-the-loop. The goal is to demonstrate how weaknesses in human cognitive processing can be compensated for by fusing human processes with text analytics and web crawling systems, which ultimately reduces analysts' cognitive burden and increases mission effectiveness.

Keywords: Text analytics · Intelligent web crawling · Decision making · Cognitive consistency

1 The Challenge of Data Analysis

While the prevalence of easily accessible information via the internet and large databases has allowed for unprecedented advances in societal knowledge, the sheer volume of data available leads to difficulties in locating the correct information that is relevant to a task at hand (i.e. finding the needle in the haystack). This sifting process is most commonly accomplished today using search engines (e.g., Google®) by submitting a single query

Disclaimer. Sandia National Laboratories is a multi-program laboratory managed and operated by Sandia Corporation, a wholly owned subsidiary of Lockheed Martin Corporation, for the U.S. Department of Energy's National Nuclear Security Administration under contract DE-AC04-94AL85000, Sandia Report SAND2016-1652C. Approved for public release further dissemination unlimited. This research was funded in part or whole by an Interagency Agreement between the Transportation Security Administration and the Department of Energy.

© Springer International Publishing Switzerland 2016
D.D. Schmorrow and C.M. Fidopiastis (Eds.): AC 2016, Part II, LNAI 9744, pp. 414–420, 2016.
DOI: 10.1007/978-3-319-39952-2_40

and iteratively visiting results in a single list to determine whether the supplied result contains relevant information or represents a false positive. This process continues iteratively through multiple queries until the information required has been found or the human analyst gives up. While such a process is useful, the overall approach itself suffers from a number of problems; (1) the analyst is required to possess a moderate understanding of the subject matter being sought; (2) the analyst is limited by the query interface provided and must possess astute abilities in constructing queries with a few words to seek out that subject matter; (3) the analyst is limited by the fact that a single prioritized list is presented based on an unknown underlying search algorithm; (4) in many cases, search algorithm results are tailored either to the global mean, or tailored to the analyst, both of which may be undesirable when searching for obscure and little known information; (5) the analyst is limited to that information which the search engine has deemed worthy of indexing, also based on global demand (e.g., Google® only indexes a small fraction of the known internet)[1].

1.1 The Challenge for the Analyst

Even the most experienced analysts are unable to be completely consistent and accurate when sifting through large amounts of information. A single analyst faces a number of cognitive hindrances. An analyst will use heuristics, such as scanning for words they have determined to be relevant, in order to gauge information importance[2]. However, this method is inconsistent. At the start of the analysis process, an analyst can decide a document is relevant because of the words in a piece of text, but later on, after they have been sifting through information, they decide a similar piece of text is not relevant because their notion of what is relevant has matured. Similarly, relevancy is based on what the analyst knows to be important and therefore is biased to their limited knowledge base on the subject of interest. A single analyst must also spend large amounts of time examining and filtering large amounts of documentation, and even then he or she is unable to synthesize and process all of the data, especially when there is a limited amount of time to make important decisions[3].

The cognitive hindrances increase for a team of multiple analysts. Between analysts, there are different heuristics and various strategies for finding information. The amount of time spent searching is multiplied by how many analysts are on a team, which can make searches for relevant information expensive. In addition, biases towards determining what information is relevant increase because of differences in experience, knowledge base, and perspectives[4]. Conflict may also arise if there are conflicting opinions of documentation relevance. Finally, if an automated method for tracking information examined is not used, then analysts may have overlap in the material they have covered[5].

---

[1] http://www.webanalyticsworld.net/2010/11/google-indexes-only-0004-of-all-data-on.html.
[2] Goldstein and Gigerenzer (2002).
[3] Pope et al. (2000).
[4] Marchionini (1997).
[5] Howard et al. (2009).

1.2   The Challenge for the Decision Maker

Ultimately, when a single analyst or team of analysts present the information they have determined to be relevant and their assessment of it, it is inevitable that they have not located all relevant information. Therefore, conclusions based on analysts' information are automatically biased, limited in scope, and skewed to the cognitive perspective of the analysts. This creates a challenge for decision-makers because they need to be able to justify their conclusions. In order to make defensible decisions, the decision-maker needs to have access to analyses and conclusions that are accurate, quantitative, justifiable, and thorough. This holistic assessment provides the pathway for decision-makers to not only make decisions, but also anticipate and respond to potential issues that the data alludes to as well as predict how and why situations may evolve.

This need for complete data does not point decision-makers to a fully automated system. Such a system could not spot the nuances in the data that a human analyst so naturally does. Instead, decision-makers need to keep the human-in-the-loop to leverage analysts' intuition, ability to calculate possible options in connection to the scenario at hand, and create a continuous pathway from the data to solutions.

Overall, the decision-maker as well as the analyst needs to reduce the amount of data processed by humans and therefore cognitive load to increase effectiveness, accuracy, and speed.

1.3   The Problem with Search Engines

When searching for relevant information on the open web, a primary question when presented with intelligent web crawling is, "What about search engines?" This question stems from an underlying assumption that search engines are enough to satisfy analysts' needs. However, if one thinks about this assumption in a deeper way, it becomes evident that search engines, even the best of them, are not the end-all solution for sifting through large datasets for relevant information.

Imagine you as an analyst are going to use a search engine to find information on a topic of interest such as the spread and impact of your academic thesis. If you search for the title of your thesis to find relevant information related to your thesis topic, you would receive a single list of webpages that have the words from your title on them. Your search will probably return your institution's academic repository and possibly the journal where you may have published your thesis. From there, the list may be your personal website, and then from there a list of other websites. You do not really know why the search engine listed the other webpages except that there are a few keywords matching your thesis title on the webpage. Your job is now to sift through the results, probably going through the list of pages top-down to determine what is actually relevant to the question you are asking. If you have multi-dimensional parameters (e.g., wanting to find related publications and individuals who have quoted your work), this list of search results will not efficiently respond to both parameters. You will probably have to do multiple queries to answer each of these parameters. Analysts quickly find that a single metric such as a search engines' list of results is not enough to ascertain the quality of the results you are looking for.

Another problem with search engines is the lack of transparency. The reasoning for why a search engine presented a list of search results can be partially or completely hidden from the user.

Search engines also transform results according to user's location, personality, past purchasing and browsing behaviors, global and/or local trends, and are influenced by search engine optimization by third parties. Results are also dependent on the parameterization of the search engines' crawlers and search engines make tradeoffs to crawl/index less to save money. Furthermore, you do not have access to the full content available on the internet. The actual size of the internet already has made effective indexing infeasible[6] and Google specifically only indexes a small fraction (~.004 % as of 2010) of the internet (see Footnote 1).

2 Huntsman

Sandia National Laboratories has attempted to solve the challenges faced by analysts and decision-makers by developing an intelligent web crawler called Huntsman. The use of web crawling and text analytics helps to both imitate as well as enhance human analysts by using text algorithms to develop consistent metrics to search and analyze large datasets. The search also eliminates bias, is parallel across computing machines, and returns the best matched information relative to all the data searched. Intelligent web crawling finds the most pertinent information and quantitatively pushes it to the forefront of the analysts' attention. This way, analysts are still in the loop to examine a smaller, more relevant dataset and validate findings.

Huntsman acts as a personal research assistant by browsing the internet or offline datasets in a way similar to the human search process, only much faster (millions of pages per day), by submitting queries to search engines and assessing the usefulness of page results by analyzing full-page content with a suite of text analytics. Huntsman uses the results of these analyses to order future downloads, allowing it to hone in on important information quickly. In this way, Huntsman provides a triage of information through analyzing the full content of each document to assess relevance to the task at hand. Upon completion, Huntsman provides various subsections of the data, based on the various analytics performed, to a human analyst, allowing them to focus only on the most useful information at hand.

2.1 Background

Intelligent or focused crawling is not a particularly well researched topic. Chakrabarti et al. (1999) first described a focused crawler that utilized a classifier to identify relevant documents, and a distiller to identify nodes which access several relevant documents within a few links. Zeinalipour-Yazti and Dikaiakos (2002) describes the idea of using web crawlers as middleware for users to gather relevant content based on a user profile.

---

[6] Chakrabarti et al. (1999), Henzinger (2000).

Where Huntsman differs from these previous approaches is in its focus the human in the loop. Huntsman focuses on leveraging the humans' abilities in pattern matching and intuition, while eliminating tasks in which the human does not excel by removing the burden of mentally processing large amounts of data, the bulk of which is not relevant to the task at hand. Another area in which Huntsman differs from other approaches is in comprehensiveness. When data is processed with Huntsman, the analyst and the decision maker have much more confidence that all relevant information has been taken into account as part of the analysis.

2.2   How Huntsman Works

Unlike regular keyword-based analysis using search engines, intelligent web crawling helps alleviate analysts' tasks that are most subject to cognitive hindrances (biases, inconsistency, etc.) and keep analysts in the loop where they are most critical (intuitive decision-making, option calculating, etc.).

The process of using Huntsman begins with crawl parameterization. This includes identifying known documents and keywords and phrases of interest. The documents of interest are then passed through a suite of text modeling tools to create signatures that target both generally relevant, as well as specific content. Keywords and phrases are used to enhance these signatures by scaling their influence based on overall document relevance.

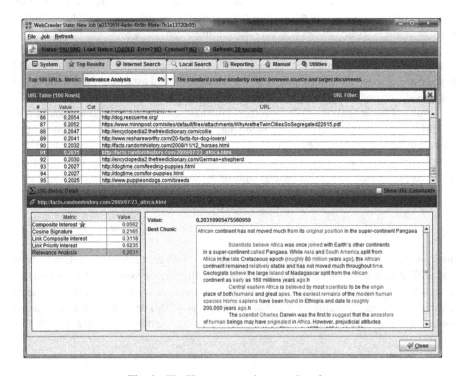

Fig. 1.   The Huntsman analyst user interface

All of these parameters are passed to Huntsman to begin the crawl. Huntsman submits keywords and phrases to various search engines to seed the crawler with good starting places on the internet. As Huntsman is crawling, each downloaded page is compared against the target signatures using a suite of text analytics. Throughout the crawl, the analyst is able to view the most relevant findings through the graphical user interface (see Fig. 1). Huntsman also provides document excerpts and other explanations to the analyst regarding its reasoning for presenting this information to the analyst, allowing the analyst to make quick decisions about the importance of the information, as well as redirect the crawl as necessary. This interaction between the analyst and Huntsman continues until the analyst decides the quality of the data collection is sufficient.

After the crawl, the analyst is able continue to review and annotate the results, and is able to automatically generate a report with the most relevant findings and annotations for documentation or to present to others. This process can be seen in Fig. 2.

Fig. 2. The intelligent web crawling process

2.3   Huntsman as a Personal Research Assistant

In a sense, Huntsman can be viewed as a personal research assistant. This approach provides several distinct advantages; (1) analysts are able to perform a search that is targeted on the entire content of the documents, rather than just the presence of a few keywords; (2) Huntsman allows analysts to perform a more nuanced analysis of the document contents by applying a suite of text analytics and presenting the results to the analyst, as well as easy to understand explanations for why each document was considered interesting; (3) While Huntsman leverages the results of search engines, it moves beyond what search engines provide by analyzing all pages crawled and providing a rollup of the best results to the analyst; (4) Huntsman's search focuses on the content, not a search engine's assessment of the page's potential interest to the masses or to the individual; (5) Huntsman can peruse enormous quantities of information, saving the analyst time and allowing the analyst to better remain in context by providing focused results and reasoning behind those results.

2.4   Huntsman Is Applicable to Various Contexts

Huntsman can be applied to multiple contexts such as data science, social modeling, business analysis, and field operations – essentially any situation that utilizes large datasets to make rapid, high-consequence decisions.

3   Conclusion

There are many benefits of using web crawling and text analytics in the analysis of large datasets. A web crawler is able to locate non-indexed information and does not rely on a search engine to serve as a middleman for compiling web data in a single dataset. Instead it uses search engines as a starting point and then crawls out from there to find any relevant data available on the open web.

Overall, there is a need to accurately and efficiently synthesize large amounts of information to enable decision-making. Huntsman is a versatile capability that has been developed and used across various contexts to assess large amounts of interesting information, which ultimately reduces analysts' cognitive burden and applies findings to increase mission effectiveness.

References

Chakrabarti, S., Van den Berg, M., Dom, B.: Focused crawling: a new approach to topic-specific web resource discovery. Comput. Netw. **31**(11), 1623–1640 (1999)

Henzinger, M., Heydon, A., Mitzenmacher, M., Najork, M.: On near-uniform URL sampling. In: Proceedings of the 9th International World Wide Web Conference, pp. 295–308. Elsevier Science, Amsterdam, Netherlands, May 2000

Jasra, M.: Google Has Indexed Only 0.004 % of All Data on the Internet (2010). http://www.webanalyticsworld.net/2010/11/google-indexes-only-0004-of-all-data-on.html

Zeinalipour-Yazti, D., Dikaiakos, M.: (2002)

Najork, M., Wiener, J.L.: Breadth-first search crawling yields high-quality pages. In: WWW 10, Hong Kong, 1–5 May 2001

Goldstein, D.G., Gigerenzer, G.: Models of ecological rationality: the recognition heuristic. Psychol. Rev. **109**(1), 75 (2002)

Pope, C., Ziebland, S., Mays, N.: Analysing qualitative data. BMJ **320**(7227), 114–116 (2000)

Howard, N., Spielholz, P., Bao, S., Silverstein, B., Fan, Z.J.: Reliability of an observational tool to assess the organization of work. Int. J. Ind. Ergon. **39**(1), 260–266 (2009)

Marchionini, G.: Information Seeking in Electronic Environments, vol. 9. Cambridge University Press, Cambridge (1997)

Using an Augmented Training Event to Collect Data for Future Modeling Purposes

Samantha Napier[1(✉)], Christopher Best[1], Debra Patton[1], and Glenn Hodges[2]

[1] Army Research Laboratory Human Research Engineering Directorate,
Aberdeen Proving Ground, USA
samantha.j.napier.civ@mail.mil
[2] Training and Doctrine Command Army Capabilities Integration Center, Fort Eustis, USA

Abstract. During materiel development, limitations of soldiers and their inter-actions with tasks and equipment are often inadequately considered until after product development. This can result in poor requirements generation and thus inadequate specifications [1]. These flaws have produced the largest cost driver in acquisition programs: performance requirement changes [2]. The Army has begun work to incorporate the human dimension into future materiel development of both equipment and training systems. Modeling and Simulation (M&S) have been viewed as ways to train soldiers and to predict performance before money has been invested in creating and fielding new products. The success of early M&S in reducing cost hinges on understanding how the human, task, and equipment work together and impact each other. In addition, their relationship must be linked to cognitive aspects of performance, especially under high arousal condi-tions. The Army currently lacks a way to describe these relationships. The goal of this project is to create a methodology to define the data needed to describe the relationship between levels of stress or arousal and soldier performance using a live training event. The methodology should provide the training and modeling communities with information on gaps in their technologies that prevent effective training or accurate predictive analysis through modeling efforts. The method-ology will also help define measures of performance needed to assess training and correctly model performance.

Keywords: Modeling · Requirements generation · Affordances · Attributes

1 Introduction

In 2013, the Honorable Heidi Shyu, United States Assistant Secretary of the Army (Acquisition, Logistics, and Technology), signed a memorandum emphasizing the need for early involvement within the Department of Defense acquisition process of the Army's formal Human Systems Integration (HSI) program [3]. She also emphasized a Systems Engineering approach and an analytical decision based model to conduct trade off analysis to make better informed decisions [4]. This sentiment was echoed by General Walker, who stated the need for the Human Dimension (HD) community and material solutions communities to intersect [4]. In addition The US Army Human Dimension Concept's [5] number one "Key Required Capability" states: "Future Army organizations

© Springer International Publishing Switzerland 2016
D.D. Schmorrow and C.M. Fidopiastis (Eds.): AC 2016, Part II, LNAI 9744, pp. 421–430, 2016.
DOI: 10.1007/978-3-319-39952-2_41

require the capability to integrate and synchronize Human Dimension initiatives (training and education, science and technology, medical, and personnel policies, programs, and initiatives) to ensure they are effective and efficient in providing adaptable, trained, and resilient forces that meet the Army's challenges in the future operational environment." It also stated "it is critical that individuals and units understand how stress affects their performance."

According to 2015 Executive Order [6], the term Human Dimension was defined as "the cognitive, physical, and social components of Soldier, Army Civilian, leader, and organizational development and performance essential to raise, prepare, and employ the Army in Unified Land Operations." The cognitive component was defined as "States, traits, and processes that make up the subjective experience, and include typical ways of problem solving, framing events in life, intelligence, and emotional self-regulation." The Physical component was defined as: "Traditional aspects of physical fitness and holistic health and fitness, with an approach that considers the mental and medical contributions to physical performance." The Social Component was defined as: "Elements that allow an Army professional to serve the nation honorably." Cognitive Dominance, now Agile and Adaptive Leaders, was defined as: "Optimizing cognitive, physical, and social strength to achieve advantage over a situation or adversary."

This project was created to address some of these issues. Until recently, human capabilities requirements were based on the performance of the system. The cognitive processes underlying the performance were not addressed. For example, a marksman would use a weapon to shoot a number of targets. The performance would be recorded. The cognitive process behind how to shoot a weapon effectively and do it in dynamic, stressful situations was not addressed. Thus there is a gap between shooting in a controlled situation and shooting in combat. Some models have attempted to address some of the cognitive processes.

2   Modeling Tools

The Improved Performance Research Integration Tool (IMPRINT) is a human performance modeling and cognitive workload prediction tool and used by human factors practitioners to assess and compare system designs and their effects on operator performance. An IMPRINT model is based on a detailed representation of the mission in the form of a task network containing the tasks that soldiers are likely to perform using system capabilities according to conceptual system designs. The task network enumerates the tasks performed and are connected according to the order in which tasks are performed in the field, and can represent concurrently-executed tasks. Each task is then annotated with a time of execution or probability distribution of execution times, values for the workload incurred while performing the task, and other information. Alternative designs are often built into the IMPRINT models reflecting independent variables of an experimental design. These alternatives can be modifications to equipment used by the soldier, reflected in task properties, or allocations of tasks to operators, reflected in changes to the task network or operator assignments. The result is a functional simulation of different experimental conditions that produce predictive performance data [7].

IMPRINT allows analysts to predict quantitative performance metrics including execution time and cumulative and resource-specific workload values during task execution. While the IMPRINT stressor parameters allow the analyst to specify certain conditions such as heat, cold, or noise, which can affect the output metrics, no option is currently built into IMPRINT to account for a holistic stress level experience under high-arousal contexts and adjust the predicted values. However, the tool does include a flexible plug-in architecture that allows for the adjustment of predicted values, which could be calculated based on an independent model of stress effects on performance [7].

3   Existing Methodology

In order to better predict how design changes may impact the performance of a soldier in a stressful situation, the relationship between Soldier, Task, and Equipment must be better defined. This paper provides an update on the progress and testing of a methodology for illuminating this relationship. The components needed to create this methodology are: (1) a way to relate Soldier, Task, and Equipment; (2) a way to quantitatively measure stress in a way that allows it to be related to performance metrics; and (3) an augmented training event to provide empirical data to combine the first two components.

The Systematic Team Assessment of Readiness and Training (START) was chosen as a baseline method for relating Soldier, Task, and Equipment. The Naval Aviation community faced similar issues while assessing simulation tools within the training community several years ago [8] when budget cuts forced the Navy to look for alternatives to live training. Simulation was an option but presented its own set of challenges. The requirements generation strategy created a never-ending list of changes as problems were discovered. Previous efforts to correct these issues had focused on the scenarios or use-cases aviators might encounter. Even that approach led to capability gaps and dissatisfaction with the training devices because a user centered understanding of the tasks making up the scenario was not developed. The way that the aviators interacted with the task and their own equipment was not well understood. The training devices didn't correctly represent important aspects of the real world cues needed by the end users to do their tasks [9]. In general, the acquisition and systems engineering communities have focused on technical problems while largely ignoring the front end analysis needed for the soldier [10].

The [8] goal in developing START was to create a framework that linked requirements to the Mission Essential Task (MET) list by way of the attributes required to perform the task and create more representative Measures of Performance (MoPs). Tasks were things that people do while attributes were the system sensory cues that initiate and affect task performance [11]. Soldier Subject Matter Experts (SMEs) were used to rate the tasks' and attributes' importance to performing the mission [8]. The ratings were combined to produce descriptions of fidelity and a rating of importance that could be used by Systems Engineers (SEs) to update simulators for training. The attributes led to increased realism in the simulators and increased training effectiveness [11]. Aviators were able to receive training and readiness credit for flight times after recommended upgrades were made to the simulators. This process was so successful at allowing human behavior specialists to identify gaps and define recommendations to other disciplines (particularly SEs) in an understandable and meaningful way that it has been used and modified by several other groups.

The START tool can also be modified to address both testing and training requirements for United States Marine Corp (USMC) systems [12]. By working with human behavioral specialists, budget analysts and SEs, it is possible to locate the gaps in several training systems and demonstrate the cost effectiveness of various upgrades to their training system.

While the Army recognizes the need to incorporate the Human Dimension and best practices of human behavior specialists into design work of the systems engineers, there is no framework to help them understand how to incorporate the human into their work early in the process. A framework must be developed that users across the Army can leverage and modify for their own needs. Understanding the tasks soldiers complete and how they complete them under stressful conditions is an appropriate starting point. Whether the goal is to design a training system, test new equipment, or correctly model the impact of various changes to the system, the task the human is doing must be well-understood in terms of what the human uses to do it. In addition, to model particular aspects of dismounted infantry, the impact of stress and resilience on performance must be studied.

4   Adapted Methodology

This effort proposes to modify the START process to create a methodology and analysis tool that can be leveraged by many practitioners to ensure the Human Dimension is incorporated into their work. To meet these goals and assess the ability to modify the START methodology to a modeling domain, we chose a use-case from an ongoing program to leverage. The training community currently has a program that addresses the desired social, cognitive (dominance), and physical parameters. The program and its background are described below.

Tactical Combat Casualty Care Training for Readiness and Resilience (TC3-TR2) is a training program aimed at training members of platoons, squads, medics, and combat life savers to collectively adapt their tactical decision making while managing Combat Casualty Care (C3) under highly stressful conditions. Currently, medics and combat life savers receive their training independent of the unit they are assigned to assist. The goal of TC3-TR2 is to integrate medic and combat life savers into unit training that will enable them and the squad to learn how to become resilient and adaptable while dealing with the C3, tactical, and emotional problems that result when their fellow soldiers succumb to injuries and casualties. This work was based on a previous effort called Squad Overmatch (SQOM).

In FY13, Squad Overmatch (SQOM) successfully investigated how to improve existing training technologies to provide combat realistic exercises and experiences to reduce Post Traumatic Syndrome (PTS) and potential suicides [13]. Working with the Army Maneuver Center of Excellence (MCoE) in FY14, the study team developed and evaluated a SQOM Stress Exposure Training (SET) demonstration and generated requirements for building squad situational awareness and stress management skills [14]. These include team skills, individual skills, and decision skills. SET is a three-phase training program designed to provide information, skills training, and practice to enable the warfighter to cope and perform (be resilient) while exposed to combat and emotional stressors. SET instructional content, delivery, and sequencing are critical to learning. In the second and third phases of SET, practice takes place under graduated exposure to stressors [15]. The second phase emphasizes obtaining skills needed for coping with stress, making decisions under stress, and the adaptability of individuals and teams. Emotional, social, cognitive, and physiological skills as they relate to performance are also addressed. The third phase focuses on practicing these skills within a training scenario that triggers tasks that use those skills. This approach addresses the social, cognitive, and physical aspects needed to meet our goals.

Leveraging the work in TC3-TR2, will allow a unique opportunity expand the START process and collect data on resiliency. START will be modified to address the specific needs of modeling by including traits and Human Abilities (HAs) of a soldier that allow the soldier to complete the task. Traits often referred to as personality types, are characteristic patterns of one's behavior, thought, and emotional response [16]. They are stable over time, across individuals, and often predictive of an individual's behavior to overcome unknown or stressful events. HAs are enduring attributes of the individual that influence performance [17]. They were developed as part of an umbrella taxonomic effort attempting to standardize the way human performance is described [18]. Currently 52 HAs exist that are grouped into four categories of cognitive, physical, sensory, and psychomotor. Affordances will be incorporated as well. Affordances are properties of the environment, but properties that are scaled to the organism. Affordances are objective, physical properties" [19]. This information is important for systems engineers as they need to understand the impact of redesigning a piece of equipment on the affordances of the equipment that allow the soldier to do the task. There is some overlap between affordances and cues. Including both allows us to choose the appropriate one for a particular task. The new information will be added to the process and assessed. This will better allow assessment of the capability of a modeling tool to correctly represent events for a predicative analysis. Basing the tasks on those performed in the TC3-TC2 training environment allows us to validate the modifications to START and assess the gaps in modeling tools. Once the gaps are adequately addressed the model can be run. The model's predictions can then be validated against what happened in the training event. We can then address differences between what the model predicted and what was actually seen and modify our methodology as necessary.

5   Method for Initial START Analysis

5.1   Identify and Decompose Tasks

The first step was to identify and decompose tasks to the appropriate levels. Efforts were made to decompose both basic infantry and the additional tasks that a combat life saver would need to address. Tasks from a previous START effort were incorporated. Tasks that were part of the TC3 scenario were chosen for further analysis.

Additionally as part of this step, a human ability analysis was conducted on the tasks and subtasks to identify what kind of activity the task was (e.g. physical, cognitive, sensory, or psychomotor). Having this insight helps to scope the identification of necessary cues, affordances, and constructs in the second step. Measures of Performance (MOPs) and Measures of Effectiveness (MOEs) that can be directly linked back to the tasks will be determined for both training and modeling needs.

5.2   Establish and Verify Attributes, Affordances, and Cognitive Constructs

The next step will be to establish and verify attributes of the tasks. In past training efforts, attributes were defined as the sensory cues that triggered or impacted task performance. Realism in a scenario and simulation is directly related to those attributes [11]. The previous START effort leveraged had sensory cues already associated with it. They will be applied as appropriate to the medical tasks.

In addition, START will be modified to look at skills or traits of the soldiers needed to effectively perform the task. Cognitive skills and processes will be addressed in order to find way to represent them in models. We will ensure items that may only pertain to modeling efforts are addressed along the way, as well as the skills or traits of the soldiers themselves to ensure enough detail to model them later. There will be special emphasis placed on cognitive and social resilience skills. This will allow incorporation of modifications into the methodology to answer modeling questions.

This additional information is needed for modeling teams to be able to effectively model the task and the human. In the case of modeling tools it tells the modeler what has to be represented and to what fidelity. It also gives them information about whether the tool could be used as it stands now.

5.3   Criticality Ratings

Previous efforts by the training community had SMEs rate the cues' criticality to the tasks. This effort proposes to include affordances, human abilities, and traits in the rating. The effort will be focused on the criticality of the attributes of the tasks and abilities of the human required to do a task proficiently that must be modeled correctly in order to get valid results. The cognitive abilities associated with resilience and decision making will be emphasized. The MOPs and MOEs will be used to start determining how abilities impacting resilience etc. could best be represented in the model.

5.4   Capability

Previous efforts by the training community had the SMEs rate training simulators on how capable they were of representing the critical cues. The modeling community will work with SMEs to determine a model's capability to represent critical tasks and the associated cues, affordances, traits, and human abilities, as well as their associated MOPS and MOEs necessary to predict performance.

5.5 Apply Algorithm and Analyze

After verifying that the correct algorithm is being used, it will be applied to determine the criticality scores for task and for attributes.

5.6 Analyze the Output of the Scores

Capability and criticality allow the systems engineers to focus and prioritize their efforts in the areas that will provide the biggest impact for the money spent. The team will look for patterns of gaps to guide them in areas to address. Systems engineers can then develop options, costs, and recommend courses of action based on the most important areas to address. This step will guide the engineer's Analysis of Alternatives (AoA) and start to show areas where research is needed to populate the models.

6 Collecting Stress and Arousal Data

The next part of the methodology was to determine a way to relate performance and stress. The task's Identification (ID) in the live event and START will be used as a starting point.

Stress is a key component of performance. Therefore, stress must be considered when identifying the interaction between users and systems. Stress can be defined as a state produced when stressors tax or exceed and individual's adaptive resources and is multifaceted, dynamic, and interactive with both psychological and physiological dimensions [20, 21]. Because of its multifaceted nature, it is important to measure trait and state psychological and physiological stress during the event of interest. These results can then be compared to real situations with known values of a stress response.

To identify traits of soldiers, measures of: coping [22], such as problem-focused, wishful thinking); dealing with uncertainty [23], such as emotional uncertainty, need for cognition; and trait stress [24], such as anxiety, depression, hostility, positive affect, and sensation seeking) will be collected. These traits are part of one's personality that are considered to be stable over time and are predictive of how a person handles, interprets, and moderates the effects of a stressful situation. They are collected from the soldiers during a time not related to any experimentation or testing.

State measures of arousal are assessed to determine the effect of a particular action or set of actions on one's stress response. To do so, they are collected at several key points during the experimentation. Measures of state stress include both the psychological and physiological. For instance, psychological measures include one's self-confidence to perform well, how they feel in terms of anxiousness, depression, frustration, positive affect, risk taking and overall negative affect during the event or right at that moment. Numerous studies over the past 25+ years have reported psychological stress responses to varying levels of stress reported by military personnel during different types of military events [25, 26]. Through the results of these studies it is possible to identify low, moderate, and high levels of stress. These psychological measures have shown high correlations with physiological responses produced by autonomic nervous system [27, 28].

Psychophysiological measures are collected through a variety of measures: Electroencephalogram (EEG); Functional Magnetic Resonance Imaging (fMRI); and Electrocardiograms (ECG). This ECG system is an unobtrusive wearable device and continuously records. Measures derived from an ECG include but are not limited to Inter-Beat-Interval (IBI), Heart Rate (HR), and respiration rate. IBI measures the peak-to-peak interval of heartbeats, represents vagal tone, and is linked to cognition [27]. IBI variability reduces compared to baseline indicating cognitive arousal. Heart rate is the number of heart beats occur in a minute. This measure increases when the body is experiencing physical stress and shows to be the reverse of IBI. Both IBI and HR are controlled by the respiration rate. HR will increase briefly during inhale and decrease briefly during exhale. This then influences the distance between the peaks of beats in the HR.

Another psychophysiological measure is salivary alpha amylase (α-Amylase). α-Amylase is produced in the salivary glands in response to circulating epinephrine and norepinephrine. The nature of α-Amylase lends to a solid measure of acute stress because it is activated and returns to normal quickly. Salivary amylase concentrations are predictive of plasma catecholamine levels and can be used as a measure of stress [28]. Measurement of amylase concentration in saliva includes the observation of chemical color changes according to standard photometric procedures developed by Andrology Labs and Northwestern University. This measurement is a quantifiable physiological measurement of stress arousal. Saliva samples are collected by placing a 1" × 1" square sponge in your mouth or spitting directly into a specimen vial.

All these measures will provide an understanding of how the human is responding to the interaction with the event, system, or training. By understanding this interaction practitioners can take into account where an event, system or training is responsible for too high a level of arousal resulting decrements in performance or mission failure.

7 Conclusion

The Army Systems Engineering community currently falls short to adequately and accurately define and characterize tasks and skills of soldiers within an operational environment in a way that would allow SEs to use the information and correctly represent the human within a systems engineering architecture. This representation can be used for training purposes, designing new equipment, or as a baseline for modeling efforts. Developing this tool through collaboration between the modeling and training communities significantly benefits the Army by developing and demonstrating a front end tool that can be used for training and system development to reduce requirements creep. The methodology can feed many Systems Engineering activities and definition of the relationship between the Soldier, Task and Equipment allows them to be addressed early on when changes are still possible. It will augment the training effectiveness enterprise efforts to determine ways to assess system requirements as well as MOPs and MOEs that are appropriate for analysis of training. These will directly impact modeling and system development efforts. A new tool will help researchers decompose Mission Essential Tasks (METs) into task and soldier attributes necessary to trigger task completion. These can be used in system development to ensure a change doesn't negatively impact the soldier. It also provides a baseline of the capabilities of modeling tools for predictive analysis. In addition, tasks and attributes are rated for importance and fidelity thus giving SEs information for AoAs to upgrade or modify equipment or models. It will provide a baseline to make tradeoff analysis.

References

1. Sage, A.P.: Systems Engineering. Wiley, New York (1992)
2. Hearing before the Senate Committee on Armed Services, Testimony of John Young, Under Secretary of Defense (Acquisition, Technology and Logistics) 3 June 2008. http://armed-services.senate.gov/statemnt/2008?June/YoungA%2006-03-08.pdf
3. Shyu, H. (2013) Memorandum. Assistant Secretary of the Army for Acquisition, Logistics, and Technology, Washington, DC
4. Soldier Systems Engineering Architecture Science and Technolgy Objective. NSRDEC, R.NSR.2015.01 (2014)
5. U.S. Army Human Dimension Concept. TRADOC Pam 525-3-7. TRADOC, FT Eustis, VA, May 2014
6. HQDA EXORD XXX-15 Human Dimension (2015)
7. Mitchell, D.K.: Mental workload and ARL workload modeling tools, DTIC Document (2000)
8. Sheehan, J.D., Merket, D.C., Sampson, T., Roberts, J., Merritt, S.: Human system capabilities-based training system acquisition. In: Naval Aviation Proceedings of the 2009 Human Systems Integration Symposium, Annapolis, MD (2009)
9. Salas, E., Rosen, M.A., Held, J.D., Weissmuller, J.J.: Performance measurement in simulation-based training a review and best practices. Simul. Gaming **40**(3), 328–376 (2009)
10. Hodges, G.: A novel approach to determine integrated training environment effectiveness. In: Proceedings of Interservice/Industry Training, Simulation, and Education Conference (2014)
11. Pfeffekorn, E.: Army live test and training pre-project Alignment combat realism assessment working group. Naval Air Warfare Center Training System Division, Orlando (2014)
12. Johnston, J., Dunfee, D., Keppeler, J., Torgler, D., Jarvis, D.: A capabilities-based assessment tool for USMC squad immersive training. In: Proceedings of Interservice/Industry Training, Simulation, and Education Conference (2012)
13. Butler, P, Osborne, R, Sivek, R., Zabek, A, Kemper, B., Ogden, P., Parrish, R., Napier, S., Rhodes, S.: Integrated squad training to optimize human performance and discourage post-traumatic stress and suicide. MITRE, Orlando, Fl, November 2013
14. Johnston, J.H., Napier, S., Ross, W.A.: Adapting immersive training environments to develop squad resilience skills. In: Schmorrow, D.D., Fidopiastis, C.M. (eds.) AC 2015. LNCS, vol. 9183, pp. 616–627. Springer, Heidelberg (2015)
15. Johnston, J.H., Cannon-Bowers, J.A.: Training for stress exposure. In: Driskell, J.E., Salas, E. (eds.) Stress and Human Performance. Erlbaum, Hillsdale (1996)
16. Kassin, S.: Psychology. Prentice-Hall Inc., USA (2003)
17. O*NET Online. http://www.onetonline.org/find/descriptor/browse/Abilities/. Accessed 24 Jan 2016
18. Fleishman, E., Quaintance, M., Broedling, L.A.: Taxonomies of Human Performance: The Description of Human Tasks, 1st edn. Academic Press, Orlando (1984)

19. Flach, J., Warren, R.: Active psychophysics: the relation between mind and what matters. In: Flach, J., Hancock, P., Caird, J., Vicente, K. (eds.) Global perspectives on the ecology of human-machine systems, p. 195. Lawrence Erlbaum Associates, Hillsdale (1995)

20. Lazarus, R., Folkman, S.: Stress, Appraisal and Coping. Springer Publishing Company, New York (1984)

21. Fatkin, L., Patton, D.: Mitigating the effects of stress through cognitive readiness. In: Performance Under Stress. Ashgate Publishing Limited, Aldershot, (2008)

22. Vitaliano, P.P., Maiuro, R.D., Russo, J., Becker, J.: Raw versus relative scores in the assessment of coping strategies. J. Behav. Med. **10**(1), 1–18 (1987)

23. Greco, V., Roger, D.: Coping with uncertainty: the construction and validation of a new measure. Pers. Individ. Differ. **31**, 519–534 (2001)

24. Lubin, B., Zuckerman, M.: Manual for the MAACL-R: Multiple Affect Adjective Check List—Revised; Educational and Industrial Testing Service, San Diego, CA (1999)

25. Fatkin, L.T. Hudgens, G.A.: Stress perceptions of soldiers participating in training at the Chemical Defense Training Facility: the mediating effects of motivation, experience, and confidence level. ARL-TR-365, U.S. Army Research Laboratory, Aberdeen Proving Ground, MD (1994)

26. Patton, D.: How real is good enough? Assessing realism of presence in simulations and its effects on decision making. In: Schmorrow, D.D., Fidopiastis, C.M. (eds.) AC 2014. LNCS, vol. 8534, pp. 245–256. Springer, Heidelberg (2014)

27. Morgan, C.A., Aikins, D.E., Steffian, G., Coric, V., Southwick, S.: Relation between cardiac vagal tone and performance in male military personnel exposed to high stress: three prospective studies. Psychophysiology **44**, 120–127 (2007)

28. Chatterton, R.T., Vogelsong, K.M., Lu, Y.C., Ellman, A.B., Hudgens, G.A.: Salivary α-amylase as a measure of endogenous adrenergic activity. Clin. Physiol. **16**(4), 433–448 (1996)

The Art of Research: Opportunities for a Science-Based Approach

Austin R. Silva[✉], Glory E. Aviña, and Jeffrey Y. Tsao

Sandia National Laboratories, Albuquerque, NM, USA
`aussilv@sandia.gov`

Abstract. Research, the manufacture of knowledge, is currently practiced largely as an "art," not a "science." Just as science (understanding) and technology (tools) have revolutionized the manufacture of other goods and services, it is natural, perhaps inevitable, that they will ultimately also be applied to the manufacture of knowledge. In this article, we present an emerging perspective on opportunities for such application, at three different levels of the research enterprise. At the cognitive science level of the individual researcher, opportunities include: overcoming idea fixation and sloppy thinking, and balancing divergent and convergent thinking. At the social network level of the research team, opportunities include: overcoming strong links and groupthink, and optimally distributing divergent and convergent thinking between individuals and teams. At the research ecosystem level of the research institution and the larger national and international community of researchers, opportunities include: overcoming performance fixation, overcoming narrow measures of research impact, and overcoming (or harnessing) existential/social stress.

Keywords: Research · Divergent thinking · Convergent thinking · Science of science · Creativity · Analogical distance · Research narrative · Scientometrics · Data analytics · Research teams · Research ecosystem

1 Introduction

Research is an estimated $1.6T/year world enterprise [1], supporting a community of approximately 11 million active researchers [2] and, most importantly, fueling a large fraction of wealth creation in our modern economy [3]. Despite its importance, however, it is practiced largely as an "art" [4], passed down from one generation to the next. We learn how to do research from our professors, managers, mentors and fellow researchers, just as they did from theirs.

In recent years, a community has been growing around a field that might broadly be called the "science" of research [5–8] – the understanding of the human and intellectual processes associated with research and its societal impact. Until now, however, the two communities (the practitioners or "artists" of research and the "scientists" of research) have advanced with minimal interaction, despite the possibility that they might benefit each other enormously. Artists of research care deeply about how effective they are, and what better way to improve their effectiveness than to apply scientific principles; while

© Springer International Publishing Switzerland 2016
D.D. Schmorrow and C.M. Fidopiastis (Eds.): AC 2016, Part II, LNAI 9744, pp. 431–441, 2016.
DOI: 10.1007/978-3-319-39952-2_42

scientists of research care deeply about their scientific under-standing of research, and what better way to test that understanding than to try to apply it to improving how research is actually done.

The Art & Science of Science and Technology Forum & Roundtable held at Sandia National Laboratories [9] acknowledges opportunities to discover and apply principles governing effective research throughout the research environment. To expand upon those principles laid forward from the Forum & Roundtable, we will focus on two research hypotheses and objectives.

Our first working hypothesis is that divergent and convergent thinking [10] are the foundational yin and yang of research. Research, broadly defined as the production of new and useful ideas and knowledge, proceeds via iterative, nested, and complementary cycles of idea generation followed by idea filtering, refining and retention [11]. For simplicity, we use for these complementary cycles the common terms divergent and convergent thinking, with the understanding that they are related (but not identical) to other terms: blind variation and selective retention (BVSR) [12, 13], abductive versus deductive reasoning, generative versus analytic thinking, discovery versus hypothesis-driven science [14], creativity versus intelligence, thinking fast versus thinking slow [15], foraging versus sensemaking [16], exploration versus exploitation [17], and learning versus performing [18].

Our second working hypothesis is that divergent and convergent thinking occur at multiple levels of the research enterprise: the cognitive science level of the individual researcher; the social network level of the research team; and the "research eco-system" level consisting of the research institution and the larger national and international

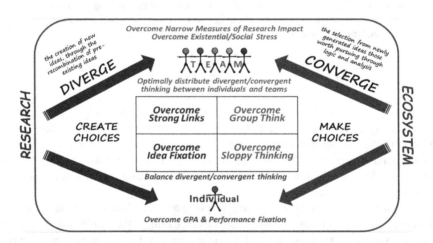

Fig. 1. Our working hypothesis is that research proceeds as iterative, nested, and complementary cycles of divergent and convergent thinking. Shown is a schematic of one such cycle, along with examples of the challenges that each kind of thinking faces at the three levels of the research enterprise: the cognitive science level of the individual researcher; the social network level of the research team; and the "research ecosystem" level of the research institution and the larger national and international community of researchers.

community of researchers. These three levels map to the micro, meso, and macro scales associated with research [5].

At all three levels of the research enterprise (individual researchers, research team, research ecosystem), we give examples of challenges to divergent and convergent thinking faced by the art of research – challenges that in turn represent opportunities for the harnessing of the science of research. Our hope is first, by articulating these challenges and opportunities, to catalyze active work on them in both communities and, second, by articulating these working hypotheses, to catalyze active work to test them (Fig. 1).

2 Individual Researchers: Overcoming Human Cognitive Constraints and Biases

2.1 Divergent Thinking: Overcoming Idea Fixation

Divergent thinking, in essence, is the creation of new ideas, mostly (perhaps always [19]) through the recombination of pre-existing ideas. But humans have cognitive constraints and biases [15] which can make divergent thinking difficult, among them idea fixation [20]. Though extremely productive researchers de-fixate themselves at key stages of their research process, such researchers are rare and are generally unable to teach others how to do the same.

There is thus opportunity for understanding the cognitive basis for idea fixation and then engineering strategies for idea de-fixation. Of particular interest are strategies associated with engineered exposure to new ideas. The ideas should be far enough away in analogical space [21] to catalyze shifts in perspective – either because they come from different disciplines or from different "translational" (science, technology, applications) communities. The ideas should not be so far away in analogical space, however, that conceptual and language gaps are too difficult to bridge.

This exposure to "optimal-analogic- distance ideas" strategy seems obvious in principle, and is in fact practiced by many in a qualitative way. However, advances in modern data analytics, combined with the sheer quantity of digitized knowledge, open up new opportunities for making this practice more quantitative. One opportunity might be scientometric clustering analyses of publications based on bibliographic connectivity. Another opportunity might be lexical clustering analyses based on syntactic/semantic regularities [22], word-order-based discovery of underlying ("latent") constituent topic areas [23], and mutual compressibility [24]. These analyses could lead to algorithms that go beyond those that power today's search [25] and recommendation [26] engines by feeding researchers ideas not just within their comfort zone, but optimally distant from their comfort zone.

2.2 Convergent Thinking: Overcoming Sloppy Thinking

Convergent thinking is the selection from newly generated ideas those worth pursuing through logic and analysis. Of course, easier said than done, because human cognition is subject to sloppy thinking and errors of logic and analysis.

There is thus opportunity for understanding the cognitive basis for these errors and for developing strategies to correct for them. Of particular interest is a strategy that might be called the "research narrative" strategy. Research narratives – storylines which knit together background, hypothesis, methodology, analysis, findings and implications – are essentially tools for logical thinking. They are important at the end of a research project, when a paper is being written for the scientific community and posterity. But research narratives are just as important at the beginning of a research project. Emerging cognitive science suggests that narrative and stories are the evolutionary optimal tools for communicating not only with others but even with ourselves [27]. A coarse story-board of the title, abstract, figures, and key references of the anticipated outcome of a research project forces clarification of many of its aspects – including those that have been hypothesized [13] to be critical sub-components of creativity, such as originality, perceived utility, and surprisingness.

This "research narrative" strategy seems obvious in principle, and, just as the "exposure to optimal-analogic-distance ideas" strategy just discussed, is also practiced by many in a qualitative way. But modern data analytics creates opportunity to practice it more quantitatively. For example, machines might someday dispassionately evaluate research narratives just as they are beginning to dispassionately evaluate essays in academic writing courses [28]. Or, perhaps more likely, a combination of machines and humans might someday efficiently and accurately evaluate research narratives via machine curation of Yelp-like peer reviews.

2.3   Balancing Divergent and Convergent Thinking

Divergent and convergent thinking are by themselves difficult, but perhaps even more difficult is our ability to know when to switch between the two. On a large scale, the history of science is replete with scientists who were on the wrong track and would have been more productive switching from convergent to divergent thinking [29]. But the history of science also has its share of scientists who prematurely abandoned ideas which later proved to be correct [30].

On a small scale, researchers with an immediate narrative of what to expect in one day's laboratory experiment or theoretical calculation, upon being confronted with something unexpected, must choose whether to stay the course (convergent thinking), whether to treat the unexpected as an opportunity to reconsider possibilities (divergent thinking), or whether to withhold judgment while waiting for additional data or in-sight.

To some extent, we all gravitate towards thinking styles with which we are most comfortable, and researchers are no different. Those who are more comfortable thinking divergently will tend to reconsider too soon; those more comfortable thinking convergently will tend to stay the course too long; and perhaps a rare few will be comfortable doing neither.

In fact, because of our modern education system's emphasis on deducing single answers using logical thinking, modern researchers might be biased towards convergent thinking. To avoid this bias, some institutions that value creativity now deliberately hire on the basis not of grade point average and SAT scores, but of more balanced thinking styles [31].

There is thus opportunity to understand and engineer strategies to compensate for intrinsic biases towards either divergent or convergent thinking. For example, at a qualitative level, the research narratives discussed earlier might not just be powerful tools for logical, convergent thinking, but might also be powerful tools for under-standing when to cycle between divergent and convergent thinking. If the train of thought that follows from one or more divergent new ideas does not hold up to the cold logic (or mathematics) of the research narrative, then it very likely would benefit from new ideas and divergent thinking.

At a quantitative level, some of the lexical analytical techniques mentioned earlier, applied in real time to evolving research narratives and other generated knowledge trails, might be able to discover not only whether divergent or convergent thinking is happening, but whether divergent or convergent thinking is appropriate for the stage of the problem at hand.

3 Research Teams: Overcoming Social Constraints and Biases

3.1 Divergent Thinking: Overcoming Strong Links

Groups can draw upon the diverse ideas of individuals to create new ideas. And, because much of the knowledge of individuals is tacit [32] and not accessible in formal codified form, closely interacting groups which can share this tacit knowledge informally can be yet more productive. MIT's Building 20 [33], Bell Labs' "Infinite Corridor" [9], the Janelia Farm Research Campus [34], Pixar's Emeryville campus [35] and Las Vegas' Downtown Project [36] are examples of how informal interactions probabilistically enhanced through intentionally engineered or serendipitously designed physical spaces are thought to enhance divergent thinking and tighter communities through understanding the psychosocial space as clearly as the physical space [37].

However, research teams also bring inefficiencies to divergent thinking. When individuals on a team become too familiar with each other's knowledge domains and ways of thinking, they no longer serve as sources of new ideas to each other. Moreover, homophily is common in social networks: we seek those who think as we do and avoid those who do not think as we do [38]. For divergent thinking, exposure to the less familiar is important, and weak links [39] in one's social network can be more powerful than strong links.

Thus, similar to the opportunity identified at the individual researcher level, data analytics may provide an opportunity to identify not just ideas that are an optimal analogic distance away from the current team's ideas, but people who are an optimal analogic distance away from people in the current team.

3.2 Convergent Thinking: Overcoming Groupthink

Just as with divergent thinking, convergent thinking in research teams can in some situations be more but in other situations be less productive than convergent thinking in individual researchers.

Convergent thinking requires logical deductive thinking, the deeper and more first-principles the more accurate and often the more surprising [40]. On the one hand, multiple minds can find and fix reasoning errors to which an individual researcher might be blind [41]. On the other hand, the depth of knowledge necessary for such thinking, and the degree to which the knowledge is tacit and difficult to articulate, the more easily it can be done within a single mind than across multiple minds. For example, the research narrative discussed earlier, a powerful tool for convergent thinking, benefits from input and criticism from multiple minds but in the end is usually most tightly and coherently articulated by fewer, even single, minds.

Moreover, teams are subject to group- think, in which groups, because of various social biases, converge prematurely and inaccurately on less-good ideas [42]. Such social biases probably evolved in humanity's pre-history for good reason: there are many situations for which quick consensus, conflict avoidance, and social cohesion are more important than accuracy. Those situations likely do not include among them research and the accurate convergence onto the best ideas, however. There is thus opportunity to understand the conditions under which teams can over-come groupthink.

3.3   Distributing Divergent and Convergent Thinking Between Individuals and Teams

Most importantly, research teams have more options for accomplishing divergent and convergent thinking than do individuals. Teams are composed of individuals. Hence, if some aspect of thinking is best done by a team or by individuals, teams can in principle assign it to the appropriate level. For example, if individuals are indeed relatively stronger at convergent thinking while teams are relatively stronger at diver-gent thinking, it could be optimal for divergent thinking to be performed more at the team level, but for convergent thinking to be performed more at the individual level [43]. To take advantage of this strategy, however, it will be necessary to first under-stand more deeply the relative strengths and weakness of individuals and teams at convergent and divergent thinking for what types of problems, in what situations and environments, and using what interaction tools.

Teams also have more options in how their individual members are rewarded. Individual researchers not in a team would individually bear the consequences of risky too-divergent thinking, but in a team could actually be rewarded for taking on such risk. However, research teams have fewer options for oscillating back and forth between divergent and convergent thinking during the life cycle of a research project. They inherently have more inertia, and thus the decision of what kind of thinking to emphasize and at what level, individual or team, is more serious.

For all the above reasons, team leadership is crucial. Throughout the life cycle of a project, a team will move through various quadrants of individual/team diver-gent/convergent thinking, with opportunity for the team and its leader to optimally allocate resources across those quadrants.

For example, with modern data analytics, can we quantify: where in its life cycle a research project is; the degree to which divergent or convergent thinking is needed; and how well the team's current composition and cognitive constructs [44] match the desired degree of divergent or convergent thinking? Just as the "quantified self" movement [45] seeks to use physical technology to monitor the manifold pulses of a person's daily life to optimize health and productivity; a "quantified team" movement might seek to use data analytics technology to monitor the manifold pulses of a re-search team's daily life [46], to better match the team's composition and organization to the research problem at hand, and ultimately to optimize the research team's health and productivity.

Indeed, understanding how to optimize the balance between individual and team, and between divergent and convergent thinking, might borrow from advances in emerging models for information foraging [16]. For example, if useful information is "patchy," a forager might first seek to look broadly for useful patches, and then focus in on a few of the most useful patches. Or, for example, the risk associated with not finding a patch in a particular time horizon, or the amount of resources allocated for the foraging, might determine which stage of the foraging is best done by individuals or by a team.

4   Research Ecosystems: Understanding and Assessing

At the research institution and community- of-researcher level, there are outsized opportunities for optimization, because it is this level that defines the overall research ecosystem. Individual researchers, research teams, and research managers/leaders are drawn from, and engage in divergent and convergent thinking within, the research ecosystem.

Note that in introducing the phrase "research ecosystem" we deliberately make the metaphor to "biological ecosystem" and hence to the importance of both the individual researchers and the environment which sets the boundary and interaction conditions for the researchers. There are opportunities for understanding and assessing both.

4.1   Individual Researchers: Overcoming Performance Fixation

Regarding the individual researchers within the research environment, hiring and nurturing are both key.

With respect to hiring, the imperfect correlation between school grades and creativity is well known [47]. One possible reason: grade point average (GPA) and scholastic aptitude test (SAT) scores select for strength in convergent rather than divergent thinking, while in research both are necessary. There is thus opportunity to devise new measures that go beyond GPA and SAT scores for assessing separately those qualities which underlie excellence in divergent or convergent thinking [31].

With respect to nurturing, the profound difference between learning and performance goals is well known [18]. Learning goals are more compatible with an out-ward/ community orientation, and with an openness to new ideas and divergent think-ing. Performance goals are more compatible with an inward/self orientation, and with a focus on known correct ideas and convergent thinking. In other words, divergent and conver-gent thinking applies not just to research problems but to researchers themselves. Partic-ularly as knowledge landscapes change increasingly rapidly, it is not just a researcher's competence in knowledge domains of current importance that is important, but his/her "absorptive capacity" [48] for assimilating and building on new ideas and thus for building competence in knowledge domains that will be important in the future.

One key opportunity is thus: can we measure qualities such as absorptive capacity, and then incorporate improvements in those qualities into metrics for the success of research projects themselves? The analogy here is to sustainable manufacturing, but applied to the "manufacturing" of knowledge: the output of research is not just knowledge, but also a strengthening of the researchers themselves. Though the ultimate goal is long-term output of great research, the proximate goal to accomplish that research output sustainably is researchers with high and continuously increasing absorptive capacity.

4.2 Research Environment: Overcoming Narrow Measures of Research Impact and Overcoming Existential/Social Stress

Regarding the research environment surrounding the individual researchers, the easy tautology is that a great research environment is one which produces the best research that a given set of researchers is capable of, and that assessing the research environment is equivalent to assessing research impact itself.

Assessing research impact is difficult, however. In science, the current state-of-the-art assessment metric is bibliometrics of formal written documents: publication and citation counts, H and other indexes, and journal impact factors. We know, however, that bibliometrics is limited [49]. It does not measure research impact on the larger world beyond formal written documents, especially the worlds of engineered products and human capital [50]. It converges slowly, because of the slow cycle time of formal written documents. And it is inaccurate, partly because of "obliteration by incorporation" [51] and partly because it is subject to human cognitive biases.

One opportunity is thus to move towards a more real-time and holistic view of research impact that goes beyond bibliometrics and beyond formal written documents. Data analytics is sure to be at the forefront of this move. Identifying the most valuable pieces of knowledge and the sources of those pieces of knowledge are at the heart of modern search analytics. Overall, extending such analytics to the narrower world of research should in principle be possible.

Limitations in our understanding of how to assess research impact, however, should not keep us from improving our understanding of how to assess research environment. Both efforts in parallel will feed on each other, and enable causal connections to be made.

Understanding research environment is non-trivial. From the discussion throughout this article of the importance of divergent and convergent thinking in individual researchers and research teams, it seems clear that a great research environment is not one in which researchers are "comfortable." Divergent and convergent thinking require individuals and teams to go beyond their intellectual comfort zones into Kuhn's "essential tension" [52]. This is another example of how understanding and fostering the psychosocial space of the research environment can have positive impacts on the communication, collaboration, and innovation of the research ecosystem.

5   A Vision for the Future

Research, the manufacture of knowledge, is complex, but not significantly more complex than the manufacturing of other goods and services requiring a high level of creativity. As science (understanding) and technology (tools) continue to be developed and applied to the manufacturing of those other goods and services, it is natural, perhaps inevitable, that they will also be applied to research.

At every level at which research is done, there are opportunities for improved understanding and improved tools. At the individual researcher level, examples are: how to overcome idea fixation and sloppy thinking, and how to balance divergent and convergent thinking. At the research team level, examples are: how to overcome strong links and groupthink, and how to optimally distribute divergent and convergent thinking across individuals and teams. At the research institution level, examples are: how to overcome GPA and performance fixation, and how to overcome (or harness) existential/social stress.

Moreover, we have focused in this article only on the direction from "science to art," in which the emerging science of research is harnessed to improve the art of research. Ultimately, even greater opportunity will be unleashed when the other direction from "art to science" is also exercised simultaneously and synergistically – when improvements in how research is actually done are used to test our understanding of how research is done.

We recognize that all research institutions are different and will have a different landscape of actionable possibilities. Many research institutions will likely share a discomfort towards opening themselves up to social scientific study. However, there are existence proofs of research laboratories opening themselves up at least to social science observation [53] if not yet experimentation. And, most importantly, the benefits to these research institutions of a science-based approach to research are potentially enormous: an enhanced productivity that, despite declining funding for physical science research, might nonetheless enable breakthroughs needed for humanity-scale grand challenges.

Acknowledgments.   We acknowledge Toluwalogo Odumosu, Travis Bauer, George Crabtree, Curtis Johnson, Thomas Picraux, Keith Sawer, Chistian Schunn, Gregory Feist, and Venkatesh Narayanamurti for the valuable insights at the Forum & Roundtable that assisted in the formation of this paper. The authors also acknowledge Charles Barbour, Julia Lane, Laura McNamara, Julie Phillips, Steve Rottler, Rick Schneider, Jerry Simmons, Rickson Sun, Mike Wanke, Rieko Yajima, and Laura Diaz Anadon for their suggestions and helpful discussions.

Sandia Corporation, a wholly owned subsidiary of Lockheed Martin Corporation, for the U.S. Department of Energy's National Nuclear Security Administration under Contract DE-AC04-94AL85000, Sandia Report SAND2016-1630J.

References

1. Grueber, M., Studt, T.: 2014 global R&D funding forecast. R&D Mag. **16**, 1–35 (2014)
2. Haak, L.L.: A vision to transform the research ecosystem. (editage) (2014)
3. Jones, C.I.: R & D-based models of economic growth. J. Polit. Econ. **103**(4), 759–784 (1995)

4. Beveridge, W.I.B.: The art of scientific investigation. WW Norton & Company, New York (1957)
5. Börner, K., et al.: A multi-level systems perspective for the science of team science. Sci. Transl. Med. **2**(49), 4–24 (2010)
6. Fealing, K.: The science of science policy: A handbook. Stanford University Press, Palo Alto (2011)
7. Feist, G.J.: The psychology of science and the origins of the scientific mind. Yale University Press, New Haven (2008)
8. Sawyer, R.K.: Explaining creativity: The science of human innovation. Oxford University Press, Oxford (2011)
9. Tsao, J.Y., et al.: Art and science of science and technology. In: Proceedings of the Forum and Roundtable Conference on Science, Technology, and Public Policy Program, 5–7 June 2013, Belfer Center for Science and International Affairs, Harvard Kennedy School
10. Cropley, A.: In praise of convergent thinking. Creativity Res. J. **18**(3), 391–404 (2006)
11. Toulmin, S.E.: Foresight and understanding: An enquiry into the aims of science. Greenwood Press, Westport (1961)
12. Campbell, D.T.: Blind variation and selective retentions in creative thought as in other knowledge processes. Psychol. Rev. **67**(6), 380 (1960)
13. Simonton, D.K.: Creative problem solving as sequential BVSR: exploration (total ignorance) versus elimination (informed guess). Think. Skills Creativity **8**, 1–10 (2013)
14. Medawar, P.B.: Is the scientific paper a fraud. The Listener **70**(12), 377–378 (1963)
15. Kahneman, D.: Thinking, fast and slow. Macmillan, London (2011)
16. Pirolli, P., Card, S.: The sensemaking process and leverage points for analyst technology as identified through cognitive task analysis. In: Proceedings of International Conference on Intelligence Analysis, Mitre McLean, VA, pp. 2–4 (2005)
17. March, J.G.: Exploration and exploitation in organizational learning. Organ. Sci. **2**(1), 71–87 (1991)
18. Dweck, C.S., Leggett, E.L.: A social-cognitive approach to motivation and personality. Psychol. Rev. **95**(2), 256 (1988)
19. Arthur, W.B.: The nature of technology: What it is and how it evolves. Simon and Schuster, New York (2009)
20. Linsey, J., et al.: A study of design fixation, its mitigation and perception in engineering design faculty. J. Mech. Des. **132**(4), 041003 (2010)
21. Fu, K., et al.: The meaning of "Near" and "Far": the impact of structuring design databases and the effect of distance of analogy on design output. J. Mech. Des. **135**, 021007 (2013)
22. Mikolov, T., Yih, W.-T., Zweig, G.: Linguistic regularities in continuous space word representations. In: HLT-NAACL, pp. 746–751. Citeseer (2013)
23. Blei, D.M., Ng, A.Y., Jordan, M.I.: Latent dirichlet allocation. J. Mach. Learn. Res. **3**, 993–1022 (2003)
24. Cilibrasi, R., Vitányi, P.M.: Clustering by compression. IEEE Trans. Inf. Theory **51**(4), 1523–1545 (2005)
25. Salton, G.: A theory of indexing. SIAM (1975)
26. Bennett, J., Lanning, S., Netflix, N.: The netflix prize. In: KDD Cup and Workshop in Conjunction with KDD (2007)
27. Gottschall, J.: The storytelling animal: how stories make us human. Boston's Back Bay, Houghton Mifflin Harcourt (2012)
28. Foltz, P.W., Laham, D., Landauer, T.K.: Automated essay scoring: applications to educational technology. In: World Conference on Educational Multimedia, Hypermedia and Telecommunications, pp. 939–944 (1999)

29. Isaacson, W.: Einstein: His life and universe. Simon and Schuster, New York (2007)
30. Jaynes, E.T.: A backward look to the future. Phys. Probab., 261–275 (1993)
31. D'Onfro, J.: Here's why google stopped asking bizarre, crazy-hard interview questions. Business Insider (2014)
32. Polanyi, M.: The tacit dimension (1967)
33. Lehrer, J.: Groupthink: the brainstorming myth. The New Yorker (2012)
34. Anonymous: Janelia Farm Research Campus: Report on Program Development. Howard Hughes Medical Institute (2003)
35. Catmull, E., Wallace, A.: Creativity Inc: Overcoming the Unseen Forces That Stand in the Way of True Inspiration. Random House LLC, New York (2014)
36. Singer, M.: Tony hsieh: building his company, and his city, with urbanism. AIArchitect **21** (2014)
37. Emmanuel, G., Silva, A.: Connecting the Physical and Psychosocial Space to Sandia's Mission. Sandia Report, SAND2014–16421 (2014)
38. McPherson, M., Smith-Lovin, L., Cook, J.M.: Birds of a feather: Homophily in social networks. Annual Review of Sociology **27**, 415–444 (2001)
39. Granovetter, M.S.: The strength of weak ties. Am. J. Sociol. **78**(6), 1360–1380 (1973)
40. Lucibella, M., Blewett, H.: Profiles in versatility: part 1 of two-part interview: entrepreneur elon musk talks about his background in physics. APS News. The American Physical Society (2013)
41. Dunbar, K.: How scientists think: on-line creativity and conceptual change in science. In: Ward, T.B., Smith, S.M., Vaid, J. (eds.) Creative Thought: An Investigation of Conceptual Structures and Processes, pp. 461–493. American Psychological Association, Washington (1997)
42. De Dreu, C.K., De Vries, N.K., Gordijn, E.H., Schuurman, M.S.: Convergent and divergent processing of majority and minority arguments: effects on focal and related attitudes. Eur. J. Soc. Psychol. **29**(23), 329–348 (1999)
43. Shore, J., Bernstein, E.S., Lazer, D.: Facts and Figuring: An Experimental Investigation of Network Structure and Performance in Information and Solution Spaces (2014)
44. Dong, A.: The latent semantic approach to studying design team communication. Des. Stud. **26**(5), 445–461 (2005)
45. Swan, M.: The quantified self: fundamental disruption in big data science and biological discovery. Big Data **1**(2), 85–99 (2013)
46. Waber, B.: People Analytics: How Social Sensing Technology Will Transform Business and what it Tells Us about the Future of Work. FT Press, Upper Saddle River (2013)
47. Chamorro-Premuzic, T.: Creativity versus conscientiousness: which is a better predictor of student performance? Appl. Cogn. Psychol. **20**(4), 521–531 (2006)
48. Cohen, W.M., Levinthal, D.A.: Absorptive capacity: a new perspective on learning and innovation. Adm. Sci. Q. **35**(1), 128–152 (1990)
49. Lane, J.: Let's make science metrics more scientific. Nature **464**(7288), 488–489 (2010)
50. Lane, J., Bertuzzi, S.: Measuring the results of science investments. Science **331**(6018), 678–680 (2011)
51. Merton, R.K.: The sociology of science: Theoretical and empirical investigations. University of Chicago press, Chicago (1973)
52. Kuhn, T.S.: The structure of scientific revolutions. University of Chicago press, Chicago (2012)
53. Latour, B., Woolgar, S.: Laboratory life: The construction of scientific facts. Princeton University Press, Princeton (2013)

Author Index

Printed in the United States
By Bookmasters